About the Underground Guide Series

Welcome to the underground!

Are you tired of all the fluff—books that tell you what you already know, ones that assume you're an idiot and treat you accordingly, or dwell on the trivial while completely ignoring the tough parts?

Good. You're in the right place.

Series Editor Woody Leonhard and Addison-Wesley bring you the Underground Guides—serious books that tackle the tough questions head-on but still manage to keep a sense of humor (not to mention a sense of perspective!). Every page is chock full of ideas you can put to use right away. We'll tell you what works and what doesn't—no bull, no pulled punches. We don't kowtow to the gods of the industry, we won't waste your time or your money, and we *will* treat you like the intelligent computer user we know you are.

Each Underground Guide is written by somebody who's been there—a working stiff who's suffered through the problems you're up against right now—and lived to tell about it. You're going to strike a rich vein of hard truth in these pages, and come away with a wealth of information you can put to use all day, every day.

So come along as we go spelunking where no book has gone before. Mind your head, and don't step in anything squishy. There will be lots of unexpected twists and turns . . . and maybe a laugh or two along the way.

The Underground Guide Series

Woody Leonhard, Series Editor

The Underground Guide to Word for Windows™:
Slightly Askew Advice from a WinWord Wizard

Woody Leonhard

The Underground Guide to Excel 5.0 for Windows™:
Slightly Askew Advice from Two Excel Wizards

Lee Hudspeth and Timothy-James Lee

The Underground Guide to UNIX®:
Slightly Askew Advice from a UNIX Guru

John Montgomery

The Underground Guide to Microsoft® Office, OLE, and VBA:
Slightly Askew Advice from Two Integration Wizards

Lee Hudspeth and Timothy-James Lee

The Underground Guide to Telecommuting:
Slightly Askew Advice on Leaving the Rat Race Behind

Woody Leonhard

The Underground Guide to
Telecommuting

Slightly
Askew
Advice
on
Leaving
the
Rat
Race
Behind

Woody Leonhard

ADDISON-WESLEY PUBLISHING COMPANY

Reading, Massachusetts • Menlo Park, California • New York • Don Mills, Ontario
Wokingham, England • Amsterdam • Bonn • Sydney • Singapore • Tokyo
Madrid • San Juan • Paris • Seoul • Milan • Mexico City • Taipei

The cool cartoons here are from Metro Image Base. For more info, contact your favorite software shoppe, or call 800-525-1552. The Image Club Catalog, which includes these and many other pieces of clipart, plus Adobe fonts, stock photos, and much more, can be yours for the price of a phone call: voice 800-661-9410 in the United States, or fax 403-261-7013 outside the United States.

Library of Congress Cataloging-in-Publication Data

Leonhard, Woody.
    The underground guide to telecommuting : slightly askew advice on
leaving the rat race behind / Woody Leonhard.
      p. cm. -- (Underground guide series)
    Includes index.
    ISBN 0-201-48343-2 (alk. paper)
    1. Telecomuting. I. Title. II. Series.
HD2336.3.L46 1995
658'.041--dc20   95-9089
                                                  CIP

Written in WinWord 6.0. Final page layout in PageMaker.

Series Hack: Woody Leonhard
Sponsoring Editor: Kathleen Tibbetts
Project Manager: Eleanor McCarthy
Production Coordinator: Deborah McKenna
Technical Editors: Jeff Rosler and Trudy Leonhard; Martha Steffen
Cover design: Jean Seal
Text Design: Kenneth L. Wilson, Wilson Graphics & Design
Set in 10 point Palatino by Rob Mauhar, CIP of Coronado

1 2 3 4 5 6 7 8 9 -MA- 9998979695
First printing, July 1995

Addison-Wesley books are available for bulk purchases by corporations, institutions, and other organizations. For more information please contact the Corporate, Government, and Special Sales Department at 800-238-9682.

*D*edicated

To Linda and Justin, of course.

To Trudy, whose technical book-writing debut appears here as Chapter 4. Not as easy as it looked, eh?

And to Kathleen Tibbetts and Claudette Moore, the two people in the book biz who keep me propped up and pointed in the right direction.

In 1959 the Communist Chinese invaded Tibet, driving its 24-year-old leader, the Dalai Lama, into exile. The Chinese unleashed a pogrom of ethnic and cultural genocide. Millions of Tibetans were imprisoned, tortured, murdered; their artistic, religious, and cultural heritage reduced to rubble. Reliable estimates place the number of Tibetans slaughtered since the Chinese invasion at 3,000,000. According to Amnesty International and other leading human rights organizations, arbitrary arrest, torture, and Chinese government-sanctioned killings in Tibet continue to this day.

The Dalai Lama settled in northern India. Millions of Tibetans followed him into exile. Most moved into refugee camps scattered throughout Nepal and India. Life in the camps is hard. Few families have more than one room to call their own. Many eke out a hand-to-mouth existence as subsistence farmers, manual laborers, handicraft workers, traders—often with "shops" consisting of no more than a couple of pieces of bamboo and a plastic tarp.

The Tibetan Children's Fund was founded in 1993 to provide food, shelter, and education for Tibetan refugee kids living in northern India. TCF's center of operation is in Darjeeling—renowned to westerners as a source of tea, but better known to Tibetans and many other Asians as a respected center of education. For more than a hundred years, English-language boarding schools in and around Darjeeling have prepared leaders of government, education, and commerce.

As of this writing, TCF sponsors almost 100 Tibetan children around Darjeeling. The kids are chosen for their scholastic ability and financial need. TCF volunteers (who pay for their own trips to India) interview the children and their parents, select the children, and monitor their progress in school each semester. Scholastic evaluation emphasizes proficiency in English, math, the sciences, and humanities.

A little hard currency goes a long way in India. $60 will sponsor a refugee kid for a full year in one of the government-run schools. $250 covers a full year—including tuition, room, and board—in one of the top English-language schools.

TCF is an all-volunteer organization. Overhead expenses are paid by TCF's corporate sponsors. Every penny donated by individuals goes straight to the children. If you would like to help a deserving Tibetan refugee kid, please contact:

Tibetan Children's Fund
Post Office Box 473, Pinecliffe, Colorado USA 80471
voice, 303-642-0492; fax, 303-642-0491

Part of the profits from the sale of this book are donated to the TCF.

Contents

Acknowledgments

This book—the first of its kind, as far as I can discern—owes its existence to the intestinal fortitude and foresight of the folks at Addison-Wesley: Steve, Keith, and particularly Kathleen, who could find the diamond in this rough. Ellie played the role of shepherd. Out in the real world, Claudette shaped the book, gave it a voice and a perspective, and kept it on track. Thanks, y'all.

As you'll soon see, the *Underground Guide to Telecommuting* relies on the real-world experiences of people who are pioneering the field, pushing the envelope every day—not on pontifications by self-anointed experts. I've drawn heavily on the experiences of telecommuters Jeff ("the moose man") Rosler and his wife Trudy ("I've never seen a moose") Leonhard, who telecommute daily from their home in the Colorado wilderness to San Jose; Martha Steffen, an urbanite who works on the left coast but telecommutes to the right; Alfred Poor and Sarah and Chris Wright, who were telecommuting before telecommuting was cool; and especially the telecommuters who participate in my own virtual corporation: Vince Chen, Kate Edson, Lee Hudspeth, Scott Krueger, T.J. Lee, Ken Mocabee, and Eileen Wharmby, collectively known as the WOPRFolk.

My ongoing thanks and admiration to the blue-ribbon Underground brain bank of telecommuters, entrepreneurs, contractors, consultants, and freelancers, who have given invaluable advice and assistance throughout the development of this book, sometimes without even realizing it: Kevin Collins, Helen Feddema, Gil Gordon, Durant Imboden, Scott Leonhard, James McDonald, Ray Moore, Judy Rapp-Guadagnoli, Bill Sharp, Elizabeth Sharp, Ted Roche, Randy Walling, Rick at Aerostar, and Janet Attard on Microsoft Network.

And of course, as with all the *Underground Guides* that rely on "the straight scoop at all costs," there were those who chose to remain anonymous. (No, not *all* of them work in Redmond.) My hat's off to y'all. Anonymously, of course.

Any errors or inanities you may find here are all mine. The really good stuff can be attributed to one or more of the above fearless sources.

Do YOU Need This Book?

> Today's workers need to forget jobs completely and look instead for work that needs doing—and then set themselves up as the best way to get that work done.
>
> William Bridges
> *JobShift*, 1994

Have you ever thought of completely chucking it all, moving to the boondocks, hanging out a shingle, and trying to make a go of it? Good. This book is for you.

Have you ever wondered why you waste a couple of hours driving to and from an office every day—when you could get your work done just as well *if not better* by staying at home? Good. This book is for you.

Have you been thinking about popping the big question to your boss—asking her if you can just try to telecommute for a while, to see if it'll work—but can't quite get up the guts, don't know how to be persuasive? Good. This book is for *her*.

Has your boss decided to make you telecommute, whether you want to or not? Not so good. This book is for both of you.

Have you ever considered the possibility that all the talk about the Information Superhighway and Virtual Corporations and CyberSurfing is, to put it politely, crap? Are you skeptical that anybody working for you, doing real work, can really get anything *done* without coming to the office? Good. You're in the right frame of mind.

YOU AREN'T ALONE

Depending on whom you talk to—and whom you believe—somewhere between two and ten million American workers telecommute. That's a significant chunk of the American workforce, and the numbers are growing exponentially. The Society

Everybody's doin' it.

There goes telecommuter number 10,000,001.

for Human Resource Management reports that 42 percent of the major American companies—those with more than 5,000 employees—already have telecommuting programs.

It's clearly the way of the future, and rapid advances in technology are fueling the growth. Ten years from now telecommuting may well be the norm, not the exception, for the developed world's burgeoning "information worker" class.

This *Underground Guide* will help you stake a claim in the brave new world.

WHAT HATH THIS UNGODLY ROT?

Lies, damn lies . . .

Does telecommuting work? Good question. And there's no simple answer.

There are lots of statistics floating around: pick up a business magazine and you'll read that telecommuters are 23.7615 precent more productive than non-telecommuters, or you'll see how telecommuting saves companies $10 zillion bucks a year. Most of the numbers you see are hogwash. The people who publish those statistics usually have a vested interest in promoting telecommuting; few of them have the slightest idea what it takes to make a business or organization hang together.

"Yes, the Net *has* been a bit slow lately. Why do you ask?"

An example, if you will. You might've read about the AT&T survey that disclosed 76 percent of all telecommuting AT&T employees were "more produc-tive" than those in the office. What you probably didn't read is that the survey asked the *telecommuters*, not their bosses, if they were more productive. (Which box would *you* check?) It didn't define the word "productive" in any objective way. And—get this—the people being surveyed had just completed *one day* of telecommuting. They were first-time telecommuters, with a whole day of experi-ence under their belts.

If you're looking for a mindless regurgitation of meaningless numbers—or (what amounts to the same thing) a quick, easy answer to your every telecommuting question—you're in the wrong place. It's a tough problem, and I won't pretend to have any facile answers.

TELLIN' IT LIKE IT IS

> It's very hard to shave an egg.
>
> John Clarke
> *Parœmiologia Anglo-Latina,* 1639

Most of what's been written about telecommuting deals with the "soft" side of the topic: how to set up a telecommuting program in your company; what kinds of committees have to meet and which details they need to thrash around; checklists for this 'n that; how to answer the phone; that sort of thing.

This is a "hard" book.

I won't bore you with the "soft" stuff. Much of it is obvious, and the parts that aren't obvious have already been covered in books such as Paul and Sarah Edwards's *Working from Home* (Tarcher/Putnam, 1994).

This *Underground Guide* takes on the "hard" part of telecommuting. Why your company should—or should not!—let a specific employee telecommute. What you really need to connect to your office's network. Whether whiteboard systems are worth the (considerable!) expense. How telecommuting arrangements can get screwed up, and how to unscrew them. Running a project from your home office. Taking advantage of on-line systems. Peaceful co-existence with the corporate IS department. Security. And on and on. The tough stuff.

After I've hashed over the nitty-gritty of traditional telecommuting—where an employee working for one company works at home or in a satellite office—I'll introduce you to the advantages and disadvantages of breaking out on your own.

The *Underground Guide* covers the tricky transition from working as an employee to becoming an independent contractor for your current employer. I'll go into detail about using telecommuting to run your own consultancy. I'll cover the "hard" tax and accounting problems you'll encounter.

Finally, I'll give you an in-depth look at a real, working virtual corporation, where independent telecommuters band together to keep the wolves from the door.

COMPUTERUS REX

> Computers will get you through times of no telephones
> Better than phones will get you through times of no computers.
>
> Pensées Pinecliffius

If you don't (or won't) use computers to telecommute, just put this book back on the shelf. You aren't quite ready for it. Yet.

I'm going to assume that you use a computer, swear at it, and depend on it to keep the business going. It needn't be your best friend, or even a welcome guest.

But at the very least, it should be an accepted necessary evil. Kinda like the IRS, if you know what I mean.

The family that plug 'n plays together stays together.

The acid test
There's a simple test to see if you're ready for the *Underground Guide to Telecommuting*: Unplug your computer (or computers) for a day. If you're screaming bonkers by the end of the day—or, more likely, if you give up the experiment in disgust before the day is out—you need this book.

The technology of telecommuting these days revolves around computers in general, and PCs in particular. Technology brackets both the bare minimum of what you should be able to get accomplished outside of the office, and the far expanses of what is and will be possible for the unfettered worker.

You needn't be a computer genius to follow along. If you have a computer and know that you should be using it more, but tend to get befuddled by all the talk of I-ways, MPC specs, and Class 3 fax modems (not to mention ISDN, firewalls, and V.42*bis*), welcome to the club! I'll step you through the bafflegab, and try to give you an educated guess about what you need to consider, and what you can safely ignore.

While the *Underground Guide* isn't exclusively for computer jocks, it tackles many of the toughest technical problems in getting telecommuting to work. It gives some solid answers to computer-related questions. And if you aren't yet convinced that a computer is vital to running your at-home business—telecommuter or not—well, someday soon you will.

Think "hard."

TRUTH WILL OUT

> Among all the world's races, some obscure Bedouin tribes possibly apart, Americans are the most prone to misinformation. This is not the consequence of any special preference for mendacity, although at the higher levels of their public administration that tendency is impressive. It is rather that so much of what they themselves believe is wrong.
>
> John Kenneth Galbraith

I'm not going to try to convince you that telecommuting is *always* the way to go. It ain't. Some people don't adapt well to the telecommuting life: A few don't have the self-discipline; even more really need the social interaction. Some jobs aren't conducive to telecommuting. Some bosses can't handle the strain of managing by results, instead of physical presence. Some customers won't take you seriously if you don't have a downtown office. Some business deals get blown when your six-year-old, home sick for the day, grabs the phone. It happens. I won't tell you otherwise.

Telecommuting is *not* for everyone.

Instead, I'm going to show you what's involved—what works, what doesn't, where the hidden problems lie—and introduce you to a handful of people who have been around the block a few times. I'll teach you their tricks, and warn you about their failures. Then you can decide for yourself if you're up to living in the cyburbs.

It ain't a bowl of cherries.

I won't tell you how to interview a secretary, organize your life, or decorate your office. But I will go into considerable detail about the concepts and technologies that drive telecommuting: phone links, on-line services, software, and the like. Forget the fluff. Like the rest of the *Underground Guides*, this is gonna be down and dirty, with advice from people who have been there, and lived to tell about it.

Some of the tips in this book (and one chapter!) are specific to the United States. Given the huge variation in laws, customs, currencies, and acceptable behavior throughout the world, there was little choice. I've tried to include country-specific notes and warnings where they seemed appropriate, but no doubt I've missed a few.

Welcome to the ether!

*Usus est optimum magister.**

Woody Leonhard
Coal Creek Canyon, Colorado

---

* Experience is the best teacher.

Conventions

The man who aims to speak as books enable, as synods use, as the fashion guides, and as interest commands, babbles.
Let him hush.

R. W. Emerson
Address at Divinity College, July 15, 1838

From time to time I'll hit you with an idea that, in and of itself, should pay for this book.

I'll mark those ideas with a wizard's wand, like this one. Keep your eyes peeled for wizardly ideas. Many of them bear the imprimatur of pioneers in the field— and contain information laden with their blood, sweat, and tears.

Other times I'll warn you about potentially disastrous mistakes, effectively warning you about what lies ahead before you, uh, step in it.

Borrowing on my computer roots, those areas fraught with danger are marked with a bug, like this. Be extremely cautious when walking in these areas. Dæmons await! Thar be tygers here. . . .

1 The Long Drive Home

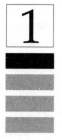

Live where you want.
Do what you love.

> Jeff Duntemann
> *PC Techniques* magazine

Ten years ago I moved into a modest house on top of a mountain, four miles up a dirt road in the Colorado Rockies. I vowed then and there I'd never live in the city again. Telecommuting has worked for me. Ten years and several renovations later, the house is twice as big as it once was—hey, *I've* added a little girth, too—and my life has changed in many ways, but I'll still be damned if I'll live in the city.

Woody at work (editors' view)

Not that telecommuting from the mountains is all sweetness and light. Far from it! The local newspaper—it's a monthly because there isn't enough going on around here to support a weekly—says that some yahoo, last week, threw a beer bottle through the Quik Mart's plate glass window. Last month somebody broke into the newspaper's office and stole their computer, an AT clone with a DeskJet Plus printer. This ain't Mayberry, RFD, folks. Crime has come to Coal Creek Canyon.

There's trouble in River City.

1

It's not just crime. We mountainous types suffer through other annoyances, natural and unnatural. Last week the Colorado high-country weather gods graced us with a monster hail and lightning storm that fried four of my five telephones. Yesterday the local cable TV company refused once again to run cable to my house because it's too far off the beaten track. The U.S. Postal Service won't deliver mail up here, even though UPS, FedEx, Airborne, and DHL all make daily visits.

As Kurt Vonnegut would say, "and so it goes."

Still, the air here is crisp and clear. The only drive-by shooting I've ever heard about involved a tourist from Texas, a long-neck brewskie, and a defenseless jackrabbit. Sixth graders honestly believe "crack" is the sound of a bat on a baseball. We have a parade every year for the Fourth of July, where the folks in the volunteer fire department can roll out their shiny truck, and the kids get into big trouble zapping each other with water guns.

Corny? Yeah. Sure.

I wouldn't have it any other way.

Your vision of a great place to live may differ greatly from mine. I know one telecommuter who wouldn't live anywhere but on a beach: If his surf board strays out of arm's reach, his palms start itching. Another good friend lives in one of Seattle's gay communities; he wouldn't live anywhere else. Then there are the telecommuters who insist on living in Manhattan . . . *meshuggeneh. . . .*

FREEDOM

> Man is born free—and everywhere he is in irons.
>
> J. J. Rousseau
> *Du contrat social*, 1761

More than mere hype   Telecommuting, to my way of thinking anyway, is synonymous with "freedom." Freedom to choose where and how you live. When and why you work. Whom you'll interact with, whom you'll ignore. Freedom to figure out what's important in your life, and if you play your cards right, the freedom to reach for that proverbial brass ring. Heady stuff.

We've come a long way, baby.

"I sentence you to Nine-to-Five."

A Brief History of Western Culture

> Hegel remarks somewhere that all great, world-historical facts and
> personages occur, as it were, twice. He has forgotten to add: the first time
> as tragedy, the second as farce.
>
> Karl Marx
> 1852

In the early nineteenth century a rapid series of mechanical inventions brought a
tidal change in the way people live and work: The Industrial Revolution, aided in
no small part by agrarian changes, drew entire populations of subsistence farmers
away from the fields and made large urban centers possible . . . indeed, necessary.
Most people worked in the cities, and lived a short walk away.

In the early twentieth century improvements in transportation made it possible for factory and office workers to extricate themselves from urban squalor.
Commuting from the suburbs became commonplace, and the more adventurous
moved to the exurbs, trading a better living place for a longer rush-hour commute. Most people worked in the cities, but lived in bedroom communities, or
even in the boonies.

All I need to know about history I learned in kindergarten.

How's that for a two-paragraph review of the Western world's achievements
over the past 200 years?

The Cyburbs

> The first settler in the woods is generally a man who has outlived his
> credit or fortune in the cultivated parts.
>
> Benjamin Rush
> *Essays,* 1798

As we enter the twenty-first century, improvements in computer and communications technology make it increasingly irrelevant where you work, and thus where
you live, as long as you're connected. I call the whole concept the *cyburbs.* And I
firmly believe it's the next step in the evolution of how humanity works, literally
and figuratively.

The first 20,000 years of human history brought civilization from extended
families to tribes to extended tribes to big tribes called cities. (Or is that "the
urbs"?) The next 100 years spread us out to suburbs and exurbs, which naturally
led to the pit barbecue, fenced back yards, designer bottled water, and the four-
hour commute.

Now we're faced with dealing with the cyburbs, where the person working
right next to you may be physically located down the hall, or halfway around the
world. Your coworker might've just stumbled out of bed, and could still be

What it's really like in the cyburbs. No. Really. Trust me. *Heh heh heh.*

wearing pajamas—or nothing at all. He could be a she, or she a he; might not speak your language, or possibly not be able to speak at all; could be of any race or combination of races imaginable; might be much older or much younger than you, or skinnier or taller or uglier; a natty dresser or a complete slob; and you're going to find out, pretty damned quick, that *it doesn't matter.*

Call off your old, tired prejudices.

Egalitarianism rules in the cyburbs. If you carry your old, tired preconceptions and prejudices into the realm of telecommuting, you'll get burned—and surprised!—over and over again.

It goes further than that. The cyburbs form the foundation of the world's first meritocracy —or at least the cyburbs make such a wild-eyed idea (which has only been around for, oh, 2,500 years) a bit more feasible. An example: I was once very pleasantly surprised by the talents of a programmer who had just begun exploring the ether. This guy was knocking out some bodacious programs, and we struck up a friendship. I tried to get in touch with him one day and couldn't. I learned later he was off line to study for a test. He'd just started high school, and his parents were insistent that he stop "playing" on line!

So put your prejudices aside. They'll only get in your way.

Getting to and from the cyburbs

The mechanics of commuting from the suburbs—cars and cell phones and clover-leaf intersections and helicopter traffic reports and fast food joints—evolved over the past fifty years, as a reaction to the problems physiocommuters* encountered. The mechanics of telecommuting from the cyburbs, by contrast, have yet to be defined, much less refined.

We're all on the bleeding edge.

---

* I've coined the term "physiocommuter" to include those unfortunate souls who don't (yet!) telecommute. If you know any physiocommuters, be kind to them. Some day they'll qualify for protection under the Endangered Species Act.

Bahn, Bahn, Bahn, On the I-I-Bahn

> Er, how fast were you going when Mr. Adams jumped from the car?. . .
> Seventy-five?. . .
> And where was that?. . .
> In your driveway?. . .
> How far had Mr. Adams gotten in the lesson?. . .
> Backing OUT?
>
> Bob Newhart
> *The Driving Instructor*, 1960

There's been a lot of garbage in the press about the "Information Revolution" and the "Information Highway" and the cyber-this and virtual-that. By and large, most of what's been written is wishful thinking from people who have never actually tried to practice what they preach.

Maybe you're one of the ten people in the world who can actually get some real work done with a cellular fax machine while tooling down the freeway at 100 clicks an hour. Maybe you're the type who already has a satellite up-link at home, and a 10 Gbps leased line to the main office, just in case. If so, I salute you, and hope you've found good insurance for the kids' matching Mercedes and weekend yacht.

All hooked up, nowhere to go

But if you're like most of us working schnooks, you're going to bump up against resource constraints (that is, a finite supply of money) sooner rather than later, and your primary reason for using the I-way will be to make, or save, money. Good. That's as it should be.

There's a fundamental shift going on in the way the world works. As businesses strive to become more competitive the concept of "work" has changed. More and more, work is something you *do* — not a place you *go to*. That's an important distinction, one that lies at the heart of the explosive growth in telecommuting, one that frees us from the shackles of nine-to-five and redefines the ways employees contribute to their companies' prosperity.

It doesn't matter where you are, as long as you have electricity and a phone line.

Semantics

> Mr. Watson, come here. I need you.
>
> Alexander Bell
> March 10, 1876

So what, you ask, is telecommuting?

Excellent question. To which there is no simple answer.

The first telecommuter   In a very literal sense, a telecommuter is someone who uses telephone technology to get to work, or (perhaps its antithesis) to get work done. Using that definition, though, just about everybody has performed some telecommuting, from Alexander Graham Bell and his first telephonic utterance—a telecommute to the adjoining room, intended to get some work out of Watson.

"Stop goofing around, Watson!"

On the other hand, some people would have you believe that telecommuting is exactly the same as working at the office, except you don't have to drive or ride to work. *NOT!* People who think that way have never telecommuted and don't have much of a clue what's going on.

On the third hand, some folks believe that you have to be self-employed to make telecommuting work, and that just isn't true. I'll introduce you to a telecommuter in the next chapter who's as loyal an employee as any you've ever met. Conversely, some self-employed people I know are the worst office-bound drudges on the face of the earth; they'd be terrified of telecommuting, even to their own offices!

A better definition   I prefer to think of telecommuting in terms of freedom. To me, telecommuters are people who can get their work done just about anywhere there's a phone line, people who have the freedom to work anyplace they can find a phone. They can roam or stay put; pull an all-nighter or take the day off; work in bed, or poolside, or in the den, or at the bar, with the stereo blaring at full volume, the kids screaming in the background, or out in a field of daisies, as the mood dictates. Telecommuters are the modern corporate Steppenwolfen, if you will—and the only real concern in anyone's mind is whether their work gets done, and done well.

That definition covers quite a bit of ground, admittedly, but if you have ever found yourself sitting in the office wondering why you couldn't be doing the same work from the comfort of your house, well, you've nailed the essence of telecommuting!

The Telecommuting Continuum

> No one is free save Jove.
>
> Æschylus
> *Prometheus Bound,* ca. 490 BC

I've found a huge variety in telecommuters' arrangements: It wouldn't be exaggerating to say that every telecommuter, and every telecommuter's situation, is unique. In general, though, I tend to think in terms of the relationship between the telecommuter and his or her work, placing each along a line I call the Telecommuting Continuum. See Figure 1.1.

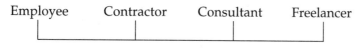

Figure 1.1 The Four Tele-Categories

Each category has its nuances, working considerations, and legal and accounting ramifications, as well as its more esoteric pluses and minuses.

Telecommuting *employees* may work at home just one day a week, with the rest of the time in the office. Or they may live in Timbuktu, only dropping by the office once a year. Regardless, as employees, they have to be concerned about performance reviews, promotions, career paths, office politics, downsizing . . . in short, everything any other employee would worry about. In exchange for the mental drain, they usually get all the benefits of "regular" physiocommuting employees, including health insurance, paid holidays, savings plans, premature heart attacks, and time off for good behavior. They're paid by the week or the month, just like an employee, often with bonuses for extraordinary work. **Telemployee**

Most of this *Underground Guide* focuses on this traditional employer/employee telecommuting arrangement. By far the largest percentage of telecommuters today fall into this category, and the concerns of these traditional telecommuters generally apply broadly to all telecommuters.

A telecommuting *contractor* generally has one or two big clients, and operates with more autonomy than an employee. ("Autonomy" here is a relative term, with legal overtones: While contractors will be called into the office less frequently than employees, they'll get the shaft just as often — maybe more so.) Contractors may charge by the hour or by the job, and should be making more money than their employee counterparts, simply because they don't get the same benefits and (at least theoretically) have less job security. **Telecontractor**

A telecommuting *consultant* usually has a handful of clients and may make a living building or fixing systems (the grunt work of the category); training by **Teleconsultant** writing course material, giving talks and seminars; or simply doling out advice to anybody crazy enough to pay for it (the glitz of the category).

Telefreelancer   A few people manage to escape into tele*freelancing*. A freelancer has no identifiable "boss," although—believe me—it doesn't usually feel that way when you're freelancing. Many book writers and magazine contributors fall into this category. So do the folks who write and distribute software packages. While their jobs may appear idyllic, don't be fooled: Every single one of them is working without a net; their next paycheck is totally dependent on what they can do today. It's scary.

Nobody's going to fit into one single category, and at various times in a given career, any or all of the categories may apply. But by taking an explicit look at all of the categories I hope to show you what opportunities exist and prepare you for problems that may lie ahead.

ROUNDING OUT THE BOOK

> The problem with Einstein's maxim, "Imagination is more important than knowledge," is that it's most often invoked by those who lack both.
>
> Pensées Pinecliffius

Okay, okay. Enough for the preliminaries and stage setting. It's time to dig into the meat of the book.

Setting up a bitchin' office   Chapter 2 will take you where no book has gone before, into the belly of the virtual office. We'll look at setting up an office and equipping it with gizmos that actually work and pay for themselves. I'll give you very specific recommendations on what to get and what to avoid, what works for me, and what doesn't seem to work for anybody. You'd be amazed at how much junk there is out in the ozone that doesn't work any better than a government spending freeze, but still (for reasons best known to advertising and marketing mavens) manages to sell by the boatload.

Woody at work (actual picture)

Chapter 3 gives a broad overview, and very specific recommendations, on what you should be looking for in a telecommuting PC. If you're about to buy a PC for the first time, or if you're looking for ammunition in the budgeting battles (what? the boss thinks all you need to work at home is a 286 with a 20 MB hard drive?), this is the place to start.

In Chapter 4 we'll look at the communications side of things: phone lines and services, funny boxes that talk over phone lines in 1s and 0s, what's available now, what may be available soon (or some day), and what will probably never get off the ground. We'll go over the kinds of things that may be installed at your central office, and how you might go about getting connected to it, with hardware and software. And we'll end Chapter 4 with the *topic du jour*—connecting to the I-way, in ways that won't cost an arm and a leg, in ways that will pay for themselves.

Talkin' turkey over the wires

Chapter 5 examines telecommuting from the vantage point of the poor, overwhelmed employee. What to get straight before you start telecommuting. What can go wrong. How to head off problems. And we'll have lots of tricks from successful telemployees, things they have found to make a big difference in the way they're treated by the folks back at the ranch.

Telemployee blues

Chapter 6 puts the stiletto-heeled show on the other foot: It talks about telecommuting from the teleboss's point of view. The *real* reasons for setting up a telecommuting program—reasons that will hold up when Big Boss 'n the Bean Counters come knocking. Figuring out who can handle telecommuting, who can't. Where things can get screwed up, and how to unscrew them before they get out of hand. When to pull the plug. Where to get help.

Teleboss stuff

Chapter 7 covers transitions, what's involved in changing the kind of work you do. If you work in the computer biz—and even if you don't!—change is (to borrow a well-worn cliché) the only constant. You need to learn to adapt, both within the context of an employer/employee relationship and, if need be, to become an independent contractor, consultant, or freelancer. Why would you change the kind of relationship you have with your employer? When is it good for *both* sides? Where are the pitfalls? If you're going to make a go of hanging out your own shingle, how much money does it really take? How much work is involved?

Ch-ch-ch-ch-ch-changes

Where all the money goes

Schedule A or Schedule C?   In general, tax laws were written to deal with the workplace of the late 1940s. A few rules have actually been updated to reflect reality of the 1960s—the last time so many of our most powerful representatives in Washington held a real job. Other than the occasional sop to modernity (such as Form 1040PC, a boon to compujocks), you're going to find yourself slogging through rules and regulations that make absolutely no sense in the modern world. Chapter 8 guides you through tax considerations, laws, and accounting topics apropos the telecommuter. What you can get away with. How Uncle Sam will ding you. Whether you should incorporate. What can be done about the home office deduction. What's an "employee" and why that's important. Zoning laws. 1099 forms. Bookkeeping. Hiring an accountant who speaks telecommuting.

Shoveling it in   After you've discovered that more than half of your income will go to feed the government—and another 10 percent or more will go to the accountants and lawyers who keep you out of tax court—you're going to be in a mood to drum up more business. (I mean, how else will you increase the 30 to 40 percent of your income that you actually get to *keep*?) Chapter 9 talks about the Internet and whether there's any money to be made on the I-way (for working schnooks like us, I mean—not the multi-billion-dollar companies that already have their hands in the I-till).

Yeti, Inc.   No doubt you've heard of "virtual corporations," groups of professionals who band together to benefit from each individual's strengths and telecommute to even out the workload. The virtual corporation is the Abominable Snowman of the Business Press: Everybody talks about them, but nobody seems to be able to find one. We'll take a look at a real, thriving virtual corporation in Chapter 10.

Blah, blah, blah   I've tried to isolate all the blue-sky stuff and put it in the last chapter. It's a short one, focusing on where all this telecommuting stuff is headed. If you're curious about the way much of the western world will work twenty or thirty years from now—and don't mind a bit of SWAG* speculation—Chapter 11 may surprise you.

Unnatural resources   Appendix A lists a whole bunch of stuff—much of it free—that you can get to help with the "soft" side of telecommuting: books, magazine articles, case studies, newsletters, government reports, conferences, and on and on. If you're in charge of setting up a telecommuting program, Appendix A will give you a head start.

T.C. phone home   Finally, you'll find a handy little phone book in Appendix B, one that provides numbers for the hardware, software, and business of telecommuting and should point you in the right direction wherever you may be heading.

Enjoy!

---

* Strictly Woody's Abysmal Guess

2 Command Central: The Virtual Office

I like work; it fascinates me.
I can sit and look at it for hours.
I love to keep it by me:
the idea of getting rid of it nearly breaks my heart.

Jerome K. Jerome
Three Men in a Boat, 1889

My first telecommuting job required an IBM PC, and I was thrilled. I ran out and bought the best machine I could find at the time—an original true-blue IBM PC, a real souped-up model, with two (count 'em, two!) floppy drives, 64K of memory, and a fancy color monitor. Well, truth be told it was a sorta-color monitor: It displayed 80 amber characters on each of 25 lines, all on a black screen.

A quick history

Another boring day workin' at home

I put the beast on a small, rickety table in our one-room efficiency apartment. It was springtime of 1985, I was out working for myself for the first time, and I worked like a man possessed. Some of my best writing and software came from that machine. It also gave me a severe case of eyestrain; prolonged, crushing headaches; and back pains and a bout of carpal tunnel syndrome that took nine years to overcome.

 You want to learn about ergonomics? You think that carpal tunneling is a psychosomatic problem? Ha! Lemme tell ya. Stick a classic IBM PC on a rickety table in a cramped room, pull up a kitchen chair, and work under those conditions nonstop for a few months. You'll learn fast, believe me.

My second office marked quite a step up from the table-and-kitchen-chair-in-a-corner standard. My own "electronic cottage" was a converted shed with a bad habit of sweltering in summer and freezing in winter. I worked from a real desk, though, bought an "office" chair, and crammed that and all my electronic goodies into an eight-by-twelve-foot space. I got a second phone line, and managed to turn out several books and run a software company with six-figure sales volume from ninety-six square feet.

Can you get away with a little office? Yes, it can be done. No, it ain't easy. I knew my time in ninety-six square feet was coming to an end when three Addison-Wesley execs dropped by for the day, and all four of us squeezed into that little office for a conference call. Fortunately, they all had a sense of humor and didn't mind laughing in shifts. We survived the experience. Somehow.

I spent eight wonderful years in that office, made a lot of mistakes, and learned a lot about making a small space work. In this chapter, I'll show you some of the tricks that worked for me, and introduce you to a handful of ideas from other telecommuters that you can put to work, whether you telecommute from your kitchen table, a 96-square-foot shed, or a custom 1,000-square-foot addition to your home.

This chapter won't talk about communications: telephones, phone lines, modems, comm software and services, and the like. We'll save that for Chapter 3. I'll also skip over the stuff that's covered *ad nauseum* in all the "How to Organize Your Office" books and magazine articles. Instead, I'm going to tackle the tough problems of establishing and outfitting an office, specifically from the telecommuter's point of view.

Satellite offices Some companies and several government organizations have established offices in suburban areas, allowing workers to commute just a short distance to well-stocked offices near their homes. If you're "telecommuting" to a teleworking site, satellite office, neighborhood work center, or whatever those offices may be called this week, skip the next section of this chapter, "Office Placement." You probably don't have any control over your working space or its contents—at least no more than you would have in a "normal" office. The powers-that-be just moved the office a little closer to your house. Cool. But you might as well move ahead to "Getting Organized."

OFFICE PLACEMENT

One of the symptoms of approaching nervous breakdown is the belief that one's work is terribly important. If I were a medical man, I should prescribe a holiday to any patient who considered his work important.

Bertrand Russell
Autobiography, 1968

One of the greatest advantages to telecommuting is that you're at home: There are far fewer drop-in distractions; meetings (both in person and via phone) tend to be better scheduled and more pointed; you can switch the incoming phone off the hook and get some work done without fear of offending the boss or coworkers.

One of the greatest *dis*advantages to telecommuting is that you're at home: Kids, neighbors, and spouses feel much less inhibition about interrupting you; there's no spillover space if you suddenly need to store an unexpected pile of resource material; there's nobody to ask to pitch in with copying or running the odd errand. You run the whole show, and you have to take control of the situation—or it will overwhelm you, I guarantee.

It's all about control.

The key to taking control is in how you set up your office.

A Workin' Fortress

The idea behind "the portable office," or the remote office, is to replicate the environment in the central office at some remote location—at home, in a hotel room across the ocean, or in a customer's office across town.

Computer Dealer News
July 27, 1994

Horsepucky.

Pensées Pinecliffius

If you put together your home office to "replicate the environment in the central office," you're doomed from the start. May as well toss this book in the garbage can and get ready to start physiocommuting again.

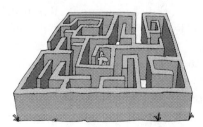

Replicate the environment in the central office.

Interruptions are the rule, not the exception, in central offices.

Most central offices consist of a random hodgepodge of walls and cubicles, set up (more or less) to make it easier for people who work together to talk with each other. Typically, central offices funnel heavy traffic through a maze of cubicles, exposing each worker positioned on the maze to a nonstop parade of noisy, distracting guests.

How is it in *your* central office? If you want to see the person in charge, can you get off the elevator (or open the door), and walk straight into their office, without bugging a dozen people as you go by? Are things strategically laid out to minimize unwanted noises, stave off unwelcome interruptions?

Yeah. I thought so.

Two Keys to Location   Your telecommutin' home office must be designed to discourage interruptions. Assuming you have any choice in where the office will be located, you're best off putting it in the least-traveled, least-used, least-bugged part of your house.

Most of the books and magazine articles you'll read sternly warn you to avoid using the kitchen or master bedroom as your *sanctum sanctorum*. That's a crock. Plenty of successful home offices share their space with the oven or the family dining table. But the best ones are always positioned with two thoughts in mind.

Office as haven during workday

First, the best offices are removed from all work-time activity in the house. If you live alone or your spouse and other family members are away while you're working, you can put the office any place you like. But if the kids get home at 3:30 and you don't knock off until 6:00, there'd better be a lot of insulation between you and the TV.

If your spouse is normally around the house during the workday, you'll need a door that can be closed, or at least enough *lebensraum* to let each of you get things done without bothering the other. No "Honey, could you shoot me a copy?" No "Darling, would you put away the dishes?" Minor interruptions like that, replayed five or ten times a day, put a huge strain on even the strongest relationship. And they can absolutely kill your productivity.

And then the office disappears at night.

Second, when the workday is over, the best offices can be placed out of sight and out of mind. For some folks that means being able to close the door on a spare bedroom; for others it means flipping a divider screen around so you don't have to look at the office junk.

I know one person who works on the kitchen table, but religiously removes everything at the end of the workday, stacking it all in neat piles in a closet. The all-in-one mobile computer desks you see in office supply stores can make this kind of hiding easier: Fold down the lid, scoot the desk into a corner, and everything is safely out of the way until the next day.

Sure you need to worry about power cords and phone jacks and lighting and heating and cooling and square footage and access and safety and all that. But if you've ever hooked up a computer, those are a given; you knew about 'em already. (If you don't know about 'em, check out *Working from Home*, described at the end of this chapter.)

> **The *important* things to remember when you're picking a telecommuting office location are to make sure (1) it's away from household hubbub during the workday, and (2) that it's hidden after working hours.**

Rock Around the Clock

> Between the dark and the daylight,
> When the night is beginning to lower,
> Comes a pause in the day's occupations,
> That is known as the Children's Hour.
>
> I hear in the chamber above me
> The patter of little feet.
>
> > H. W. Longfellow
> > *The Children's Hour,* 1860

Before you settle on an office location, it pays to spend a whole day looking at the ebb and flow of activity around your house. Take a while to grok* the environs. You'd be surprised how many times people think they know "the obvious place" to put an office, but then end up changing location within a few weeks.

Larger ain't necessarily better.

The best way to check for migration patterns is to simply sit and watch while people go about their daily business. If you don't have the time or patience to observe first-hand, check out the wear pattern in your carpeting. Yeah. Sounds silly, but it works. You don't want your office located anywhere near the high-traffic areas.

Observing movement

When looking into the sound situation, nothing beats the real thing. If you're worried that you won't be able to concentrate with the TV going in the other room, try it. Turn on the TV; crank it up to as high a level as your kids are likely to want. Then nudge it a bit higher. Now, grab a dull book and try reading it in your planned office area. Can you stand it? Only you know for sure.

Checking out sounds

Do you have somebody in the household who spends a lot of time on the phone? It's easy to tell if the gabbing in a particular location will drive you bonkers. Get a portable radio, plug it in next to the offending phone, tune it to a talk station, and turn the volume up to normal telephone conversation level. Then

---

*__grok__ \grók\ *vt* To understand profoundly through intuition or empathy. Coined by Robert A. Heinlein in his *Stranger in a Strange Land. The American Heritage Dictionary of the English Language, Third Edition.* "Grok" gets my vote as the most important nontechnical term created in this century.

nudge it a bit higher. Grab that same dull book and try reading it in your planned office area. If you can't tolerate the noise level from that radio, I guarantee your live-in gabber's talk will drive you nuts. Either move the phone or move the office.

I don't think I'll get married again, dahhhling.
I'll just find a man I don't like and give him a house.

Times to Monitor   I break the major interruption periods into six categories. You should consider how your new office will hold up during each of these time slots.

As the worm turns   First, think about how your home office will hold up before the house wakes up. If you work early in the morning or very, very late at night, this may well be your most productive time. In the wee hours, you have to be concerned about whether your noise will wake up other members of the household. If there are small kids to consider, you must also be sure that they can get to you in case of an emergency. There's nothing worse than a four-year-old waking up from a nightmare, and then not being able to find the parental unit.

Morning madness   Between the time the house starts stirring and the time everybody who's going (kids, physiocommuters, hungover guests) is gone, you won't get any work done. Don't worry about it. Just make sure that your office stuff can be put out of the way easily during the interlude.

Normal hours   Most of your work will probably be done between breakfast and the time the afternoon rush starts. If you're trying to figure out where to locate an office, you need to be concerned about stay-at-homes, of course (see "Kids" and "Parents" later in this chapter). But you should also be concerned about other common interruptions.

Pets, in particular, are something that nobody seems to think about. If you have a pet who's a member of the family, though, you'll know how annoying they can be. Your pet will go wild the first week you're in a new office. Any change in routine will drive most pets nuts. If you can keep the pet in your office, more power to ya. But if you have to put the pet somewhere else, make sure there's enough of a sound barrier: A pet clawing on the door or barking at the moon adds spice to a business telephone conversation. Don't forget that the sound of your voice may actually set the pet off, so the sound barrier works both ways.

I'm no distraction. Ya wanna play? Pleeeeeeease. . . .

Other kinds of interruptions are pretty obvious, and their solutions equally so. If you live next to a freeway, you'll want to locate your telecommuting office on the quiet side of the house. If you're distracted by the view of your garden— every time you look at the flower bed, an irresistible urge wells up to go pull weeds—make sure the office doesn't overlook the garden (or board up the offending window). If you have neighbors who drop by unannounced, put your office someplace that can't be seen from the street and disconnect the doorbell. And on and on.

Honey, I'm home.

When the kids, the spouse, or any other away-for-the-day residents of the house return, you'll want to break what you're doing and give them a little time. Trust me on this one. You may think that the kids will be able to let themselves in, turn on the TV, take care of themselves until dinner, and let you keep working. Wrong. The trick is to give them the time they need, make sure everything is fine, and then make a clean break back to the office. If your kids habitually watch TV, play video games, plunk around on the computer after school, shoot some hoops, or do anything else that makes noise, you'll need lots of sound insulation between you and the distraction. Locate your office accordingly.

Dinner madness

You won't get anything done around dinner time. Don't even try. When you decide on a location for your office, make sure it won't get in the way of dinner. An occasional spate of late-night work might force the family into eating dinner in an unusual place—Mom's late work night may always signal a trip to McDonald's— but trying to make dinner on or around your office desk is a sure recipe for disaster.

Into the night

The final time slot to consider is the one immediately after dinner, extending well into the night. During the children's hour, ol' Henry Longfellow may have been able to retreat to his darkly paneled library and savor the patter of little feet— disciplined by the firm hand of the family nanny. You, on the other hand, will be forced into your cramped, jury-rigged office, where you will no doubt contend with the scuffling of rival siblings, the crash of mutilated furniture, and the occasional yelp of a tormented family pet.

Plan your "office environment" accordingly.

Tax Considerations

> The income tax people are very nice.
> They're letting me keep my own mother.
>
> Henny Youngman

While it never makes sense to make a decision based solely on its tax conse-quences (or so my accountant tells me; sorry, Pat, but I *still* don't believe it), an injudicious choice of location may completely hose your home office deduction.

Playing by Uncle Sam's rules

If you're a "traditional" telecommuter—an employee who works at home because *you* want to—you won't qualify for a tax deduction. Don't even think about it. Put your office wherever traffic patterns dictate.

If you don't fit in the "traditional" mold, though, you may well qualify for a home office deduction. It won't be much money. And it'll raise a red flag on your tax return. But if you qualify, you should go ahead and exploit the rules to your advan-tage! Heaven knows the government can use your money better than you can.

Anyway, if you're not a "traditional" telecommuter, check out Chapter 8 to see if the location of your telecommuting office might affect its deductibility. For example, if you put your home office in a spare bedroom and let your nephews sleep on the floor when they come to visit, you're SOL.* Similarly, you lose the deduction if your office is in the garage, and your lawn mower is in the garage, too. But you may qualify for a deduction for that same garage office if there's a torn, dirty rag hanging from the ceiling on two rusty nails—as long as the rag sits between your office and the lawn mower. See the difference?

May as well pick a place for your office with both of your eyes open, and know about the hoops the government will expect you to jump through, *before* all the furniture gets moved in.

GETTING ORGANIZED

> Early to bed, early to rise
> Work like hell and organize.
>
> Al Gore
> Presidential campaign slogan, 1988

Remember that, as king of your virtual office, you're a one-organism band. At various times you'll play receptionist, engineer, accountant, office administrator, purchasing department, custodian, and systems administrator.

---

* Strictly Outta Luck. One of those fancy computer terms you've heard about.

The trick lies in getting things organized from the get-go, so you can devote as much of your time and energy as possible to actually getting work done. By avoiding the myriad traps and time sinks that float around a home office, you'll accomplish more "real" work, and maybe have some time left over for the spouse and kids.

Time sinks

Maybe.

One Big, Happy Telefamily

> Childhood knows the human heart.
>
> Edgar Allen Poe
> *Tamerlane*, 1827

Childcare is childcare, and a worker with kids is going to need childcare from time to time — whether the worker telecommutes, physiocommutes, or gets by with simple astral projection. Arranging for childcare is just as complicated whether you work at home or not: When you're working, you're working.

Guilt Trip   You should never, ever feel guilty about seeking childcare while you work at home. Toddlers and work simply don't mix. With very rare exceptions, you can have a two-year-old at home, or you can work at home. You can't have both. Trying to baby-sit a toddler while you're working gives short shrift to the job and — more importantly — to the child!

That doesn't mean you have to kick your daughter out of the house if she gets sick for the day. Telecommuting gives you some options.

The books and magazine articles will tell you that kids and telecommuting are totally incompatible — on any given day you can have kids at home, or you can work at home, but not both.

That simply isn't true, and you mustn't accept the gross oversimplification. The truth is, it all depends on the child, the job, the parents' expectations, and how well a child can adapt to the inevitable rivalry between time demands for the job and for the kid.

Dad! My tongue's stuck! Get off the phone RIGHT NOW.

Although every child matures at a different rate, I've seen four very different stages in a child's growth, vis-à-vis the telecommuting parent.

Pre-toddlin'   ***The First Year***   Once your child sleeps reliably through the night, but before your child can walk, juvenile interruptions can be localized—if not eliminated. Many parents find it isn't too difficult working at home with a pretoddler, at least half time, providing the work can be arranged to fit the child's schedule.

You won't be able to answer the phone every time it rings. You won't be able to drop everything during the midday feeding and run some numbers for the boss. But you will be able to work out a schedule that gives you an hour or two of uninterrupted concentration, followed by a break, and then another hour or two, once or twice a day. If your child will play quietly in a playpen in your office— and many will—the pretoddling times are quite compatible with telecommuting.

Toddlin' to terror   ***To First Grade***   From the time your child starts walking until he becomes quite independent, you won't be able to get anything done in a home office while the child's at home. Nothing at all.

I've seen three solutions to this Kid Teleconnundrum.

Most commonly, telecommuting parents will arrange for childcare, preschool, kindergarten, or some other combination of baby-sitting and schooling outside the home. It's traumatic, for both parents and children. It's expensive. It's difficult: Finding the right care giver is tougher than finding a good lawyer.

Some telecommuting parents are able to trade off childcare responsibilities with their spouses, and those responsibilities can be woven into the working parts of the week. In my experience, this approach doesn't stand a chance of succeeding unless there's a firm, set schedule—for example, Dad gets the kids on Monday, Wednesday, and Friday mornings, and Tuesday and Thursday afternoons; Mom picks up the flip side; and the rare exceptions are negotiated days in advance. Without a schedule that's respected by all parties, one spouse or the other gets dumped on, and the resentment builds quickly.

The third arrangement I've seen that works well is a scaled-back work day with in-house childcare. A friend of mine has a son who took a nap every afternoon, like clockwork, from about noon to 2:00. She simply closed up shop in the mornings—phone calls went straight to the answering machine—and worked from noon until 6:00 or so every day. She hired a neighbor to come in and baby-sit from 2:00 to 6:00. The child knew, once he woke up, that Mom was working and couldn't be disturbed. (It took a while to reinforce that structure; Mom and the baby-sitter had a harder time with it than the boy!) Mom's back to teleworking full days now, and business is booming.

Can I eat this, Mommy? Can I, huh?

Between Seven and Twelve The latchkey years can be difficult for kids with physiocommuting parents. Young kids, sometimes just six or seven years old, are expected to let themselves into the house, put together a snack, and watch TV until their parents get home from work. **The virtual latchkey**

Telecommuting parents have a real edge up on physiocommuters when their kids reach the latchkey years. They can break from work when the kids arrive home from school, get them something to eat, and set them up with something to do. Most kids from the age of six or so can keep themselves occupied for a couple of hours while Mom or Dad finishes off the workday.

Twelve and Older Hell, once they're teenagers you'll be lucky to get 'em to come home, period, right? The only problems I've heard about with telecommuting parents and teenagers is the inevitable tendency to workaholism, and how teenagers can take that personally. I'll talk about workaholism later in this section. **Teens**

> A child develops individuality long before he develops taste. I have seen my kid straggle into the kitchen in the morning with outfits that need only one accessory: an empty gin bottle.
>
> Erma Bombeck
> *If Life is a Bowl of Cherries — What am I Doing in the Pits?*, 1978

In Defense of Dad Let me get on my soapbox one more time before turning to other topics. Most telecommuting programs seem to assume implicitly that the work-at-home parent of an infant or toddler will always be the mother. That's a shame, really. I was a work-at-home Dad. My wife and I split childcare responsibilities fifty-fifty for the first three years of our son's life. And I'll gladly tell any recalcitrant Dad out there that being involved, day to day, in the first few years of your child's life can be the most rewarding time you've ever spent.

The Daddy Track   The number of Dads opting for telecommuting because it gives them more of a chance to participate in their kids' rearing is growing every day. Dads, don't be bashful! The Daddy Track is a noble and virtuous calling.

If your boss can't accept that fact, remember: You can always find another boss.

Taking care of Mom and Dad   *Parents*   Eldercare in the telecommuting milieu hasn't received anywhere near the attention that childcare draws. As our population ages, though, it's inevitable that more and more telecommuters will struggle with the elder problem: how to take care of an ailing Mom or Dad while making a living at home?

The short and easy answer, of course, is to get them involved in what you're doing. Unfortunately, if you've been caring for a parent, you probably know that it's much easier said than done.

Many of the tips I gave for the kids of telecommuters can apply, *mutatis mutandis,* to parents, as well, particularly if the parent is suffering from a mental or physical limitation.

You can get information on available programs in the United States by looking in your phone book under State Government, Human Services Department (or sometimes Social Services Department). Many larger counties and cities also have similarly named services, and the American Association of Retired Persons (listed in the business section under AARP) will help, as well.

The only additional bit of advice I can offer to telecommuters caring for live-in adults is to consider one of the formal Eldercare programs that are springing up around the country. Seniors seem to be particularly responsive to programs that run in conjunction with kids' care programs: There's something comforting in rubbing elbows with tikes.

Creating an Identity

> Trying to define yourself is like trying to bite your own teeth.
>
> Alan Watts
> *Life,* 1961

Once you've picked a location for your telecommuting office and decided how to handle those who will be displaced—or at least inconvenienced—by your choice, it's time to start making decisions about how you're going to run your business, and what sort of image you'll be projecting to the outside world.

It's not as easy as it sounds.

Your Dark Secret   The pivotal first decision you must make is whether you're going to let the world know that you're working at home. If you're a traditional telecommuting employee, your boss may have hard-and-fast rules. For example, it's not unusual to let your coworkers know which days you'll be at home, but keep outside customers in the dark. Every office handles it a little differently.

If you're starting your own business, the to tell or not to tell decision is by no means clear. Many customers won't think less of you (indeed, some will think *more* of you) if they know that you're working from the house. But there's still a small, hard core of prospective customers who may think that you can't "really" be working if you're based in the house. And there will always be a little bit of bias: If folks know you work at home, and they get an answering machine instead of your bright, sparkling voice, the immediate conclusion will be that you're out somewhere goofing off.

Anti-home prejudice

Which is probably true, but *hey!* that's why you work at home, eh?

SnailMail* Address

Traditional telecommuting employees have to work out, with their bosses, how to handle interoffice mail and SnailMail that should go directly to the telecommuter's primary place of work—which is often their house. I don't know anybody who's really solved this problem: Mail that should go to the central office comes to the house; mail that belongs at the house ends up at the bottom of a coworker's in basket. Expect a lot of screw-ups.

> **One friend of mine has reported limited success in getting his mail routed to him at home by bribing the mail guy in the central office. Well, "bribe" may be overstating the case a bit, but you get the idea. A bottle of wine every now and then lets the mail folks know you care—and keeps them from saying, "Who da hell is this Leonhard character? Guess I'll stuff his mail in the Human Resources box and let them worry about it."**
>
> **Curious about how your mail is being treated? In the United States, it costs only $3.00 to find out. Send yourself a Priority Mail package, and see how long it takes to get routed to your home!**

If you're setting up your own business the situation is, if anything, worse. Curbside mailboxes are notorious for rip-offs and vandalism: You'd be better off trusting your important business mail to a gang of pimply prepubescent geeks. (Come to think of it, that's *exactly* what you're doing with e-mail, but never mind.) You might be able to get a drop box—a heavy metal contraption with a key—but if you do, the mail delivery person will curse your very existence. Drop boxes are terribly clumsy. Besides, using a drop box is just like scrawling "YO, KIDS! LOOK AT THIS! THERE MUST BE IMPORTANT STUFF IN HERE!" in neon colors all

Drop boxes

---

* That is, mail delivered by the "neither snow nor rain nor . . ." postal service.

over the box. Check with your local post office if you think a drop box might solve your problems. But don't say I didn't warn you.

It's a tough nut to crack. I don't know of *any* reliable way to ensure high volume, secure mail delivery to a residence. So the next best choice is . . . don't have mail delivered to your residence!

P.O. Boxes Renting a box from the post office, or from franchises like Mail Boxes Etc., has both advantages and disadvantages. They're considerably more secure than curbside mailboxes, of course, and some of those franchise operations let you use a prestige address like "10000 Fancypants Drive, Suite 321" instead of "POB 321." That fools your customers for, oh, at least five seconds. The gullible ones, anyway.

The downside of P.O. boxes   When it comes to advertising and order forms, many states require you to use a physical address in addition to the P.O. box number. I know some consumers who won't order products unless there's a physical address on the order form. Many delivery services refuse to deliver mail to P.O. boxes (even if it turns out the P.O. box is with a franchiser, and thus readily accessible); sometimes they won't even pick up a package unless it has a street address. So a P.O. box number is far from a panacea.

On the other hand, sometimes you simply must have a P.O. box. If your community has zoning laws or restrictive covenants that prohibit home offices (see Chapter 8; better yet, *move!*) using a street address for your business simply waves a red flag in front of your nosy neighbors. A P.O. box won't clear you from this type of ludicrous restriction, but it may reduce your chances of getting caught.

Many telecommuters in the U.S. find that a combination of P.O. box and physical address works best: they give out both addresses simultaneously.

> **Woody's WorldWide Web Widgets**
> **123 Someplace Drive**
> **P.O. Box 456**
> **Coal Creek Canyon, CO 80403-0456**

U.S. Postal Service regulations require the USPS to deliver mail addressed in this way to the address nearest the zip code. In this case, the piece would be delivered to P.O. Box 456. But if a customer used the same address to send a piece by, oh, FedEx, the FedEx driver is smart enough to know that the parcel should go to 123 Someplace Drive.

I've used this method of addressing packages for ten years now — physical address for parcels, P.O. box for mail, both addresses given out simultaneously — and it's worked pretty well. Occasionally the postmaster will throw a monkey wrench into the works, but it takes a stupendously incompetent postmaster to really screw things up.

We *do* have a stupendously incomp. . . well, let's just say that the local postmaster and I have locked horns numerous times, but that's another story.

Forwarding Mail Think through how you'll use the mail, should your telecommuting activities increase. Keep in mind that P.O. box franchises like Mail Boxes Etc. will only forward your mail for thirty days, and they may well charge an arm and a leg for the service. After thirty days, the next box holder is likely to receive all your mail. Giving your mail to the next guy is perfectly legal and, as I understand it, that kind of service is the rule, not the exception.

The U.S. Postal Service, on the other hand, is required to forward most mail addressed to you for a full year. See Figure 2.1. If you live outside the United States, similar rules probably apply, but you should call the local PO to find the precise details.

When is your mail not your mail? When it belongs to a mail box franchiser.

Type of mail	Forwarded free of charge for
Express Mail	One year
First Class Mail	One year
Priority Mail*	One year
2nd Class (periodicals)	60 days
3rd Class (catalogs, books under 16 oz.)	Not forwarded. With few exceptions, this stuff is just simply thrown away
4th Class (16 oz. or more)	Forwarded free locally, but you get to pay postage due if you move outside the local area

Figure 2.1 USPS Forwarding Regulations

The USPS forwarding service is free, and in my experience works pretty well. If you want to have mail forwarded, go to the nearest post office and ask for a change of address form. Fill it out and leave it with the postmaster.

Within a few days you'll receive an "Official United States Postal Service Change-of-Address Kit." Save the envelope the kit comes in—the one with your new address—just in case there's ever any question about whether you filed the form properly. The computer-generated code that appears above your name on the kit is your proof that the USPS computers have been notified.

---

*Priority Mail is just First Class mail weighing more than twelve ounces; if your Priority package weighs less than twelve ounces, it's simply billed at the twelve ounce rate. Priority and First Class service are the same. Another triumph of marketing over reality.

Note that you *don't have to move* to have your mail forwarded. Little-known fact, but it's true. If you decide you don't want to have mail left in your curbside mailbox anymore, but want it to go to a new post office box, you are perfectly within your rights (in the United States anyway) to have mail forwarded to the post office box. Just submit a change of address form.

But wait. It gets better.

You can tell the USPS to forward letters addressed to a specific person or a specific business. Say your telecommuting company, Woody's WorldWide Web Widgets, grows so fast that all those registration checks have your old curbside mailbox groaning under the weight. Go out and rent a P.O. box. Then submit a change of address form, but be careful to specify that only the mail addressed to Woody's WorldWide Web Widgets is to be forwarded. Ta-dum. For the next year all first class mail sent to WWWWW at the curbside mailbox should magically appear in the P.O. box.

And . . . pssssst . . . you didn't learn this from me, okay? I hear that it's possible to keep the mail-forwarding routine going almost indefinitely, well beyond the one-year time limit, if you monkey around with the computer program the USPS uses to track forwarding addresses. Submit a change of address form today, say, for all mail going to 123 Someplace St. Then a year from now submit a similar change of address form, but do it for 123 Some Place Street. A year later, try 123 Someplace Str. Get the idea?

Will it always work? I dunno. Is it legal? Probably not. Am I advising you to use devious, underhanded means to circumvent the proper operation of the U.S. Postal Service? Who, *moi*?

Three phone lines are *de rigeur*. *Phone* I'll go into lots of detail about phone lines, types of service, prices, pros and cons, in Chapter 4. Suffice it to say here that you will probably want two *more* lines run to your house, to handle the telecommuting workload (one for business use, another for the fax and modem). Get those phones in, and get on the list to have the lines installed, like, now. There's nothing worse than having a business all ready to go, with your phone lines sitting in your hands.

There's a way to fake it with caller ID—and we'll talk about that in Chapter 4—but if it takes six months to get a phone line installed in your area, the time to start working on it is right now.

If you're a traditional telecommuter, and will be using those lines strictly for business, consider having the bills sent straight to the central office for payment. That's just one less detail for you to worry about.

Return to sender . . . address unknown . . .

E-mail   Your on-line persona may need a new identity, as well. There are several cyberthings to check when setting up your new office.

First, do you need new IDs? Some companies may require you to change your ID when your means of getting onto the office network changes (for example, from local to dial-up). Find out early, because you'll need to notify all of your e-mail buddies of the change as soon as possible.

The id

Second, how long has it been since you changed your password? Really. You should be ashamed of yourself. If you're going to have remote access to your central office's computer, that's a big step up on the "potential security risk" continuum. Go change your password now. And change it again once your telecommuting office is set up.

The ego

Third, your usage patterns are going to change enormously. For many people that won't make much difference. But if you belong to an on-line service with multiple billing options (CompuServe comes immediately to mind), you may end up with humongous first-month bills if you choose the wrong option. When you start telecommuting, what used to be the right option may suddenly become way, way wrong. Check it out before the bill arrives!

The superego

Rest of the Image   If you're setting up your own telecommuting business, you'll have a whole host of problems that dog every business startup. Chances are very good you'll want to start by hiring an accountant versed in the needs and traps of small business, and possibly an attorney.

It's all in the image

If you're doing business in the United States, you'll have to decide if you want to incorporate (see Chapter 8). You'll need a business name, and you'll probably have to file it with the county (call the County Clerk's office). You may need a tax resale certificate, even if you don't resell anything (they'll know when you file your business name). You should apply with the IRS for an Employer Identification Number (an "EIN"; call 800-829-3676 and ask for Form SS-4). You'll want to get all the IRS publications that apply to small businesses: Publication 334 is a good start.

Logo   A good logo will probably set you back several hundred bucks, but it's better to get it sooner than later. Make sure you hire somebody who knows what they're doing, and insist on getting an electronic copy of the final product.

All of this is in addition to the usual business startup problems: product development, pricing, marketing, business plans, and on and on. Entire wings of business libraries are filled with tomes on those topics. Have fun!

Your Image on Paper

> Men are valued, not for what they are, but for what they seem to be.
>
> E. G. Bulwer-Lytton
> *Money,* 1840

With the possible exception of setting up software, you'll waste more time and money hassling over office supplies than any other aspect of establishing your telecommuting office.

Letterhead   Even if you're a traditional telecommuting employee, you may find it useful to print letterhead stationery with your own address on it. Using the company stationery and crossing out the central office address with a pen looks pretty tacky.

Roll your own   Designing your own letterhead on a computer is pretty easy. If you're handy with a "draw" program like CorelDRAW!, or if you know your word processor very well, designing decent stationery can take a day or less. (In particular, if you use Word for Windows, check out Chapter 8: The Underground Template of *The Underground Guide to Word for Windows* (Addison-Wesley, 1994) ISBN 0-201-40650-0.) Simplicity counts: A single, simple, understated design will work better than a garish display of ego.

If you don't feel like doing it yourself—or if you want a multicolor design that's beyond your abilities on the PC—any local print shop can whip up something in a nonce. Or ask your local graphic artist to take on the job. In either case, if you can sketch out a few ideas, bring along samples of letterheads that you like, or take a camera-ready copy of your logo to the shop, you'll save a lot of time and money.

Before you sign the work order, make sure you tell the people at the print shop that you'll be using the letterhead on a laser (or inkjet, as the case may be) computer printer. There are two important reasons for alerting them.

- Some inks used in "quickie" print shops—particularly the kind of inks that are used for a raised effect, like engraving—are completely incompatible with lasers; the ink will melt and run when it hits your laser's fuser, possibly screwing up your fixer roller, and definitely causing you no end of hassle and expense.

- Some papers used by printers don't work very well with laser or inkjet printers. Inkjets, in particular, are notorious for "wicking," producing blotchy print when used with very porous papers. Lasers have a hard time fusing onto textured paper: The print can "crack," particularly along fold lines; it can also rub off.

Checking Paper Quality   Before you spend a lot of money on a print job, there's a little trick you should consider trying. I learned about this the hard way. I spent almost $2,000 on a print job that produced lovely letterhead, but whenever I ran the paper through my HP LaserJet, the resulting print would "crack."

The paper tester from hell

Here's the seven-step Underground paper sanity check. It's vital if you're going to blow some significant bucks on a print job. But it's also a good approach to follow if you're just combing through a paper store to pick up usable business paper for your laser or inkjet printer.

1. Go down to the print shop you're going to use to print your letterhead and choose two or three kinds of paper that appeal to you.

2. Have the print shop give you two sheets of each type of paper. In the best of all possible worlds, they'll have "spoilage" handy—paper that's already been printed, but was rejected for whatever reason. You want a couple sheets of spoilage to test-print on your laser or inkjet printer. It's best to work with paper that's already been through the print shop's presses because the nature

of the paper can change subtly when it goes through those presses. If they don't have spoilage, though, don't worry about it. Just get a couple sheets of each of your favorite papers.

3. If it's possible, get a couple of matching envelopes for each type of paper. Generally matching envelopes have to be specially ordered, but in some cases the printer may have some samples lying around. When it comes to testing envelopes, the color of the paper isn't nearly as important as matching the paper itself—the weight, texture, finish, and the "fit" of the finished envelope.

4. Take the paper and envelopes home and write letters to yourself. Feed the paper through your printer. Make sure it feeds properly, and doesn't bunch up in the rollers. Take a close look at the finished print. That's what your customers will be seeing. Is it good enough for you? Address the envelopes to yourself. Do the envelopes feed through the printer without jamming or sliding? Do they crinkle, creating "the smudgies?"

5. Fold the letters and stuff them in the envelopes. Make sure some of the folds go right through the middle of the lines of print.

6. Mail the letters to yourself, preferably from a variety of post offices or mail boxes.

7. When the letters come back, first check the face of the envelope. Has any of the print smudged? Is any of it cracked? If the post office applied a machine readable bar code, is it legible? Next, check the letters themselves. Did the print on the folds crack? Can you see a faint "ghost" image, where print on one side of a fold transferred to empty areas on the other side of the fold?

If your envelopes or letters come back blotched, cracked, spotted, discolored, "ghost"ed, or torn to pieces, it's time to rethink your choice of paper! Far better that you learn about the paper's shortcomings before you've paid for 10,000 sheets, eh?

Fahrenheit 451   *Ex Post Facto*   What, you already spent a gazillion bucks on fancy paper, and it fails the seven-step Underground paper sanity check? Yeah, me too. Not to worry. A friend of mine has found a trick that eliminates cracking and ghosting on almost every type of paper. I *don't* recommend that you use it: You can burn your fingers, or even burn down the house. But it does work on every type of paper I've seen.

When all else fails, toast it.

If your stationery has a nasty habit of cracking or ghosting, or if your envelopes smudge like there's no tomorrow, get down to a hardware store and buy a paint stripper. No, I'm not joking. You want a heat gun rated at 1200 watts or so—the weekend painter's version of a super-duper industrial strength hair dryer. My friend claims he's had a lot of luck with the Milwaukee 1200 Heat Gun.

As soon as each page rolls off your printer, put it on a heat-resistant and fireproof pad (my friend uses a Corian countertop), and hit the page with the heat gun. It takes a bit of practice to get the heat just right: too little, and the print won't get "fused" to the paper; too much and the paper will crackle and turn yellow (or, presumably, catch on fire!). Watch your fingers.

Again, I do NOT recommend this approach. It's too dangerous. But if you're a trained fire-fighting professional, it *does* work.

What to Have Printed   If you think things through a bit, you can save hundreds— even thousands—of dollars on printing costs by judicious separation of the work to be done by the print shop and work that you can do on your laser or inkjet printer.

In general, a print shop can do a bang-up job on complex graphics, maybe your logo, and any multicolor printing you might want on your letterhead or envelopes. All of that stuff is hard to do on your laser or inkjet printer. Complex graphics on a laser (even at 600 dpi) won't turn out as sharp as work done by a good print shop. Color printing on a laser tends to look washed out; color printing on a dye-sub printer is enormously expensive; and color printing on an inkjet printer (other than, oh, an occasional line or accent or two) probably won't look like much.

> Complex graphics and color should be done by a print shop.

So have the print shop do the complex graphics and color. But *don't* have them print your company name, address, and the like.

You can do it yourself!

If you use your laser or inkjet printer to print your company name, addresses, phone numbers, e-mail addresses, and 'most everything else on your letter-head and envelopes, changing little things won't cost a lot of money. You can move your office—or switch from a street address to a P.O. box—by simply modifying the word processor template you use for creating business letters. Want to change your fax number? It's easy if the number isn't preprinted on your letterhead. Adding a second voice line? Piece o' cake. Creating a second business, with a slightly different name? No sweat. Use the print shop to do what they do best. But save the rest of the work for your word processor!

I use my business stationery for personal letters (with my name on top, replacing the company's name). It also works just fine, with a few minor modifications to the template, for press releases, product announcements, and just about any other formal business communication. By relying on the print shop to produce an eye-catching color logo and using my word processor for everything else, I've saved myself thousands of dollars, months of waiting for special "rush" jobs, and at least half a head of gray hair.

You'd be surprised how many companies in the telecommuting business change their names or addresses and are still using white-out to bring their letterhead, envelopes, and brochures up to date. Telecommuting companies are, by definition, mobile. Keep your options open. Don't throw away your money by having the print shop do things you can do at home!

Paper Direct   *Preprinted Paper*   No doubt you've seen the Paper Direct brochures. Paper Direct (for phone numbers, see Appendix B) pioneered the colorful, preprinted, laser-ready paper business. Hundreds of different letterheads, envelopes, brochures, business cards, and the like are available, in a bewildering array of colors, designs, and styles.

A typical Paper Direct letterhead will cost fifteen to twenty cents. Envelopes run about twenty-five to thirty cents apiece. That's about the price you'll pay for a top-notch custom print job, if you're willing to buy stationery in quantities of 1,000 or more, but Paper Direct sells in quantities of 50 to 100.

Remember that you're only buying the paper, fancy though it may be. You'll have to use your laser printer to add your own logo, name and address, phone and e-mail numbers, and the like. Paper Direct sells prebuilt templates for various word processors, but (and I'm something of a template snob, so don't take my word for it) they're not much.

Image Street   Moore Business Products has a new division called Image Street that offers the same shtick, at about the same prices, with one interesting twist: They'll print your logo, business name, address, and so forth, on any of their papers for about five to ten cents each (minimum quantity 500; call for details). They'll also convert your 35mm photograph into a roll of self-adhesive labels—suitable for sticking on business cards, brochures, letterhead, whatever—for about twenty to sixty cents per label. Note that the photograph doesn't have to be a person's portrait: You can use a picture of your product, or your service, or Uncle Jed with his funny Groucho Marx glasses.

Generic preprinted papers   The big paper manufacturing companies were a little slow to catch on to the preprinted laser paper craze. That's one big reason why the paper is so expensive. Gradually, though, they're learning. Check with your local discount paper supplier. You may be pleasantly surprised by their competitive prices.

 One little warning. These papers are generally designed specifically for laser printers. If you're considering using an inkjet printer with any preprinted papers, make sure you specifically ask if the paper you're interested in will work with your kind of printer. Some paper that works beautifully with laser printers smudges badly with an inkjet.

Business Cards No discussion of preprinted papers is complete without a warning about business cards. Paper Direct and Image Street will sell you sheets of colorful business cards for about four cents per card. Ten cards (2 by 3½ inches) fit on a standard 8½-by-11 sheet of paper. They're "micro-perfed" with small, nearly invisible perforations, to separate easily, once you run them through your laser printer.

Some people think the cards are great. Certainly, they're colorful—in fact, you can often coordinate the cards' color and design with your letterhead and envelopes. But some folks, including me, think they fall short of the mark. The micro-perfed edges don't feel right. The cards themselves are pretty thin.

Anyway, a word to the wise: Before you order preprinted laser business cards, make sure you hold one in your hand. Judge for yourself if they're up to your exacting standards. In particular, compare them to the cheapie business cards you can have made at any print shop for a penny apiece or less.

If you do decide to print your own business cards, be sure to check out Rockford! Pro, the premiere business card software ($30 from OsoSoft; voice 805-528-1759). It will help you come up with a good design and have you printing cards in no time.

DIY Color Speaking of cheapie print jobs. My wife came up with this idea while trying to minimize overhead costs for the charity she heads.

Adding a splash of color to a plain black-and-white print job can be as easy as running a color marker over a printed design. Many print shops have pre-fab clipart you can put on your letterhead, envelope, or business card. If the design comes out on the finished piece dark enough (and most do), running a Hi-Liter or similar light-color marker over the artwork will produce a very convincing imitation of a two-color print job. You can color in a drop-down hollow letter, or swipe a daring neon squiggle through a line of conservative black type. The black shows through, and the splash of color can be most attractive.

STAYING ORGANIZED

>Don't agonize. Organize.
>
>Florynce R. Kennedy
>1973

As a telecommuter, your life will be ever more pleasant if you not only take pains to get organized in the first instance, but also strive to stay organized as the work piles up.

Easier said than done, eh?

An accepted method for staying organized

How do you PIM?

Time Management   So much has been written on the topic of time management that you start to wonder where all these experts came from. And I often wonder if there isn't more time wasted on setting up those time-calendar-personal-information-management software systems than their users ever recoup by putting the software to work.

Personally, I keep a handwritten to-do list for project management and a little desk calendar for appointments. Phone numbers and addresses are on the computer, of course, so I don't have to type them in every time I write a letter. I use a simple, single-purpose program called Metz Phones to keep track of 'em. That's it. Anything more for me is overkill.

As you switch from the hustle and bustle of the corporate office, with its time-sliced coffee breaks and three-deep meetings, you may find your needs changing, too. Don't ever be afraid—or ashamed!—of throwing away your fancy-schmancy appointment book or Totally Cool Personal Information Manager.

KISS

Your needs may be different, of course. Don't let me talk you out of your Day Timer or PackRat 5.013. Just keep in mind that you may waste more time organizing your time than you'll spend simply doing the work and not worrying about organizing it.

Scheduling   While scheduling is rightfully considered a subset of time management, it presents special problems for telecommuters. Not to put too fine a point on it, "scheduling" refers to your ability to apply butt to chair, and get some work done.

While there are plenty of distractions in a typical main office, there are lots of "get back to work" cues, too. The boss or a coworker walks by. The crowd around the coffee machine starts shuffling back to their cubicles. The guy down the hall starts screaming epithets at his computer. The clock strikes one. Somebody calls an impromptu meeting. Many different external triggers can remind you to get back to work.

Anything but work

Telecommuters don't have those kinds of triggers. If you go off on a tangent—you're working on a report and suddenly remember that all the window sills need dusting, or you're pulling together a critical spreadsheet and this overwhelming urge comes over you to defrag your disk—there are no subtle cues to bring you back to the work at hand.

If you have these kinds of distraction problems, you may find it worthwhile to come up with a written Schedule. (Note the capital "S"!) At the beginning of each day, review what needs to be done and block off portions of the day to accomplish each task. Write it all down and stick the Schedule someplace where you have to look at it, like right next to your computer monitor.

If you feel that a computer can help to apply discipline where a vacuum now exists, look into Lotus Organizer. It's one personal information manager that doesn't seem to have gone off the deep end, with solid phone book, calendar, and scheduling functions, and little pretension to taking control over your computing and noncomputing life.

What me worry?

Personally, I've never written down a Schedule, and doubt that I'd follow one even if I had it. If you fall into that category too, don't despair. It gets better after awhile. Well, that isn't necessarily true. If it doesn't get better, telecommuting probably isn't your cup of tea. Regardless, "think time" is time well spent, even if you're washing the dishes or mowing the lawn or looking out the window.

Hey, I should be telling you.

Some of my best ideas just kinda pop into my head when I'm driving, staring at the mountains, sleeping, or watching some dumb movie—just about anytime when I'm not "working." The same thing will happen to you, too, when you stop thinking of "work" as a place you go, and start accepting it as a natural part of your telecommuting lifestyle.

Getting Going

> Whenever I find myself growing vaporish, I rouse myself, wash and put on a clean shirt, brush my hair and clothes, tie my shoe-strings neatly, and in fact agonize as if I were going out—then, all clean and comfortable, I sit down to write.
>
> John Keats
> 1819

The worst time for most telecommuters is at the very beginning of the day. There's no burning rush to get out on the freeway in time to get to the office before the boss arrives. You want to linger over that latte grande. Read the paper. Wash the car. Pull some weeds. It's terribly tempting.

I have four friends with the getting-started blues. They've found four very different ways to overcome the problem. Perhaps one of them will work for you.

Like Keats some 175 years ago, one well-known computer writer (whose name you would recognize in a second) found it easiest to get in the mood for work by getting up according to his old schedule, dressing in a suit and tie, and walking into his home office. He would close the door, work a long day, then return "home," only removing the tie once the workday was over.

Fortunately, he grew out of it.

Another friend could never drag herself into the office in the morning until she coerced a coworker in the main office to call her every morning, just as the coworker arrived. Worked like a champ. The fear of appearing to be a slacker got her schedule going in the morning.

Your approach needn't be quite so draconian.

Another friend of mine has a mental alarm clock, triggered by her favorite morning TV show. She always, always heads to the office when she hears the "outro" music on the *Today* show. By the time Bryant Gumbel is off the air, she's sitting behind her computer, warming up to the day ahead.

My fourth friend is, uh, let's call him frugal. If he can find a way to save a buck, he'll go to the ends of the earth to make it happen.

When he discovered that the phone company generally charges 40 percent less for long-distance telephone calls made before 8:00 a.m., that's all the incentive he needed. He now gets into the office by 7:30 every morning. He immediately jumps on the phone, making calls and sending faxes before the magic 8:00 cutoff point. (He lives on the West Coast, which helps.)

I bet he saves hundreds of dollars a year by simply adjusting his schedule so the long-distance calls go out before 8:00. More importantly, though, I bet he's *made* thousands of dollars because he's in his office early, reliably, every day, and by the time 8:00 rolls around, he's primed and ready to get to work.

Diffr'nt strokes for diffr'nt folks, I guess.

Circadian Rhythms

> The morning is a friend to the muses.
>
> Desiderius Erasmus
> *Colloquia*, 1524

As a telecommuter, you often have free hand to work the hours that suit you best. Yes, some traditional telemployees are expected to be available to answer the phone during "core hours." But by and large, having the flexibility to determine where you work also gives you a lot of flexibility in deciding when you work. Use it!

Most computer jocks are night owls: Their most productive hours come long after the sun sets. I'm exactly the opposite. I work best from around 4:00 a.m. until the early afternoon. My mind turns to mush by dinner time, and I'm asleep mentally, if not physically, by 8:30.

Morning people, night people, and times of the living dead

Scientists call the daily ebb and flow of energy your "circadian rhythm." It's a very real, measurable effect. Yeah, "circadian" sounds like some pop psychologists' excuse for writing a book. (*I'm OK, You're Circadian*, eh?) But in fact circadian rhythms exert enormous control over how well you can work. If you've ever experienced jet lag, you know how powerful the daily time rhythms can be.

Physiocommuters have to shoe-horn their natural circadian rhythms into the hours they're supposed to be working. If you're a night person and you're expected to physically show up for work at 8:00 a.m., you probably won't get anything done before 10:00, at best, but you'll be raring to go about the time everybody leaves. I expect that's one reason why caffeine is the computer jock's breakfast of champions.

March to the tune of your own drummer.

I like my morning latte straight.

This may be the most important productivity-enhancing tip in the *Underground Guide*. If you want to get the most out of your working day, follow your own circadian rhythm. Adjust your starting and ending hours until you find the times that *you* work best. Be aware of the fact that your optimum work times will change, most frequently before and after long plane trips (usually in conjunction with jet lag), and around the days when the rest of the world goes on and off daylight savings time. Oh yeah, it happens.

Keeping on Track

> Make no little plans; they have no magic to stir men's blood and probably themselves would not be realized. Make big plans; aim high in hope and work, remembering that a noble, logical diagram once recorded will never die, but long after we are gone will be a living thing, asserting itself with ever-growing insistency. Remember that our sons and grandsons are going to do things that would stagger us.
>
> Daniel H. Burnham
> *London, 1910*

As a telecommuter you're running your own minibusiness, even if you're a traditional employee. As the owner of a business (or at least the baton holder of your own one-organism band), it's very important that you identify where you want to be headed and verify periodically that you're still on track.

Some people call that "planning," others call it "goal orientation." I just call it common sense. Your business will suffer if you don't have a very clear vision of where it should be going and how you'll get it there.

Once a week, every week, you should devote some "quality time" to planning out the course of your business and evaluating whether you're doing what needs to be done. Block out at least fifteen minutes. Turn off the phone. Close the door. Get away from all the weekly distractions. And . . . in the words of Thomas Watson Sr., THINK.

Letting Go

> It's alright letting go,
> As long as you can let yourself back.
>
> Mick Jagger

Funny as it may sound, for most people the physiocommute serves one very positive purpose: It acts as a psychological buffer, so you can brace yourself for the day ahead while on the way to work, and wind down a bit on the way home. Shift gears.

When you start telecommuting, though, you often don't have that nice, clean—albeit frustrating and draining—delineation between "it's time to work" and "it's time to stop working." The distinction between work and nonwork tends to blur.

Workaholism Oscar Wilde was fond of saying that work is the bane of the drinking class. I'm beginning to believe that workaholism is the bane of the telecommuting class. It's more than a little ironic: Most people new to telecommuting fear that they won't have the intestinal fortitude to make themselves work, while many old hands find their biggest problem is that they haven't the intestinal fortitude to *stop*.

Some people (present company certainly included) are workaholics by nature. Obsessed. Type 1. Whatever you want to call it. You know the symptoms. Workaholics have a hard time cutting off; they get to the office early and stay late; all of their entertainment and most of their social interactions come at work; they can't tell the difference between a business associate and a friend; they tend to talk about nothing but work; they measure their worth as a human being by how well they feel they're doing on the job; and they're forever taking work home.

Symptoms

When your work is *at* home, letting go gets much harder.

> **I've only found two tricks to make me quit working. First, if I promise somebody that I'll do something "at 5:00" or the end of the work day, it's hard to go back on the promise. (Kids are especially good about it: "But Daaaaaad, you said you'd play Donkey Kong Country with me at 5:00.") Second, I have to turn off the bloody phone, or I'll be answering it all night. Weekends, too.**

That's about it. Quitting is tough, eh?

The Wider View It's a cultural thing, I guess. I've lived in several Asian and Middle Eastern societies where the distinction between "work" and "nonwork" is even more tenuous than it is for the typical American telecommuter. Long hours on the job without breaks are hallmarks of traditional Japanese and Korean business life. The Chinese "godown"—a work-at-home storefront on the bottom floor, with cramped living quarters on the upper floor—has formed the backbone of Asian retailing for centuries. In many Arab and Indian communities your job determines just about everything in your life—it can be even more constricting than your caste—and working like a dog is the only socially acceptable way of life.

Is it really a problem?

In some of these societies, the concept of "taking a break" is quite foreign. A Korean businessman may go out for a night of drinking and carousing. . . yet still be working the whole time. A rural Indian businessman may work in the lower-level storefront part of his home, living with a large extended family upstairs, and spend years hardly venturing beyond his front door. Farmers in the more fertile parts of Asia will work twelve hours a day, seven days a week, for years on end, to feed their families. If they're fortunate, several years' work may net enough to buy a small TV set.

Which is all by way of saying that working hard isn't the *worst* thing that can happen to you. People all over the world work a hell of a lot harder than you do— or at least a hell of a lot harder than *I* do—and still manage to lead productive,

Keep it in perspective.

meaningful lives. While there's plenty of pressure in the West to take time off and relax, there's no conclusive evidence that failing to do so is terminal.

Remember, though: Working hard isn't the same thing as working smart. Don't lose sight of your goals.

If you're working too hard, raise your rates!

Productivity Tips

> The laziest man I ever met put popcorn in his pancakes
> so they would turn over by themselves.
>
> W. C. Fields

Over the years I've collected ideas from folks who seem to get a whole lot of work done, in spite of the slings and arrows of outrageous interruptions. You know the kind. The Ones Who Never Sleep.

Before we leave this section on Staying Organized, I wanted to present you with the suggestions I've found most useful. So here, in no particular order, are my favorite hints for boosting your productivity, specifically adapted for the telecommuter.

. . . and that's just the *important* stuff

Trash It   Paper piles up: Toss it early, toss it often! Almost all of the paper that crosses your desk is dispensable. Why keep it? Unless you can think of a specific, compelling reason to hold onto a piece of paper, waste it—preferably the first time you see it. The junk just piles up and makes it harder to find the important stuff.

Ignore It   Most of the phone calls you get aren't time-critical. By answering the phone every time it rings, you not only disrupt your work, you're actually encouraging folks to call for noncritical reasons.

The telephonic driver's seat

Do yourself and your business associates a favor. Encourage them to use electronic mail or the fax machine; failing that, force them to use voice mail or the answering machine. That way *you* get to choose when you want to be interrupted.

Adapt It   Are you tired of all the distractions a day in the telecommuting office brings? Here's a trick: Adapt your work schedule. If the boss and/or the job permit it, start working late in the afternoon and continue through the night. Or get up before sunrise and get eight hours in before most folks are at lunch. Adapting your schedule to avoid predictable interruptions can work wonders on your productivity.

Bunch It   Most folks find they work more effectively if they "bunch" tasks. Let your SnailMail sit for a few days, then tackle it all at once. Leave your e-mail for the end of the day, and only check it once. Check your voice mail just once a day. You get the idea. Switching from task to task entails a certain amount of overhead—both physical and mental—and bunching often minimizes the grind as you switch gears.

Get Away   Sometimes a change of scene can help you "focus," particularly on difficult jobs. When I need to edit a book manuscript, for example, my favorite haunt is the local Chuck E. Cheese, the animatronic pizza-parlor-*cum*-madhouse, "Where a kid can be a kid." Somehow, the sound of thousands of screaming kids—and my own young'un playing—forces my mind to concentrate in a way that I could never maintain in my home office. Weird? Yep. But it works.

The Chuck E. Cheese solution

You're probably different, of course. You may "focus" better in a park or at the beach. Some folks are at their most creative while they're driving in the country or jogging around the block. Seek out different locations, and see if they help you work better. The results may surprise you.

Part of the problem is psychological: When you work at a central office, going home offers a retreat of sorts. (Well, at least a change of scenery.) When you work at home, there's no retreat effect: You jump out of the office frying pan into the familial fire, as it were.

Stay Away   Sometimes family members can't take a hint: They'll come barging into your office at any hour, for the most trivial reasons. (Sounds a lot like the central office, eh?) One trick that works for some telecommuters is to rigidly identify times when it's OK to interrupt. You might take a hint from Lucy and stick a note on the door saying, "The Doctor Is In. Five Cents Please." when it's

You blockhead, Charlie Brown

OK to interrupt. Or you might simply leave the door ajar. One friend of mine swears he's rigged the door handle on his office to deliver a potent shock if it's touched during the hours of 9:00 to noon, and 1:00 to 4:00. I think he's joking, but with him you never can tell.

Can I interrupt now, dear?

Whatever you do, though, don't overreact. No matter where you work, or what you do, you'll get interrupted. Having the spouse bug you to take out the trash isn't materially different from having the boss call you into an unscheduled meeting—and tossing the trash may, ultimately, be far more worthwhile.

Deliver Us from Evil   Another type of interruption you might not think about is the daily grind of delivery people. If UPS and FedEx and Airborne and DHL and the like visit you a couple of times a week, and each rings the doorbell every time there's a package, the cumulative effect can be most distracting. I have a friend who solves the problem by placing a yellow sticky-note that says "I accept delivery of the package. John Q. Smith" on his front door every morning, then disconnects the doorbell. That takes care of almost all interruptions of the door-knocking variety. He reasons that anybody else who really needs to get in touch with him will know his phone number and call.

It's keeping me waiting.   ***Anticipation***   If you telecommute only a few days a week, a little bit of planning can help you take advantage of your telecommuting days. If your kid starts coming down with the flu, and it looks like you'll be spending a few days at home taking care of her, be sure you pack a few days' work in the car. (Flu can take a kid out of circulation for four or five days; chicken pox, measles, and the like can land you at home for a week or more.)

If you need to see the dentist, and the dentist's office is near your home, a full-day interruption in your physiocommuting schedule could turn into a short hour or two out of your telecommuting day.

Just Say YO!   When you start telecommuting, it won't take long before friends, family, and neighbors all start thinking that you have lots of time on your hands. Shortly after they come to that realization, you'll be approached about all sorts of things—baby-sitting your long-lost nephew, raising money for the local Temperance Union, serving on the board of the Nuke the Unborn Baby Whales Foundation. (That's pronounced "NUB-waif" and, oh, while I got your attention, do you want to join? I mean, you aren't commuting any more, and it really isn't that hard, ya know? You just have to come to these meetings and vote sometimes. That's all. It'll only take about an hour a month. Promise.)

MOM always liked you better.

Beware the time sinks. Learn to say, "no." It ain't easy, but it's necessary.

Put Your Idea Here   More than anything, an effective telecommuter must look for time-saving ideas, and aggressively put them to use. When you're dancing to your own tune, every minute counts.

A PLATFORM FOR YOUR PLATFORM

> Know thy ass, for it bears thee.
>
> John Muir
> *How to Keep Your Volkswagen Alive*

I want to devote an entire section of this chapter to the focal point of your telecommuting office: the parts that support both you and your computer, both physically and logically. If you're like most telecommuters, you'll spend more time with your computer, office desk, and chair than anywhere else in your house. It's critical that the platform for your computer is designed to help and not get in the way.

The Switched-On Desk

> Now landsmen all, whoever you may be,
> If you want to rise to the top of the tree
> If your soul isn't fettered to an office stool,
> Be careful to be guided by this golden rule—
> Stick close to your desks and *never go to sea,*
> And you all may be Rulers of the Queen's Navee.
>
> W. S. Gilbert
> *HMS Pinafore,* 1878

You might think that the determining factor in a good telecommuter's desk—that is, one suitable for your computer, one you can work at for eighteen hours at a stretch—would be its solid appearance, its fancy precut holes for computer cables, or its pedigree as a genuine "ergonomic computer desk."

What makes a telecommutin' desk?

Not so. Not so.

Fact is, you can work on a pair of sawhorses and a slab of plywood just as well as you can work on an intricately carved rosewood antique—indeed, *better* than you can work on the antique—providing you keep two things in mind:

- Your desk must be rock-solid.
- The keyboard has to sit below normal desk height.

That's it. You don't need cable channels or a tilt-and-swivel landing spot for your monitor. No wire cages to catch printouts. No side-caddies to hold your CPU or little half-height shelves for your diskettes. Most of that stuff just gets in the way. As long as you concentrate on stability and height, the rest will follow like night unto day.

The best desks are sturdy, with the keyboard down low.

The right stuff   *Stability*   Unfortunately, most of the desks you'll find in furniture stores, office supply houses, and computer warehouses are made of particleboard—in other words, they're compressed sawdust, held together with glue and a prayer, with a pasted-on piece of paper on top that's printed with a design that's supposed to look like wood.

Yeah. Sure.

Unless the manufacturer has gone to extreme lengths, particleboard simply doesn't hold up. Yes, it looks good on the showroom floor. Yes, it'll be pretty stable for a year, or maybe two. But sooner or later, screws and other connectors in the particleboard will work loose. Legs start flopping. Every time you bump the desk it wiggles. Eventually the mere act of typing on a keyboard placed on the desk will start the monitor jiggling like a bowl full of jelly.

The higher-quality (read: more expensive) desks that you'll find in most furniture stores are made of the same particleboard, but have a one-sixteenth-inch-thick piece of real wood on top. Don't be fooled. They don't work any better than their sawdust brethren.

Ideally, you'd want a desk that's solid wood, with expertly machined, tight-fitting joints, or one that's steel with strong legs and connectors that won't loosen with age. Unfortunately, desks of this ilk—they were common in the 1960s, but are very hard to find today—tend to cost $1,000 or more.

An expensive solution

If you're very, very picky, you may be able to find a desk with a particleboard (the ads say "laminate") top and steel legs that will last for years. Such desks are very much the exception: You can look at hundreds of junky particleboard desks without encountering a single solid one. The good ones have two distinguishing characteristics. First, the steel base and legs form a structurally complete unit—they don't rely on the wood top for stability. Second, they have oversized anchors buried deep in the particleboard wherever metal connects to the top.

A not-quite-so expensive solution

Some of the best desks you'll find are old steel klunkers, the kind that weigh 300 pounds and are sold for scrap metal at used office equipment auctions. I've seen hundreds of them go for $10 or $20 apiece, the only catch being that the purchaser had to remove the bloated monsters from their old locations. If you aren't overly concerned about making the cover of *Interior Decorator Magazine*, or having the world's most gorgeous office, take a close look at the old, old furniture. Bargains abound. Rent a trailer, and take a big friend and a dolly or two.

Keyboard Height   The typical desk stands 30" (about 76 cm) or so above the floor. That's a great height for writing (by hand, with a pen, remember how to do that?) or reading. But it's way, way too high for a keyboard. If you try to put your keyboard up at 30", your wrists will flop down onto the desktop, and you're just begging for repetitive motion problems.

Depending on your height and the height of your chair, you'll probably find that you work best with the keyboard 25" to 26" (63 to 66 cm) above the floor. I can't over-emphasize how important it is to get the keyboard at the right height: sticking your keyboard on top of a 30" desk could lead to years of agony. True fact. It happened to me.

If you have a perfectly good 30"-high desk with enough free room to hold a computer, don't fret: Just remove the center drawer and replace it with a pull-out adjustable keyboard holder ($12 from MEI Micro Center, SKU #900464; see Appendix B). Make sure the keyboard holder drops low enough—or jury-rig a couple of spacers between the holder and your desk when you mount it.

My Recommendation   A good telecommuting desk needn't be terribly expensive. I spent years looking for an "ideal" computer desk, and finally came up with one that costs $250 for the 48" x 30" version, $275 for the 60" x 30" size, plus

An unabashed plug for a great product

shipping. It's solid (laminated top, steel legs and sides), adjustable, and has a cut-out keyboard rest for moving the keyboard to almost any height. The desk is 29" high, but the legs can be raised or lowered a full inch. The keyboard tray moves 3".

Contact Global Equipment Company and ask about the 50070X series "Bi-Level Ergonomic Workstations." Nope, the price doesn't include casters, drawers, or any of the fluff: It's a workhorse, pure and simple.

If you order a "Bi-Level Ergonomic Workstation," make sure you get the shelf—it adds a great deal of stability to the finished product.

Desktop Real Estate

> Always leave room for the mouse.
>
> H. H. Munro ("Saki")
> *The Square Egg,* 1924

Before you rush out and buy a new desk, though, make sure it will hold all your telejunk! Desktop real estate in an era of 120-pound monitors must be allocated with the wisdom of Solomon.

What you see is what you got.   *Monitor*   If you have a 14" or smaller monitor, you'll probably want to stick it on top of the main computer box. Contrariwise, most 15" or larger monitors should stand by themselves; you'll have to find another place to put the CPU.

You're going to want the front of the monitor to be 15 to 30 inches from your face, with the top of the monitor screen just about even with your eyes. (Smaller monitors go closer, bigger ones farther back, of course.)

In my experience, those swing-away monitor arm things don't work very well; they tend to accentuate even a tiny wobble in the table. But there's nothing wrong with propping up your monitor with a book or a rack, as long as it doesn't develop a nasty tendency to slide off the table. Tilt 'n swivel bases are nice—but if you're the only one using the monitor, you can pretty much put the monitor wherever you want, and forget the fancy base.

Be careful to orient the monitor to minimize glare. If you can see the reflection of overhead lights, or if you can see light from outdoors reflected in the screen, you'll regret it. Get shades for the window, change the overhead lighting, or move the monitor.

The main attraction   *CPU*   "Desktop" computer cases are designed to lie flat on a desk. "Tower" cases sit upright. Mostly, though, the orientation question is marketing smoke and mirrors. You can put a "desktop" case upright, even if it doesn't look like it was designed to work that way. You can put a "tower" on its side, too, as long as you remember to turn the machine off before you flip it!

No, you don't need a fancy bracket or anything of the sort. Just make sure you aren't covering up any vents, so the air continues to flow freely, and double-check to see if the floppy drives are still accessible.

You can put the main CPU box on the floor, too. Either flat or on its side, no big deal. It may gather a little more dust down on the floor, but as long as you don't kick it (or kick it too hard), the computer will never know the difference.

Phone **While you're plotting the positioning of items on your desk, there's one little productivity-enhancing idea I wanted to toss your way. I read about it years ago, and it really works. If you're right-handed, put your phone on the left side of the desk. If you're left-handed, put the phone on the right. You'd be surprised how much of a difference it makes: The cord doesn't get tangled as easily, the numbers are easier to see and use, and your neck won't hurt as much. Works like a champ.**

The Throne

> If a man has good corn, or wood, or boards, or pigs to sell, or can make better chairs or knives, crucibles or church organs, than anybody else, you will find a broad hard-beaten road to his house, though it be in the woods.*
>
> R. W. Emerson
> *Journal*, 1855

What's the single most important piece of equipment in your virtual office? That whiz-bang Pentium multimedia computer, you say? Nope. You can struggle along with an obsolete computer for months, even years, and still get useful work done. The telephone? Wrong again. On a pain scale from one to ten, lousy phones are hardly a minor nuisance. Not even poor lighting or unreliable electricity or a malfunctioning heater or a leaky roof will cause you anywhere near the pain and frustration brought on by a bad chair.

I hear it time and again, from telecommuters of every persuasion: The most important piece of office equipment is the lowly chair. Spend one hour in a bad chair and you'll feel it for the rest of the day—if not the week.

Nice to see you're back from the front.

Choosing a Chair With all the money wasted every year on bad chairs, you'd think there would be a *Consumer Reports*-style guide to the latest models. Not so. Not possible, actually. There are so many different chairs made available to the public every year that merely cataloging all of them, much less evaluating them, would be a Herculean task.

---

* Emerson is said to have mentioned "a better mouse-trap" during one of his lectures, but that phrase didn't appear in print during his lifetime.

Telecommuters have all the needs of a typical chair buyer, plus one that's often overlooked: If you spend most of your day in front of a computer, make sure that the chair you buy will let you slide under your keyboard without banging your knees. Most (but by no means all) chairs adjust up-and-down far enough to clear your knees. Similarly, most (but, again, not all) desks and computer hutches have enough clearance side-to-side to accommodate even the widest chairs and knobbiest knees. When you go out shopping for a chair, it would behoove you to ensure that you can return it if it just won't fit.

How to pick a good chair? It isn't easy.

Lumbar street

Start by sitting in the chair. Does it have good lumbar support—that is, can you feel a firm pressure in the small of your back, that conforms to the curve in your lower spine? If not, I'd advise you to move on to the next chair. Flat-back (or, worse, no-back "secretarial") chairs without any lumbar support can bring on aches and pains you never knew existed.

See me.

Next, look at the chair's design. If you spend any time at all "sitting back" in your chair, the back should go up at least as high as the middle of your shoulder blades. Arms are optional—some people swear by them, others swear at them— but if the chair has arms, they should stand no more than an inch below your elbows: sit up straight, and if *your* arms don't rest comfortably on the *chair's* arms, pass this chair by.

Feel me.

Now get the "feel" of the chair. Is there enough room for your hips? Can you get in and out of the chair without bruising yourself? Are the tilt and swivel comfortable? Move around a bit. Would you feel comfortable sitting in this chair for eight, ten, twelve hours a day? Many telecommuters spend more time in their office chairs than in their beds.

Touch me.

Next, check the construction. If it rolls, make sure the chair has at least five rollers: You'll tip over with four. How are the arms attached? Wood screws will give out over time—welded metal or doweled wood last longer. And on and on. Your friendly local salesorganism will give you an earful.

Heal me.

Finally, watch out for the covering. Don't ever get leather, unless you know for an absolute fact that the leather will "breathe"—and even then, make sure the manufacturer will let you return the chair a month later, when you find out that it

Lumbar support, the hard way

doesn't really breathe, and the salesperson was blowing smoke. Vinyl tends to be just as clammy as the worst leather. If you work in short pants or short sleeves and your skin will come in direct contact with the chair, avoid leather and vinyl like the plague! For my money, a tightly-woven, smooth cloth beats all the fancy finishings, and artificial blends (nylon, polyester, and the like) wear best.

"Big Man's Chair"   No, this isn't my chauvinism showing through. It's an industry term. If you weigh more than, oh, 150 pounds, chances are very good that the first thing to wear out on your chairs is the bushing, the round metal whozamajigger that holds the rod connecting the bottom of the seat with the casters. You'll know the bushing is wearing out when your chair starts wobbling a bit. For telecommuting heavyweights (present company certainly included), the bushing goes kaput long before the fabric wears out.

Hey, it ain't your fault. Most office chairs are made for petite secretaries and the occasional 90-pound horse jockey. They're intentionally built to be light and portable—and inexpensive.

Chairs for the fashionably thin

It may surprise you to find out that there's an entire class of chairs made for the post-anorexic telecommuter. (Something else they didn't tell you in B-school, eh?) They're called "big man's chairs"—that's the official, technical term. Their main distinguishing characteristic is in the diameter of the rod that connects seat to casters, and in the heft of the bushing that holds the rod.

Most salespeople at most office warehouses (at least in my experience) don't have a clue about "big man's chairs." But if you walk into an office supply store that carries an extensive line of office chairs, you'll probably be able to find somebody who understands the term, and its implications.

> **If you weigh more than 200 pounds—certainly if you weigh more than 250 pounds—it's well worth the hassle and expense to get a "big man's chair." Ditto if you wear out the bushings on a chair long before the fabric, regardless of your weight. Even more so if you simply wear out chairs every year or two.**

Adjusting a Chair   Every chair needs adjusting. If you're lucky, the salesperson who's getting a commission on your generosity will be able to adjust your chair before you buy it. If you aren't so lucky, you'll have to do it yourself, or talk a family member or friend into working with you. Not to worry. It will only take a few minutes.

Height

First, adjust the chair up-and-down so your feet fall flat on the floor, and most of your thighs rest on the chair seat. Your knees should be up just enough to lift the front part of the thigh above the seat. Typically this adjustment is made by turning the bushing at the top of the casters so the rod moves up and down. You may have to loosen a screw before the bushing will turn.

Depth, arms   Once the height is right, move the arms and back into place. If you sit up straight, the chair's arms should fall just below your elbows. The back should be moved to give you good lumbar support while your butt—the center of weight—lies directly over the rod.

Tilt   Finally, tighten the big handle on the bottom of the seat so tilting all the way back requires a little bit of pushing. You should feel comfortable leaning back, with support all the way, but you shouldn't feel like you need to shove.

At home   The salesperson should help you with all those adjustments, but there's one last, crucial adjustment for folks who spend a lot of time at a keyboard. When you get home, move the chair up to your PC, and stick your hands on the keyboard. Your elbows should be at 90 degrees. If not, adjust the height of the keyboard or desk first. Then adjust the chair, if necessary, and use a footrest if your feet come off the floor.

It's nice to have your feet resting on the floor. But it's crucial that your elbows extend at 90 degrees (to avoid repetitive motion problems), and that your thighs rise slightly off the seat (to keep the circulation going in your legs). If push comes to shove, fake it with a footrest—don't compromise on your elbows or thighs.

The Price of Perfection   I bet you scoffed at the price of chairs the first time you saw them. It's hard to believe that folks at the central office would cough up $200 or $300 for an office chair, when you can pick one up at Ye Olde Discount Furniture Parlor for $39. No *way* you'd pay three hundred bucks for a chair, you said.

My path to seated enlightenment   Well, the joke's on you. Or at least it's on me.

I bought a cheap chair once. It lasted about a week, and my back complained every minute. So I bought a $100 chair at a discount club. It lasted a few months, until the bushing gave out. I threw it away.

So I bought a $250 chair from an office warehouse, and it held up for a couple of years. Finally the bushing started wobbling. Then an arm broke off. I finally got the arm reattached (thanks, Dad!), and gave the chair to my wife.

I finally, uh, sat down and figured out that I was averaging $125 per year on office chairs—a considerable expense, especially because I was never really happy with the chairs.

Another unabashed plug for a great product   So I bit the bullet and blew $600 on a "big man's chair," a La-Z-Boy office chair. (Yep, La-Z-Boy makes office chairs. Nope, they aren't the recliner/lounger/kick-back consumer chairs you associate with the name "La-Z-Boy"; they look like they belong in a boardroom, or on the floor of the Senate. And several are. Some of them list for $1,000 or more, but if you look around you can find 'em at steep discounts.) I've been sitting in that chair for two years now, and it feels as good as the day I bought it. Bet it lasts ten more years.

Don't get disillusioned. Expensive chairs aren't necessarily better than cheaper chairs. There's no good reason to pay for a name—the big-name lines have klunkers just like the no-name manufacturers. But it's worth waiting to get a good chair. The clincher: You won't really know if you have a "good" chair until you've been in it for a week.

Power and Light

> I had rather be shut up in a very modest cottage, with my books, my family and a few old friends, dining on simple bacon, and letting the world roll on as it liked, than to occupy the most splendid post which any human power can give.
>
> Thomas Jefferson
> 1788

While most of the other aspects of setting up a telecommuting office are pretty obvious, I'd like to warn you about a few potential problems every telecommuter's office faces.

Power If there's any way you can get a separate office electrical circuit—that is, a set of wires that physically runs from your circuit breaker panel to your office— do it!

    To the people

There are two types of power interference that can be particularly painful in a telecommuter's office.

RFI, or radio frequency interference, generates the "static" that you hear on a radio or see on a TV. Small home appliances often give off lots of RFI. Generally, a cheap $10 surge protector will prevent RFI interference from affecting your computer. (While it's true that some computers create enough RFI to screw up radio or TV reception, the solution is usually as simple as moving the radio or TV antenna away from the PC.)

    RFI

EMI, or electromagnetic interference, is a horse of a different color. Typically caused by heavy machinery, something as innocuous as a garage door opener or refrigerator can create enough EMI to bug your PC. EMI is the main reason why you'd like to have your telecommuting office on a separate circuit.

    EMI

> **If you can't put your office on a separate electrical circuit, make sure you get your PC, fax machine, phone equipment, and answering machine hooked into a UPS. (See later in this chapter.)**

HVAC Heating, ventilation, and air conditioning are important anywhere you keep electronic equipment. It's particularly important to keep computers and phones at room temperature—say, under 80 or 90 degrees. Cold can take its toll, too. Computer boards shrink when they get cold, and the contacts can work loose. I've seen memory modules, hard disk controllers, and system BIOS chips all fail when they were allowed to get too cold. In each case, warming them up brought them back to life.

It's more than mere machines. Heat, cold, and humidity affect your productivity, too. Don't skimp. Even if you live someplace that rarely needs air conditioning, you may find an AC unit is vital to keep your PC healthy. Avoiding one hard disk crash will pay for an AC unit, and then some.

Smoking destroys hard drives.

Don't crash your drive with smoke particles.

Well, OK, I lied.

I haven't found any correlation between room smoke and hard drive crashes. But it's a good excuse (if you need one) to keep from smoking—or to keep a guest from smoking. I won't lecture you. I just want to see you live to tell your grandkids about the *Underground Guides*. OK?

Noise Some folks can't stand noise—and others go nuts when it's too quiet!

If you suffer from too much noise, consider using solid core doors, double-pane windows, and sound-absorbing wall and floor coverings.

Noisebuster

You might also try the sound-canceling earphones that are on the market. They work by feeding a "negative" sound, designed to offset ambient noise, through a large pair of headphones. They're not cheap—the Noisebuster, available at most computer stores, retails for about $120. I find the big headphones annoying and the sound-canceling technology far from effective outside a very narrow range, but your experience may be quite different from mine. Some people swear by 'em.

If you can't stand the whine from your PC's hard drive or power fan, and don't want to tear out the offending components, consider *making your office noisier*. Seriously. A fish tank can make enough white noise to drown out most whining fans. Small, battery-operated waterfalls can, too.

And if you really, really miss the sounds of the old central office, you can always make a tape recording of the ambient noise at your old desk, replaying it in your home office. To ensure that you don't get too nostalgic about the wonderful ol' office days, though, make sure that you include a good clip of your boss screaming, the guy in the next cubicle snorting as he calls the Exotic Ladies line, and Snardfarq in Accounting whining about the way you filled out your expense report.

Light   Natural light is best of course, and it's always nice to orient things to take advantage of your own zero-cost light source.

> **You'll find many home office books and magazine articles extolling the benefits of fluorescent light. It's cheap, it's soft, it's cool. Telecommuters, though, have a special concern you rarely hear about: flo lights *pulse*. Some people are very sensitive to the pulsing. When I work at a monitor that reflects overhead fluorescent light, I get splitting headaches in no time flat. The pulse of the flo light somehow synchronizes with the flicker of the screen, and the combination makes for a four-martini headache. You may not have the problem. But it's best to check before the computer and light fixtures are in place, eh?**

Safety

Smoke Detectors   How many smoke detectors are in your telecommuting office? If you said, "None," I want you to put this book down, run out *right now* and buy a handful. Seriously. You need at least two for the office—one right above the computer, one on the other side of the room—and one for each hallway connecting to the office (two if there's a stairwell). Get 'em. Use 'em. That rat's nest of wires behind your computer can catch on fire and burn faster than a politician's soul.

How long has it been since you checked your smoke detectors? If it's been more than a month, I want you to put this book down, run over *right now*, and test them. Push the button and listen for the beep. No beep? Try a new battery. No battery? Get a new detector.

It really is important.

Fire Extinguishers   When smoke detectors come up, can fire extinguishers be far behind? I keep two types of fire extinguishers around the office, and recommend that you do likewise.

First are the electrical extinguishers, in little pressurized canisters, about the size and weight of cans of shaving cream. They're rated 2BC (the "2" means there isn't a whole lot of gunk in the can; "B" means it's OK for a liquid or grease fire; "C" means it's for electrical fires). They contain a pressurized gas—something like halon—that will extinguish a small fire without completely destroying electronic equipment. Think of the pressurized gas extinguisher as your first line of defense against electronic fires, should a wire get melted or a board go kablooey.

Surgical firefighting

Pulling out the stops   Second are the full-fledged guys, the 10ABC extinguishers ("10" meaning there's a lot of gunk; "A" signifying it's good for wood and paper fires). If the time ever comes that I need to haul out the big guns, these are the guns. They'll blast a small paper file to hell—and, alas, take your computer along with it. Don't point a 10ABC extinguisher at a PC, fax, phone, or other piece of electronic equipment unless you're willing to kiss it good-bye. Conversely, never hesitate to hose your PC if it's gonna torch your house!

Security   In addition to all the usual security concerns, telecommuters need to be worried about having machinery visible from outside the house. Thieves have a strangely inflated concept of the value of PCs, faxes, and fancy phone systems. Don't tempt them.

For More Info

> When you know a thing, to hold that you know it, and when you do not know it, to admit that you do not—this is true knowledge.
>
> Confucius
> *Analects,* ca. 500 BC

While there's very little written material specifically designed for the high-tech telecommuter, there are two excellent sources of information on working out of a high-tech home.

Home Office Computing magazine   The best way to stay up-to-date on the latest wired home office developments is to subscribe to *Home Office Computing*, one of the few popular magazines that manages to deliver a lot of effective information, eschewing both the patently obvious and the utterly useless.

Working from Home   For a general reference on the ins and outs of establishing and running an office in your house, it's hard to beat Paul and Sarah Edwards's classic *Working from Home* (Tarcher/Putnam, 1994, ISBN 0-87477-764-X). While the Edwards's coverage of the technology of telecommuting is light (hey, that's why I wrote *this* book!), when it comes to home office nuts and bolts—particularly the "soft" stuff like laying out workspaces, keeping the house clean, even choosing a business, should you ever need that kind of advice—*Working from Home* is the ultimate reference.

3 TelePC

Alice sighed wearily. "I think you might do something better with the time," she said, "than wasting it in asking riddles that have no answers."

"If you knew Time as well as I do," said the Hatter, "you wouldn't talk about wasting *it*. It's *him*."

C.L. Dodgson
Alice's Adventures in Wonderland, 1865

Nothing in the computer realm so resembles a riddle *sans* answer as the perennial question, "What should I buy?"

In this chapter we're going to look at computer hardware and software selection problems that bedevil most computer buyers, and particularly at considerations peculiar to the telecommuter. If you're about to buy a telecommuting PC and need a quick refresher, or if you're trying to show the boss what kind of PC you'll need to get *real* work done at home, this is the place to start. I won't even try to go into the subject of selecting and buying a PC in depth: It would take an entire book as long as this one to do the subject justice.

Once over, lightly

Computer! Computer! Take a letter, wouldja?

You needn't be a computer geek to select the "right" computer, any more than you have to be Mario Andretti to pick the "right" car. This chapter will take you through the basics, warn you about specific problems for telecommuters, and leave you armed with enough information to make an informed decision about buying or requisitioning a PC.

MOM knows best.

If you're looking for detailed guidance on evaluating and selecting the computer and components that are right for you, and you're willing to spend a few days coming up to speed on the topic, check out the latest edition of *The Mother of All Windows Books* (by Woody Leonhard and Barry Simon, Addison-Wesley, 1993). Mom and the crew will take you through the tough parts, and—unlike your local computer salesperson—leave you smiling.

The Big SOHO Lie

> *Tota in minimis existit natura.**
>
> Latin Proverb

"SOHO"—Small Office/Home Office—has become quite a buzzword among the computer cognoscenti. In an attempt to impress shareholders, computer manufacturers claim that certain lines of their wares will appeal to the SOHO crowd. Software manufacturers take great pains to cater to the SOHO market. Magazines target SOHO. Marketers slice and dice SOHO statistics, in pursuit of greater sales and fatter profits.

SOHO products tend to be scaled-down versions of industrial-strength best sellers. They're meant to be easier to learn, easier to use, possibly cheaper, certainly more accessible. Sound like something you'd be interested in?

NOT!

Say NO to SOHO.

The simple fact is that SOHO folks need all the computer power available in big offices *and then some.*

That's not to say everything labeled SOHO is bad. Far from it. But if you, as the single operational stuckee running your telecommuting office, feel that scaled-down products are good enough, well, you're selling yourself short.

 Beware the SOHO siren song. You're every bit as smart as the typical office worker. You need all the horsepower of your multi-billion-dollar competitors, right there in your telecommuting office, and you need to learn how to use that horsepower better than they do. Don't let the size of your operation cow you into making a bad business decision.

---

* All of nature is to be found in the smallest things.

COMPUTER HARDWARE

Let's start with the basics, the hardware—the stuff that you can touch. The good news is that it's hard to buy a really *bad* PC. The bad news is that it's even harder to find a really *good* PC.

Rule 1: Keep the hardware happy.

You might've heard the old saw that you should choose your software first, and then pick the right hardware to run it. Well, times have changed. The market has already made the decision for you. And the answer is: Windows. Never mind what the question was.

Like it or not, Windows rules the roost.

You thought otherwise?

Mac versus PC

> Beauty is rather a light that plays over the symmetry of things than that symmetry itself.
>
> Plotinus
> *Enneads,* ca. 250 AD

"Should I buy a Mac or a PC?"

Wish I had a nickel for every time I've heard that one. It must be the most-asked question I've encountered. Fortunately, it has a simple—not simplistic—answer.

Unless you have absolute, definite, between-the-eyes requirements for a Mac (say, you need a certain type of software that only runs on the Mac; or your main service bureau won't take PC disks; or the whole office uses Macs and translating your files would be a huge pain), you're much better off in both the short and long run getting a PC.

It's a religious issue more than anything. I'll confess to being extremely biased in favor of Windows and the PC. But in the same breath I'll insist that a PC is cheaper to buy and almost as easy to learn and use. The software is better. And cheaper. You're much more likely to have a buddy who's a PC genius, to pull you out of the tight spots. The add-on hardware is more plentiful. And cheaper.

In short, there's a reason why Intel-compatible (or IBM-compatible, if you prefer) PCs hold a 90 percent market share: more bang for your buck.

"Is the PC better?" you ask.

I dunno. Does it matter?

PC, PowerPC, Apple, and OS/2, Too

> You can run some of the software all of the time,
> And you can run all of the software some of the time,
> But you can't run all of the software all of the time.
>
> Pensées Pinecliffius
> *Ode to an Emulator,* 1995

Win-on-Mac   You've seen the ads. Apple ab-so-lutely guarantees that its Macs will run PC software. Didja see the guy on the TV? He sticks a PC disk into his Mac, and *voilà!* Windows magically appears, dancing to the Mac's tune.

Win-on-Warp   You've seen the ads. IBM ab-so-lutely guarantees that OS/2 will run Windows software. "Better Windows than Windows tut-tut!" There's a different guy on TV, explaining why you need to pay more for OS/2 so you can run your Windows programs right out of the box! Well, sometimes, anyway.

Win-on-RISC   You've seen the ads (or you will soon). IBM, Apple, and Motorola have developed a new RISC chip called the PowerPC. They ab-so-lutely guarantee that the PowerPC will run Windows software. There's yet another guy on TV, showing you how Reduced Instruction Set Computing will make Windows run like the win! . . . uh . . . wind!

Malarkey, I say.

All of these assaults on the Intel-Microsoft hegemony (not to mention assaults on your intelligence) rely on something called **emulation**, a technique that makes one computer behave as if it were a different kind of computer.

Uhuru Urdu   The concept's pretty simple. Just think of what you, as an English speaker, would have to do to emulate . . . oh, say Urdu. You'd hire an Urdu translator, right? Your Urdu translator would walk around with you, listen to what folks are saying in Urdu, and translate the words real-quick-like into English. Then you'd give the translator your answer in English, and the translator would respond to the original inquiry in Urdu.

Except . . . well, have you ever seen how on-the-fly language translation works in practice? The translation isn't perfect. Lags and pauses develop in the strangest places. Inflections and nuances drop out. Carrying on more than one conversation simultaneously leads to all sorts of interesting consequences. In the best of all possible worlds, the participants will end up with a close approximation to the actual conversation. But there's always a chance for error—and sometimes the errors can be disastrous.

Computer emulation works the same way. Whether it's a Mac trying to run DOS programs on an emulated Intel 80386 instruction set, OS/2 trying to get out of the way when Windows applications make Win32 API calls, or the PowerPC trying to do both simultaneously, the possibility for errors increases enormously.

Emulation is nothing new. Bill Gates made his first $10,000 on a PDP emulator, and Gates was hardly a pioneer in the field. In all the years of emulators and emulating, I haven't seen one emulator that's bullet-proof, and precious few that were anywhere near robust. Admittedly, I'm biased here, too: I've written thousands of pages detailing bugs in major software packages *running in their native environments*. Emulation adds another layer of complexity. I shudder to think what kinds of bugs and problems lurk in the emulation realm.

Emulation's checkered history

Caveat emulator.

There are exceptions, of course. Windows NT, for example, is supposed to run precisely the same way on both the Intel i486 and the PowerPC (and MIPS and . . .). Personally, I don't believe it for a second, but you never know: The people moving NT to all the other computers are very smart, and "porting" like this isn't the same thing as emulation. If you're going to use Windows NT, the PowerPC may not be a bad choice. But if you're that advanced, you don't need my advice, eh?

NT and the PowerPC

The Computer

> Happy is the man that findeth wisdom,
> and the man that getteth understanding.
>
> Proverbs III
> ca. 350 BC

The preceding two pages were simply preamble to a simple conclusion, one you've probably reached already.

What computer should you get? Whether you're buying new or schlepping a machine home from the office, you should get the best multimedia PC you or your company can afford, with Windows already installed.
It's really that simple.

The only wiggle word in that pearl of knowledge is "best" (you noticed it, too?). Since "best" is so hard to pin down, and varies widely depending on how much you have to spend, I'm going to spend the rest of this section dealing with "minimum," and concentrating on what to *avoid*, as well as what to get.

When you go out shopping for a new machine, or when you start wrangling with the IS department over how much of a PC you need to take home, show them these pages and use them as leverage.

Central Processor

CPU   At a minimum, you'll want a 486 DX2/66 or better computer. "Better" means a 486 DX4/100 (or some number greater than 66 over on the right-hand side). If you can afford it, get a Pentium P-90 or faster computer—it'll run twice as fast as a 486. But avoid the Pentium P-60 and P-66; they won't give you much more bang for your buck, compared to the 486, and they have a bad reputation of running hot, a cardinal sin.

 NOT!

Intel's competitors (and particularly IBM) would have you believe that the early Pentium P-90 chips should be avoided—citing something about errors in obscure floating point unit calculations. If you're agonizing over P-90 flaws, well you can forget about it. Unless you spend most all day, most every day, doing complex mathematical modeling or exacting, repetitive high-precision division, you're more likely to be struck by lightning than a P-90 calculation error. In spite of what Intel's competitors would have you believe.

Cache Memory   At a minimum, you'll want 128K (that's about 128,000 characters) of "L2" or "Level 2" cache memory. Cache memory lets the CPU run faster. Don't pay much extra for more cache memory. And don't buy a machine with less than 64K cache.

Main Memory   Get 8 MB (that's 8 megabytes, or about 8,000,000 characters) of main memory. You'll need that much to run Windows effectively. If you find you have a few shekels left in the budget at the end of this exercise, splurge on 8 MB more, for a total of 16 MB.

Slots and Bus   Most telecommuters can get along just fine with a plain vanilla ISA architecture. (The **architecture** dictates how the machine is put together internally; it also controls what kind of add-on cards you can use.) If you don't understand the architecture alphabet soup, don't worry: 'Most any new machine you find for sale these days is ISA. The only real alternatives are almost extinct. EISA costs too much. MCA is a big, expensive, true-blue joke.

VLB versus PCI

You'll need **local bus**, as well, but again 'most any new machine you find for sale today has local bus. The local bus lets certain privileged add-on cards—in particular, video cards—get at the main part of the computer faster than other add-on cards. There are two competing types of local bus: VLB and PCI. The differences between the two don't matter much. Conventional wisdom says you should get a VLB bus with an i486 system, and a PCI bus with a Pentium computer. Who am I to knock conventional wisdom?

Finally, make sure that your machine, fully configured with all the installed options, still has a few extra slots left, for new add-in cards. Depending on the size constraints on your desk, you may opt for a smaller, "desktop" box, and thus fewer slots. But if you have a choice, get a full-size tower, with lots of extra slots ready for the inevitable time when you want to add more capability to the machine.

Setting up the Furshlinger Fruzahumus/66 is easy, sir. We just forgot to degauss the meriphister head. You can do it. Got a screwdriver handy?

Setup, Delivery, and Maintenance   If you're taking an office machine home, make sure you set it up *in the office* before you lug it home. It's a whole lot easier shaking out minor problems when you're sitting next to the office guru. Make sure you iron out who will deliver the beast, and when, and who's going to take care of anything that goes kablooey.

Disk Storage

Figure out how much you need.
Add a hundred percent.
Then double it.

Pensées Pinecliffius
Dem Gigabyte Blues, 1995

How Much Space?   With hard disk drives running well under forty cents per megabyte, now is not the time to skimp on disk space. At the central office you may have twenty different apps on the server, but your telecommuting connection could take forever to download what you need. Indeed, you may spend more in a few months' worth of downloading phone bills than it would take to buy a 1 GB drive (that's about 1,000,000,000 characters).

I recommend that you start out by planning on a 700 MB drive, and add on from there if you have any unusual requirements. 500 MB may not hold all your apps—much less all your data!—so why put the squeeze on when hard drives are so cheap?

What Brand?   It doesn't matter. All the major brands work about the same. Faster access time (the average time it takes to find a piece of data on the disk) is nice, but don't pay extra for it. Once you have all your disk caching in place, you won't notice the difference between 12 ms and 15 ms access times. On-drive cache (memory inside the disk that makes it run faster) is nice, but the cache that's automatically set up on your computer is better—and it doesn't cost any more. Mean Time Between Failure (a theoretical figure that's supposed to tell you how long the drive will last) doesn't mean squat. IDE (the cheapest kind of drive) works just as well as SCSI (a more sophisticated, more expensive kind), and you won't need to add a SCSI adapter card.

Don't sweat the details. Buy plain vanilla. Go for price per megabyte.

Monitor and Video Card

> In the beginning darkness existed, enveloped in darkness.
>
> Rig Veda
> ca. 1300 BC

Monitors vary widely in quality. Some people can't stand fuzzy monitors; others don't seem to notice. If you're like most telecommuters, you'll spend a lot of time staring at your monitor. Take the time to make sure you get a good one.

Monitor size is measured diagonally.

What Size?   With rare exceptions, there's little (if any) difference in usable size between a 14" and a 15" monitor, so don't get hung up on size in the low end. Most telecommuters would benefit from a 17" monitor: If you need to have more than one program visible on the screen simultaneously (and most interrupt-driven telecommuters do!), 17 inches can make you considerably more productive. Ron White wrote the definitive return-on-investment analysis for larger monitors; you can find it in the November 1994 issue of *PC/Computing*, pp 196–215.

Dot pitch is key.

A monitor's **dot pitch** measures the distance between same-color dots on the screen. A large number means the picture comes out grainy; a small number indicates a finer picture. You want a monitor with a dot pitch of 0.28 millimeters or less. (Sony Trinitron tubes —available from Sony, Nanao, and a few other manufacturers—use slightly different technology; there are no dots, and thus no dot pitch. Not to worry. Trinitron tubes are all excellent.)

If you're buying a computer in a store, make sure you see the monitor in action before you pay for the machine. If you're buying mail order, scan the magazines for reviews of the latest monitors, and only rely on "round up" reviews that compare numerous monitors side-by-side. (Those "first look" reviews, where one or two monitors get a quick once-over, don't tell the whole story. It's the same way when you're choosing a TV: You can't really see the difference between models unless you compare them side by side.)

What 14 hours at 14 inches feels like.

Which Video Card?   You're going to have more problems with your video card than with any other single part of your PC and sometimes you won't even know it's the video card that's doing the trashing. All of the major vendors turn out cards with buggy drivers: the card itself may work, but the program that Windows uses to drive the card will go belly-up at all the wrong times. Some vendors issue updates to their drivers once a month. Dozens of different versions are the rule, not the exception.

Any video card you get these days should be a **local bus** card—one suitable for use in a VLB or PCI computer. (Assuming you have a VLB or PCI computer, of course.) The amount of memory on board the card will control how many dots you can see on the monitor, and how many colors will be displayed simultaneously. 1 MB of video memory is usually sufficient to run at $1024 \times 768 \times 256$— 1024 dots across the screen, 768 dots up and down the screen, and 256 on-screen colors—which is what I recommend for most business applications.

$1024 \times 768 \times 256$

Get a fast video card, but don't become obsessed with speed ratings in the magazines and the ads: Card A may run 20 percent faster than Card B in Winmark testing, but you'll never even notice a 20 percent speed difference in day-to-day use.

I used to recommend the Volante Warp boards because they had super-stable drivers. Alas, I can't find Warp boards anywhere these days. (Maybe I'm not looking in the right places.)

Given the current sorry state of affairs in video driver quality control, I can't do much but leave you to the wolves: You're going to have problems no matter which card you buy. When you buy a new card, just make sure you find out where to get the latest drivers.

Put 'Em Together   There's one more video spec worthy of your attention: the **refresh rate**. As you probably know, video images are drawn on a screen by an electron beam that sweeps quickly, row by row, painting colors as it whizzes by. (Televisions work the same way.) If the beam sweeps too slowly, the screen starts flickering—a most annoying distraction. Most people find the flicker intolerable if the beam sweeps the whole screen any slower than about 70 times per second. Or, to put that in computerese, you want a "refresh rate of at least 70 Hz."

What's the refresh frequency, Kenneth?*   Unfortunately, the sweep speed is a function of both the monitor and the video card, and it varies depending on how many dots are being shown on the screen. Unless you're very good at reading technical documents, the only way you can find out how fast the beam will sweep is to ask a knowledgeable salesperson. And, with all due respect to the many fine salesorganisms out there, 'tis a rare, rare techie who will know the answer to your question.

Nonetheless, the question must be asked and answered. You should formulate it like this: "Dear Ms. Salesperson. If I buy this here video card, and that there monitor, and I run it at 1024×768 resolution, what's the refresh rate?" The answer should be something like, "Oh wise one, that combination will run at 74 hertz." If the number comes in between 70 Hz and 100 Hz, you're in fat city. If the number is lower than 70 Hz, pass the card and monitor by. If the number is over 100, less than 50, or comes in some unit of measurement other than hertz, your sales organism is out to lunch. Best to replace it.

With all that techie folderol behind us, I recommend that you get a 17" monitor, 0.28 mm dot pitch or smaller, and use it to run Windows at 1024×768 resolution. Get a fast local bus video card with 1 MB of memory. And make sure that the whole shebang will run at a refresh rate of 70 Hz or higher.

Another unabashed plug for a coupla great products   If you can afford it, go for an NEC or (my favorite) Nanao monitor. Year in and year out, Nanao and NEC make top-rated monitors. It's easy to see why. They're built like shirt brick houses. (What, you never seen a shirt brick?) They don't come cheap, but your eyes will thank you every day for your wise choice. I use a 21" Nanao T660i, recently reincarnated as the T2-20, and it's as lovely a piece of computer equipment as exists on the face of the earth.

New Age   Did you notice how I didn't mention anything in my recommendations about MPR II emissions, or Energy Star compliance? There's a reason for that.

Energy Starlet   Energy Star is a standard recently established by the U.S. government that specifies lower-energy "sleep" states for monitors. If your monitor sits idle for so

---

* With apologies to Dan Rather (who was mugged by someone repeating, "What's the frequency, Kenneth?") and REM (who know a good hook line when they hear one).

many minutes, and it complies with Energy Star, it should switch into a low-power-consumption standby mode. I still maintain that the best Energy Star capability is the "off" switch: If you're going to leave your monitor sitting, just switch it off. Most monitors consume less power than a 100 watt light bulb. So it's very much a matter of degree. While reduced waste of natural resources is a laudable goal—and the Energy Star program is run by folks who really do have our best interests at heart—I just can't motivate myself beyond the loud yawn stage.

MPR II compliance is another question altogether. Monitors emit all sorts of radiation. So do TVs. Microwave ovens. Electric blankets. Overhead power lines. Portable telephones. And on and on. Then there's all the natural sources of radiation: cosmic rays, radon, trace amounts of uranium in drinking water. That's just for starters. Nobody knows, really, how much radiation of what kind is harmful, and it seems clear that there's no simple relationship (if there's any relationship at all!) between exposure to monitor emissions and, say, cancer or miscarriages.

Monitor mutant zombies

MPR and MPR II compliance merely state that a monitor gives off very, very low levels of radiation of all known types. It's a Swedish standard that's been adopted simply because nobody else has been willing to establish concrete numbers. Sort of a standard in a vacuum, if you will.

MPR certification

What to do?

Hell, I dunno. I punt. I look for MPR II certification. I don't necessarily recommend that you do. (But then again, I won't use an electric blanket, so who am I to say?) There's simply too little evidence to make a definitive statement one way or the other. If you're naturally paranoid about such things, go for MPR II.

Printer, Copier, Scanner, Hydra

> Seeing isn't believing.
> Believing is seeing.
>
> Judy the Elf
> *The Santa Clause,* 1994

Printers

Two types of printers dominate the market: lasers and inkjet printers. While you would be tempted to believe that a laser is more expensive than an inkjet, it ain't necessarily so. Yes, the purchase price is higher. But the cost of consumables—particularly, the high price of inkjet refills—brings prices of the two closer than you might imagine. It all depends on your print volume: If you do a lot of printing, the laser is actually cheaper.

Choosing a good printer is easy. Go down to your local computer shoppe. Take a look at the output from an inkjet printer. Compare it side-by-side with the output from a laser printer. If you can stand the inkjet printer's quality, buy a cheap HP DeskJet (or an OfficeJet; see the end of this section). If you can't, buy a cheap HP LaserJet.

There are a few exceptions to that rule of thumb, but not many.

600 dpi   If you print a lot of grayscale art (typically, scanned photographs), 600 dpi (600 dots per inch—in other words, high-resolution printing) is nice. No, the people reading your business letters won't be able to see the difference between 300 dpi and 600 dpi. Don't pay much extra for it.

Color   Sometimes color printing makes a difference: I've seen schematic diagrams printed in color, for example, and the color, used sparingly, can really help. Most of the time, though, color comes across as amateurish and jarring. High-quality color (dye sublimation) printers cost many thousands of dollars and produce stunning results. Low-quality color (laser and inkjet) printers are only a little bit more expensive than their black-and-white siblings, but the color isn't much— and if you don't use the colors in your inkjet cartridge frequently, it'll gum up.

High Volume   If you run a couple of thousand sheets through your printer every month, the high price of DeskJet ink cartridges will drive you over the edge. Laser cartridges are much less expensive, per copy. At some point (and it varies on a whole host of considerations, but certainly around 100,000 copies over the life of the printer), you'll actually pay more to run a DeskJet than a LaserJet. For a detailed analysis, take a look at the discussion in the hardware chapter of *The Mother of All Windows Books* (Addison-Wesley, 1993).

Non-HP Printers   Hewlett-Packard has many worthy rivals, and if you see an exceptional buy on a competing printer, you might want to think about getting it. Personally, I'll take HP. They're well built, and last forever. The drivers work (most of the time anyway; don't get me started on the DeskJet Win31 driver version 5.0). If you have problems, help is never far away. It's a tough act to beat.

Not Worth Getting   **I'd never spend more hard-earned money for a printer with any of the following bells and whistles.**

- Extra Fonts. (Fonts are different kinds of type: This is Arial. This is Times New Roman. *This is Times italic.* All are fonts.) Windows has all the fonts most telecommuters will need, and then some. If you need to do some fancy desktop publishing, good—even excellent—TrueType fonts may be had for pennies apiece.

- PostScript. (**PostScript** is a printing language; its primary competitor is **TrueType**. Some typesetting machines only "speak" PostScript. If you want your office printer to speak PostScript, you'll pay hundreds of dollars extra for the privilege.) TrueType works every bit as well as PostScript, and it's free— although you may be forced into using PostScript if you employ a service bureau that's stuck in the technology of the 1960s.

- Additional printer memory. Most come with enough memory to handle anything you're likely to encounter.

If you print a lot of envelopes, the envelope feeder may be worthwhile, but for most telecommuters it's a waste. Ditto for the extra paper trays. If you have extra money in the budget, spend it on something else.

Copier

Those little personal copiers are getting more reliable every day. Only one little   **The others**
tip: Check out the costs of consumables before you buy. Toner can make a big difference in the final cost of a copier.

Scanner

If you're going to do any serious scanning, get a flat-bed scanner. The handheld units simply can't compare in scan quality or ease of use. Although the market may change significantly by the time you read this, I'll put my money on the HP ScanJet. Excellent quality. And cheap.

Scanner: Two-seventeenths of a Hydra Haiku

Logitech also has a scanner that's well adapted to the cramped office. The Logitech ScanMan Power Page (that's what they call it) is a single-sheet job, but it's small, and it comes with Windows software that pops up on your screen whenever you put a piece of paper in the scanner. Combined with a fax modem, you can choose to scan, copy, or fax the inserted sheet, all at the click of a button. Nifty.

Hydra

Near the end of the Pliocene epoch, a rather dull Olduvian anthropoid named Grik-lak discovered that a copier is nothing but a scanner with an attached printer. It was soon conjectured that a fax machine is a copier with a modem, and that a scanner is a copier that can send the image to a computer. Rocket science.

Some day in the not-too-distant future, we'll have one machine that combines all the functions of a printer, a copier, a fax machine, and a scanner. 'Tho the machine doesn't yet exist, it already has a name: it's called a "hydra," the Swiss Army Knife approach to PC output. Instead of buying four pieces of office equipment, we'll only need one—and it will take up one-fourth the space of the old ensemble. Unfortunately, the day of the hydra isn't here just yet.*

HP OfficeJet   HP, imitating Mel Brooks's vision of Young Dr. Frankenstein ("that's Frahn-ken-STEEN"), has taken bits and pieces from various other HP products and assembled a proto-hydra that's surprisingly talented and urbane. HP's entry, dubbed the OfficeJet, combines a single-sheet copier, a plain paper fax machine, and a DeskJet printer, all for under $800. Unfortunately, the OJ misses two important hydra components: It won't let you fax something directly from your computer (you have to print it first, then turn around and feed the paper through the fax machine), and it won't let you capture images scanned by the copier. With those two exceptions, though, it's a very impressive combination. (The single-sheet limitation isn't much of a problem, in my experience, because you'll probably head out to the local copy shop if you need to copy many pages.)

Save the Carpals: Keyboard and Mice

> Give me your hand and let me feel your pulse.
>
> Shakespeare
> *The Comedy of Errors*, 1592

Designer keyboards   There's been a lot of talk in the computer press about ergonomic keyboards, particularly the fold-apart split board variety, and the camel-back version (a Bactrian camel, if you will, not one of those *<sniff!>* dumb Dromedaries†) popularized by Microsoft.

The designer 'boards sure do look sexy, but do they work?

---

* You expected any less? Vanquishing Hydra was, after all, the first Herculean task.

† Okay, okay. I'll try not to be so obscure. Dromedaries are single-humped camels; they're the snarly, mean, ugly, smelly, spitting "ships of the desert" romanticized in so many movies about the Middle East. Bactrians, from Central and Southern Asia, are double-humped, hairier, just as smelly, but considerably better behaved than Dromedaries. The "ergonomic" Microsoft keyboard has two humps. Or at least it should. All three bite.

The simple answer: Nobody knows. There's anecdotal evidence that some people benefit from using nonlinear keyboards. But nobody's done a scientific study. Indeed, what isn't known about repetitive motion problems *in general* far outstrips what is.

Since so much of the ergonomic debate centers on anecdotal evidence, I'm going to inflict you with my own anecdote — based on years of excruciating pain and numbness (and, the worst, painful numbness) caused by long hours at the keyboard. The greatest relief for me came when I finally stopped placing my keyboard atop my 30" desk and lowered it to 26 inches above the floor, simultaneously adjusting the chair so my elbows extend at 90 degrees. The second greatest relief came when I discovered something called Power Putty, a Silly-Putty-like gob of squeezable stuff designed to exercise the hands and forearms. You can find Power Putty at most sports shops. Between the two, the aches and pains in my arms and hands have completely disappeared. Phenomenal.

Which Keyboard?   Find a keyboard you like and stick with it, even when you change computers. If you like crisp, clicky keyboards check out the Lexmark (available at any computer store) or — my favorite — the Northgate Omnikey (voice 800-526-2446, fax 612-943-8332). If the click leaves your teeth chattering, try the Gateway keyboard (voice 800-846-2000 or 605-232-2000). If you're tempted to try the Microsoft Bactrian camel keyboard, or any other odd ergonomic keyboard for that matter, by all means do so, but make sure you can return it if you decide you don't like it. One little tip: Any keyboard that costs more than $100 or so has "sucker" written all over it. **Keys to happy clickin'**

If you get a keyboard with a new system, go ahead and keep it, even though the keyboards that ship with most new systems leave a whole lot to be desired. The first time you spill a cup of coffee on your keyboard, you'll be most thankful for the backup. **Keyboard backup**

Genus Mus   Some mice, like some keyboards, develop a fanatical following. The Microsoft Mouse II — the Dove Bar mouse — has many aficionados, myself included. I've also had very good luck with the Logitech Mouseman Cordless. Make sure you keep 'em clean, and they'll reward you with years of dependable service.

Again, save the cheap mouse that comes with a new system. You never know when your mouse will turn tail-up. Even a cheap mouse is better than no mouse at all.

Other Hand Savers   I haven't had any luck with wrist rests (those foam gizmos you put in front of a keyboard to hold your wrists up) once the chair and keyboard height are adjusted correctly. Ditto for the mouse corrals (the little ledges that **Wrist rests, mouse corrals** surround the mouse, elevating your wrists while you click), but some people swear by 'em.

For serious carpal problems   If you start having wrist and hand problems, and your elbows are working at a 90 degree angle, you might want to try wrist splints. Surprisingly, you don't need a prescription to get them; most sporting goods stores carry excellent splints. But if you have continuing pain in your wrists or forearms, or numbness in your hands or any finger, get thee to a doc who knows about this stuff!

A good friend of mine suffered from carpal tunnel syndrome. She took her complaint to the doctor—a company doctor, it turns out. The doctor told her it was all psychosomatic, that (variously) a week off, a change in job duties, wrist splints, and heaven-knows-what-all would alleviate the pain. She spent years fighting that doctor, as her problems got progressively worse. Lemme give you a tip. If your doctor tells you that repetitive motion problems are psycho-somatic, your doctor *doesn't know what the hell he/she/it is talking about*. Get another doctor. Quick. Even if you have to pay for the referral yourself.

Other PC Stuff

> You know what I hate, man?
> When you go to see the great gold Buddha
> And you pick the leaf *with the virus on it.*

> Ad for Burn Cycle
> "It's not just a game—it's an infection!"

CD-ROM is a necessity.   *Justifying a CD Drive*   Every telecommuter needs a CD-ROM drive. You can tell your boss, "Woody said so." What, you say the boss won't be convinced? Okay. Try this on for size.

Installing Microsoft Office Pro—a product with thirty-four disks—can take an hour or more. The CD version, on the other hand, installs in about twenty minutes, and you can go do something else while you're waiting for it to finish.

Not good enough? Alright. Try this.

Several good dictionaries (and a few so-so encyclopedias) come on CD. They cost about as much as the print version, but you can get at the entries noticeably faster on your PC than with the hardcopy. And if you need to copy information from the dictionary, it goes much faster working with the CD.

Still not good enough? Hmmmmm. . . . You've got a tough boss.

There's a huge amount of information now that's available only on CD. If you're in the software biz, the Microsoft Technet CD will pay for itself (compared to, say, on-line time) in a few uses. If you're a writer, several reference CDs will become indispensable. If you're a graphic designer, clipart and fonts on CD sell for a fraction of their diskette cousins. And on and on.

And if that isn't good enough to convince the boss, go out and buy a CD player *with your own money*. You won't regret it.

Sound   On the other hand, I don't know of any particularly good business justification for sound, just yet.

Computer-generated sound is neat. Yes, there are little programs that will read back rows of numbers from a spreadsheet, so you can proofread them. But why not simply print out the numbers and double-check visually?

Voice recognition—the other half of most sound boards' repertoire—still has a long, long way to go. Yes, there are programs that will respond to your limited voice commands. But is it really easier to say, "File" <pause> "Open" than to click a couple of times?

> **The days of accurate conversational speech recognition are at least a decade off. Maybe more. What passes for speech recognition nowadays bears no more resemblance to true speech recognition than a skateboard resembles a Maserati.**

Don't get me wrong. I have sound boards on all of my computers, and I use them extensively. Sound *can* help alert you to unusual situations, or warn you when processing is over and it's time to turn your attention back to the PC. But for most business users, sound is still a luxury.

Unless you can figure out a way to justify Doom II as a business expense. . . .

Two Important Peripherals   I always keep two more peripherals handy. First, I have a cheap calculator that sits underneath my monitor. Yeah, Windows has a calculator. Yeah, you can flip over to it and calculate to your heart's content. But why bother? A $5 calculator can travel to where you need it; it's always on; and it won't interrupt your concentration the way swapping computer programs so often does.

High tech, high touch: the perfect peripheral

The second peripheral? A cheap $6 stopwatch, which I attach with Velcro to the front of my monitor. When processing times seem to slow to a crawl, the

Sound is worthwhile, but not in the same league as CD.

Calculator

Stopwatch

stopwatch helps me keep my perspective. When I'm spending endless hours on hold, waiting for some tech support weenie, the stopwatch reminds me that it's only been ten minutes. It's a sop to what's left of my sanity. Try it. You'll like it.

Keepin' the Beast Alive

> The Buddha, the Godhead, resides quite as comfortably in the circuits of a digital computer or the gears of a cycle transmission as he does at the top of a mountain or in the petals of a flower.
>
> Robert M. Pirsig
> *Zen and the Art of Motorcycle Maintenance,* 1974

If your telecommuting office is in the middle of a major metro area, your computer and communication equipment maintenance problems won't be any worse (or any better!) than those of the companies around you.

PC repair droids don't telecommute. But maintaining computers out in the boonies—even in a suburban home—has its own unique problems, its own, uh, challenges.

Maintenance Basics If you're buying a brand-new computer, phone system, peripheral, or the like, it will no doubt come with a 7- to 30-day return policy. Take advantage of that policy by unpacking the equipment as soon as you get it home, and running the beast as hard as you can for the entire return period. It's a strange truism that most electronic equipment will break down early if it's going to break down at all. Coercing it into breaking down during the warranty period can help fend off industrial-strength headaches later.

Catch the problems early. If you're bringing a computer home from the office, it's also best to exercise all of it as soon as you can. Why? Because the guru at the central office who got your system going is more likely to remember what your machine looks like and how to fix anything that goes bump in the night.

I'm here ta fix that Pentium floating point unit, Toots.

Maintenance Contracts   Some people swear by them, other people swear at them. On-site maintenance contracts can be very expensive, and if you have the temerity to take your PC outside the repair company's "normal territory," they may refuse to honor the contract (read the fine print before you sign!).

On-site repair in the boonies is a very iffy proposition: You may find that the repair truck will only come out your way once a week, or once a month. Some on-site repair contracts require you to first send the offending part to the manufacturer and wait while the manufacturer determines if (in their opinion) the problem you're experiencing is really caused by their equipment. Other on-site contracts require you to contact the manufacturer so they can send a new part to you, and you can schedule an on-site visit only after you have the part in hand. It's a jungle out there. Finger-pointing can take weeks or months to resolve.

On-site repair

On the other hand, if you're a telemployee and the central office is many miles away, an on-site maintenance contract may be the only viable choice. (Depending on your central office IS department's reputation for responding to support calls, it may be the only viable choice regardless of where you live!) You may find it beneficial to work out some sort of repair cost ceiling with your boss ahead of time. Anything under $100, say, could be written off on an expense report.

There's nothing wrong with using a local repair organization. The big national organizations will often contract with local companies anyway—so a maintenance call to ACME International Repair may actually bring you a repair person from Joe's CompuShack.

I haven't found a foolproof way of deciding whether a maintenance contract on a new machine is worth the expense, but a friend of mine has developed an interesting way of shaking out some of the worst problems. Here's how it works.

- Before you buy the machine—when you have the most leverage—ask the sales clerk exactly how the repair policy works. You say, "Step me through it. It's Friday afternoon and my monitor stops working. What do I do? Then what do you do?" Take good notes.

- Hang up the phone and call the vendor's tech support number. Keep track of how long it takes until you're speaking to a real, live tech support engineer.

- Tell the tech support droid, "I'm about to buy a PC from your company, but I need to know about your maintenance policy. It's Friday afternoon, and my monitor stops working. What do I do? Then what do you do?"

- If the story you get from sales even *remotely* resembles the story you get from tech support you're probably in good shape. Chances are mighty good you'll be surprised at the discrepancies.

You need
authorization.

RMA   Remember that you'll need something called an **RMA** (for "Return Merchandise Authorization") number to return malfunctioning equipment to the manufacturer. The tech support people will give you an RMA number when they're convinced that the product is faulty. An RMA number lets the manufacturer track each defective product. Not coincidentally, it also ensures that you've jumped through the manufacturer's hoops in trying to get the product to work: They won't give you an RMA number until they've exhausted all avenues for repairing the product over the phone.

Make sure you print the RMA number on the outside of any package containing returned product. Also make sure that you keep a permanent record of the RMA number and the products you've sent.

The Boonies   If you live outside the on-site repair companies' normal service area, you can always use UPS as your maintenance contractor: Just pack up your PC and ship it overnight to the manufacturer. In many cases, it'll be faster to send the unit UPS or FedEx to specialists who know what they're doing, than to wait for an on-site repair person who may or may not understand your particular problem.

If you live a long way from the closest PC repair shop, there's nothing that compares with keeping multiple PCs on-site, just in case your main machine goes belly-up. The backup PC needn't be anywhere near as powerful as the main machine—its primary function in life may be for communications, or it may double as a game machine for the kids—but when your #1 computer dies, having a #2 handy can be a lifesaver.

Computerettes

The pound of flesh, which I demand of him,
Is dearly bought; 'tis mine, and I will have it.*

Shakespeare
The Merchant of Venice, 1597

I'll talk about the travails of being a Road Warrior, and various on-the-road tricks, in Chapter 5; right here I'd like to talk about the Road Warrior's steed, the portable computer.

Your one and
only?

While many industry pundits would have you believe that a portable computer is really all you need—that portables provide all the amenities of desktop

---

* Amazingly, the phrase "pound of flesh"—key to the plot of *The Merchant of Venice*—does not appear on the Microsoft Bookshelf CD (or in any version of Bartlett's, electronic or printed, that I could find). This citation comes from the *Much Ado About Shakespeare* CD, from The Bureau of Electronic Publishing.

computers; that your first (and only!) PC should be a portable—in my experience it just isn't true. Portables are considerably more expensive and less capable than desktops. Most new technology appears first for desktops. And the price curve for that technology falls much more steeply on the desktop than in a portable.

> **Some people have a crying need for a portable: If you are on the road all the time, and the computer has to come along for presentations, research, or e-mail, you're definitely portable material.**
>
> **What surprises me, though, is the number of people who have little use for a portable, but go out and buy one anyway, thinking they'll get a lot of work done on the odd cross-country flight. Bah. If you work at a desk almost all the time, a portable will only get in your way. Unless you have a nearly infinite budget, think of a portable as your second computer. Treat it as you would a second car or a second TV: not really a necessity, in most cases, but mighty nice to have when you need it. Even with all the fancy docking stations, full-size keyboards, and plug-in high resolution monitors, the portable still lags behind its big brothers.**

Notebooks and Laptops　Every extra ounce in a portable computer extracts a pound of flesh from the person who has to carry it. Since the *raison d'être* for carrying a portable is, uh, portability, the first thing you must consider when evaluating a portable is its weight. There are two weighty trade-offs: diskette drive or no drive; CD or no CD. Personally, I dump both of them (I use a diskette drive that plugs into the back of the notebook, and leave it in the suitcase), but your circumstances may be different.

　If you're going to buy a portable or pilfer one from the central office, make sure you get a i486SX2/50 or better ("better" meaning a number higher than 50 at the end), at least 8 MB of main memory (yeah, I know it'll cost more), a 300 MB hard drive, a PCMCIA slot for a modem, and Windows pre-installed. A black-and-white ("monochrome") screen will suffice for pedestrian uses, but if you intend to get some serious work done you'll want active matrix color.

De minimus

> **The most important point: Before you settle on a portable, make sure you *try* it. In particular, check for the feel of the keyboard and the clarity of the screen under several different lighting conditions, and make sure you can live with the mouse. Both Toshiba and IBM have been making award-winning portables for years. That's a good place to start.**

PCMCIA　Most cards plug into notebooks via something called a "PCMCIA slot"—essentially an opening in the computer that accepts credit-card-size add-on modems, hard drives, network adapters, and who-knows-what-all. Way back in the early days of PCMCIA slots (say, a year ago), there were horrendous compatibility problems: Certain cards would only work with certain slots on certain computers. Fortunately, many — but not most! — of the compatibility problems have been conquered. You'll still have problems getting an off-brand modem, say, to work with an arbitrarily selected notebook computer.

There are two different kinds of PCMCIA slots available nowadays, and they vary in the thickness of the slot: a Type II slot holds a 5 mm thick card (the size of a typical modem card); a Type III slot holds a 15 mm thick card (the size of a typical hard drive).

Choosing between Type II and Type III
If you have to choose between Type II and Type III slots, the primary consideration is the capacity of the hard drive. If it looks like you're going to need more hard drive space, go for the Type III slot. Otherwise, Type II will suffice.

PDAs Personal Digital Assistants and pen-based computers had a real run of glory a while back. The concept's great. The execution leaves much to be desired. Handwriting recognition is still in its infancy. Tiny hand-held computers still behave more like toys than serious computers. (Not that there's anything wrong with toys!) Some day they'll be ready for prime time. Come back in ten years.

Surfing the Channel

> Tim was so learned that he could name a horse in nine languages.
> So ignorant that he bought a cow to ride on.
>
> Benjamin Franklin
> *Poor Richard's Almanac*, 1750

If you find yourself in the position where you have to go out and buy a computer, taking the time to ferret out the right kind of supplier—the right "channel"—can make a big difference.

Would you buy a used PC from this man?

Computer Boutique It's tough being chief cook and technical bottle washer, particularly if you find little pleasure in the care and feeding of your electronic equipment. For those who need a little hand-holding (and who doesn't these days?), the upscale computer or electronics shop can't be beat.

Upscale computer stores distinguish themselves by having a stable staff of knowledgeable clerks who are willing and able to listen to your specific needs, and lend a hand when you need it most. Sure, you'll pay a little more for your hardware and software. But when you need help, you won't be forced into hiring a $100-an-hour consultant to sort out the pieces.

The staff makes the difference.

If you're shopping in an upscale store, you shouldn't be looking for a computer as much as you're looking for a competent helper. The expertise of the staff — and their ability to answer your questions in short, intelligible phrases — is much, much more important than the features of any particular computer. Don't forget it!

Mass Merchants   On the other hand, if you don't want to pay for the dubious honor of holding the hand of a computer geek, you're probably better off with a mass merchandiser. You can tell you're shopping at a mass merchandiser when the staff changes every month or two — and all the clerks have terminal acne. All the clerks, that is, except for Joe (as in, "I don't know the answer, sir, you better ask Joe"), and Joe is only on the floor between 9:30 and 9:45 weekday mornings.

Everybody, it seems, is in the computer business these days. Sweep past the counter of espresso machines, down the aisle with the air conditioners, and there you'll find computers. If you're lucky, some of them will actually be plugged into the wall.

Seriously, mass merchants — from the old office supply warehouses to the new computer superstores — generally offer good products at excellent prices. If you don't want the boutique hand-holding and don't require any super-fancy hardware or software, the warehouses and superstores are probably your best source. You can see precisely what you're buying. You can pick up the equipment, haul it home, and get it working immediately. If something goes wrong, you can storm back to the store and talk to a real human being, eyeball-to-eyeball.

Mail Order   At the top of the channel food chain, mail order companies (actually, telephone and fax order companies) offer the latest equipment at the lowest prices. The best mail order companies have customer service reps who will help you select the right product — and they're often more specialized, and thus more knowledgeable, than the clerks in mass merchandise stores. You can order precisely what you want, at prices that range from reasonable to cutthroat.

On the downside, you have to take quite a bit on faith. You won't be able to see or feel a product before you buy it — an important step in buying a keyboard or a monitor. It can take weeks to put together a custom system and ship it to you. If something goes wrong, you may spend hours and hours on hold, waiting for tech support.

If you decide to go the mail order route, avail yourself of the mother lode of mail order knowledge: Get a copy of *Computer Shopper* magazine. You may break your back schlepping it home. And you're certain to feel guilty about all the trees that gave their lives to create the *magnum opus*. But there's no better source of mail order information on the planet.

Credit Cards   No matter where you buy, no matter what you buy, always, always use a credit card. Period. If something goes wrong, the credit card company will go to bat for you. Don't let any vendor talk you into using cash, or even a check. The protection of a credit card far outweighs its expense.

COMPUTER SOFTWARE

> To know yet to think that one does not know is best;
> Not to know yet to think that one knows will lead to difficulty.
>
> Lao Tzu
> *Tao tê Ching*, ca. 250 BC

Instant karma's gonna get you.

There is no simple solution to the software puzzle: Just about the time you think you've figured out how to use a particular application, something will happen that'll send you back to square one. I know: PC software oddities have been hitting me upside the head for nigh on a decade. Anybody who tells you it's easy doesn't know what they're talking about.

You'll lose more time on lousy software than on any ten bad pieces of hardware. The trick is to come up with a collection of software that you can learn and use without consuming inordinate amounts of time or effort.

Much easier said than done.

I am the ghost of software future.

Looking at the world thru Woody's rose-colored windows

Once you've settled on Windows—and for 90 percent of all telecommuters, Windows is the best way to go—the choice of basic application software is pretty straightforward.

I'll talk about general software in this section, and leave communications software for the next chapter, after we've had a chance to look at the polyglot world of on-line access. As with the preceding section on hardware, I won't even try to make this section comprehensive. Instead I'll focus on specific products you'll need, with emphasis on concerns peculiar to telecommuters, and warn you about products to avoid.

Suite Things

> One of our defects as a nation is a tendency to use what have been called weasel words. When a weasel sucks eggs the meat is sucked out of the egg. If you use a weasel word after another there is nothing left of the other.
>
> Theodore Roosevelt
> 1916

Most telecommuting computer users spend a great deal of time using one or more of the common "core" computer programs:

The hard core

- Word processors, for writing and correspondence
- Spreadsheets, for manipulating numbers and graphing
- Databases or Personal Information Managers, for keeping track of large amounts of information
- Communications software, for connecting with the central office, on-line services, or clients' computers
- Presentation graphics packages, for creating presentations

Your basic application software packages—the software you use every day to write letters, keep track of information, and the like—should work similarly, and work together. When you learn something fundamental about your word processor, you should be able to apply that knowledge to your spreadsheet program or to your database program. When you need financial information from a spreadsheet, it should be easy to paste that information into your word processor.

Interconnection

Synergy is a must.

Works   Several software companies sell combined "Works" packages geared to the small office user. These packages combine word processing, database, and spreadsheet capabilities, often with rudimentary communications functions.

The Works packages are long on easy interconnection—indeed, sometimes it's hard to tell which part of the package you're using, they're so thoroughly interconnected—but they're stunted applications, short on functionality.

Suites   Most of those same software companies sell collections of full-fledged application programs, commonly called "suites." Suites are typically two or three times more expensive than integrated "works" packages, but the individual programs in the suites are full-fledged, state-of-the-art applications. Now that suites sell for less than a single application cost just a couple of years ago, suites have taken over the office application scene.

Works nixed   It's hard to recommend integrated Works packages these days, particularly for telecommuters who typically need all the computing horsepower they can get. They're a bit cheaper, but not much. While it's true that it will take longer for you to learn about all the applications in a suite, using a suite isn't significantly more difficult than using an integrated package, and the greater power available to suite users can make a big difference when the going gets tough.

If your basic computing needs are very rudimentary, and you have little reason to swap computer files with other folks, and it's likely to stay that way, go ahead and get one of the Works packages. But if you want to get the most out of your computer, get a suite, and take the time to learn how to use it.

Unless you're facing overwhelming reasons to the contrary (for example, everybody at the office uses WordPerfect, or you're stuck with exchanging data exclusively in 1-2-3 format), get Microsoft Office, the granddaddy of all the suites. Individual applications in the MS Office suite are stellar; they work together pretty well (better than the competition, anyway); and Office is the hands-down best seller, so you're more likely to find help when you need it.

Besides, why waste the time learning a Works package, when you're going to outgrow it in a couple of years anyway? The extra hundred bucks you spend on a full-fledged suite like MS Office will repay itself time and again.

Keeping the Books

A beggarly account of empty boxes.

Shakespeare
Romeo and Juliet, 1594

Every telecommuter will need some sort of bookkeeping software, even if only to keep track of phone calls and the odd deductible expense.

There's no question in my mind that Quicken is the best checkbook-balancing-style accounting program for the telecommuter, or for anybody who runs a small office. If your activities increase to the point where you need a chart of accounts, trial balances, and the like, QuickBooks will do yeoman's work.

Special Purpose

> Man's yesterday may ne'er be like his morrow;
> Naught may endure but Mutability.
>
> P. B. Shelley
> *Mutability*, 1821

Telecommuters have several other special software needs.

ZIP Ah, the vagaries of mutability! Most of the things computer jocks toss around the wires is full of hot air. Using a technique called **data compression**, programs can squeeze repetitive pieces of data out of files. Companion decompression programs reconstitute the data to its original form. A typical data file can be reduced to half its original size, thereby saving half of your on-line time and cutting your phone and connect-time bills. If your communication software doesn't automatically compress and decompress data — and few do — you'll need a package like PKZip ($47 from PKWare; voice 414-354-8699, fax 414-354-8559).

> **Reduce on-line time by shrinking files.**

While PKZip is the de facto PC standard for squishing data destined for transmission over phone lines, the program itself is a bear to use, especially when you're accustomed to nice, cushy Windows programs. WinZIP ($29 from Nico Mak; CompuServe 70056,241) puts a nice face on PKZip's snarl.

> **WinZIP**

Antivirus One of the unfortunate facts of telecommuting life is that the folks back at the central office (particularly the ones charged with keeping the central computer and/or the networks running) are going to think of you as a primary source of viral infections. While you're no more likely to encounter a virus than anybody else, the fact that you're dialing into the main office from a "dirty" machine (that is, any machine that doesn't reside physically within the central office) will bring all sorts of unwanted attention your way.

You're going to need some sort of antivirus software—like Norton Anti-Virus or one of the many competing products—in addition to the antivirus software that comes with your machine. Don't rely on your operating system's capabilities alone, as that will be the first antivirus software to be cracked by new strains. Learn to use the antivirus software, and routinely scan any new data that comes onto your system. Even if you never catch any offensive viral critters, the people back at the central office will sleep better at night.

> **Norton Anti-Virus**

Licensing Considerations

Those that dance must pay the music.*

John Taylor
Taylor's Feast, 1638

Let me conclude this short discussion of software with a look at one of the thorniest issues facing telecommuters: How many different copies of a piece of software do you need to buy?

Surprisingly, for an industry so embroiled in sweeping advances and so in tune with the changes in working arrangements like telecommuting and flextime, the software biz is running way behind in its billing practices.

Telecommuters in general, and traditional telemployees in particular, must take great care to avoid running afoul of software licensing restrictions.

A plethora of requirements
Life would be much simpler if software manufacturers would get together and decide on one licensing policy applicable to all commercial use. Unfortunately, that isn't the case: There are as many different kinds of software licenses as there are software manufacturers.

Some licenses will let you run a copy of the central office software on your home machine, providing there's no chance that both the office copy and the home copy will be running at the same time. In industry parlance, these licenses let you "treat software like a book"—you can take it with you, move it around, do whatever you like, so long as only one copy is being used at any given moment.

Concurrent use
So-called "concurrent use" licenses require a company to license the maximum number of copies that will be in use at the same time: If 20 people are connected to a server, say, but only five use the package at a time, the company need only license five copies. Typically, concurrent use licenses don't even consider the possibility that some employees may be working at home.

Most licenses will require your company to buy two separate copies of a software package if you're going to use it on two different machines—say, an office machine and a home machine.

Other licenses, though, won't even let you make backup copies!

License violation penalties are stiff. Be aware of the differences in licenses, and make sure you stay within your license requirements. If all else fails, call the manufacturer to clarify any questions you might have about telecommuters' licenses. Chances are good the software folks haven't even thought about it!

---

*. . ."pay the piper" is more common today, but didn't appear in print until 1670.

FAXES

> Already we Viewers, when not viewing, have begun to whisper to one another that the more we elaborate our means of communication, the less we communicate.
>
> J. B. Priestley
> *Thoughts in the Wilderness, "Televiewing," 1957*

Before we tackle the on-line milieu in the next chapter, there are a few hardware odds 'n ends that merit your telecommuting attention.

Fax Machines

> Everything is stolen these days.
> A fax machine is just a waffle iron with a telephone.
>
> Grampa
> *The Simpsons*

I don't know how people ever survived without fax machines. Seriously.

Sure, they're a poor substitute for e-mail. Yeah, they tend to jam at the worst possible time. Nope, they aren't the greatest manifestation of humanity's technological innovation. But, *damn!*, they work. They're everywhere, from the front counter of the local pizza shop to the back streets of Luang Prabang. They've played a pivotal role in several revolutions and near-revolutions—the real kind, with tanks and guns. They're the closest thing the world has to reliable, cheap, ubiquitous communication.

The greatest common denominator

So would somebody please tell me why so many telecommuters skimp when it comes to buying a fax machine?

Man, the details on these plain paper faxes are amazing!

The debate rages.   There are two schools of fax thought among telecommuting PC cognoscenti. One group feels that a good-quality (that is, plain paper) standalone fax machine is a modern business necessity. The other group gets along just fine, thank you, with a fax modem and no independent fax machine; they're content to have faxes fed directly into their computers.

The fax machine as a separate appliance   *Standalone*   Advocates of the standalone side have several things going for them. First and foremost, standalone fax machines (or hydras, discussed earlier in this chapter) can work with paper documents; fax modem users need expensive and potentially troublesome scanners to be able to send hardcopy.

They'll also point out that they can leave their fax machines on 24 hours a day, consuming much less power than leaving a PC on 24 hours a day. If the PC goes belly-up, they still have a fax—and vice versa. And faxes stored on disk can take an exorbitant amount of space.

Fax as a subset of tele-communications   *Fax Modem*   Most fax modem users insist that they only send out documents generated on their PC. In the rare instance that they need to fax a hardcopy, they'll pop on down to the local copy center or grocery store and pay the dollar or two.

The modem fans can also rightfully claim that most faxes need never be printed, and the ones that are printed will automatically come out on plain paper—their PC's regular printer. Fax modems are hundreds of dollars cheaper than fax machines. They take up much less space (typically, no space at all). Sending a fax from Windows is as easy as pushing a button; in fact, sending dozens of faxes can take just one click, and you can schedule the software to dial out during time periods when long distance charges are cheaper.

It's a floor wax! It's a dessert topping! No, wait! It's both!

Personally, I have both a fax machine and a fax modem, and use both of them regularly. The fax machine is a necessity because I frequently need to send out documents that weren't created on my PC (for example, magazine articles, reviews, preprinted forms, legal papers, and the like). The fax modem comes in handy when I'm sending out pages generated by the PC—and it's a real life saver when I have to broadcast the same fax to a dozen or more different phone numbers. Best of all, the fax modem was free: Most modems these days have fax capabilities; when you buy a modem, the fax is thrown in gratis.

All my incoming faxes go straight to the fax machine and are printed immediately. They're too important to leave whirling around on a disk, where injudicious punching of a "Delete" key could send them to Bit Blot Heaven.

Most telecommuters—at least telecommuters who don't live next door to a copy center or grocery store—should consider using both a fax machine and a fax modem, taking advantage of the benefits of both.

Just one little note on buying a stand-alone fax machine: Get plain paper. Don't even think about futzing with the shiny, smelly, curly stuff. If you can't afford a plain paper fax right now, hold off buying one until you can.

Line Switching/Sharing Devices

> "Know thyself" is a good saying, but not in all situations.
> In many it is better to say, "Know others."
>
> Menander
> *Thrasyleon,* ca. 300 BC

So you only have one telephone line, and the phone company says it'll take six months to get you another one?

That's where line splitters come in. A line splitter is a little box that hooks into your telephone line. You plug your fax machine, a telephone, and an answering machine into the other side. When the phone rings, the line splitter "picks up" the line and listens for a fax squeal. If it hears the fax squeal, it automatically routes the call to your fax machine; the fax machines do their handshaking dance, and out pops your fax. If the line splitter doesn't hear a fax squeal, it routes the call to your telephone. Then, if you don't answer the phone after a predetermined number of rings, the line splitter routes the call to your answering machine. **Why split lines?**

Line splitters work by using a little electronic sleight of hand. In case you've ever wondered what *really* happens, well, it goes something like this: **How a line splitter works**

John Smith dials your phone number. He hears the phone ring in the usual way, *b-r-r-r-r-ing,* but the first ring is very short. No big deal. Happens all the time.

Your Line Splitter Maximus hears the ring from John's call and answers the line real quick, before any of the phones in the house start ringing.

You're sitting in the house and have no idea any of this is going on.

The Line Splitter Maximus starts listening for a fax squeal. Here's the tricky part. While it's listening for a squeal, it generates a noise that sounds like the phone is ringing! *B-r-r-r-r-ing. B-r-r-r-r-ing.*

John Smith doesn't realize it, but somebody (er, some*thing*) has picked up the phone, is listening on the line, and is sending out these ersatz *b-r-r-r-r-ing* sounds. If John's very attentive, he may notice that this *b-r-r-r-ing* doesn't quite sound the same as a normal phone ringing, but what the hey.

Ma Bell is sitting at her coffers, chortling. John Smith doesn't realize it, but the call has already gone through, and if it's a long-distance call, the meter is ticking.

You're still sitting fat, dumb, and happy (well, at least *I* would be). You don't have the slightest idea what that machine is doing.

Line Splitter Maximus waits a few seconds for the squeal. Since this is John calling, the Splitter won't hear a squeal, but it keeps John happy by sending out the fake *b-r-r-r-ing* sounds. When the Splitter finally decides it isn't talking to a fax machine, it starts ringing your phone.

You hear the phone ring. John hears a fake *b-r-r-r-ing*. All the humans are happy with their delusions.

You pick up the phone, and the Splitter drops itself out of the loop. "Why, John!" you say, not knowing that John's been wondering why the hell you didn't pick up the phone, "How nice of you to call!"

· Great theory, eh?

Only one problem. I've tried lots of line splitters—including several that have received rave reviews in the major magazines—and for the life of me, I had Hobbes' time getting any of them to work. Maybe some of them work better than they used to, but color me skeptical. Don't rely on a line splitter. Go out and get another phone line, even if you have to wait six months.

UPSs

> Power is precarious.
>
> Herodotus
> *Histories,* ca. 430 BC

You may be one of the twenty-seven people in the world who have clean, reliable power—and if you do, it's probably coming from a bank of batteries the size of a Southern California subdivision, or a multi-million-dollar generator with a dedicated natural gas feedstock. If you're among the other 5,499,999,973 inhabitants of this planet, chances are good that the local power supply quivers and dips like a 1950s teenager at the senior prom.

Surge protection
Chances are good that you already have a surge protector plugged into your important equipment: at a minimum, your computer, modem (if it's a standalone modem, residing outside the main computer), and fax machine. Surge protection is nice (if you get a good surge protector; check out the latest review of surge protectors in *PC Magazine*), but, alas, for telecommuters working in the home, surge protection alone isn't good enough.

You need a full-fledged uninterruptible power supply, or a UPS.

UPS ups and downs
A good UPS will not only protect the family PC jewels from power spikes—the province of surge protectors—it will also iron out the normal ups and downs in the power company's voltage, and keep your machines running for five or ten minutes after the power goes out completely. They are, to put it simply, indispensable.

Once upon a time, UPSs were an extravagance, a luxury few could afford. In fact, if you go to your local power company and ask them to provide a UPS for your computer, chances are pretty good you'll be quoted a price of $500 to $1,000 or more. The power company folks will talk about clamping spikes and feedback loops and all sorts of devils that are assumed to inhabit less-expensive UPS devices. It's pure poppycock. The UPS you can buy from your local computer shop, or from 'most any mail order house, will work just as well as any fancy-schmancy UPS the power company can pull out of a brochure.

UPS capacity is measured in kVA.* I could give you a bunch of technical mumbo-jumbo, but the bottom line is pretty simple: If you have a normal PC, a 250 kVA unit will work fine; if you run a big screen, or have lots of power-sucking cards and add-ons in your machine, the 250 kVA will probably work, but splurge a bit and go for the 400 kVA. A 250 kVA unit should cost about $100. The 400 kVA shouldn't be more than $175. That's the whole UPS shtick.

I swear by American Power Conversion's Back-UPS series. They're cheap, and they work great. In fact, they work so well I bought a second one for my TV and a third for my stereo. Excellent, cheap insurance.

When you get your UPS, plug in your computer, monitor, and inkjet printer; your modem, powered speakers, or CD-ROM drive (if any of them are outside the main PC box); and your fax machine, answering machine, and telephone (if it takes power). Go ahead and load 'em up: The additional power requirement for an answering machine or a phone is minimal. They won't put undue stress on your UPS.

But don't plug in your laser printer! The power-on cycle of a laser printer draws enough juice to fry most UPSs. Besides, most laser printers (and all HP LaserJets) are built with strong power supplies, able to withstand all but the most egregious fluctuations. Your UPS doesn't need the laser printer, and the printer doesn't need the UPS.

FOR MORE INFO

> Would you convey my compliments to the purist who reads your proofs and tell him or her that I write in a sort of broken-down patois which is something like the way a Swiss waiter talks, and that when I split an infinitive, God damn it, I split it so it will stay split, and when I interrupt the velvety smoothness of my more or less literate syntax with a few sudden words of bar-room vernacular, that is done with the eyes wide open and the mind relaxed but attentive.
>
> Raymond Chandler
> To Edward Weeks, ed., *Atlantic Monthly,* 1948

---

* kVA=thousands of Volt-Amps. Another meaningless unit of measurement.

One last plug for MOM   I would be remiss in my duties as doting parent if I failed to mention the two best all-around references to selecting, installing, and using PCs: *CD-MOM, The Mother of All Windows Books, CD-ROM Edition* (by, ahem, Woody Leonhard and Barry Simon, Addison-Wesley, 1993)—which deals with the daemons within Windows —and *PC Mom: The Mother of All PC Books* (by Woody Leonhard and Barry Simon, Addison-Wesley, 1995)—which tackles all things PC, save Windows, including CD-ROM, multimedia, and the like. As their names imply, these are weighty tomes, but for depth and breadth of coverage, they can't be beat.

Wired   And if you're starting to wonder whether you're the only sentient organism on the planet who's still struggling with all this techno-crap, you'll find plenty of kindred spirits haunting the pages of *Wired* magazine. Hip, cool, iconoclastic (literally and figuratively), and refreshingly dead-on accurate, *Wired* is brought to you by people unafraid of telling it like it is.

If Raymond Chandler were writing today, he'd be writing for *Wired*.

Worried about losing your sense of perspective? Your sense of humor? Your sense, period? The solution's simple. Get *Wired*.

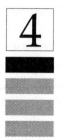

4 Over the Wires

There is no excellence without difficulty.

Ovid
Ars Amatoria, ca. 2 BC

In this chapter we'll tackle the technology of telecommuting—phone lines, equipment, software, products, and services, including the Internet—that help you reach out and touch someone. Or something. Anything.

No matter how you slice it, this stuff is *complicated*. If it weren't so damned important—indeed, if it weren't at the root of what you can and will do as a telecommuter—it's the kind of thing you could snooze through and hardly miss a beat. Unfortunately (or fortunately, I guess, if you're of the pointy-head persuasion) this technology will define what we telefolk can accomplish over the next decade or so. If you brush it off now, or just kind of ignore your telecommuting destiny and relegate it to the phone company, it'll come back and bite you in a year or two.

The defining technology for the next decade

So we're going to dig into the thick of the tele-phony alphabet soup, and try to knock some of these high-falutin' concepts down a notch or two, so normal people like you and me can understand 'em.

Trudy versus TCP/IP

Help from a guru's guru

I've enlisted the help of Trudy Leonhard, my sister, to help make some sense out of the bafflegab. Trudy's been doing networks and communications for almost as long as I've been doing computers. Scary thought, that.

Oh. Don't worry. Trudy won't befuddle you with ten-syllable words and inscrutable explanations. You'll see. Plain talk (and a slight streak of insanity) run in the family.

Take it away, Trudy!

WHERE WE'RE GOING

Between us, we cover all knowledge;
he knows all that can be known
and I know all the rest.

Samuel Clemens
Autobiography, 1908

So *that's* why he has tire tracks down his back.

Woody's always been scared he'd end up as intellectual roadkill on the Information Superhighway. Telecommunications technology really ain't that tough. I'm going to prove it by taking you step-by-step through the concepts that constrain your telecommuting capabilities today, and those that will shape your telecommuting future — if or when high-tech companies finally get with the system.

I'm going to start by explaining the various telephone services available these days, from Plain Old Telephone Service* to leased lines, ISDN, and ATM. Then I'll talk about things you can attach to phone lines, from (surprise!) telephones and headsets to modems and strange boxes for your PC. Then I'll look into things you can do with the whiz-bang technology, like hooking into your office network, videoconferencing, whiteboard systems, and the like — with a special emphasis on what works now, what's likely to work in the future, and what you can do now to prepare for the future. Finally I'll tackle the world beyond the office: on-line services, electronic mail, and getting hooked into the Internet.

I'll show you how to use the stuff that works, and how to avoid the stuff that doesn't. I'll let you know if you should be jumping up and down, demanding that the phone company upgrade its service to your doorstep. And I promise I won't ever — not even once — refer to more than two obscure concepts in a single sentence.

Hey, if Woody can understand it, you can, too. . . .

* The technical term is "POTS." No joke.

TELEPHONE SERVICE

> Remember, my friend, that knowledge is stronger than memory,
> and we should not trust the weaker.
>
> Bram Stoker
> *Dracula,* 1897

In this section I'm going to try to give you an idea of how the telephone system evolved, try to explain why it's stuck somewhere in the intellectual Mesozoic era, and then show you what kinds of phone "service"—that is, the capabilities of various kinds of phone circuits—are either available now, or will soon be available at a location near you.

A Brief History of Lines

Before we get going, I have to confess something. Once I was a BellHead. You remember Ma Bell, don't you? Well, the telephone company used to have a big (really *big*) research group called Bell Labs. Then came the break-up and suddenly Bell Labs metamorphosed into AT&T Labs and BellCore, the combined research effort (arm? heinie?) of the seven regional telephone companies.

My life as a dog

I worked at BellCore, hence my confession. BellCore housed *hundreds* of frustrated Ph.D.s. Bell collected 'em like bugs. Oh sure, there were a few doctorateless—after all, Bell's an equal opportunity employer—and some Ph.D.s specialized in things like nuclear engineering, which doesn't have much to do with *my* telephone. I hope. Still, the Labs were Doct-O-Rama.

Now let me explain the Bell Method for brewing morning coffee.

Think about it. What would be a Ph.D.'s worst nightmare? After years of beating your head against an academic wall, you just got the 'ole degree, and your friends and family are so excited 'cuz you landed a job at *the* preeminent engineering research group. Life's so cool you gotta wear shades.

Then you show up at work and find out *everybody* has a Ph.D. Your boss. Your coworkers. The women in the hall talking about Beavis and Butthead. The guy who designed the company's expense report form. Doctor so and so? Big, bloody deal. Nobody's impressed.

Then it strikes you after about a week. The work you are doing, Dr. Nobody, is um, well, dull.

An anachronistic anachronym factory

What to do? What do Ph.D.s do in the real world? Why, start writing papers! With big obscure words. Even better, create acronyms. Really cryptic acronyms. Ones that, even when you know the words the acronyms refer to, you still haven't a clue what it means. Publish 'em. *Journal of Irreproducible Results*. The *Bratislava Mathematical Monthly*. Anywhere. Everywhere. Soon people refer to your acronyms. Power! Prestige! Immortality. Just like academia.

When I first joined BellCore, a fellow colleague actually showed me seventy pages of acronyms he had waded through while working there. I kid you not! So indulge me if I slip now and again. Telephony acronyms are second only to standards names in nonsense. Remember the frustrated Ph.D. frantically scribbling when you suffer through 'em. At least they made *somebody* happy.

Forward, into the past

The story of Ma an' the Baby Bells is an evolutionary song of woe. Imagine yourself sitting in a stuffed chair, sipping Courvosier XO, strains from *The Rites of Spring* blasting at full volume, with the TV running a continuous silent loop of the Keystone Cops. The drama unfolds. . . .

Highways, Byways, Tolls, Trolls, and Bandits

> Why should I have to pay a troll, just to cross a bridge?
>
> B. G. Gruff
> *MythDirections*

The elbow is connected to the arm bone.

First there was Alex Bell and Watson with their equivalent of two paper cups and a piece of string. You spoke into a handset. The gizmo in the handset moved back and forth, varying the amount of electricity going through the phone line. On the other end, a similar gizmo vibrated in concert with the electricity in the phone line, reproducing what was spoken on the other end.

That's the basis of analog phone signals: a vibrating gizmo on one end causing fluctuations in electric current on a piece of wire, which in turn make the gizmo on the other end vibrate, re-creating the original sound.

It hasn't changed since 1876.

Central Office

Soon, Bell realized that having a private line for everybody you wanted to talk to wasn't practical. So he cut the phone lines into halves, brought the half lines into one place—a Central Office or CO (it's starting!)—and created a switch board. If you wanted to talk to somebody you notified the switchboard operator. Then the operator switched you to your destination party. Usually without listening in on your conversation.

Woody likes to make jokes about his Mom . . . uh, *our* Mom. Truth is, our own Mom was a telephone operator. In addition to being a switchboard operator, connecting calls manually, she spent one hour a day telling the time, live, in 15-second increments. For this, she was paid 30 cents an hour. Only later did Alex Bell's Mom finally figure out how to use recordings to tell time.

When the two half-phone-lines were connected together they formed a closed **circuit**. Thus was born **circuit switching**—a manual process involving patch cords that connected the ends of these half-phone-lines. The wires running from your house to the Central Office was called a **local loop**. A hundred years later, the process of connecting halves of phone lines together is still called switching, and the halves of lines are still called local loops.

<aside>Circuit switching on a local loop</aside>

Facing the near-impossibility of housing all the switchboard operators, Ma Bell got clever and created mechanical switches to automatically connect people. The things were noisy, clacking continuously. But, using a new-fangled technology called "phone numbers" and radical rotary dials, they could automatically switch analog calls to the proper circuits. The collection of CO switches and lines and loops was called a **network**. A Public Switched Telephone Network. 'Course the telephone companies don't call it that. To them it's the PSTN.

<aside>Polly wants a clacker.</aside>

An activated PSTN termination device

This was great up until the fifties. The only computerlike device that tried to use the phone lines was the teletypewriter, the telecommuter's Model T. (Hey, Bill Gates used one to build his first empire. Can't knock it too hard.)

Then came along the computer. Contrary to popular belief the computer is a dumb animal. Want to say something intelligible to a computer? You have to translate it into ones and zeros. Digital. Type "Tiptoe Through the Tulips" into your computer, and it turns into a bunch of bits.

<aside>Did Rosie the Robot have ears?</aside>

Compare that to the way humans communicate. It'd be pretty hard to confuse Tiny Tim singing "Tiptoe Through the Tulips" with, say, James Earl Jones. That's why analog signals are so nice. They get the message and the madness.

A modem, as you probably know, converts the computer's ones and zeros—which won't work on a phone line—into the analog pulse that phone lines adore. The side that plugs into the back of your computer works with the computer's ones and zeroes; the side that plugs into the wall has a telephone gizmo that

<aside>Enter the modem.</aside>

speaks to other modems in a high-pitched squeal. The modem converts digital data into a sound, and then converts the sound back to digital.

Digital is cleaner than analog. That static you hear on the phone wreaks havoc with high-quality analog signals. Digital is also more reliable. Digital data goes across the PSTN, er, phone network, in packets: Every message one computer sends to another is divided up like a jigsaw puzzle, with each puzzle piece numbered. If anything happens to one of the pieces, the receiving computer tells the sending computer to resend it.

More than that, digital is *fast*. Audio CDs are digital. A cheap computer inside your CD player merely converts the ones and zeros on the CD into the analog signal expected by your speakers. That cheap, slow computer can spit a lot of ones and zeros out in the time it takes for Tiny Tim to sing "Tiptoe Through the Tulips." Imagine what would happen if you used an expensive, fast computer.

Is it Tiny Tim? Or is it live?

You are in a maze of twisty, turny paths.

So is it any surprise to find that the telephone companies went digital? They took all our voices and digitized them, with sound so good you can hear a pin drop. All the switches are digital, too. The clacking in the CO has been replaced by the silent sound of electronic switches.

Unfortunately, all our phones are still analog: They still have those little gizmos that expect to push electricity along a wire, and in turn be pushed by the tiny analog pulses. The switches expect analog pulses from your phone's gizmos. So the local loop, the half-phone-lines from your house to the CO, remains analog. But the rest of the phone system is digital.

Consider the irony.

When you want to make your computer talk to another computer, you have to convert your computer's digital data to an analog signal so it can go across your local loop to the telephone switch to be converted to digital so it can go across a bunch of digital switches, only to be converted back to analog at the other end's local loop where that person is using a modem to convert the analog back to digital!

What a convoluted, contorted pile of crap.

I'd like to say the phone companies did that because they wanted to keep our country's landfills from overflowing with defunct analog phones. I'd like to say that.

But why?

Actually, the phone companies made it this way because the move to digital switches—or *anything* new in the phone companies—happens gradually.

Patience, grasshopper.

Telephone switches cost around $1,000,000. Phone companies like to keep 'em until they keel over . . . usually about twenty years. Digital switches arrived on the scene in the early 1970s, and they were still cohabiting with the old clackers in some places into the early 1990s. Evolution in the phone biz runs slow: Compared to the computer biz, it's glacial.

Things were going (or suffering) along like this for many years. Then something happened. The government decided to split Ma Bell into AT&T and the Baby Bells. Suddenly AT&T had to compete with other long distance carriers like MCI. The regional phone companies, the RBOCs (Regional Bell Operating Companies, pronounced "arrrrrr-box"), remained regulated monopolies. This was tough on the RBOCs (so they whined) because long distance calls used to subsidize local calls. Companies make most of the long distance calls, but they were finding ways to skip the RBOCs altogether, so the RBOCs were losing money. Time to drum up some business.

The D-I-V-O-R-C-E will be final today.

One way was to provide data networks for companies. One such networking method, called X.25, was heralded for awhile, because it was an international standard. Global digital communications and all that. But X.25 didn't turn out to be as successful in North America as elsewhere. So the RBOCs went trolling for more business.

The other approach was to hit the mass markets. Create popular services anybody can afford. Have you heard of Call Waiting? Call Forwarding? Those are simple capabilities of digital switches, which have been available almost everywhere for a long, long time. Why did these services only pop up recently? The phone companies didn't realize how much you'd pay for them!

Take Caller ID. It's a simple application of **out-of-band-signaling**.

Out-of-band-signaling. Say what? It sounds complicated, but really it's quite simple. The phone companies established out-of-band signaling to keep from tying up expensive full-voice-grade circuits with trivial things like ringing the phone.

Band on the run

The beginning of every telephone call goes like this: Yo! Some dudette in Colorado is dialing a number. She's calling New Jersey. Got the number. OK. Which switch is that? Got it. Better ring the phone. *B-r-r-r-ing.* <sound of a switch twiddling its thumbs> *B-rrr-r-r-ing.* Is anybody gonna pick it up? *B-r-r-r-r-ing.* Oh <expletive deleted>, they did pick up the phone. Better stop the ringing sound, and start billing 'em.

Why waste a whole voice circuit on something so trivial—something that can be handled by the switches, exchanging tiny packets of information among themselves? That's what the phone company did: They set up a separate network, independent of the PSTN network, just to handle little no-account stuff like ringing the phone. It's called out-of-band-signaling, Signaling System 7, or (I can just see you waiting for the acronym) SS7.

But wait. With out-of-band-signaling the switch at the receiving end needs to know who's doing the calling so it can set up a voice circuit. Hey! How's about using the caller's phone number? Bingo. Caller ID.

Mo' money   SS7 features brought in the bucks, but that wasn't enough money to satiate the RBOCs. They had stockholders. They had company bonuses. They had other things to invest in, like cable and movie portfolios and speculative real estate. They needed more dough.

I found IT!   In stepped Integrated Services Digital Network or ISDN (pronounced "eye-ess-dee-en"; we'll talk about it extensively later in this chapter, in the part marked, uh, ISDN). It was the RBOC savior. The answer to each and every question. ISDN provides all sorts of capabilities at your doorstep, not the least of which is the ability to carry a digital signal all the way from your house to the switch. Once it's at the switch, the rest of the phone network is digital anyway. No need to detour through messy—and abysmally slow—analog signals. A digital service from end to end. Available at a curb near you. Some day. Maybe.

ISDN marks the Modern Period in the phone company's history, an evolutionary process that is probably still occurring at a phone switch near you. First they upgrade the switches to handle SS7 out-of-band-signaling with other switches. You know that your switch has SS7 capabilities when the phone company says you can get Caller ID. Then they upgrade the switches to handle the ISDN protocol straight to your doorstep. That's when the phone company says you can get ISDN.

About a year or two (or three or four) later, fully 10 percent of the people who work for the phone company can spell ISDN, and 10 percent of *them* know what it means.* We haven't yet reached that point in telephone evolution where I live— just got off the phone with yet another phone company employee who said, "I'm sorry, but U.S. West doesn't offer, what did you say that was? ICBM?"—but that's another story.

So much for the Compleat History of Telecommuter's Telephony.

Choices,   The telephone companies can now soak you in several ways, for various
choices   kinds of telephone lines: analog, ISDN, several varieties of leased lines, or if you

---

* That isn't too bad, really, for some of the local phone companies. ISDN has only been around for, oh, ten years. Twenty, I guess, if you really get right down to it. But it takes a long time for the phone companies to develop training courses, ya know? And then people actually have to go to the courses, and well. . . .

are desperate, possibly X.25. Which brand should you buy? And, having chosen a type of line, what options should you get?

Ah, Woody warned me. You *do* ask the tough questions.

A Chicken In Every POTS

> When you are skinning your customers you should leave some skin on to grow again so that you can skin them again.
>
> Nikita Khrushchev
> 1961

There are several ways to get from here to there and back again. One is Plain Old Telephone Service, or POTS. That is just a regular line from your house — an analog line on the local loop. To send data you use a modem. To talk you use your phone and typically your mouth.

The POTS thickens.

It was good enough for my great gran'pappy an' it's good enough for me.

This is the path of least resistance. If you do not need a lot of data transmission power (say to connect to the company LAN for applications and e-mail), and your file transfers don't run much more than a few megabytes a day, POTS is OK.

On the other hand, if you connect more than half an hour a day via long distance, POTS is expensive. Check out ISDN.

Should you end up with POTS, at least for now, most telecommuters need to consider a second (or even a third or fourth) line.

Why get a second line? To drive your local phone company installer guy crazy? Maybe.

Split personality — multiple lines

A second phone line means separating business from pleasure. You can leave the business to the answering machine after 5:00 p.m. Or, if you're one of those workaholic types, you can drive family members crazy by only answering the business calls after 5:00 p.m. A second phone line also helps keep the IRS stuff or expense reports straight, and it's the only way to deduct the cost of a phone line (see Chapter 8).

Most telecommuters can use three lines: the personal line, the business line, and a fax/data/emergency-outbound-long-distance line.

We have three phone lines, many two-line phones, a fax machine, and several modems, and organize the lines like this:

- The personal line rings in the main part of the house and in the office, but we will often turn off the ringer in the office.

- The business line only rings in the office, but the line runs to all the phones in the house, just in case.

- The fax machine picks up the fax/data line, the modems are hooked to the fax/data line (outbound only, for security reasons we don't let anybody dial in to the computers), and one phone in the office (with the ringer turned off) is connected to the same line.

At least it's moderately *organized* insanity.   That gives us a lot of flexibility, without going overboard. More often than not the phones ring when and where we want them to, so we don't get distracted by nuisance calls. And it's a rare day, indeed, when we don't have all three lines going simultaneously at least once.

'Course, a second phone line doesn't guarantee you'll keep anything else in your business straight. We have three lines. We're still workin' on the organizing part. Mumble.

Extra-Cost POTS Services

> If you reflect for a moment, you will see that it isn't merely probable but absolutely certain that one desires what one lacks, or rather that one does not desire what one does not lack.
>
> Socrates to Agathon
> Plato's *"The Symposium,"* ca. 350 BC

Telecommuters lack a lot.

It's only money.   There are a slew of optional "You pay, we play" phone company services for regular ol' POTS lines. (Many of them are included with ISDN phone service, discussed in the next section, but you'll have to ask the phone company which ones they offer . . . this week. . . .) Let's delve into what services your friendly local telephone company can provide. Hopefully, they'll even know what they can provide, too.

While some of these services can be replaced by a trusty phone, answering machine, or fax, some require Ma Bell. Unless you've been asleep the last ten years (Hi, Rip!) you'll be familiar with many of 'em. The boring ones we'll breeze through à la Cliff Notes. Some others may surprise you.

Most phone companies offer Call Waiting, Call Forwarding, Call Conferencing, **The offerings**
Voice Messaging, Speed Dialing, Priority Calling, and Distinctive Ringing services, all of which you are probably familiar with. In addition, many can provide
Caller ID in states where that is deemed legal. They also can often provide
personal 800 service, business lines, and multiple fax services.

**The operative word here is MOST. If the switches in your CO aren't relatively
new—say installed more than 20 years or so—you're stuck with whatever the
switch can handle. Maybe the type and age of the switch your house is
connected to should be included in the Multiple Listing Service, so you really
know what kind of house you're buying. "Oh my, not only is the house located
near nationally recognized schools but it has a fully featured AT&T 5ESS
telephone switch! You won't want to let this one get away!"**

That AT&T 5ESS bit does it every time.

While living in the backwaters, as we do, may affect when the switch is **YMMV**
replaced, location is not the only factor. Yes, even people in New York City—
especially people in New York City—may have to wait years for a phone line,
much less optional services. Call it Universal Unaccess. The phone switch costs
millions and millions of pennies and the telephone companies like to hang on to
'em. So, while we will talk about each of these services, remember YMMV (Your
Mileage May Vary).

Useful Basic Extras

Speed Dialing's for those who forget numbers. **Call Conferencing** allows you to
conference three to six people on the phone. Any decent phone you buy today has
both services, so why pay monthly for 'em? Telemployees usually have the
company conference *them* in. Only a virtual corporation may think they need
megapeople conferencing. But they're probably too bright to fall into the meeting
rut, anyway.

Call Waiting   **Call Waiting** lets you know if somebody else is trying to call you when you're already on the line by interrupting your conversation with a "CLICK." You can choose to make the first person hold while you answer it (which annoys some egos) or you can ignore the click (in which case why did you get the service?). It's nice if you have a phobia for missing calls, or if your boss is *really* edgy about telecommuting. I can live without it.

Call Forwarding   **Call Forwarding** forwards some (Selective Call Forwarding) or all of your calls to another number when you are out or the phone is busy. It's useful if you are a telecommuter who travels, especially since you can forward to a cellular phone (bloody *expensive*, but convenient), or if you live in a telecommuting telecommune (like us) where you can forward the call to the spouse's line.

That forwarding to the spouse makes for interesting intros. "Hello. This is Trudy Leonhard, president of the premier software consulting company Snowbound Computing, primary shareholder, and otherwise a Very Important Person. Oh, and receptionist for *der Dingsda*.* How may I help you?"

Distinctive Ringing   Another phone company starlet, **Distinctive Ringing** mucks with your "B-r-r-r-ing" sound. In Distinctive Ringing you can have up to four different phone numbers on the same physical line, each with its own special "B-r-r-ring": the number 555-0001 may ring as a "Bring . . . Bring . . . Bring . . . Bring," while 555-0002 goes "Moooooooan," 555-0003 sounds like "Bring-Bring . . . Bring-Bring," and 555-0004 goes "Brrrrrrrrrrrrring." You get the idea. The phone numbers are dummies: They all ring on your one line, the only difference is the sound they make.

Telecommuters might want Distinctive Ringing for any of several different reasons.

For example:

- It lets you start out your business with two or three phone numbers, but only one physical phone line. Later, as the phone company installs physical lines, you can have the numbers switched over to ring on those lines.

- You can give out "distinctive" phone numbers to important clients. But before you buy into this method, compare it with Priority Ringing, discussed next.

- Used in conjunction with Call Forwarding, described previously, you can distinguish between calls coming in on this number "naturally," as opposed to calls being forwarded. It's a bit hard to describe, but easy to set up. Say you have two phone numbers, 555-0001 and 555-0002, set up with distinctive ringing on your business phone line, and a home number, 555-0003. If you set up 555-0003 to Call Forward to 555-0002, say, you'll be able to tell by the tone

* or, roughly, what's-his-name.

of the ring on your business line whether you have a "real" business call (to 555-0001), or if it's just a home call (to 555-0003) that's being forwarded.

- Unlike the line splitters that Woody dislikes so much—the black boxes that are supposed to route inbound faxes to the fax machine, and all other calls to the phones—Distinctive Ringing can give you reliable splitting of inbound faxes, voice, and data. The hardware or software that accomplishes this feat (called "Call Directing" just to confuse everybody) merely listens to the sound of the ring. If you have 555-0008 and 555-0009 set up with Distinctive Ringing on the same physical phone line, the Call Directing box listens whenever the phone rings: if the ring is for 555-0008, it can route the call to the phones; if the ring is for 555-0009, it can be routed straight to the fax machine. Cool.

You won't see **Priority Ringing** advertised very often, but it can solve a very specific problem that plagues many telecommuters. Priority Ringing lets you set up a "hot list" of inbound phone numbers: Dial *61, and the computer will step you through the method of adding and deleting numbers from the hot list, right there on the phone. If any of the people on the hot list call you, the phone will ring with a distinctive tone. For example, the boss's number could be recognized so her "B-r-ring" will stand out from the regular riff-raff.

Priority Ringing

Ohmigod. Is that the Cosmic Boss ring? Or the hairdresser?

In addition to distinguishing calls from your boss (like distinguishing a fire?) and separating your business calls from the spouse's you could also use it, in the way just described for Distinctive Ringing, to split inbound faxes.

The local phone companies have a service that many of our FAFTCC (Friends and Family Telecommuting Calling Circle) swear by. Actually, they jump up and start rolling around on the floor over it. This is a personal 800 service: an 800 number that simply rings on whatever line you choose.

1-800-FREECALL

It's great for home-based businesses that have business far from home. It makes the company look *big*. Gotta be big and well known if you can afford an 800 number, no? Used to be true. Not any more. That new 1-800-BUY-MYSTUFF number rings at little ol' 303-555-0001. But, hey, why tell your customers?

Another great thing about personal 800 service is that customers from other cities who would otherwise hesitate to call long-distance will call: "Well, I'm not sure if I need a Hekbib, in fact I don't really know what they are, but hey! it's a free call." There's another interesting twist. . . .

One FAFTCC says he finds an 800 number very useful for his consulting business. Because he teleconsults, he has to rely on the client company's employees for much of his information. In some companies the employee's long distance calls are monitored or prohibited. He said that once he got an 800 service the calls—and information—started flowing in. It was one of his best investments.*

Caller ID   Another great feature, if you can get it, is Caller ID service. (Our illustrious Sponsoring Editor *hates* Caller ID, but that's because she doesn't have geeks calling her at all hours of the day and night.) Yes, there are weighty moral questions, pro and con, about "exposing" the name and number of the caller to the callee. But, dammit, the next time you get three back-to-back solicitation calls on the business line from the *Rocky Mountain News*, you're gonna want Caller ID, too.

If you haven't seen Caller ID in action, it's pretty simple. Call the phone company and get the service started (assuming it's even legal where you live). Schlep on down to the local poor excuse for a computer store and shell out $30 to $50 for a Caller ID box. Plug it into the wall. The next time somebody calls, their name and phone number appear on the box, before you pick up the phone. Unless . . .

U.S. West   Unless you have phone service with U.S. West. Man, this one pissed me off!
Caller ID is a U.S. West takes out these big ads in the local paper. "Free installation of U.S. West
fraud. Caller ID" they say. "Act Now!" Down in the fine print at the bottom, it says, "Not all callers will be identified." That's cool: There's an override code a caller can punch into the phone to keep their number from appearing in the Caller ID box. Some folks get their phone numbers permanently blocked. No problemo.

I get Caller ID service. I buy a $50 box. Plug it in and . . . guess what? I can only see the number and name from local callers! Anybody who calls me from outside the Denver local calling area shows up as "Out of Area": no phone number, no name, no nothing. Man, what a fraud!

I called to complain, to see when U.S. West can get me *real* Caller ID—the kind available all over the country. Three, four, five different numbers. Nobody at U.S. West knows what I'm talking about. I finally find a U.S. West rep who says it's a problem with my long-distance carrier. I call AT&T, and they say it's U.S.

---

* The other big boon for his teleconsulting business was the condo he bought. It let him get away from a house of five females. Even his goldfish are female. Now he feels he can male bond by going to the condo's gym. Not that he has. Maybe I should get him a spittoon. Not that he would ever use it. Ah well, the girls have forgiven him because the complex has a huge pool. But I digress.

West. Several hours later, I finally find out the truth: U.S. West has *never* had real Caller ID—their Caller ID service has never been able to identify callers outside the Denver metro area, since the first day it was available. They just, uh, neglect to mention that little detail in any of their ads. Golly gee.

Even outside the U.S. West fallout zone, sometimes the **&^% thing won't work, usually because the calling party's switch or some path between them and you does not provide the service. Not much you can do about it.

You can use Caller ID service to screen calls ("Its Beavis again, let's have the modem answer!" *hehe-hehe-hehe*). On some voice messaging software you can have the Caller ID trigger applications such as a contact database so you can have information on the client pop up on your PC as you answer the phone. Let them identify themselves and then ask them about their fishing trip. They'll think you've been dying to know all week if they caught a steelhead or not.

Caller ID's other virtues

Notice I said to let them speak first. It's disconcerting to call somebody up and have them say "Well, hi, Lisa!" before you get a word in edgewise. You tend to look around and make sure you don't have food between your teeth—in case they can see you, too. Anywho, you can wow them a lot better if you don't let on you know who they are or that your notes on them just popped up with "ask about steelhead." Hey, they don't have to know you can't tell a steelhead from a pollywog.

As Caller ID becomes more common, the need for separate Caller ID boxes will disappear: Already there are phones, voice messaging boxes, and software to handle it. It's only a matter of time before Caller ID is built into everyday office phones.

"Why Bother" Extras

So much for something worth buying. Now let's take a look at a couple of extra-cost services that rarely, if ever, are worth getting.

Ever been tempted to blow the considerable extra bucks and get a "real" business phone line?

For a "real" business?

It's none of the phone company's damned business how you use your phone line. As long as you aren't doing something patently illegal—and in some cases, even if you are—the phone company has no right to know how you use a phone line going into your house.

By and large, having business-line service is a tremendous waste of money. The only time you have to pay for a business line is if you want a listing in the

Yellow Pages, a business directory assistance listing, and a business White Page entry in the phone book. That's it. For that you get charged out the wazoo.

Having a business line doesn't even give you faster repair service. We know. We have encountered Joe-Bob, the local telephone repairman. Occasionally it gets a bit, well, breezy around here. Saw Toto flapping around the other day. Winds at 100-plus mph. This, along with the occasional lightning strike causes phone outages ("*ZAP* I told you it was a bad idea to put a TV antenna on the roof—ah, where's the cat?"). Once my business line was out for a week. Fortunately we have three phone lines, so it was only loss of business and not loss of sanity. We asked if we could get business service so Joe-Bob could get out here a little faster. Well, we were told that Joe-Bob gets there when he gets there, and it didn't matter what the line was.

Next time I'm going to claim I'm U.S. West management. They won't know. They don't even know what each department does, let alone who's in them.

So business lines only give you limited phone book advertising. Several fellow teleconsultants have chosen to spend their advertising dollars elsewhere— especially when those dollars are few and far between. . . . Many more have regretted not spending their dollars elsewhere.

You can always send a fax to Mom. Maybe *she'll* call on the business line.

MEL: a nice guy   Here's another phone company service you can avoid. It's called Bob . . . uh, no, wrong company. It's called MEL, an acronym for Market Expansion Line. (U.S. West calls it that. YMMV.)

MEL is a combo Distinctive Ringing/Business Line without the Distinctive "B-r-ring." For businesses on a budget, supposedly. You get a separate business number (with all the business phone listing wrappings) on the same physical line as something else, like your home phone. It's cheaper than adding a second dedicated business line. You can add Distinctive Ringing (costs extra) so you can tell what type of call is coming in.

Beats me why anybody would want it, unless they absolutely had to have the Yellow Pages listing and could afford the MEL charges, but didn't have enough to spring for a full business line. MEL's a pain. If you have too many business calls or too many personal calls this configuration can be annoying, since you can only receive one call at a time. However, if you are starting a home-based business and don't expect a lot of calls or want to test the waters first, this may be a cost-saving solution. Just don't say I didn't warn you.

Long-distance Service

> I knew once a very covetous, sordid fellow who used to say,
> "Take care of the pence, for the pounds will take care of themselves."
>
> Lord Chesterfield
> Letter to his son, November 6, 1747

One last thought on telephone pipelines before we jump to cool digital telephone services. If telecommuting requires you to make long or numerous long-distance calls be aware that it's a talker's market. **Going the distance**

The long-distance carriers are scrambling for your business. Each has at least one discount plan, but they usually don't tell you about them. That is, unless you are on MCI's "trying to convert 'em" list in which case you will be notified about every five minutes.

If your long-distance calls are local long-distance—that is, the bill is completely within your local telephone company's territory—you may be able to get on a plan with the local phone company. **Local long-distance**

Where we live, local long-distance calls to our friends just over the mountain— about 20 miles away—cost *more* per minute than a call from the Colorado backwaters to San Jose, California. So anyway you slice it, it's worth trying to slice it down.

If you spend more than a few bucks a month on long-distance calls, take a moment or three and study your (real or expected) calling habits. Where will you be calling? Always to the same number—like to the corporate LAN? Will you have a mix of computer calls to the modem and voice calls to your colleagues—all in the same area code? Are the calls going to be during business hours or are you on after-hours graveyard shift? Do you make many calls—if so you may find a plan that takes minute fractions instead of rounding up. Are you using your line for both business and as your home phone? If so you should remember to count personal calling patterns. Do you have multiple phones? You may decide on different carriers for the different phones. No time to be loyal. Do you travel and need a phone card? **Long long-distance**

Once you have pondered these questions call up all of the long-distance carriers in your area. There may be others besides the big three: AT&T, MCI, and Sprint. They should be listed in your Yellow Pages under "Telephone Services— Long Distance."

Once you pick a carrier and plan, recheck every six months or so. Each carrier will go through previous phone bills with you, figuring out the best plan. Remember carriers add or change plans frequently, so continue to check periodically.

Beware of the cons and con artists. Even the big three long-distance carriers are given to, uh, flights of hyperbole.

Speaking of which. In early 1994 the big three carriers were all touting great discounts: 20 percent off, 50 percent off. What they didn't tell you was that all three got approval the month before for an across-the-board 10 percent increase! If you did not bother to call and sign up for their new programs, you got socked with that 10 percent increase. Even if you did sign up for the discounts, 20 percent was not 20 percent less than what you had paid for two months earlier, because it was 20 percent off the new price. Schnooks. Well, you can't stop such tactics but you can make sure that you get the best deal among the riff-raff. Be careful about lock-in deals (just like a lease) because they may try to change the rules on you, and check what connect/disconnect charges they'll try to foist on ya before switching carriers.

ISDN

> Public telephones in Europe are like our pinball machines.
> They are primarily a form of entertainment and a test of skill
> rather than a means of communication.
>
> Miss Piggy
> *Miss Piggy's Guide to Life,* 1981

So what is this ISDN I've been teasing you about? Should you get it? What is it good for?

If you live in parts of western Europe, ISDN is like falling off a log: When you finally (finally!) get a phone line installed, it's bound to be ISDN. Ah, aren't you the lucky one.

2B or not 2B   For most of the rest of the world, though, ISDN means "I Still Don't Know." It's a question of chicken and egg: If you're transmitting data, ISDN at one end of the phone line demands ISDN on the other end, too. If your office doesn't have ISDN, and nobody else in your on-line life has ISDN, then it makes no sense whatsoever for you to get ISDN.

In the United States anyway, ISDN critical mass has not yet been attained. But that will change—most likely in the short term. When Microsoft Network gets ISDN lines in most of its big markets and Internet service providers start seeing more of their customers become ISDN-conversant, the critical mass won't be far away. Certainly by the end of the decade, ISDN service will be fairly widespread —and telecommuters will be leading the charge.

The Innards

So how does ISDN work? That takes a little explaining.

There's a cable that runs from the telephone pole into your house. If you've ever cut open that cable, you know that it contains four separate, small, insulated strands of copper wire. For reasons I've never really understood, telephone people call that cable—that bundle of four wires—a **twisted pair**. No doubt you've suspected it all along: There's a twisted pair living in your house.

If this is your idea of a twisted pair, we need to talk.

Oh well. Could be worse. They could call it a "twisted foursome" and then you'd *really* have some explaining to do.

With a POTS system, each telephone number (each "phone line," if you will) requires two wires. Since you have a twisted foursome . . . er, twisted pair running into your house, you already have enough wires for two different telephone numbers.

Ninety-nine times out of a hundred, when you call the phone company and have a second phone line on your property set up, all they have to do is change a couple of entries on the switch's computer. No human need ever touch a single wire. For this they charge you big-time.

ISDN hijacks all four copper wires to create three phone lines. Yep, it's a little bit of black magic, but you know how fancy these electronics guys can be. Two of the phone lines are super-duper lines, each capable of handling more than twice the data of a normal analog line. The third line is more like a pothole than a superhighway.

Enough POTS already

Think of ISDN as three phone lines—or three **channels** to use the technical term—coming into your house. Two of them are called **Bearer**, or "B" channels. They carry the brunt of your data or voice. Each B channel can spit out 64,000 bits per second* (commonly abbreviated 64 Kbps), whereas even the best analog phone line with an expensive modem can only carry 28,800 bits per second (commonly abbreviated 28.8 Kbps).

---

* Usually. Until SS7 is everywhere some paths from here to there will still be using in-band-signaling. In that case, you only get 56 Kbps per B channel.

The other one, the **Delta**, or "**D**" channel, is used mostly to do all that out-of-band signaling I was telling you about. However, there is a smidge left over so the phone company lets you use it as a data-only channel at 9.6 Kbps.

2B + D = ?   Put it all together and you get ISDN 2B + D. How's that for acronymania! All of it is digital. No more digital-to-analog-to-digital modems. No more squeals being turned into bits and back again.

ISDN is good at a lot of things, but voice isn't one of them. ISDN uses a brain-dead method—developed in the early 1960s and never updated—to convert voice to digital. As a result, voice calls waste a lot of space: One voice call uses up a whole B channel. Data hog. So, for ISDN, at most you only get two voice lines at any one time. That's OK, I guess, if you're a telecommuting Han Solo, but it isn't so good if you were foolish enough to let your child become a teenager. You *didn't* let your child become a teenager, did you?

Putting the
pieces together   You can configure the three channels, the 2B + D, in a number of ways. Maybe you only want one B channel (What? You crazy?). Each B channel can be only data, only voice, or both (but not simultaneously). Your B channel can be set up as point-to-point, which means you always go to the same destination, like the corporate office. Or it can be multipoint, which means you dial out to anywhere—as long as "anywhere" has an ISDN hookup for the data.

Remember: A voice B channel can talk to anybody with a regular old telephone. But a data B channel can only talk to another ISDN data B channel.

In other words, if you're hell-bent on data transmission, you can rig an ISDN line to run at more than 128 Kbps—more than four times as fast as the fastest analog line available today. Is there any wonder why telecommuters are clamoring for ISDN?

Ah, but all this speed and glory hath its price. There may be such a thing as a zero-cost lunch, but ISDN certainly isn't it.

ISDN service isn't as simple as POTS: there's a whole lot more to it than plugging a little plastic thingy into the wall. It can take several days to get the service and equipment to all work right. Intel has something called "Intel Blue" to simplify things if you buy Intel ISDN equipment, although they, too, can run into brick walls.

Tariffs

Pricing depends on the configuration and your state's tariffs. What's a tariff? Good question. Remember that the phone companies are supposed to be regulated monopolies. Each state has regulators that will set what standard price phone companies can charge for services like ISDN. In some places, ISDN can be billed out at a flat monthly rate; in other places, you'll get hit with a per-minute charge. Depending on your state, ISDN can be billed at one price for residential customers and a completely different price for businesses (which is what they'll call a telecommuter no doubt). Every state gets to name their price.

Tariffing also affects what features you get with ISDN, such as Call Waiting and Caller ID. Some come with the basic package, some do not. If you want additional features you will have to pay extra, just like with POTS.

Parts Is Parts

There are several pieces of acronyms, er, I mean equipment, needed to work with ISDN. If you are planning on using ISDN in more than one place in your house (say, at multiple phone locations) you will need to do some rewiring in the house, because ISDN converts your twisted pair to three lines, which will require six wires inside the house. (The twisted pairs are multiplying like tribbles. AHH!) If you want any "normal" lines you may have to add some additional lines to the house, too, since ISDN uses the whole twisted pair. Good time to become buddies with the neighborhood electrician.

> **ISDN does not provide power to the telephone. On a "normal" line, power comes from the CO, but not with ISDN. If the electricity goes out in your house, your ISDN phones go out, too. Hmm, great premise for a horror film. "Oh gawd. Not only is she turning her shivering back on the ax-wielding fiend but she has ISDN with no backup power supply and he cut the power lines!"**

Uh-hem. Let's talk equipment. Now in ISDN-speak you have to worry about the U and the T/S interface by using an NT1. Put that all together and what do you get? NUTS. *Heh heh heh!* And you thought BellHeads didn't have a sense of humor.

Just a little Bell humor

Time for some terminology. The **U interface** is the point where the twisted pair from the telephone company gets converted into a 6-wire line in your house.

The **NT-1** (Network Termination-1) is the box that actually does the conversion: One side plugs into the ISDN line, the other side has three pairs of wires. One single NT-1 can, depending on the model, handle up to eight pieces of ISDN equipment. Not bad, eh? The catch is that the NT-1 only works with ISDN equipment and who has eight pieces of those hanging around in their backyard?

Bafflegab

If you want to use your analog phone, fax, or PC you have to get an adapter to go between the NT-1 and the phone, fax, or PC. The adapter is called a Terminal Adapter, or (you guessed it) a **TA**.

There is no power on the ISDN line, so you may want to get a Power Supply or **PS**. (Aren't these acronyms fun? Like spittin' up fur balls.) Often a power supply is bundled in with the NT-1, but you need to check to be sure.

<table>
<tr><td>

ISDN Daisy
Chain

</td><td>

That's the ISDN Daisy Chain: The ISDN phone line connects to the NT-1, which connects to a TA, which connects to your ISDN-conversant phone, modem, or fax. You may also want or need a PS to provide power to the NT-1.

</td></tr>
</table>

 If you are using the ISDN line strictly for high-bandwidth data—and as a telecommuter, you probably will be—you may forego all of that alphabet soup in favor of a single PC card that combines the functions of the NT-1, the TA, and the PS. It makes things easier to install. And easier to buy. The only bummer comes if you want to add something later—some PC cards don't let you attach TAs.

Some of these PC cards let you plug a regular, everyday analog phone into the back. That can be most helpful for figuring out when the line is down. But be careful if you are considering attaching a modem to the analog phone line.

 If you are thinking of attaching your fax/modem to the analog line of an ISDN PC card, or simply through a TA into an NT-1, make sure the modem manufacturer *recommends* it. Some don't. This is *muy importante* if you thought you'd use a TA to attach your fax/modem for stuff like on-line services and non-ISDN computer hookups.

ISDN is like buying a car with hidden extras. Lots of parts, each of 'em costing bucks. But it may be worth it if you live telecommuting life in the fast lane.

<table>
<tr><td>

Say it, don't
spray it: SPID.

</td><td>

Each piece of ISDN equipment needs a **SPID** (Service Profile IDentifier). It is a number issued by the local phone company to identify each piece of ISDN terminal equipment. Makes them look organized. Supposedly it can help with repairs but I ain't bettin' the cabin on it.

</td></tr>
</table>

Planning for ISDN

The Price Is Right—Or Is It?

How expensive is ISDN? How bad do you want it? *Heh heh.* All that bit pushin' comes at a price. The price of computer-based ISDN stuff is plummeting—as computer prices always do—but prices for the more pedestrian ISDN products are still floating around in the budgetary stratosphere.

An NT-1 can run $200 to $500. Power Supplies will cost an extra $100 or more if not included in the NT-1's base price. You can get NT-1s from 'most any networking or telecommunications vendor, including Black Box (see Appendix B). **NT-1, PS**

A Terminal Adapter costs around $500. Or, you can get the all-in-one PC card— with NT-1, PS, and TA functionality—for $700 or less. (PC prices being the way they are, that price may be cut in half that by the time you read this.) Black Box offers both, but you may find a wider selection and better prices by simply scanning the latest edition of *Computer Shopper*. **TA, PC**

ISDN phones run $250 to $2,000 apiece. You have to want ISDN voice really bad to spring for a phone in that range. ISDN phones have the one advantage that you can get a single software package to answer all incoming calls on both B channels—but there has to be a cheaper road to the universal answering machine. If you want ISDN phones in more than one place, the rewiring will kill ya, too. **Phones**

For two grand, you should get the butler thrown in for free.

Fax machines for ISDN lines (they're called "Group IV") cost around $2,000 or more. 'Course a Group IV fax on this side won't help much if you don't have a Group IV fax on the other side, too. **Fax**

Monthly ISDN phone service charges vary, based on tariffs. Average costs, as far as I've seen, run $125 to $150 to get connected, $40 to $100 per month as a flat charge, and if a per-minute charge is tariffed, anywhere from 1.5 to 30 cents per minute, for local calls. Usually that per-minute charge is doubled if you use both B channels—and you probably will. **Phone bills**

Yeah. You read that right. You can pay up to $100 a month simply for the privilege of owning an ISDN line, and another 60 cents a minute for local calls, should you have the temerity to use it!

Man, those high-priced local phone companies should be paying for their new switches with wheelbarrows full of cash. Wonder what they would charge for gold twisted pair?

Long distance   If you need to go long distance you have to deal with long-distance carrier charges, too. Heaven only knows what they'll charge.

When do you   So when *do* you want to use ISDN? Trudy's rule of thumb: Look to ISDN when
yell Uncle?   you hook up to the central corporate office and you can take coffee breaks after each key (or mouse) stroke. When your boss asks you what you've done all day and you can say self-righteously "I transferred a *whole* file." When, after reading the company e-mail, you get this feeling that soap operas have fast moving plots. In short, when you need bit power, and you're willing to pay (and pay and pay) for it.

Prices are falling. As more and more people clamor for ISDN, the phone companies will be forced to provide good service at a fair price—or so the theory goes, anyway. You can help drag Ma Bell kicking and screaming into the twentieth century by getting on the phone, right now, and calling your local phone company's "home office" center. Ask about ISDN. And don't take no for an answer.

Tell 'em Trudy sent ya.

 Even if you get ISDN and you are flush with channels you may *still* want a second POTS line. Why? ISDN doesn't work directly with your normal equipment. You either have to get ISDN-enabled telephones or a terminal adapter for each piece of equipment. Do you have a phone in your office and also a phone somewhere else, say in your garage, where you would also like to be able to answer work-related calls? Guess what, with ISDN that garage phone won't work. Time for the mad dash back to the office. ISDN phones are expensive. Terminal Adapters ain't cheap. It all has to be wired too. Lot of fuss just for a garage phone, but I'm sure your boss will understand. Right.

 The other reason to have a POTS line? If you want to connect to some other computer or on-line service that doesn't have ISDN access, or you don't want to pay the outrageous price for their ISDN access. It's a nice backup for all those folks you may have to communicate with who are still cruisin' at country speeds.

There's an extensive list of ISDN providers, local phone company ISDN contacts, and ISDN-related hardware manufacturers in Appendix B.

Other Alternatives

> The highest moral ideal either for a people or for an individual is to be
> true to its destiny . . . to leave the known for the unknown.
>
> Christopher Dawson
> *The Sociological Review,* 1925

For many people locked in the traditional phone company mindset, choice of   **POTS today**
telephone service is just like Ford's choice of Model Ts—any color you want, as
long as it's black. *POTS, POTS, POTS.*

Telecommuters who wither away on the line and need better data throughput   **ISDN**
will probably push for ISDN. It's a pretty safe bet that ISDN service will expand   **tomorrow—**
greatly in the near future. Who knows, ten years from now you may be able to call   **or sooner**
your local phone company and get connected immediately to someone who
understands the ins and outs of ISDN.

There are several other technologies floating around, though, and I would be
remiss if I didn't at least mention them in passing. Several are more faint echoes of
the past than strong voices for the future, but you may bump into them, and
should know both their strong and weak points.

One option is a leased line. A leased line can only go to one destination, point-   **Leased lines**
to-point. It's all digital: You'll need a separate line for voice. It's expensive because, as
the name indicates, you have a line dedicated to you. A leased line could be a
direct link between your home office and the central corporate office, or you may
want a permanent connection to the Internet.

> **Here's another Trudy Rule of Thumb: If you have to fly to get to the central
> corporate office, a leased line will be way too expensive. Buying your own Lear
> jet may be cheaper.**

On the other hand, if your central corporate office is hooked to the Net, you might
consider the Internet as a cheap, but convoluted, alternative: A leased 56 Kbps
connection to the local Internet on-ramp can be cheaper than other approaches.

The costs for a leased line are steep, but you do not have to pay on a per-call   **Bucks**
basis. You pay by the mile. So how steep is steep?

At one point when I had given up on ISDN I considered getting a leased 56
Kbps line from my home to the Internet. The access point was about 25 miles
away. U.S. West quoted me a cost of about $150 per month with an initial set-up
fee in the hundreds.

> **Prices where you live may be quite different. One poor soul in Arizona (also a
> U.S. West customer) had to pay $700 to connect and $300 a month for a line
> under 10 miles away. I swear it depends on what the guy at the phone company
> ate for lunch.**

Connecting to a leased line is a little different. Instead of a modem you will need a **CSU/DSU** (Channel Service Unit/Data Service Unit). These cost around $500. You need one on both ends, just as with modems. The central corporate office may use a hub which, amongst other gadgets, has a CSU/DSU equivalent. Most phone companies will help you find a CSU/DSU vendor or you can try the local computer store. You may need either a two-wire or a four-wire CSU/DSU device, because some phone companies need to use four wires to transmit 56 Kbps service to your house. It all depends upon how far from the CO you are and how the heck they're providing the service.

Switched 56

Like a leased line, Switched 56 is also digital, but (as the term "Switched" implies) it allows you to dial up different 56 Kbps destinations. Just like POTS you pay connection, monthly, and per minute costs. Where we live, there's a $200 connection fee (it's hard to flip those "ON" switches), $60 monthly, which includes one free hour; and 10 cents a minute thereafter. As with the leased line, you'll also need a CSU/DSU.

Switched 56 and leased line 56 Kbps are old technology, kind of like an expensive classic sportster. You may be interested in something a little newer. Something faster, and possibly cheaper. That's what ISDN promises.

X.25

Some local phone companies like Ameritech offer plug-in X.25 networks, as do Tymnet and Telenet. X.25 is an older spec that implements "Wide Area Networks." Your central corporate office (or whoever you're dialing) has to support X.25 to make the whole thing work. X.25 can run up to 64 Kbps.

There are three reasons why you may want to look at X.25 WANS. One is that it has potential to save you money, especially if your destination is far away, because the service provider has a much closer access point, generally without long distance charges. Because all your data is packetized and combined with every other customer's (just like the Internet), you share the same phone line for most of the trip. Didn't your Mom always try to get you to share? Now you know why. You achieve economies of scale. The second reason is that X.25 has some security, which is getting harder and harder to find these days. Third, you can, in some cases, bill all of the connections to the destination. If you are a telemployee, that is one less expense report. Yesss!

X.25 pricing is usually by the packet, and can be quite reasonable.

So why aren't people lined up for X.25 service, like lines in Disneyland? The reason is because it is slow. The X.25 method of handling packets assumes the telephone lines are made of string and paper cups. Not very reliable. So X.25 graciously does error detection and correction . . . at every switch. Slows the baby down. Most lines don't need the error detection ad nauseam now, but with X.25 you pay for it over and over again.

Just about everything leaves X.25 in the dust.

You may have heard about Frame Relay and something called **Asynchronous Transfer Mode** or ATM. They're often touted as the next step beyond ISDN, and from a technical point of view, they are. Unfortunately, with a very few exceptions, ATM and Frame Relay are much too expensive for the typical telecommuter: Both the phone service and the requisite hardware cost an arm and a leg.

ATM and Frame Relay

The exceptions? A few forward-thinking phone communities are implementing pilot ATM projects. As of this writing, there's one in the San Francisco Bay Area, and another in Boulder, Colorado. (The latter is code-named "BATMAN." I kid you not.)

Some day ATM and Frame Relay may change the face of telecommuting. For now, though—a time when nine out of ten calls to the phone company end in a denial that ISDN even exists*—ATM and Frame Relay are just too far out on the horizon.

EQUIPMENT

> From coupler-flange to spindle-guide I see Thy Hand, O God—
> Predestination in the stride o' yon connectin'-rod
>
> Rudyard Kipling
> *McAndrew's Hymn*, 1904

There are several connectin' rods to your desk. As the one-organism band in charge of your telecommuting activities, you need to make some home equipment decisions. You need to deliberate over the vicissitudes of such uninspiring (but vital!) products as fax machines, modems, answering machines, and telephones. They can be real or virtual, or a hazy shade of both.

If the telephone line is your on-ramp to the Information SuperHypeWay, then consider your communication equipment the Chitty Chitty Bang Bang that'll get ya there. Unlike Chitty, the equipment telecommuters use these days usually involve software at some point—the line between hard equipment and software keeps getting more and more blurred.

So before we start comparing machines to modems to software, let's take the holistic approach. You may be tempted to forget about all the equipment listed in this section, figuring that you can get software to run on your PC to accomplish the same thing: fax software in place of a fax machine, say, or a fancy telephony board to take the place of an answering machine. The problem is that there's a

Soft or hard?

---

* Or, as Woody likes to say, "Ninety-nine point nine percent of all Americans don't know what ISDN is—but why do they *all* have to work for the phone company?"

practical limit to how much you can cram on your PC. Here's what to watch for in general when considering software as an alternative to stand-alone equipment.

Whaddya mean, no space at the Inn?

Capacity   Faxes come in as images (that is, a bunch of dots that are supposed to look like something). Voice comes in as, well, voice. If you decide on using a fax/modem or voice messaging system on your computer instead of a fax or answering machine, you have to worry about storage capacity. Images and voice take a much larger chunk of disk storage space than, say, a word processing document. Incoming faxes and faxes scheduled to be sent take space. Some software has compression, which helps.

Lurkers

System Resources   In addition to disk space, the soft substitutes for hard boxes consume memory and Windows resources—and if the software is DOS-based you have to worry about TSRs.* Some of these guys use up a very limited real estate, called **conventional memory**, of which there is 640K. And just because the software claims it runs in Windows doesn't mean TSRs aren't lurking. If you don't understand all this technical gobbledygook, you'll have Hobbes' time trying to keep software substitutes running.

Like a slug

Multi-tasking   The more stuff you've got running the slower your PC can become. Be especially wary of software that claims you can do two things at once. It may not be as great as you think. After all, a dentist thinks you can talk *and* keep your mouth opened wide, but I wouldn't make a habit out of it. On the other hand, if you want to be able to do multiple communication tasks, it is better to get software that handles it.

Bigger 'n better

Upgrading   Compared to stand-alone machines, equipment that uses software has a better chance of continually improving, albeit for a price. On the other hand, a stand-alone may be reasonably priced enough that you'd rather toss it and get a new one when the time comes.

So don't automatically assume that a software solution on your PC is *ipso facto* better than a cheap, reliable, stand-alone box. Just 'cuz it's cool doesn't necessarily mean that it's good.

---

* TSR = Terminate-and-Stay-Resident program. An archaic (but still common) method for allowing several DOS programs to run more-or-less concurrently.

Telephones

> There was a young man with a hernia
> Who said to his surgeon 'Gol-dernya,
> When carving my middle
> Be sure you don't fiddle
> With matters that do not concernya.'
>
> Heywood Broun
> Limerick written while waiting for an operation

With all the high-fallutin' talk about digital this and multioperational that, there's still no substitute for a good, solid, noise-free telephone, with a handset that doesn't jump out of your hand, and a few simple, worthwhile capabilities. Speed dial. Speakerphone. Hold. Last number redial. The easy stuff.

Beware the "softphone" siren song! If you have been scouring magazines and newspapers for the ultimate office equipment you will read about softphones, or CTI (Computer Telephony Integration). The CTI folks promise to replace your phone, your answering machine — and probably your coffee maker and first-born child, too — with a single box that takes care of everything. High Tech! Multimedia!! Blah. Blah. Blah.

While CTI may rate as a so-so replacement for your answering machine, I would not trade the whole passel of those softphones for my Panasonic KX-T3185. It has two (count 'em — two) lines — which already outdoes the softphone. It has conference calling, speed dialing, hold, speakerphone with mute, and a clock to boot.

The plain ol' phone, still hangin' in there.

Actually, CTI does bring two useful features to the telecommuter: Caller ID Pop-ups — which pop up information from your PC-based Personal Information Manager (PIM) whenever someone calls — and call logging, which can keep accurate track of who you're calling, and when. A third CTI application automatically dials the phone number from your PIM, but that's a toss-up because some telecommuters claim manually dialing a phone number is the only exercise they get.

The good side of softphones

But if the latest whiz-bang technology doesn't deliver much, what should you do? Go back to the old-fashioned business phone, the one Ma Bell used to use?

Well, yes and no.

A Tale of Three Phones

I'm hard on my telephones. The weather up here can give 'em a run for the money, too: Lightning strikes are not uncommon, and phones seem to get fried more often than any other appliance in the house. Let me tell you about my quest for the ultimate telephone. You may find a bit of yourself in this story, too.

The four-line GE
I started by installing the most advanced four-line phones I could find, a General Electric model. Man, they had everything: intercom, timers, one-touch this, and hands-free that. I plugged each one into its own 120-volt surge suppressor and protected the phone lines themselves with their own surge suppressors. Each of the six phones in the house started looking like the back of my PC: wires going here and there, stretching all over the place. I even figured out how to use some of the fancy features on the phones. It was great.

Until we got our first big lightning storm. One lightning bolt fried four of the six phones. It took me an entire day to trace down which surge suppressors had given up the ghost, and which phones were still working. (Checking the six 120-volt surge suppressors and twelve phone line suppressors was easy, it's all the permutations and combinations of six phones and their intercom circuitry that drove me nuts!) I was so mad I could hardly talk: an entire wasted day.

So I traded in the four fouled-up GE phones for four new ones, and . . . predictably . . . the next lightning storm knocked out two of them, too. I rounded up all six of them and returned them to the retailer, in a huff.

The three-line AT&T
I traded them in for the top-of-the-line three-line AT&T model, which had just been released for retail sale. Keeping the old (and still functional) surge suppressors, I plugged all six of them in. Programmed them. Learned a bit about their advanced features, and . . . .

The next lightning storm knocked out three of them. Fried. I swapped out the three, knowing good and well that the next round of lightning would probably zap them, too. It did.

The two-line Panasonic
So I moved down, to the Panasonic KX-T3185. Neat phone. Lots of features, but no intercom. Half the price of the AT&T. And they've been working for more than a year, with nary a hiccup.

 I don't claim to know exactly what killed those phones, but I'm willing to make a big bet. I'll betcha just about anything that the fancier phones, with more interconnecting stuff, and more advanced circuitry, are far more susceptible to minor fluctuates in phone-line voltage. Those fancy phones didn't stand a chance in my hostile environment.

Woody lives in a lightning-prone area, too. He swears by his two-line Panasonic KX-T3280, which includes an intercom. (If you'd ever seen his house you'd understand why: Seems like it's a quarter-mile hike from the family room to the office.) Personally, I hate the KX-T3280—the intercom requires that all the phone lines in your house be wired from a single point—but it's a free country. Woody can be wrong if he wants to be.

In general, I recommend that you chose the *lowest*-tech phone you can find that meets your purposes. Get a 30-day no-questions return guarantee. And if you take it home and the phone sounds the least bit scratchy, or you don't like the delay on the speakerphone, return it!

Headsets

> A good listener is not only popular everywhere,
> but after a while he knows something.
>
> Wilson Mizner

Are you ready for the single most important recommendation in this book?

You need to get a hands-free telephone headset, the kind that slips over your head. Plantronics and AT&T make them. The basic models cost less than $100. If you're telecommuting, I *guarantee* that the very first day you use one, you'll wonder how you ever survived without it.

Right on, Trudy! Right on!

Unless you have three hands

Most telecommuters use the phone a lot. Most telecommuters use their computers a lot. And, at least part of the time, most telecommuters need to use both their phones and their computers, simultaneously. When that happens, there's simply no substitute for a headset.

Once upon a time headsets were scratchy things, uncomfortable, and the sound quality lagged somewhere near the dog-screeching category. Not so any more.

Most headsets have a base that plugs directly into the side of the phone—where your handset goes—and the handset plugs into that base. Sometimes you'll have to adjust a couple of switches to get the handset and headset to work.

Instructions in the Plantronics box are written in some cryptic English variant, so I called Plantronics and asked for an explanation. Basically, if the headset and handset don't work immediately when you plug them in, you have to slide the switches marked "I" and "II" until you can hear the dial tone. Both "I" and "II" can be On or Off, so you have four choices: I On, II On; I On, II Off; I Off, II On; and I Off, II Off. If none of those four choices work, return the headset.

If you can't get the kind of headset that plugs into your telephone to work, there's a second type that simply plugs into the wall, just like a phone. It has its own keypad, with last number redial. It costs about $25 more than the plug-in-the-phone kind, but will work anyplace a regular phone will work.

There are three kinds of headsets: the kind the kid in the picture is wearing, which you've probably seen in long-distance service TV commercials (and can buy at any phone supply or AT&T store); the kind that fits in your ear like a hearing aid (Plantronics calls it "The Mirage"); and a cordless unit that looks like a Buck Rogers prop.

The spousal unit likes the hearing aid type. It doesn't cramp his style: The earpiece won't cramp the style of long-haired hippie freaks. If you can't find this kind of headset at your local business supply shop, get in touch with HB Distributors (voice 818-882-0000, fax 818-700-1808) and ask for their latest Plantronics catalog. Under $100.

Woody, on the other hand, swears by the 900 MHz cordless flavor. (You doubted it?) As of this writing, it's only available in the United States from a company called Hello Direct (voice 800-444-3556 or 408-972-1990, fax 408-972-8155, e-mail xpressit@hihello.com), and runs an outrageous $349. But that includes an extra-comfy leather earpad.

Hey, it's deductible. . . . .

Modems: Talkin' V. Talk

> We call them Twinkies. You've seen them on television acting the news,
> modeling and fracturing the news while you wonder whether they have
> read the news—or if they've blow-dried their brains, too.
>
> Linda Ellerbee
> *And So It Goes*, 1986

If you've ever encountered a modem manufacturer's marketing brochure you **Twinkie talk**
know Twinkies aren't confined to the news. These brochures ("2,000,000 megabits
per fortnight! MNP 7*bis* compliant! V.FCC standard!") quote data rates that belong in
Ripley's Believe It or Not. They talk letters and numbers. Voltages. This and That
standards. When you see hype like that, remember: The Marketing Twinkies are
rolling back on their heels, thumbs hooked in their britches, goin' "Ah, yes.
Bafflegab at its best!"

So let's dissect and decipher the gibberish. Bring it back to plain English. And
I'll try not to sound like a Twinkie.

There are several styles of fax/modems. There are internal modems that fit **Modem types**
inside your computer, external modems that connect with a cord to your computer's
backside, external "pocket" modems that are lightweight and can be used with a
laptop; there are PCMCIA (sometimes called "PC-Card") modems for laptops
only; and there are voice versions of all of the above. There are also different types
of wireless fax/modems and modems internal to the notebook computer.
ARGGGGGHH!

So, what to buy? What to buy? Well, modems all pretty much cover the same
bases. You have your data rate, your data compression and correction schemes,
your fax class, and your compatibility problems. That's about it, really.

Standards

All this is affected by standards. Standards are important because they increase
the chances that your modem will work with everybody else's. Standards are
good for you. Like eating liver.

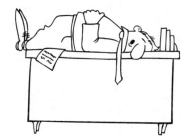

Wake up! Standards aren't *that* bad.

There are modem standards and there are fax standards (well, there are other standards but let's not get carried away). By the way, this might be a good time to refill the cup o' caffeinelike substance you prefer. Unfortunately, talking standards can be almost as boring as making them. Oh well. At least it doesn't take as long.

I need some class. Let's start with the fax part of fax/modem standards because they are relatively short and sweet (I said *relatively*). Note that we're talking about fax/modem standards: fax *classes* are another breed of cat entirely, and we'll look at them in the next section, the one on fax machines.

Fax/modem standards revolve around the driver that does the processing between the fax and the computer. Avoid SendFax since it is old and lame. Class 2 is the precursor to Class 2.0. Intel has a standard called CAS. It is similar to Class 2 and 2.0. All three use the modem to do most of the processing. This is good when you are faxing in the background since it has minimal impact on the computer's processing.

BFT The most interesting fax/modem standard is Class 1, however. It moves much of the CPU crunching onto the computer, so you may experience slow-downs while faxing. The slow-down should be less noticeable with fast CPUs, particularly Pentiums. The coolest thing about Class 1 is that it supports Binary File Transfer (**BFT**). This enables the fax/modem to send binary files instead of images: A Class 1 modem trying to send a file looks to see if the receiving modem understands Class 1. If both modems support Class 1, they automatically decide to send *the file itself,* instead of a picture of what the file would look like if it were printed.

Say you want to send a Word for Windows file to somebody, so the other person can edit it. You can fax it Class 2, and the receiver can print the fax, then scan it using OCR (whiach teimds to miz words in the transltin), and ultimately try to edit it on her PC. With Class 1 modems on both ends, though, the file itself is transmitted. No OCR. No garbled scans. The formatting comes through. Cool stuff.

There's a big catch: At least two different BFT standards are floating around. One is an official Standard, called T.434, supported by the big international standards organizations. Microsoft has the second flavor, in Windows for Workgroups and Windows 95. Ne'er the twain shall meet. If you want to use Windows 95 to run BFT, you had better make sure the fax/modems on both sides support the Microsoft version. Does Microsoft *ever* play with the other kids?

Rising to a higher standard Since we've already entered the muck, let's talk modem standards, of which there are three general categories. You've got your I-own-the-market-or-I-am-Microsoft-so-what-I-say-goes-nanner-nanner De Facto standards; your I-can't-wait-until-you-guys-finally-quit-bickering-and-finish-this-pre-standard standards;

and your bona fide Standard standards, promulgated by a national or international standards organization. Guess what? In the current fun world of modem standards, you have to worry about all three.

There are two main sets of standards to watch for with modems. One set is called **MNP**. The other is **CCITT**.

MNP refers to Microcom Networking Protocol—Microcom being an early pioneer in modem technology. The MNP standards are a set of de facto standards: they weren't established by a committee; they just kind of grew up around what was going on at the time—the stuff that Microcom was looking for.

CCITT, on the other hand, is a Standard standard. CCITT stands for Consulate Consolidated Concrete Committee mumbmumble Telephone and Telegraph mumble. Pardon my French. You can pronounce it "see-see-eye-tee-tee," but I prefer "sit" because it is more descriptive. CCITT is an international standards committee that likes to come up with enlightening standard names like the "V" series, which is for modems. They often have a *bis* version (*bis* being French for "half"), which means it came later. So you have V.OMMP and V.OMMP*bis*. Sort of new and improved.

CCITT updates their standards every four years in color-coded books. I think this is the year of the banana slug yellow. Recently, CCITT changed its name to ITU, but nobody seems to have noticed. Besides, ITU sounds like my cat sneezing. Regardless, CCITT is the premier international standards body. They ensure international interoperability.

Both MNP and CCITT standards cover three independent areas: basic data rate, data compression, and data error control.

Basic Data Rate   This is the standard defining the transmission rate of the modem. The best data modem can run at 28.8 Kbps. Don't let the marketing brochures fool you. By comparison, the first widely used modems clocked it at 0.3 Kbps, while ISDN can run at a little over 128 Kbps. Standards you'll probably see on currently available modems are

- V.32*bis* is the CCITT standard for 14.4 Kbps transmission speed, which is currently the most widely used modem speed. On a good line, V.32*bis* modems can send or receive about 100K bytes of PKZIP compressed data per minute.

- V.32terbo is a De Facto standard that appeared after V.32*bis*. It's supposed to be faster than V.32*bis*, but support for V.32terbo is disappearing quickly.

- V.FC, which means "Fast Class," is a preliminary standard for 28.8 Kbps transmission by Rockwell International that is rapidly being replaced by the true Standard V.34.

- V.34 is the CCITT standard for 28.8 Kbps transmission speed. On a good line, V.34 modems can handle about 150K bytes of PKZIP compressed data per minute (Note: that isn't twice as fast as a V.32*bis* modem!).

- V.34*bis* is on the way, with more bleach and fresh pine scent. No hint yet as to what, precisely, it will contain.

Squishing the data by modem

Data Compression   This is one of the two ways to get more bits for your dollar. Data compression allows modems to increase throughput without increasing transmission speed. The sending modem compresses data (such as redundant data) into a compact form. The receiving modem decompresses the data back to its original form. Files already compressed with tools like PKZIP (see Chapter 3) will not gain much throughput increase: If you usually send and receive .ZIP files, instead of plain text, this standard doesn't really mean much.

- V.42*bis* is a CCITT data compression standard for high-speed modems. It compresses data by as much as 4:1. Sometimes it's referred to as the Lempel Ziv compression scheme. V.42*bis* compression doesn't have any effect on PKZIPped files.

- MNP 5 is an older De Facto standard that provides compression up to 2:1. It can actually slow down transmission of PKZIPped files.

Data compression can only occur when two modems use the same compression scheme. The modems will negotiate at connection time, choosing the most powerful scheme they have in common.

Data Error Control   The telephone lines were developed for voice and can be "noisy." One zap of static can hurl many data bits to the bit netherworld. To provide error-free transmission there are error detection and error correction methods. Together they give you error control.

- V.42 is a CCITT standard method for error control based on something called LAP-M, or Link Access Procedure (Modem).

- MNP 4 is a De Facto standard error control scheme that doesn't let the modem automatically correct scrambled data as easily as V.42.

Most V.34 modems will use V.42 but fall back on MNP 4 if necessary. Some modems can also adjust transmission dynamically based on line noise.

While I recommend getting a V.34 modem at 28.8 Kbps you might check what other standards the specific modem is backward-compatible with. This is particularly important if you are using an on-line or Internet service because they tend to lag behind in high speed modems: Many will only support V.32*bis* speeds, that is, 14.4 Kbps.

Windows Binary File Transfer is the way of the future. It's fast, it's accurate, and it will appear soon on a desktop near you (if it hasn't already).

One other thing you will find in marketing blather is the **Data Transfer Rate** or **Data Terminating Equipment (DTE) rate**. DTE refers to the speed at which the modem and computer talk to each other. It is *not* the transmission rate, although the ad copy on the box may make you think that the DTE number is a competitive advantage. In reality, the DTE should be set by the modem's manufacturer at the basic transmission rate multiplied by the compression rate. For example, a V.34 modem with V.42*bis* will be 28.8 × 4 = 115.2 Kbps.

DTE Marketing Hype

The Hardware

So now you know enough about modem and fax standards to wade through any modem vendor's marketing brochure and make an informed decision. The last thing to consider is type of modem. Do you want an Innie or an Outie? External modems cost $50 or so more than internal but they do not require opening up the computer, and the lights on the front panel are useful. Numerous times they have let me confirm my suspicions that Carbon Copy had gone out in the weeds. Sometimes it surprises me that the file transfer really *is* still going on. At these times I tend to whimper "I want ISDN" under my breath.

Are you an Innie or an Outie?

Pocket modems are light (LITE?) and can be used on laptops as well as desktops. PCMCIA cards are geared for portables like laptops but are only good as paperweights for desktops. If you really, really need to be mobile there are modems for wireless phones. They are either cellular or mobidems (radio modems). The cellular modems that support MNP 10 are more reliable.

> **Before you run out and buy a modem, go through all the software you might need first. You want to make sure that the modem will work with each software package. It simplifies installation and hassles. Yes, it's bassackwards. Send complaints to the cat.**

One final modem body part to worry about (or ignore) is the UART. If you are planning to access remote applications, or transfer good-sized files, you will want to squeeze every bit out of your modem. Because an external modem typically attaches to a serial port, the computer serial controller chip (also known as a UART) may be a bottleneck. If the UART can't keep up, bits get overwritten in its buffer. It doesn't take much to overpower the old version UARTs (don't blink). Wimpy, wimpy, wimpy.

Where UART there thou art.

> **Now there is a UART called 16550A that has a 16-byte buffer. If you're working with an older computer, and you're getting a new, fast external modem, consider upgrading the UART. (Internal modems have their own UARTs, and all of them these days use the 16550A.) If you are getting a new PC, insist on a 16550A. It gives you more breathing space before the modem has to overwrite data.**

Fax Focaccia

> This is a most versatile bread product in that it is great just as it comes
> from the oven, but it also makes terrific sandwiches.

Jeff Smith
The Frugal Gourmet Cooks Italian, 1993

Just the fax, ma'am

Woody's already talked about why you should get a fax (see Chapter 3). A fax is great just as it comes out of the machine (wouldn't eat it, though). Even your part-time help—the folks who think technology is a four-letter word—can use a fax machine. At the very least it's nice to have slides faxed to you before a presentation or meeting. Woody also settled the fax versus fax/modem debate, as far as I'm concerned ("And the winner is . . . BOTH!"). Let me explain why.

Trench Wars

When we originally set out to telecommute we thought a fax/modem and Logitech Scanman handheld scanner would cover all the bases. It was high tech, it was inexpensive (sort of), and a fax is a fax is a fax. Right?

Neophytes.

Appropriate technology in the computer era

Alas, the industry leader, grand pooba of fax software daunted us. Or was that dented? Delrina's fax software user interface was, well, in the words of the great technoid himself: "clunky." Call us dummies, call us idiots, call us Simpsons—we just could not remember how to do each feature for the infrequent times we faxed things. Unfortunately that was not the hard part. The Significant Other needed to fill out time cards. Sounds like a reasonable use for the new toys, er, work equipment. We would scan in a time card as a template, insert it into Word for Windows, fill in the blanks, scan the 'ole signature and viola!

It didn't work that way.

 First, we found scanning by hand awkward. A paper tray helped, but it was adding up the bill. Then we found that even with the tray, the scan was slanted. At the time, the software had no rotation capabilities (or they hid it well). Word for Windows had other ideas. Maybe it was the lines, but WinWord refused to treat the image as an editable document. Nor could we attach the signature correctly. After two days of trying, we gave up. A cheap old fax machine took only fifteen seconds to fax the time card and that included filling it in.

I wonder what the spouse put down on his time card for the two days we muddled over this. Admittedly, that was then and this is now. . . .

The deciding factors

Anyway, what I wanted to cover in this chapter is the laundry list. What to look for if you're a fax debutante, and features to trade off if you're going to be a faxaholic.

Class III or BFT

First of all, you want a Class III fax or fax/modem. Just about every fax machine sold in this decade is Class III, so you don't have to worry about it. There is a Class IV, but those are digital fax machines that are significantly faster than Class III, much more expensive, and probably not as effective for the high-tech telecommuter as simple Windows-based Binary File Transfer.

Other than that, here's a rundown of general fax features to ponder when making the big F decision.

Speed   Most stand-alone fax machines run at 9.6 Kbps, but 14.4 Kbps is available, most often with fax/modems. (The stand-alone 14.4 Kbps fax machines are still pricey, especially those with laser printer paper.) If almost all of your faxing takes place with people who fax at 14.4 Kbps (that is, they all have, and use, fax/modems), the higher speed might be useful. But if you are a telemployee and the corporate office is all 9.6 Kbps, getting 14.4 Kbps fax on your end makes no sense.

Ease of Use   Stand-alone faxes are simple. Any paper that fits into the fax tray and doesn't get stuck somewhere down in the guts of the beast is, by definition, faxable. That includes text documents, newspaper clippings, an illustration, a photograph, or your time card.

Requires some assembly

With fax/modems, life isn't so simple: Not only must you scan in any document that doesn't originate on your computer, the fax software has to help you with the difficult task of sending the scanned image over the phone lines. Software that takes over your PC effectively converts your $3,000 computer into a $300 fax machine. Software that allows faxing to run in the background can slow things down to the point that you really can't get anything else done anyway.

Another nuisance appears if you set the printer to "print" a fax and then forget to reset the printer. The next document you print will be faxed to the unsuspecting. Of course you would never print anything embarrassing. Nah.

Paper   There are three kinds of stand-alone fax machines: the inexpensive, (say $300) easily maintained, curly papered, I-just-know-this-is-cancer-causing-smelling thermal; the expensive (say $500) plain paper ink jet kind; and the really expensive (sky's the limit) and really nice plain paper laser kind. There are also stand-alone gadgets that use your computer printer.

All it takes is money.

If you choose the thermal stand-alone make sure that it has a cutter. Cutting each page of a rolled-up, incoming fax gets old *real* fast.

Stand-alone fax machines have two paper capacity limitations. One is the amount of paper it holds: Look for machines that hold 200 sheets or more. The other is how many pages the document feeder can hold before you have to sit there and spoonfeed the thing: ten pages is a practical minimum, but twenty to thirty pages or more can come in handy at times.

Fax machines and fax/modems that use regular paper have a problem if the document being transmitted is nonstandard (like if it is international). You can always ask the sender to reduce the size via a copier but be prepared to read it with your trusty magnifying glass ("Look. We got a fax from the Pinecliffe International Cultural Society! *What is it?* I think it's the Mona Lisa. *No it isn't. It's a picture of a guy taking a bath in an old whiskey barrel.* Oh. Well, it still must be cultural. Let's put it in the living room. *NOT.*")

Dialing Features   Stand-alone fax machines typically have preset speed dialing. Some machines are a bit braindead: They can't accommodate the longer international numbers. Fax/modems usually have phone books to store numbers or can interact with a PIM phonebook. Other features are auto redial (it'll attempt several times before giving up) and scheduled faxing, so you can send your faxes when phone rates are lower. Both of those features can pay for themselves in the first few days.

OCR Ogre   *Viewing/editing*   Fax software lets you do various levels of editing. This can include annotating faxes, highlighting them, selective erasing, cutting/pasting from Windows Clipboard, and designing cover sheets. For converting the image of the incoming fax to an application document, such as converting to text for a word processor, **OCR** (optical character recognition, pronounced either "oh-see-arr" or "ochre") is the technology of the day.

As far as I'm concerned, OCR is *not* ready for prime time, particularly when working with faxes. If you get an excellent inbound fax and put it through the OCR package bundled with most fax/modems, you'll be lucky to get 98 percent accuracy. That means that on a page this size, with 2,500 characters or so, fully fifty characters will be incorrect. Try sticking that in your spell checker and smoking it!

Faxboxes   Another fax feature is a fax mailbox. You can store incoming faxes in multiple mailboxes much like voice messages on voice mailboxes. Some software allows you to compress, store, and retrieve faxes in different mailboxes via searches. It's a high-priced option that may have some applicability in your home office, but be aware of the fact that the sender has to monkey around with mailbox numbers.

Status/notification   Many flavors of fax software let you see the status of your faxes—coming and going. Many provide a log of faxes, some by individual faxbox. Some have searching on logs. If you pay for a status service from your local phone company, you'll get a summary of fax usage. Serious faxaholics may find the local phone company's pager notification service useful: They'll tell you immediately when a fax comes in. A welcome addition to the social life of the fax-starved.

Never-Busy Faxing   This is a feature provided by the local telephone company— for a price. A temporary inbound fax box allows you to receive faxes when your fax machine is busy. The service takes the new incoming fax and stores it until your fax machine becomes free. It then resends the fax to your machine or to another number. Faxees never lose an incoming fax; faxers never hear a busy signal. Too bad they don't have something analogous for nuisance voice calls. Oh. I guess they do.

I'm always here.

Remote Faxing, Fax Forwarding, and Broadcast Faxing   Windows 95, most fax/modem software, some fax machines, and all the local phone companies have these features. If you've ever tried to send a two-page fax to each of 100 people, you know just how important this capability can be.

Faxback and Fax on Demand   You know the tune. A befuddled customer, say, calls into your faxback service. He punches a couple of buttons, and a few minutes later a fax that's supposed to solve his problem arrives on his fax machine. When it works right, faxback provides a lot of information with very little overhead— and none of those infinite waits on the phone, wrestling with a thousand different choices, trying to figure out which button to push.

How many facts would a fax faxback if a fax could faxback facts?

Local phone companies can arrange for faxback: They provide a voice message touch-tone menu of choices, and then connect with a fax service bureau to handle the actual faxing for you. Or you can dedicate a computer with a faxback board ($500 to $1,000, but the price is falling rapidly) to the task.

Binary File Transfer   See the standards discussion earlier in this chapter for an explanation of this feature. Over the next few years, Windows-based BFT looks like the horse to bet on, but there are other options. Delrina has both T.434 standard and Microsoft's de facto At Work Fax as well as its own proprietary version of BFT. It allows for error correction, too. Remember that BFT does not work unless both sides have it. It beats OCR technology hands down, but if you are sending a lot of editable documents via faxing you might consider if there is an easier way (e-mail, comm software, carrier pigeon) to do it.

So which should you get? Fax or fax/modem or fax/modem with nifty fax software?

Bottom-line it for me, Trudy.

Well, most telebodies don't need all those fancy features. What they want is something easy. Usually a fairly cheap fax/modem and a trusty fax machine in the corner is the best solution. And Windows provides all the fax/modem software most people will ever need.

There's an extensive list of fax hardware and software vendors in Appendix B.

Integrated Voice and Data

> The human voice is nothing but flogged air.

Seneca
Natrales Quæstiones, ca. 63 AD

Much has been made of late about integrated voice and data technology. In reality, it's the modem's equivalent of patting its belly and rubbing its head at the same time.

What is it?   Voice/data technology merely interleaves voice communication with data, using something called a voice/data modem. As is so often the case, for integrated voice/data communication to take place, both ends of the conversation must have modems that not only support voice/data, but support the same *kind* of voice/data.

Some day in the not-too-distant future, integrated voice/data may become important as a way to teleconference — voice for the humans, data for their connected computers — with a single phone call. It isn't yet clear, though, whether integrated voice/data will become an end in itself, or if it's just a quick stopping-point on the way to integrated video/voice/data.

Some groups have banded together to create, dissect, classify, and make acronyms for this latest voice technology. Yes, I'm talking standards again. Ouch! that hurt.

'Gads . . . I have to talk and calculate *at the same time*?

A lot of effort has gone into having voice and data on the same line. The technology therefore has an acronym, naturally: SVD (Simultaneous Voice and Data). If the voice stays analog it is ASVD and if the voice is digitized it is DSVD. Here are the various classes of voice/data modems:

One parts data,
two parts voice,
eye of newt

- **Class 0** defines voice/data in which two separate calls are placed. One call is for voice and one is for data — which describes you and your modem (on its own line). It also describes ISDN with 2 B channels. Rather extreme ends, but they do both meet the criterion.

- **Class 1** describes old stuff so we'll skip it.

- **Class 2** classifies interactive switched (*not* simultaneous) voice/data systems. This is used in Radish Communications Systems VoiceView, which is used by several modem vendors (US Robotics, Hayes), as well as Windows 95. The scheme interrupts voice transmission to send data when data is required. The system will not transmit voice again until the data transmission is complete, which could be quite annoying. Proponents say that in this scheme the data transmission is more accurate.

- **Class 3** describes simultaneous voice and data transmission. AT&T Paradyne's VoiceSpan divides voice and data into two separate channels. Transmission of one type does not affect the other type. However, dividing into channels severely reduces the data throughput.

There is another technology, an alternate Class 3 approach, that packetizes the voice and the data and ships them out without regards to type, race, sex, color, or religion. The melting pot of voice and data. This approach is used in Phylon Communications' SingleCall. MultiTech uses it in its product. Effort has been made to use the fewest bits possible to encode voice. Proponents of Class 3 technology point out that 60 percent of the time you're talking on the phone you are not talking (Well, for some of us, anyway). That 60 percent is used for data.

If your eyes glaze over at slick brochures (some use Brill Cream) on SVD, slap yourself. Then slap yourself again. Given the current state of the art, you would only use this technology when you want to send data and talk about it at the same time to the same person, instead of making two separate calls. It's a way to save a few pennies. Scrooged modems.

So what does it mean, Class?

> **You are compromising when you use these clunkers. SVD only works with pairs of modems (that's in the fine print). The data rate is either impaired or you have to dance around voice and data (or both). Why don't you just go bang your head against a wall?**

So while you will see phantasmic claims about voice/data, skip 'em. They should impress you somewhere's between squat and squat and a half.

But the future? Ah, who knows what evil lurks in the mind of Redmond. . . .

Just Leave a Message and Maybe I'll Call

> A people which is able to say everything becomes able to do everything.
>
> Napoleon I
> *Maxims,* 1804–1815

There is one last bit of telephone lore to mull over: the diverse alternatives in the answering machine/voice messaging genre.

Well, doc, it started when my voice messaging system began talking back.

Answering Service

Many telecommuters find it easiest to employ an answering service. It's an expensive solution but it can make your company appear large and busy, if not personable and warm. With a human you are guaranteed almost all the functions attributable to answering machines and voice messaging, without the installation hassles. Or perhaps only a portion of the installation hassles. If you think an answering service is The Answer, then shop around. A bad answering service can be worse than an answering machine with a lobotomy. Get recommendations and check them out.

Inhuman Alternatives

If you are a telecommuter who could care less about impressing the masses (or need to impress on a budget), there are four choices open to you: an answering machine, Voice Messaging service, a voice messaging box, or voice messaging hardware/software for the PC. Each has its benefits and (considerable!) drawbacks.

Here are the voice features to consider when putting them all to the test.

Greetings and Salutations If you are long winded (who? *moi*?) you may want to watch for greeting message length limitations. Digital answering machines can be quite limited. Computer-based systems impinge on disk space.

Some voice messaging solutions allow you to prerecord multiple greetings and switch between them.

Ring-number Settings Not sexy, but if you are sharing your voice line with other equipment, such as a fax, you will want to be able to set the number of rings before the machine picks up the phone line.

Screening Calls and Pop-ups/Call Blocking   Screening can be achieved through caller ID, the caller entering a secret password number, or a snoop feature. In the latter you can eavesdrop on the caller leaving a message and choose to answer. Some voice software can trigger phone book pop-ups based on caller ID that give you information about the person calling you. Even better, some connect with PIM products, like PackRat and ACT!, or databases.

She says to tell ya she's not here.

Call Blocking allows you to block specific calls based on caller ID: They can leave a message, but you'll never know it.

Taking Messages/Voice Mailboxes   Answering machines with a tape are limited by the tape, digital answering machines by memory capacity. More capacity always costs more money. Available capacity affects the number of messages and possibly the length of a message. Some systems will limit the length of a message—with no warning.

Hello! You just won the 10 - million-dollar sweepstakes! Please call us at "CLICK"

The other feature to consider in message taking is the ability to have multiple mailboxes. Number of mailboxes, individual greetings, and passwords are the things to look at. A general greeting instructs callers to press the key for their intended recipient. Each mailbox owner then listens only to his or her own messages using a personal code. If you are the one, the only, the sole telecommuter in your household you may still use this feature to separate business from personal voice mail.

> **Some people do not like to listen to long messages. "Hello. My name is Inigo Montoya. If you are the six-fingered man, press one and prepare to die. If you are not, press two and have a nice day . . . Blah-Blah-Blah." Impatient people (you know who you are—and so do we) start punching buttons to see if they can cut through the fluff (it works on some PBXs). If that doesn't work they hang up. Next time you get a dial-tone message or several strange beeps, it's time to change the greeting.**

Message Notification   A Voice Messaging service typically indicates if you have a message by giving a special tone when you pick up the phone. For those prone to lapses in memory (I won't mention Woody by name), this may not be enough. A PC can pop up an indicator on the screen. An answering machine can have blinking lights, a digital display of number of messages waiting—and some models can beep.

Remote Features   Any remote capabilities should require PINs to access messages. The longer the PIN, the harder to crack. It is also better to be able to choose your own PIN and to change it when you like. This is not only a privacy issue. This keeps people from changing your greeting to direct the operator to accept third-party calls. Gives new meaning to discount rates—for them.

Speaking of which, some answering machines have a nifty feature that saves bucks. You set the regular messaging on the machine to kick in after four rings or so. Then the machine will ring only twice if you have messages, four times if you don't. When you call in to check messages, if it rings three times you can hang up. You know you don't have any. No call. No charge. Great way to avoid long-distance charges.

Many Lines, One Solution   Some answering machines provide the two-line, one-messaging solution: It can answer incoming calls on two different phone lines. The only thing to watch for is how the machine reacts when it is taking a message for one line and the other line needs to leave a message.

Message-forwarding   If you like to have message indicators zap you when you walk in the door, have been referred to as the absent-minded professor, or cannot remember how old you *really* are, this feature is for you. Activate message-forwarding and, when a caller leaves a message, the system calls you, you punch in your PIN and viola! you hear your message. Another forwarding feature is where the system will send a message to your pager. For integrated voice/data/fax software systems the message can even indicate if it is voice, fax, or e-mail.

Power/reliability   If the electricity goes out, reserve power in answering machines kicks in to preserve digital greeting and messages. Make sure it is with batteries that recharge themselves. For voice message boxes, such as Intellect Telephone/PC Link, there is battery backup. For PC messaging systems a PC UPS is required. Of course, with Voice Messaging service you do not have to worry about power outages—except for the occasional terrorist bent on blowing up CO equipment. The same goes for reliability of service; most likely the local phone company service doesn't break down. Most likely.

Member, Technical Agnostic Society
Any PC-based phone answering dohickeys require that the equipment be kept on at all times. For those of you who believe in turning off the PC at night, a computer-based solution poses a problem. It can also be frustrating for those of you who really don't believe in anything but tend to be on automatic pilot by the end of the day.

Taking Messages When You Are Popular   Most equipment cannot take messages when you are on the line already. But the phone company's Voice Messaging service can.

DTMF is Voice Messaging software that recognizes touch-tone tones and can respond when the caller presses keys on their phone ("Press 1 for the Ginsu special . . . ."). DTMF can be used for your own faxback service, line splitting ("Press 1 if you are a real person") and complicated greetings.

Universal Mailboxes and Desk Clutter   Finally, an asthetic component. The more equipment, the more clutter. Some of us define ourselves by the clutter quotient. Others consider it a genetic defect. There are numerous combo gadgets coming out that reduce desk clutter. The phone answering machine, phone/fax, phone/fax/answering machine/coffee maker/hair dryer/breakfast maker,* and so forth. Software solutions and Voice Messaging service do not devour valuable desk real estate.

Another advantage of the combination software solution is the concept of a universal mailbox. The decluttering of the virtual in-box, if you will. The PC can take phone messages, receive faxes, and store e-mail all in one folder or box. Theoretically.

There's a lot of cool stuff available. You probably don't need any of it: By and large, the bells and whistles will make your life more difficult, and offer little if anything in return.

Bottom-line it again, Trudy.

A simple, relatively cheap, reliable answering machine is usually the tele-commuter's best choice. Make sure you get a machine with two tapes: one for recording the outbound "greeting" message; the other for recording inbound calls. Really cheap answering machines that rely on digitizing your greeting message may lose the message entirely every time the power goes out, and may lack really important features such as greeting message cutoff. Avoid the cheap-cheap machines.

Local phone companies offer Voice Messaging services—essentially a telephone answering machine that you pay for by the month—as do some independent companies. I talked about Voice Messaging earlier in this chapter, under "Extra-Cost POTS Services." If you'd like to get messaging, but you want an alternative to the phone company, look in the yellow pages under Telephone Services.

Voice Messaging service

The next step up from standard answering machines (whether operated by you or by the phone company) are voice messaging boxes. Two companies currently have such boxes on the market: Intellect and OCTus.

Voice messaging boxes

Each try to incorporate softphone features with their product, which is a waste of their time and your money.

Intellect actually expects their product to be used with your local phone company's Voice Messaging service. OCTus requires an extra voice messaging module. Both make some use of Caller ID capabilities and call logging. Intellect connects Caller ID with more PIMs than most. While they have the *potential* to be

---

* The breakfast maker automatically makes coffee, toast, and sunnyside-up eggs. What, you think I make these things up?

quite different, in their current incarnations at least, they aren't much different from a voice fax/modem. The only advantage they have currently is that they can be run while the PC is off. Big deal. Saves a few electrons. Otherwise their features are comparable to almost any other answering machine solution.

Voice messaging on the PC

PC-based voice messaging is poised for an explosion in capabilities and a meltdown in prices, all to be brought on by the promulgation of Windows-based telephone standards.

In the corner wearing the Big Britches: TAPI

It's a knock-down drag-out boxing match. In one corner is NetWare. In the other corner are Microsoft and Intel. Clash of the Titans or David and two-headed Goliath? You be the judge.

Microsoft's Windows has a Telephony API (application programming interface—essentially, a standard set of programming conventions that make it easier to build new programs) called, appropriately, TAPI (pronounced "tappy"). This, along with a new board and possibly a handset, enables application providers to create software that runs on your PC to mimic the phone.

The Hype starts. Your computer can place calls, receive calls, forward, and conference calls (big deal). Caller ID can trigger applications, contact information, or databases (this might be something). You can have rule-based call routing so that, say, after 5:00 p.m. the voice messaging system has one greeting "We're closed. Go away." and another for business hours "Hello, this is friendly Blob, your business etiquette seminar specialist!" Hype. Hype. Hype.

But the Windows Telephony API is geared strictly for individual computers. Great for a one-woman business that uses one phone line for business voice/ data/fax and personal calls. Not so good for the person who dares, heaven forfend, to want multiple lines. Or, say, a transfer feature and intercom for the family that teleworks together. Did we mention designer music on hold? Maybe some day the ultra-clever TAPI programmers will figure out how to put it all together. But it's going to take a while.

Anybody out dere want a little TSAPI?

And in the other corner, we have Novell Netware. Their API, Telephony Services Application Programming Interface (TSAPI; some people outside Utah, Novell's home, insist on pronouncing it "sappy"), is geared towards companies with not only Netware but a PBX. The API has all the functionality of TAPI plus inter-PC interaction. Calls can be transferred and even tracked as they make their way through the company. More features. Great. Recognition of multiple phone lines. Great. Requires a PBX. Blah. Requires a Novell Netware LAN. Blah Blah.

TSAPI

Frankly, I think they are both missing the telecommuting boat. I haven't found any TAPI/TSAPI/SVD or any other acronym that lets me do rule-based call handling on my lone PC—something that every telecommuter needs. TAPI promises but nobody's delivered. We are a veritable telecommuting commune in my house (a family that works together shirks together—ah, never mind). We have yet to find the telecommune voice-messaging solution.

And nowhere 'tis to be found a hardware/software combo that lets the telecommuter have a separate voice line that only interacts with the computer when it is necessary. This should be when a call initially comes in (for Caller ID pop-ups, rule-based call routing, and call tracking), when a call ends (for call tracking), when the telecommuter starts a call from a phone book (the PC talks to the modem/box), and when a call gets directed to the voice messaging module. Otherwise the call should not impinge on the computer (butt out!). This API would assume the telecommuter has a separate voice line from the data/fax line. The voice line box talks to the PC only when necessary, leaving the PC mostly free for important data transmissions and application crunching. The next step would be for the voice box to handle multiple phone lines. It should be doable. So far, it just isn't done. Sigh.*

DAPIR— dream API for real folks

The voice messaging systems hooked into a PBX ignore the remote telemployee. Hello out there! Anybody home! Still, with Caller ID hooks, call logging, and phonebooks, a voice messaging box or software may be better than Voice Messaging service or an answering machine. If they could only break the one-phone-line mentality. . . .

If by chance you have more than one PC in the house you might want to connect them through a peer-to-peer LAN. Many telecommuters who choose LANs choose Windows. Others are widely available. These LANs are fairly straightforward to connect. In some cases you will need a cable and Ethernet cards.

One last word on desktop communication equipment

---

* Anybody wanna start a virtual corporation?

If you are using a POTS line and need to access multiple sites you may want to add a router to the LAN. I have to recommend Netblazer PN (pick a number) with warranty service. Why? One day we came home to find our little router dead. Rigor mortis had already set in. Sad sight. Probably foul play. I yelled at the cat on general principle ("Tick-Infested Fur Ball. Bird Breath").

So, we called Netblazer and (1) we got to talk to a human almost immediately; (2) after recovering from the shock we explained the problem; and (3) they expressed us a replacement immediately. Now, whenever I am indefinitely on hold for a company where "Your call IS important to us" or they say their average hold time is two minutes and it has already been ten, I reflect on that one brief, sweet encounter with Telebit. Maybe their product doesn't have the latest whirligigs, but they come through when you're vulnerable. They got my business.

There's a lengthy list of voice messaging hardware and software manufacturers in Appendix B.

COMMUNICATION SOFTWARE

> Use what language you will, you can never say anything but what you are.
>
> R. W. Emerson
> *The Conduct of Life*, 1860

Telecommuting bleeding edge Now that you have the pipe and the equipment, what more do you need? Well, there are several types of software out there to help you get up close-up and personal in a digital sort of way. Let's look at document conferencing, videoconferencing, data communication software, remote control, and remote node software.

The rocket science section starts here.

We will reserve discussion of remote node software/equipment for the "Back at the Fort" section—which discusses concerns of the central corporate office IS staff—because it will probably be a joint decision with IS for telemployees. In other words, you may be able to make recommendations, but the propeller heads at the office are going to have final word. Fair 'nuff. They have to live with it.

Document Conferencing

> What is the use of running when we are not on the right road?
>
> German Proverb

This general category of software has an identity crisis. I prefer calling it Document Conferencing software, although the category includes software described by vendors as Desktop Conferencing, or even Whiteboard systems. Electronic whiteboard systems—where you draw on a six-foot-tall whiteboard in Seattle, and it shows up in Tucson—are quite different. An order of magnitude in bucks.

What's a document conference?

So what is document conferencing? It is proprietary software (don't even *think* about mixing vendors) that allows users to work together in real time over LAN or modem links, viewing the same file and exchanging comments. It is designed to facilitate remote presentations and conferencing. It lets you work interactively with one other person, or several people at one time. Most applications work by transferring files or images and displaying them in a shared space (on each participant's computer screen). The images can be stuffed into electronic slides or trays—much as one would sort photographic images—and each person can write comments while the others look on.

This is much like an electronic whiteboard system, except that each person is in her own little room with her own PC.

Actually, that's the problem with this technology. Any document or presentation that requires real-time interaction usually means all those physically able should get together in a room and hash things out. Why should they limit their ability to communicate by staying in their own offices and using their PCs? The telecommuter will phone in or, if it is really important, get their physio presence in the meeting too. Beam me up, Scotty.

None of the document conferencing software I've seen even holds a candle to electronic whiteboard.

Okay, okay. There are two cases where desktop conferencing technology can be useful. One is in a virtual corporation, where people are scattered all over the globe, all the time. In that case a multiperson PC conference may be just the ticket for meetings. The other is BS sessions—where the telecommuter

wants to shoot the bull with another person. If they were physically in the same room, one person might draw something on the whiteboard to illustrate a point, while the other looked on. With desktop conferencing the two respective PCs become the communal whiteboard. In this scenario the software does not have to be sophisticated. Which is good because most of this genre of software is, well, underdeveloped.

Most desktop conferencing software packages appear to be marketing department afterthoughts for videoconferencing software. Still, if you think document sharing may be useful, there are a few features to be on the lookout for.

Shake, rattle, and scroll *Display Resolution*   With any two PCs, there are potential display resolution problems. One may have a smaller screen than the other. Check how the product handles this.

Live or Memorex?   Some let you snapshot an image and annotate it, then snapshot again . . . only now you have to manually add the changes. Better are those that use remote-control capabilities to keep the image updated. This is only important for virtual corporation meetings, really, since BS sessions work better with blank canvasses than Picassos anyway.

Semiautomatics   There's automatic and semiautomatic (only one person can draw). Make sure everybody can make the changes, not just the person who initiated the session.

I want blue. *Annotation*   Get software with color markups for each person, preferably with the annotation feature that separates out annotations so you can move them and edit your edits. Even the most gifted among us can occasionally retract what we say, so make sure there is an Undo command.

Jump Start   Intel Proshare (jump) started this. One problem with all of these one-on-one software communication packages crops up when you need to rap with the multitudes. The unenlightened. The uninformed. In other words, someone who doesn't have your version of software. Some software vendors, like Intel, let you retrieve a free copy of the software from the information superhighway to give to the other person. Nice for teleconsultants, telecontractors, and telefreelancers.

Compression depression *Transfer Protocols*   As with other software dealing with images, we are talking megabytes. Slow. Unlike file transfer, you can't just PKZip every update. Image compression is nice.

Multipage Presentations   The product should have Folders, Trays, or tabbed notebook pages, to let you organize and readily refer back to groups of images with a similar theme.

> **Make sure you have a chance to try a desktop conferencing package under "live" conditions before you buy it. You may feel differently, but we just couldn't find any packages out on the market that we'd recommend.**

There's a list of more than a dozen document conferencing software vendors in Appendix B.

Videoconferencing

> We operate with nothing but things which do not exist,
> with lines, planes, bodies, atoms, divisible time, divisible space—
> how should explanation even be possible when we first make everything
> into an image, into our own image!
>
>   Friedrich Nietzsche
>   *The Gay Science,* 1887

If you are going to communicate remotely, wouldn't it be better to communicate visually? That is what 4,396,419.26 vendors are betting on. Videoconferencing is a technology in its infancy. The question is, how soon will it grow up? Desktop videoconferencing is expensive, limited, not interoperable (that is, one vendor's product won't work with any others'—and sometimes not even with itself!), and in many cases requires ISDN-type bandwidth to make it worthwhile. There are many vendors out there *and I'm not sure why.*

Monkey see, video do.

If you want a visual reminder of who you are ("We're here, we're here, we're here) to the colleagues in Whoville, why not paste a picture of yourself on their monitor? Or have a picture of you pop up when they use an electronic phonebook to call you. It's easier, cheaper, and more reliable. Besides you can get your best angle and always be power dressed.*

If you want to convey the nuances of your facial expressions, videoconferencing may work with a full screen—but the minuscule 3" × 5" window that passes for video these days just doesn't cut the mustard.

> **Besides, if visual contact is *that* important you will want your mug right there, complete with gesturing hands and posturing stances. It's called *body* language, not face language.**

---

* Much better than trying to hide the fact that you are actually wearing gym trunks and a moderately obscene T-shirt, and patting a dog on your lap. Et tu, Woody?

Hello, Mr.
Spacely.

On the other hand, anything that provides an illusion of your physiopresence may soothe the qualms of telebosses and colleagues. The question is, will the boss and IS buy it? The price is too high to cost justify equipping each employee in a home office. It also means more dispersed maintenance headaches for IS. A LAN-based solution is not practical, either. The data requirements for just a few simultaneous video conferences can saturate the LAN right into catatonia.

As affordable ISDN disseminates, videoconferencing will expand, but mostly to meeting rooms, where the costs are contained and the maintenance is easier. Once this happens telecommuters may be able to justify a desktop videoconferencing system (assuming it can interoperate). Then if they have the urge to gesticulate facially they can have the other party schedule the meeting room.

Intel's Proshare and AT&T's Vistium fall into the category of desktop conferencing software. They both require ISDN phone lines, and (as of this writing anyway) can be, uh, pricey—particularly if ISDN in your neck of the woods costs two arms and three legs. Creative Labs' ShareVision works with regular POTS lines, but the video quality is something you'd better look at before you plunk down any bucks.

There's an extensive list of videoconferencing hardware and software vendors in Appendix B.

Data Comm Packages or Remote Control?

> The heights by great men reached and kept
> were not attained by sudden flight
> But they while their companions slept
> were toiling upward in the night
>
> Longfellow
> *The Ladder of Saint Augustine*, 1858

The LapLink
genre

Data comm software originally started out with plain vanilla point-to-point file transfer. You'd start up the data comm package, and it would reliably copy a file from there to here. Some were easier to use than others, some faster, some more reliable. Then the software companies added or improved terminal emulation and on-line service access. Then some smart programmer started wondering why the data comm software didn't just hook into the remote computer and run it. Thus was born remote control software: the puppet strings that let you run one computer from another, at long distances.

The Outer
Limits

So how does remote control software work? Glad you asked. Say you are a telemployee who works out of the office a few days a week and out of the home on the other days. With remote control software, your home PC takes over the PC at the office. ("We have control of your PC. We control the horizontal. We control the vertical.") If you want to be able to access files and programs from the office, including those on the corporate LAN, you can use remote control. It's one way to access company e-mail, too.

To start a typical remote session, the host—that is, the computer in the central corporate office—is set in call-waiting mode. The home PC connects to the host via modem. The host then prompts with logon and password procedures, if the software has any. Now the home PC controls the host. Somebody on the host PC may be able to use it, too. However, you usually don't want anybody messing with it while you work, so often the software lets you lock parts of the host PC, like the keyboard.

Once control is established, the remote user can run all the applications normally available on the host system and can transfer files back and forth between the host and remote (that is, back at home). If the host is connected to a network, the remote user can also access all network resources.

It works amazingly well, as long as your phone line can handle the load.

As time went on, it became more and more clear (at least to me!) that old-fashioned data comm software all by itself wasn't very useful. After all, remote control software will transfer files from a remote PC, perform terminal emulation, and access on-line services just like the data comm software, *and* add remote control features. Besides, Windows 95 does simple data comm software-style file synching free. So who needs an old-fashioned data comm package?

The data comm software vendors wised up, and started adding things to their rapidly aging packages. Most data comm packages now include rudimentary fax software. Traveling Software has gone double fisted: On one side they have added fax to their Commworks package, and on the other they have added remote control in LapLink for Windows.

Why should data comm packages add fax? Beats me, especially since many modems bundle it in, and Windows beats 'em all. I guess if you are never going to use remote control, then a data comm package will give you file transfer without more confusing features. You just may have a confusing number of choices for fax software.

So what criteria should you use when sifting between the good, bad, and ugly? Here are some features to consider for both data comm and remote control software.

Installation   All of these packages are easy to install. At the worst you need to identify your COM port and modem, and set the transmission speed. Some products partially automate this process. They can identify COM ports and the presence of UARTs. Different packages support varying types of modems. Make sure yours is supported.

 The biggest pain with installation is how it affects your PC. Most remote control software has the audacity to change drivers on your PC. Changing the Windows video or keyboard driver is one way to intercept commands, translate them, and pass them back and forth between host and guest PCs. Look especially for SYSTEM.INI or registration data file changes.

Baby you can drive my car.

Why is this driver swap-out bad? Well, for one, if their driver is buggier than the Microsoft version, you can get all sorts of inscrutable errors cropping up out of nowhere. Different versions of Windows have completely different windows drivers—your remote control windows drivers may not work on all of them! Blah.

Add to that the fact that you have to make sure they load correctly, and if you change anything remotely affecting those drivers you may have to reinstall either Windows or the package, or both. Change video resolution? Reinstall your remote control software. Add a new video card? Reinstall. Don't know about you, but I just don't think about remote control software when I'm messin' with video. Besides, the constant urge to reinstall means you have to remember where all the disks are.

My dog's bigger than your dog.

Interoperability   Assume the worst. Each vendor has the best protocol for remote control and file transfer. At least that's what they say. Which means each uses its own proprietary protocol. No standard interface.

Some software vendors claim you can get limited functionality even though you don't have their software installed on the host. Carbon Copy is one. Some do use protocols like IPX (see later in this chapter) but not for interoperability. Too bad for the teleconsultant with multiple clients.

Go fetch.

Scripts   There are scripts for integration with on-line services, like CompuServe. Many packages have predefined scripts for the major on-line services. You just have to make sure they have your service of choice. Some allow customization. Others have script recorders. Norton's pcAnywhere has full, unattended log-on and session automation, including uploading and downloading of files and execution of all DOS commands.

Cro-Magnum mind melding

Ways to Get Stuff from There to Here   Drag-and-drop file transfer, *à la* Windows 95's Briefcase, is popular. No more commands. Just drag and drop to copy or move a file. Other things to look for are compression, and algorithms that only transfer changes to files. Some programs indicate if you are about to overwrite a file—something I do frequently. Speaking of overwriting files, Close-Up writes the original file to a backup so if a transfer goes haywire you still have the old copy. Virus detection is another file transfer feature, though it is hard to keep up with all the germs flying around.

What else? Copy based on a criterion, such as the date. Batch copy (make sure you can watch the progress for multiple-file copies). Cloning—everything in Directory A is in Directory B (B may have other files, too). Remote cutting and pasting from Windows' Clipboard is nice.

Most packages provide a display of directory trees at both ends of the connection and let you tag and send files in either direction. Most offer several file commands like delete, rename, local copy, and make directory. Most offer at least a rudimentary form of directory synchronization or updating, in which the package identifies and writes new and updated files from the directory on one end of the connection to the corresponding directory on the other, in one operation. Those are all important capabilities.

Protocols Supported/Terminal Emulation Supported Both data comm packages and remote control software offer terminal emulation modes that support modem and null modem connections* and standard file transfer protocols such as Kermit, Xmodem, Ymodem, and Zmodem. These let you log on to on-line services like CompuServe or Netcom or bulletin board systems. The data comm packages tend to offer more choices.

Remote control software also has features to compare that deal with (surprise!) remote control. Here are the main ones to watch for.

Remote rendezvous

Connecting/One for the Road If a PC starts to grab control of a host, the host can be notified about its impending servitude via pop-up alert on the screen. That's nice if there is a, uh, remote possibility you will share the host PC with somebody in the office—or if somebody at the office has arbitrarily decided that you are going to, and neglected to inform you.

Not all connections are proprietary. If you choose a road less traveled, such as an Internet or digital connection to your office, you will be interested in getting a product that will work over something other than a proprietary protocol. They are out there.

Remote Control via LAN If you see this feature in a remote control software package you can ignore it. The idea is for people like technicians at the central corporate office to access many PCs on a LAN remotely. Telecommuters need not be concerned about it.

---

* A **null modem** is just a cable that attaches to the serial ports of the two machines. It's a way to fake two computers into believing that they're connected by modem—and thus make them believe they can use normal on-line capabilities—without having to go to the bother of connecting modems to the machines and dialing one from the other.

**Whaddya mean
you have a 52"
monitor?**
PC Display Configuring   In many of the programs where the host is running a higher screen resolution, the remote provides scroll bars so you can move to all parts of the host screen. LapLink has a graphical interface to automatically adjust to different resolutions.

Another feature worth looking for is split screen session windows, and ability to view by screen or window.

Home PC Screen Updates   Remote control software has gotten smarter in how it updates the guest PC's screen. If the host sent screen updates, especially Windows images, every time a change was made on the host side the software would shove all the pixels across the phone line—a painfully slow process. Graphics are notorious bandwidth hogs. Instead of transmitting the whole screen, in most remote control software the host and guest PC do one of three things:

- Send partial screen updates. The host sends an initial full screen to the guest, followed by partial screen updates—the "deltas" as time goes by.

- Send internal Windows commands, called GDI calls, instead of screenfuls of data. The host sends an initial screen to the guest and then follows up with Windows' screen writing instructions (GDI calls). Then the guest PC updates its screen based on the GDI call.

- Cache screens. This is the most recent advance and appears to be the best. In screen caching, the guest PC stores screens (or portions of screens), so that when the same image is redisplayed, it can simply be called from the remote system's memory rather than being retransmitted.

Driver Redirection or Mapping/Printer Redirection   This feature allows you to run an application on one system using files located on the other. For example, if you want the host application to edit a file on your home PC, you can map your home PC C: drive to a D: drive on the host. Now the host application can recognize files on its D: drive.

Printer redirection is important if you ever want to print a host file out on your local printer.

**Where were we
when the lights
went out?**
Logs   Either the host may track all remote users or the guest PC may track all remote control contact, or both. This is useful for security and accounting. Some are quite fancy, like Norton pcAnywhere.

Security   Seems like every software product connecting two ends together these days allows for callback. After the remote user logs on to the host and sends a password the host will call back at a predetermined number (based on who you are). Not only does this improve security, but the host gets the phone bill—nice for those who have to worry about expense reports and invoices. A variation on this is for those on the road. It is called roving callback. In this case the caller actually enters the phone number to call back. Not as secure, but still pretty cool.

Remote control software almost always allows for passwords before connection between host and guest.

Other features include access restriction—limitations on what can be accessed, and by whom. It may be based on caller, directory, or file. It may include viewing and editing files or sending and receiving files.

The host keyboard and mouse may be disabled by the guest. That's a useful feature to keep someone from editing a file while you are trying to copy it. Sometimes you can blank the host's screen on connection.

A very important security feature for remote control is the ability to reboot the host at the end of a session, so nobody can sneak in after you're done and wreak corporate havoc. If anybody's gonna wreak havoc it should be you, no?

Session Time Mobileware has a unique approach to reduce telephone connection charges. They use messaging sent from intelligent agents on your PC to the host. The host only reconnects after the message is processed.

So much for the theory. Now for some practical, bloody-knuckle experience. Our recounting here has not been edited for family viewing; the squeamish may wish to skip down to the next section.

In our case, we were stuck with what the spousal unit's IS department decreed: the DOS version of Carbon Copy for all remote control. How should I describe to you the full feeling one gets using the product? Hmm. YUK!

Hobnobbin' with the goober snatchers

Actually, that's putting it politely. Woody wouldn't let us print what we *really* thought. The program was slow. DOS uses the whole bloody screen (imagine twenty-one inches of pure green ASCII characters). Most of all, DOS Carbon Copy was totally unreliable. We used to place bets on how many tries it would take before we could get connected. Three was the average, but once it was ten tries before it would connect. Nobody won the bet that time. Several times it froze while in the process of doing something (guess it was break time or something).

Remote control software has some advantages over remote node servers (described in the next section). One is that the application software is easier to maintain: It is on the company PC. Remote control software also uses less of the telecommuter PC's resources. On the other hand . . .

When holding a PC hostage isn't enough

Used to be that all remote control software sucked. If you only had to access the 'ole office occasionally you put up (with DOS) and shut up (in cyberspace nobody can hear you scream). The biggest problem was that the software

treated your home PC more like a dumb terminal, passing things on as it got them. With DOS that wasn't too bad, but with Windows it could be excruciating. What they really needed was a client/server model where the client and the server talked about what they wanted to bring over. You know, a little intelligence. Well, remote control software vendors have moved towards that. There are actually a few bats in the belfry now. Or is that marbles in the head?

Still, remote control has its problems. One is that the host PC needs to have a modem. (Although some allow you to use a modem pool and the LAN.) Another problem is only one person can take over one PC, so remote control ties up two PC resources in one swell foop.

A problem near and dear to the telecommuter arises when the host crashes. Naturally it would happen after business hours. Your connection is gone. If you don't have one of those remote restart gizmos attached (a TOPS unit, described in Chapter 5), you're SOL. No more manna until the next business day.

More importantly, remote control software makes IS departments nervous. It is hard to manage if the PCs are dispersed (like for the part-time telemployee) and it has less sophisticated security features. If just one schmuck telecommuter doesn't password-protect their inbound connection, it opens the host PC, and through it the company LAN, to lurking miscreants.

Still, the telecommuter will probably find both remote control and remote node servers useful. We hope the IS department will, too.

BACK AT THE FORT

> It's true, hard work never killed anybody,
> but I figure, why take the chance?
>
> Ronald Reagan
> Annual Gridiron Speech, 1987

SOHO   A lot of press has been spinning around the market opportunities falling under the general rubric "Small Office/Home Office" or SOHO. Almost all telecommuters fit the SOHO mold.

BOZO   But what about the telecommuter's central corporate office? The traditional telemployee's center of operations? In the spirit of clever acronym naming—and in memory of several places I've worked—I've dubbed this central corporate office the "Big Office/Zoo" environment, or, memorably, BOZO.

There are several products which, when safely snuggled in BOZO land, can help remote users such as telecommuters. These include remote node servers, ISDN bridges and hubs, electronic whiteboards, security equipment, and some telephony products and features not advertised during prime time. We'll look at all of them in this section.

The SOHO consumer, known in some circles as a "mark."

Many of these are high-ticket items, but they can be cost justified under the right circumstances because they give equal opportunity for use by any remote user or site or vendor or consulting companies or (well, you get the picture).

Remote Access to the LAN

> Pigmaei gigantum humeris impositi plusquam ipsi gigantes vident.*
>
> Didacus Stella
> In Lucan, *De Bello Civili*, ca 60 AD

One way to access company applications is via remote control, an approach that's especially useful if you are a part-time telecommuter. You may have applications residing locally on your office PC that you need to access, as well as the company LAN.

Getting on the BOZO bus

But there are limitations to remote control. It raises significant security questions. IS may not be enthused about maintaining it. You won't be enthused if it needs maintaining at 11:00 p.m. on a Saturday—we telecommuters never work weird hours, right?

Remote control doesn't understand client/server applications. (You mean you want to process something *before* you connect to the host? Save connection phone charges? Huh?) This is where remote node servers blast forth: Remote node servers make your computer at home think it's connected directly to the LAN, even though it's making the connection over a phone line. Remote node servers

---

* A dwarf standing on the shoulders of a giant may see farther than the giant himself.

aren't cheap. They aren't easy. And if you need to transmit at Warp speed (you can't)—ah, well, if you want to speed along you'll need ISDN.

Before discussing remote node servers and ISDN connections it is important to understand some basic networking devices and concepts. This may hurt a little. Just a slight sting, followed by numbness, but it'll go away. Trust me.

Networking for ascetics

Networks are broken up into layers of "protocols." It's the bakery approach. A good cake bakery will not sell just vanilla and chocolate cakes. They will offer several bottom-layer flavors, several fillings, and several top-layer flavors—various combinations produce many different cakes.

By layering the network into different protocols, a user, in theory, can mix and match to get the best protocol "stack." In theory.

Network layers, telecommuter point of view

For a telecommuter trying to connect to the company LAN, the layers can roughly be categorized into three parts. The lowest is the communication link, the pipeline, which we have already discussed: In almost all cases it's either POTS or digital or ISDN.

The next level is the low-level protocol: Ethernet, proprietary ISDN bridge protocols, or the Internet's (and others') PPP, and so on. The low-level protocol "carries" messages back and forth between your computer and the server. It ensures that all the traffic flows smoothly and makes sure any errors get corrected before the higher-level messages are passed along.

The highest level is the protocol that the company LAN connecting device/ server expects: X.25, TCP/IP, NETBEUI (Windows NT), Appletalk, a proprietary protocol, Netware IPX, and so on. The highest-level protocol is the actual language your PC uses to talk to the server.

Bridges. No, not Lloyd.

A **bridge** connects two LANs together at the low-level protocol (usually Ethernet): In the case that interests us most here, a bridge ties together the LAN you set up at your home with the LAN at the office. A bridge gets a packet of information and determines if it is for the local or remote LAN. If it is for the remote, the bridge sends the packet across. It does not know what type of higher-level protocol is being used. Bridges are considered to be protocol independent; in that sense they don't know and don't care what the messages flying around actually mean.

Router

A **router** is smarter than a bridge. It looks at the packet and if it is for a remote LAN it determines *which* LAN. A router can connect a local LAN to multiple remote LANs. A router is also smart enough to translate among the bewildering array of protocols: If a router has a Netware IPX packet, but it determines that the packet must be sent through a TCP/IP network, the router is smart enough to cram the IPX packet into a TCP/IP packet—and presumably the destination router will then be smart enough to strip the envelope and send the packet on its way. Since routers are aware of the higher-level protocol they are considered protocol dependent.

A **gateway** actually changes the packet from one high-level protocol to another in the process of routing a packet to a remote LAN. For example, the IPX packet would become an IP packet and the destination LAN would be expecting an IP packet.

Gateway

OK. That's the basics.

Both ISDN bridges and remote node access servers act like intelligent bridges. They both have useful features specific to the higher-level protocol used. One of those features is data compression. Another is flexible auto disconnect and speedy reconnection when the line is needed again.

While the remote control products allow the caller on a remote PC to run programs on a networked PC, remote node access products treat the remote PC as another node on the corporate LAN. They are aimed at client/server applications. As much data as possible is kept on the remote PC so the minimum is pulled across the wires.

Remote control versus remote node

The choice between remote control software and remote node access isn't an easy one: There are plenty of pros and cons. Because the application software is on the remote PC, it does make it harder for IS to upgrade and track licenses. On the other hand, no company PC is being tied up. The telecommuter is not at the mercy of an unreliable host PC (although they are at the mercy of a —we hope— robust server).

Remote access node servers do not have a lot of features to compare. Most have to do with matching the LAN and the remote PC. Here they are:

Which remote node package?

- **Client PC** The server software needs to support the client PC's operating system. Some software vendors charge more to support multiple client operating systems, some don't. A feature useful to clients and IS is the ability to customize client floppy disks for installation.

- **Server OS/protocols/WAN links** The server needs to support all potential links to it (for example dial up, ISDN, and so on). The higher-level protocol must be compatible with both the link and the LAN. If the remote node server is a software-only solution, it needs to support the operating system of the target server machine.

- **Sessions** The number of simultaneous sessions and ability to group servers is important for growth and future expansion.

- **Management** The type of management is important to IS's ability to maintain the system. Some solutions have SNMP* manageability.

- **Security Features** Password protection is important, dialback should be available, compatibility with authentication devices is best.

* And you wonder why I asked Trudy to write this chapter? —Woody

ISDN bridges   ISDN has been described as a pipeline, mainly for data. The products that you buy to implement ISDN are bridges, and possibly ISDN hubs at the corporate end.

I'm into   ISDN bridges are different from other remote node solutions. They are two-
bonding. headed beasts. The two B channels can be treated separately, or they can work in concert. Some bridges use just one head. This is a single-channel solution (clever name, no?). In a split channel the bridge can handle one B channel as data and one B channel as analog for voice. The most interesting bridge, though, is the one that can handle both channels simultaneously. That's where you get the 128 Kbps turbo bit power. The best ISDN bridges do what's called Dynamic Channel Bonding. They start with one B channel, but if the data transmission gets bogged down they add another channel.

 Intel Remote Express can have one of the B channels configured as data/ voice. It then drops the data rate from 128 Kbps to 64 Kbps so you can answer an incoming call. It provides a built-in TA so you can use a regular analog phone for the combo line. Now *that's* what I call bonding.

 Many ISDN bridges feature something called Dial On Demand. It's just a fancy name for saying that they will automatically hook you up to the company LAN without you having to dial: By all appearances you're on the company LAN all the time. Dial On Demand simply disconnects the phone when you aren't using the LAN link, and then reconnects in a big hurry when the link is needed. The magic comes compliments of drivers on your PC. Seriously cool stuff for the well-dressed ISDN buff.

MPP   What if you don't want to use ISDN bridges? What if you want to connect to the Internet using ISDN? Unix WorkStations and routers usually use the TCP/IP PPP (Point-to-Point) protocol. TCP/IP is popular because it is on UNIX WorkStations, it handles diverse machines, it is used with Ethernet, and it is the lifeblood of the Internet. PPP doesn't know about bonding. It can handle one B channel at only 64 Kbps—not so good considering the Internet is into images, and images use lots of data. The Internet folks are on the case. A new protocol called Multi-Point-Protocol, or MPP, will be able to bond. You'll be able to get all 128 Kbps with it. Soon.

 On the corporate end, the Network Express ISDN InterHub can serve multiple ISDN products simultaneously. This is unusual because ISDN remote products typically only work with their host counterparts. It hosts adapter cards, bridges, UNIX WorkStations, and ISDN routers. The InterHub can work with IBM WaveRunner, Teleos PC TA S/102, Digiboard ISDN Adapter card, Combinet Everyware ISDN Bridge, and a Sun Sparcstation to name a few. This is nice if you are a telemployee in a company committed to telecommuting no matter what the LAN/computer environment.

Security

To fear the worst oft cures the worse.

Shakespeare
Troilus and Cressida, 1601–1602

The IS department is probably quite aware of security issues. With telecommuters, like mobile users, the door opens wider. Common security measures include dial back, establishing access rights for separate applications, partitioning sensitive company information, and fire walls. Some of the remote control and remote node server software help with dial back and establishing authentication. An additional security product to consider is the SecureID card and server. It works much like a bank ATM machine card in that there are two parts to authentication. The user has the SecureID card, which is about the size of a credit card. On it is displayed a randomly generated passcode that changes every 60 seconds. The user, when logging into the corporate system, provides name, password, and the SecureID passcode. Since the password changes every 60 seconds it is nearly impossible to break.

Plastic with no limit

No, I want your password *now.*

The Internet is also a security risk, though the popular image of the Internet exaggerates its weaknesses. The PPP protocol provides two types of authentication. The first is PAP. When the telecommuter attempts to establish a connection with the central corporate office, some identification goes with the name and password the user provides. The identifying information provides a little more security, however neither it nor the password are encrypted, so an intruder with a protocol analyzer could break through. CHAP uses a three-way handshake. After the link is established, the central corporate office sends out a challenge to which the remote device must answer correctly. The LeeMah product also throws a challenge but it encrypts all messages back and forth.

I-way security

For more information on security, particularly on the Internet, take a look at *The Underground Guide to PC Security* (Addison-Wesley, due soon after this book hits the shelves).

Electronic Whiteboards

> The length of a meeting rises
> with the square of the number of people present.
>
> Eileen Shanahan
> *The New York Times Magazine*, March 17, 1968

What's an e-board? Unlike document sharing, which only works if everybody uses their own PC, the electronic whiteboard displays on the telecommuter's PC while everybody physically present gathers at one normal-looking whiteboard.

While the electronic whiteboard is only one-way communication (it would be nice if the telecommuter could annotate the PC and have it reflected on the group's whiteboard, but the technology isn't up to that point yet), the physically present participants are not adversely affected by the product.

The implementation is not difficult, at least in theory: A laser tracks the dry marker's color and position. The product is pricey. Average costs are $35,000 to $40,000. But it can be used by remote offices as well as the telecommuter.

You should avoid electronic whiteboards like Future 2000. This product uses projection. This means that while the speaker is drawing on the board, and blocking the projection, nothing can be seen. Imagine trying to draw a complex diagram blindly. Imagine trying to imagine what the heck somebody is drawing when you can't see a thing until they step away from the board. Very awkward. Very obtuse.

There's an extensive list of electronic whiteboard manufacturers in Appendix B.

Telephony

> The voice is a second face.
>
> Gerard Bauer
> *Carnets Inedits*

Advanced phone products Computer products and pipelines aren't the only tools and features at the corporate office that a telecommuter can benefit from. Telephony has some tricks in its telecommuting bag. One is teleconferencing. The other is (obscure?) PBX features and modules.

If you let your fingers do the walking it is *not* a snap. Not when it comes to teleconferencing with many people in many remote offices. Usually it is more of a fumble: an "Are you still there?" and an "Oops." Sometimes if you bridge too many people into the phone, the sound quality deteriorates drastically.

Audio conferencing

But there is a great teleconferencing product that alleviates most teleconferencing "oopses." It is called Meeting Place. The product is really geared towards a complete audio conference where everybody dials in. It can replace audio conferencing services. That's where all of its features can be exploited. But it has good features even if most meeting participants are physically present. The product connects to the company's PBX and LAN. It can handle up to 120 remote participants in any combination of meetings. The meetings are scheduled through phone, e-mail, or PC menu.

The creators of Meeting Place are currently hard at work tying the product into well-known scheduling software. When the meeting starts, somebody in the meeting room dials into the Meeting Place server. Remote participants, when they are ready to join, dial into the server, which is a single phone number that does not change. Since the meeting room dials in, it doesn't matter where the room is. Meeting place changes make no difference. Everybody dialing in means that the meeting organizer does not have to remember to call remote participants or fumble over bridging-in multiple people. The sound quality is good. And remote participants can be announced as they "enter" the meeting. Unfortunately there is no way to announce to the remote attendee who is in the room (a bane for telecommuters), although they can find out who else has dialed in. If somebody has to miss the meeting, all or portions of the meeting can be recorded.

If all participants dial in there are some additional features. This is a great product for more than just telecommuters, which is good because it is in the $35,000+ range. Hard to justify for one lone telecommuter, sure, but many companies will find it useful for vendors, consultants, satellite offices, and mobile employees too.

There is a feature most PBXs have that you, the telecommuter, may not be aware of. You should be.

PBX Paging

Most PBXs have the ability to page a pager when a voice mail message comes in. Telecommuters don't have "message waiting" lights on their home phones, but a pager beep works almost as well. You can set it so that only urgent voice mail triggers the pager, or you can set it for all voice mail.

Teleconsultants hooked to PBXs that get few, but important, voice mail messages from their clients should also consider this beeper express. The one drawback is that paging frequency must be set in advance. So if you cannot answer your page because you are in a meeting, the #$%@! thing may beep you every five minutes.

PBX
telecommuter
module

If you are a telecommuter living close to the central corporate office—say within shouting or local calling distance—there may be a PBX module that you may wish to persuade the powers-that-be to purchase. Some PBXs, such as AT&T's Definity, have an optional, extra-cost "telecommuter module." The module requires the telecommuter to log in, thus setting up a phone connection.

This connection allows the telecommuter to operate just as if she were in the office with a PBX-connected phone. Colleagues dialing the telecommuter's PBX extension trigger a "call" to the home phone. The telecommuter can also dial extensions, retrieve voice mail, and transfer calls.

Definitely worth a look if the call to your home office is toll-free.

Boogie-Boarding Cyberspace

> . . . I've got gadgets and gizmos a plenty.
> Who's-it and what's-it galore.
> You want thing-a-ma-bobs? I got twenty.
> That's OK. No big deal. I want more . . .
>
> Ariel
> *Little Mermaid,* 1992

E-mail rules   Cyberspace is the ether of the nineties. Most of it is used to send e-mail. If you're a telemployee, your IS department probably decreed the company e-mail direction long ago. However, there are some relatively new e-mail products for the telecommuter to consider—and others to avoid.

Beyond e-mail, cyberspace opens up a vast library of information. You can search and copy files, access applications from far away, post questions, and even converse real-time in a textual way. On-line services, such as CompuServe, open up some avenues of knowledge. Several companies specialize in public-access e-mail. AT&T, Sprint, and MCI all have e-mail networks.

Net   The big banana, though, is the Internet (the Net). There have been books, articles, TV stories, tomes, really terrible movies, and entire sections of libraries written about the Net. Politicians are getting involved (there goes the neighborhood — and free speech). What next? Net lingerie?

Even when all the hot air blows away, the Net *is* awesome. It's also Dante's Inferno. Chaos. Confusion. Flames. People will tell you about surfin' the Net. We are not so ambitious. We'll be boogie boarding cyberspace. So grab your nose plugs and sand buckets while we take a look at a few of the nooks and crannies of particular interest to telecommuters.

Local Mail

We do not mind our not arriving anywhere
nearly as much as not having any company along the way.

Frank Moore Colby
The Margin of Hesitation, 1921

The three big names in corporate e-mail are Lotus cc:Mail, Microsoft Mail, and WordPerfect Groupwise. E-mail is the product choice least likely to be influenced by the budding telecommuter, since the decisions were cast in stone a millennium ago. Still, if you are in the market, most features are common to all packages. However, one feature that differentiates products is the advanced rules-based processing of e-mail. A basic version allows for user-defined filters. The filters can be based on e-mail size, subject, keywords, and sender. More sophisticated rules, such as that of Beyondmail, allow for automatic forwarding and autoreplying of e-mail with predefined messages.

E-mail at the central corporate office

So how do you think big monitors make little monitors?

If you have Lotus cc:Mail and have not moved to cc:Mail Mobile for Windows, you should. It is a client/server version of the software that speeds up execution significantly. It can run in the background, you can set up rules to process mail (except they only work after you download, which steals most of the thunder for telecommuters), or you can preview mail (manually) before downloading it. The implementation has icons for various sites, and it is easy to customize icons. There is a plethora of protocol/pipeline connections from TCP/IP to X.25 to IPX to ISDN to wireless. Unfortunately, it also takes up 10 Mb of disk space.

The Lotus position

Universal Mailboxes

> Affairs are easier of entrance than of exit;
> and it is but common prudence to see our way out
> before we venture in.
>
> Aesop
> *The Sick Lion*, ca. 550 B.C.

Bringing it all together   We are living in a parallel universe. Yes, there is the fax/voice messaging universe. And there is the e-mail universe. We live in both. Each claims to have the Universal mailbox. Ah, but which universe? With e-mail it is a single in-box for all e-mail — both internal and external e-mail.

If you wish to have this type of universal mailbox don't count on E-mail Connection. The product only consolidates on-line services mail. It does not poll internal company mail because it presumes you are not a telecommuter. You have to manually connect to the office in order to "poll" company mail. In addition, it doesn't let you preview mail before downloading. But that is nothing compared to its bugs.

A fellow veteran telecommuter tried the product on her Internet account. For some reason, the product would GP fault the PC. But that was not the worst of it. First it would poll the Internet e-mail, pull it down into netherspace on the PC, *delete* it from the Internet account, and then GP fault. The mail was lost. She called ConnectSoft numerous times only to be told there was no way to trace the bug and that "Gee. Our technical people are too busy for you now. Maybe later." Numerous calls. Last I heard it had been three months. She is still waiting for a call back. Just how long do vendors expect you to stay on hold? Don't fall into the same trap. Stay away from E-mail Connection.

Microsoft's Exchange adds almost-universal e-mail functionality to Windows. While I wouldn't call it perfect, it's definitely worth a look if you haven't already. The advantages of a similar interface — even if it isn't such a great interface — for all sources of electronic communication can't be overstated.

The Internet — Gettin' Hooked to the Outside

> Knowledge is of two kinds:
> we know a subject ourselves,
> or we know where we can find it.
>
> Samuel Johnson
> Boswell's *"Life of Samuel Johnson,"* 1775

So many choices   There are also connections to the outside world: on-line services. Some are a network in themselves, such as CompuServe. Or America Online. They have their own forums, news groups, and services. Stores. Stock quotes. Magazines. CompuServe is the most popular for computer jocks, and the most expensive. On the other end are service providers that give you access to the Internet. They usually have better Net access at better prices. They may include a decent interface and a few internal news groups, but that's about it.

Which brings us to the Internet. The Ibahn. Information Scooped Up Highway. The Net.

Had to get there eventually

The Net is like an onion with many layers. And noxious fumes if you get too close. A prudent telecommuter will want to keep her distance with one (or two or three) software front ends to the Net. All on-line services provide some sort of connection to the Net.

So what is the Net? Why would a telecommuter care? And just how does one go about getting connected?

The Internet is actually many networks meshed (mashed) together. They are joined together by a common set of TCP/IP protocols, tools, and gateways. The original network, the ARPAnet, was created by the U.S. Department of Defense to provide a decentralized and highly reliable communications link among military sites. ("The Ruskies may have nuked us but we can still send war updates to the survivors, by gawd.") That was the theory. So from the beginning the ARPAnet was anarchy. No central command (it could get nuked). No central governing body (vaporizer bait).

A five-minute intro to the Net, for the telecommuter

Around the same time UNIX become popular as a computer operating system and UNIX freaks created a network of UNIX machines called Usenet. Both the ARPAnet and Usenet were decentralized. Both had certain rules of etiquette. For example, commercial applications or advertisements were a serious No-No. The networks were used mostly by researchers and undergrad students who were hotly debating which way a roll of toilet paper should be installed.* Usenet had a set of bulletin boards by subject. Users could "post" messages to the newsgroups and, using various programs, read the postings of others. Thus was born the auspicious (suspicious) NetNews.

Then the networks sort of merged with a few other networks (gently, like an avalanche), ARPAnet became the Internet, the Defense Department wanted to stop funding the Internet, and the groups that took over allowed businesses to connect to the network. Since then the thing has been growing. It's all over the world.†

Your PC connects, via modem, to a larger machine, which in turn is connected to the Internet. The people who own and operate the larger machine are called "service providers." While use of the Internet itself (as of this writing) is free,

Service providers

---

* With the paper end on top, of course. So kittens can't unroll it.

† Woody's fond of saying that he first logged onto the Net in 1974, didn't see much worth worrying about, and let twenty years go by before logging on again. True story.

you'll pay a fee to the service provider for the use of their system, typically $10 to $20 a month, plus a few bucks an hour. I'll talk more about service providers at the end of this section.

**Places to go
and people to
see**

There are essentially nine ways to exploit the Net for work, fun, profit, and to annoy your Significant Other: send/receive e-mail, including mailing lists; read and post NetNews; join an IRC chat session; read e-zines (on-line magazines); play MUD or MOO games; telnet into another machine, like the corporate office; search and copy files; and "publish" files for others to search and copy. That's about it.

File searching and retrieving takes several forms, all pretty inscrutable to read about, all pretty easy to use. There are FTP servers to explore, Gopher servers, Web servers, and to a lesser degree WAIS servers. These are client/server based. You use client software on your end called navigators or browsers.

NetNews   There are between five and fifteen thousand NetNews newsgroups depending upon who's counting and which way the sun sets. Amongst those NetNews groups offered by your service provider, you can subscribe or unsubscribe to as many as you like. Telecommuters will find numerous interesting professional newsgroups, especially if you have a technical stripe. Even if you do not find a kindred professional group, you may find groups to ask questions of — and get answers from — wizards and gurus. Some are real, some self-appointed. These groups may be from vendors of products you have acquired (and cursed). Or you may find a group of fellow telecommuters. Telecommuters anonymous.

**I like mine
well done.**

You can read NetNews postings (messages), reply to a posting privately via e-mail, or post your own messages. Before posting you should sit and watch—the official term is "Lurk"—for awhile. Get your bearings by reading, not jumping in and making a fool of yourself. Groups often post periodic FAQ (Frequently Asked Questions) files. Read them.

The Net has its own Netiquette; it helps to keep an anarchic system from being overly chaotic. You won't find Miss Manners here. You'll find flame throwers: people unafraid of making an in-your-face comment about any transgression you may commit—real or imagined. One Net *faux pas* and you're charcoal.

E-mail   The e-mail system used on the Internet is called SMTP (Simple Mail Transport Protocol). The SMTP protocol expects all e-mail messages to be in plain text (often called "ASCII") format. Until recently this usually meant you had to manually convert binary files, like programs, into plain text using a utility like uuencode. A newer, superset protocol, called MIME (Multipurpose Internet Mail Extensions) handles multipart multimedia messages gracefully. While its messages still must be in plain text, MIME-based systems usually handle the conversion for you automatically.

A MIME reader is more sophisticated than typical Internet mail readers. The MIME reader first passes the message through a parser, which identifies the components of the mail message. A dispatcher then accesses a viewer specific to the message component type (text, video, audio). An upcoming standard will even allow a user to choose which component to read (for example, "skip the video, give me the text").

MIME

You can send e-mail to anybody in the world (connected to the Net or an on-line service). It's extremely useful for contacting clients, vendors, consultants, your mother-in-law, the president of the United States, or the leaders (and revolutionaries) of many other nations.

In addition to e-mail there are mailing lists on various topics. Some are moderated (you send a message to the moderator) and some are "broadcast-my-thoughts." If you have a service provider that charges per e-mail message you should be aware that some lists are very active.

Telnet   This utility connects you to another machine—perhaps even a PC at the central corporate office—through the Net. It's a potentially inexpensive alternative for connecting to the mother planet for telecommuters who live far from the corporate zoo. Instead of paying long-distance charges, you pay for a local call to the nearest Internet access point. Some Internet providers are even establishing ISDN links (ya gotta look hard). The downside of using the Net is that throughput is unreliable. It depends on traffic. If the computer security folks at your company are paranoid (haven't met one that isn't yet) then they may think the telnet idea is as good an idea as pulling one of their teeth out. They may balk at the thought of using the unsecured Net as the medium for doing work. Personally, I haven't found too many competitors out there who send swat teams of people on the Net with network sniffers to try to sniff out the lone telecommuter using Telnet to log onto the corporate network. I can think of easier ways to commit corporate espionage — like filching a badge and changing the picture on it (if Harrison Ford can do it . . .). Still, there are lots and lots of people on the Net who have nothing better to do than poke around, trying to find mischief worth getting into.

Mission Impossible

FTP   Text files existed first on the Net. The tool to copy them is FTP (File Transfer Protocol). The means is straightforward: You go to an FTP server, log on with an ID of "anonymous" and use your e-mail address as the password, find a file you wish to copy, and then FTP it. **Anonymous FTP**, as this method is called, can be an easy way for a server to allow anybody to get on the system strictly to download public files.

A telecommuter can glean important information via anonymous FTP. You can get software upgrades and bug patches. You can use FTP to receive information from folks not directly connected to the office LAN—like consultants. Partner companies. Subsidiaries.

To help search for available, public FTP files, there is a tool scattered about called ARCHIE. It looks for the search string you provide, giving you the matching computer and file name. You can then pop over to the computer and FTP the file. ARCHIE is good if you are looking for a specific file or program, and can narrow down the search with keywords.

Another search tool, **Gopher**, gives you a hierarchical set of menus of files to retrieve (FTP). It lists different host computers and the subject area of the information they contain. A tool called VERONICA integrates the listings of all Gopher servers into a single information source. Gopher is best if you are searching for information on a broad theme.

World Wide Web   WWW, W3, or "the Web" is the latest Internet fashion statement. Files (pages) can be multimedia and the have hypertext links to other files (pages). The other pages can be anywhere in the world. Literally. The pages are created using a language called **HTML** (HyperText Markup Language). Hypertext links are highlighted in some manner. The Web protocol on top of TCP/IP is something called **HTP** (Hypertext Transfer Protocol). Web browsers start with a home page, and from there you can hop just about anywhere. The Web is big. Really big big. Because the Web lets you hop, skip, and jump hyperlinks you can get, well, lost in space.

Do the Web crawl: Do-do-do-ddo-do-do

Web catalogs help organize the chaos. Sort of. It can be daunting (read: boring) to wade through catalogs. Web search tools are at least automated. They categorize as they search. Currently search tools are all freeware but that should change quickly. Probably by the time you finish this paragraph. Robots. Spiders. Worms. Crawlers. They have different names. No flies though (unless it is you, stuck in the mire saying "Help me. Hellllp me"). They either use depth-first (start with a page and traverse every hyperlink, cataloging as you go) or breadth-first (catalog page after page after page) searching algorithms or hybrids. Whatever you call it, the search tools limit how you can search. They may allow multi-item searches (for example, a title and a key word). Different tools also differ in the amount that they categorize. Categorizing can run the gamut from just page titles all the way to every bloomin' word on the page.

Many businesses and commercial enterprises are interested in the Web, probably because a Web page sounds a lot like a cross between an infomercial and a billboard. The Web may give you the information you need for your job, or access to customers, or it just may be where you shop until you drop.

WAIS   Wide Area Information Server is a full-text indexing software that's used to index large text files, documents, and periodicals in servers. It hasn't been implemented widely. It finds and retrieves documents in databases based on user-defined keywords.

IRC (Internet Relay Chat)   A tool to have real-time conversations through the computer. Unlike NetNews there are no fixed groups. Anybody can set up a channel (group) and it lasts until the last person leaves. Many service providers have IRC clients. Most connect to a specific server. Ask them how to connect if it isn't obvious. IRC commands start with a / slash. The /help newuser group is a good place to start. Text typed without the / is assumed to be conversation and is broadcast to everybody on the channel. If IRC sounds like your cuppa tea, check out Stuart Harris's *irc Survival Guide* (Addison-Wesley, 1995).

Anyone want to take a Cyber Coffee Break?

MUDS   Multiuser Dungeons. Text-based fantasy role playing games with multiple players. The object-oriented version is called a MOO.

Armchair Warriors

E-zines   These are non-traditional magazines that are on-line. They have their own, uh, character.

General Info

Here's a bit of general Internet info to get you started. The InterNIC information services is a National Science Foundation group ready and willin' to get you out and about on the Net. This group also has Internet info to get you going on Web, Gopher, and FTP servers. Here are some sources for servers and other services:

- **Web servers**   http://www.internic.net
- **Web search tools**   NIKOS   http://www.ms.com/cgi-bin/nomad
  WWW Worm   http://www.cs.colorado.edu/home/mcbryan/wwww.html
  Jumpstation II   http://www.stir.ac.uk/jsbin/jsii
  Webcrawler   http://www.biotech.washington.edu/webcrawler/home.html
- **Gopher servers**   gopher.internic.net, gopher.micro.umn.edu
  send e-mail to listproc@einet.net with   subscribe gopher-jewels *your name*
- **FTP servers** ftp.internic.net,
  FTP to   ftp.shsu.edu go to /doc/doc-net/ftp-list and get sitelist file
- **WAIS databases**   gopher-gw.micro.umn.edu
- **Mailing Lists**   FTP to usc.edu go to /net-resources and get interest-groups file
- **E-zines**   send e-mail to e-zines-request@netcom.com
- **AT&T's 800 Number directory**   (mighty useful)   http://att.net/dir800

Once you are on the Net, there are several on-line books about the Net to guide you. The price is free, which should fit in the boss's budget. *Zen and the Art of the Internet: A Beginners Guide to the Internet* is at emoryu1.cc.emory.edu in the /computing/reference/networking/internet directory. *Hitchhiker's Guide to the*

Internet can be gophered at gopher.fsl.orst.edu. *Big Dummy's Guide to the Internet* is at ftp.eff.org.

Internet Service Providers

To get connected you need to find an Internet service provider. Bribe somebody already on the Net to get you a list of providers by sending e-mail to info-deli-server@netcom.com and put *send pdial* as the subject header. Look for a provider that gives you all the services you want (or a PPP connection) and that is a local call to access. Preferably as high a speed access as your modem. You may also consider ISDN connections to the Internet if you plan on using the Web a lot or connecting to the company machine. Then check pricing.

Service providers these days are like fleas on a hound dog's back—they're popping up everywhere. Virtually every major metro area has an independent service provider. The phone companies (notably MCI and several RBOCs) are getting into the act. All of the on-line services (MS Network, CompuServe, AOL, Prodigy, Interchange) provide some access to the Net. Getting connected has never been cheaper or easier.

A word of advice: Pick a provider that has a low set-up fee. That way, if you are unsatisfied, you can switch providers with minimal loss of money. You may need to do so. Some providers such as Netcom and AOL are notorious for having too many customers, not enough access. One telecommuter tried getting connected to Netcom in New York City for three weeks. She could not get in before 10:00 p.m. Another had troubles in Seattle. Both providers are well-known national outfits. Unfortunately that doesn't mean squat. Don't hassle it. Switch providers.

A telecommuter needs to decide between myriad types of connections when shopping Internet services.

On-line Service Account   Getting hooked is easy, services are iffy. On-line services (MS Network, Interchange, CompuServe, AOL, Prodigy, and so on) usually have their own enticements. Stock quotes. Forums. Vendor support. Shopping. On-line magazines. All of them give access to the Internet, but in different ways, and the offerings and prices seem to change from day to day. For the on-line service handholding you pay much more than you'd pay a regular Internet service provider. CompuServe is the King of On-line Services. Naturally they're also the most expensive. You pay for royalty (or is that you pay royally?).

Shell Accounts   Typically, a shell account gets you onto the Internet, but only by using a clunky text-based interface on the service provider's big computer. This is the easiest kind of account to set up and the most limiting (with the possible exception of on-line service accounts). You are at the mercy of the provider in terms of Internet services. Many don't have multimedia Web access. The front-end software can often be best described as retro-1950s-style menu-based. You may be able to get more features, such as true multimedia Web access, if the provider is willing to let you install a pseudo SLIP application. Ask the provider about The Internet Adapter (TIA) and Slipknot.

SLIP/PPP Account   This requires more effort on your end but many new software front ends, such as Internet In a Box, help. With SLIP/PPP you have full access to the Internet. As you'll see in your first ten minutes on the Net with a SLIP/PPP account, speed is everything: Those cool Web pages can take forever to squeeze themselves through your phone line. At this moment, a PPP account at 28.8 Kbps with a POTS line, or 56/64 Kbps with ISDN is the fastest dial-up account you can get. Soon there will be an MP connection available for ISDN links; it will be able to combine two B channels for up to 128 Kbps.

Nailed-up Connections   Leased lines directly connected to the Net are nice to set up mail servers that can notify you immediately when you have inbound e-mail waiting. The line generally runs at 56 Kbps. It's just like PPP only faster and more expensive.

In order to procure the most up-to-date information on telecommuting and Internet access, I took a scientific poll ("Yo. Anybody out there want to expound on their Net connect woes?").

Pointy-headed pontifications

The general response was that SLIP/PPP is great, but required a few phone calls to the service provider to get connected. Hold on to those phone numbers. Write them down someplace permanent. Other access choices were easier to connect but sometimes frustrating when the telecommuter found out they didn't have a certain Net tool. Nine out of ten said they think uploading and downloading software is as easy as doing taxes (where's the EZ form?). About as much fun, too. Many called their service providers to figure it out.

Woody swears by Internet in a Box. He spent days hassling with all those other products, and never did get on. With Internet in a Box and a SLIP/PPP account in hand (and the good help of SuperNet, his service provider), he was up and Web surfing in an hour.

Front Ends

Once you have an account, and if you are able to choose, you'll want to shop for Net browsers and combo packages. Since the Internet is growing so quickly, the software changes continually. Here is a list of currently cool features to look for in each service. One software package may not have it all.

General   Some packages offer multithreaded support—what I call multitasking. You can do multiple tasks. For example, you can download a file and send e-mail simultaneously.

E-mail Tools   Different packages have different capabilities. Filtering messages based on criteria is nice. The ability to attach files including sound and graphics (using the MIME standard) to messages really helps; drag 'n drop is even better. Customizable folders are good, better are nested folders. Being able to quote from a previous message — or not. Mail robots. Off-line mail preparation is extremely useful, as is storing drafts that you can revise and send later. Scheduled connections. Unsend feature to avoid embarrassing accidental replies. MCIMAIL has 800 numbers with no surcharges, which is nice for traveling telecommuters. Signature files automatically attach your 'signature' at the end of your messages: It's the Net of equivalent of a vanity plate, only much more ostentatious. Spell checkers. Rule-based mail polling. Sorting or searching messages by criteria like sender, subject, priority, arrival time, and so on. Mailing lists. Carbon Copy messages to others. Be sure to investigate all the possibilities and choose a package that suits your style.

NetNews Readers   Better readers allow you to filter your news messages. Some have threads — groups of messages on the same subject — that you can follow. Air Newsreader lets you look at the outline of the threads so you can collapse parts you are not interested in. Also personal newsgroup folders are nice for organizing discussions. Because NetNews generates so much noise, it is nice to have a "Kill" file capability where you skip messages by subject, person, or host site. That's a nice Net way to clamp your hand over a loud-mouthed oaf. Off-line newsreading is important to minimize connection charges. Signature files here, too. Some readers let you conduct searches based on key words.

FTP   This is a basic utility, like school scissors and paste. Not much to add. Some products give a network file manager along with the regular file manager so you can drag 'n drop to copy files.

Gopher Browsers   Not a lot to differentiate the products, but Wingopher is a little better at searching than its competitors.

Web Browsers   There are four basic browsers from which nearly all commercial browsers stem: Mosaic, Cello, Lynx, and Netscape. For OS/2 there is the IBM Web Explorer. Lynx is strictly a text-based browser so you lose all the glitz of a Web page (often used in shell accounts). On the other hand, skipping the multimedia is much faster.

Cello is faster than Mosaic but does not compare to Netscape in features. A telecommuting FAFTCC guru sent me observations on Cello. He specializes in evaluating software. Let me repeat his comments verbatim: "Jello has a shifty UI (User Interface). Was ported from X-Wintoes and looks like a port."

Could it be he used a Newton?

Mosaic is the most popular Web browser interface but it was created for high-speed links. Of course commercial versions of this browser may improve on it. Netscape is the newest browser, and one of the key people on the Netscape implementation team was a guru for Mosaic. Thus Netscape is an improved Mosaic, in a way. Netscape is geared for dial-up speeds. For one thing, it downloads text first, allowing you to peruse and scroll the text while it downloads images. Images are first outlined, then filled in. You can abort the image download if the outline doesn't look promising.

Some browsers include the Winsock TCP/IP stack with PPP that you will need to set up a PPP connection. Many require you to get it from elsewhere. Make sure your browser has been tested with the stack you buy. Other features to look for in Web browsers are:

- **Hotlists or bookmarks** to get to favorite Net spots quickly. Even better are layered hotlists, such as a menu or folders, and ones to which you can add notes, including voice.

- **File size and download progress** tool so you can tell if a file is just slow to download or if it is hung. This is a Must Have feature.

- **Print, Print Preview, and Save to File** Being able to save a document as HTML or plain text or a multimedia format is nice.

- **Customization files** so you can modify menu bars and add viewers for different types of image files. Add-in viewers will support more file image formats.

- **Multiple windows** so you can access multiple pages simultaneously.

- **History lists** of pages traveled—for current session or (even better) for any "Saved" session. The best have a map that not only lists document titles but the path you took to get there (you know, like a map). Some browsers also mark links already traversed. Great for the fuzzy headed. It is nice if the hotlist uses document titles instead of URLs.

- **OLE 2.0 support** so that you can imbed hyperlinks into a Word document and ship it out or use it to create an automated script is nice. Drag 'n drop attachments are better.

- **Scheduler/Macros** to run Scripted files at any time.

- **Selective Retrieve** only the images you want.

- **Page Caching** for quick retrieval of previous pages.

- **Search/Cut/Paste** selected text and images within a page.

- **32-bit** architecture should be faster for machines that can accommodate it.

- **Navigation buttons** for a range of pages are important, such as forward, backward, and toggle buttons. There are subtle differences among the browsers in how they are implemented.

- **WAIS gateways** to give you access to WAIS servers.

One important thing to keep in mind. The Web is so cool that *any* Web browser that works is better than no Web browser. Try it. The first time you get connected to the Web, you'll be on it for hours. It's one of the most addictive computer things ever invented. You'll see.

A few cautionary parting notes, if I may . . .

Security   Currently the Internet is an unsecured network. That's amazing, in that the original network was created by the United States military. Hmm, maybe not so amazing. There have been a few celebrated cases about just how insecure it is. Crackers sniff out or crack passwords to get sensitive information. This has been a real impediment (or godsend, depending on your viewpoint) to commercializing the Net.

I ain't puttin' my Visa number on the Net. Even if it is at its limit.

Netscape has the ability to encrypt and authenticate, but only if it is used with its Netsite Server. Some versions of Mosaic are adding security. The struggle for better security on the Net continues, but it's still a long way from reality.

Pretty good   Until Net security improves, if you need to e-mail sensitive information over
privacy   the Net you should probably use the relatively secure tool called pgp (for pretty good privacy). Subscribe to alt.security.pgp or send e-mail to pgp-public-keys@pgp.mit.edu with *help* in the subject line for more information. Pgp can either encrypt a message or embed a digital signature to verify who sent it (or both). Basically you generate a public and private key. You give your public key to the recipient. They give you their public key. To send an encrypted message you use their public key. They decrypt it with their private key. To send a message with a digital signature you use your private key. They verify authenticity with your public key. As long as the keys are genuine and untampered, and the encryption is not cracked, your messages are secure. But it is manual so it is not practical for electronic commerce.

If you want to publish on the Net, or set up shop, there are a few places to point you in the right direction. Downtown Anywhere main street can be found at http://www.awa.com. Information about the InternetMall is at http://www.mecklerweb.com/imall/about/howto.hmtl.

The CommerceNet is a consortium of high-tech companies interested in promoting product sales. Its aim is to build a business-to-business secure network on the Net. It is half research, half reality. Membership costs are not for the faint-hearted. Cost is a minimum of $5,000 (that's three zeros). Users logging into the CommerceNet WWW page are directed to a graphical catalog of products and services. Using a special secure version of Mosaic, customers can order directly over the Net. For more info send e-mail to info@commerce.net.

The OpenMarket Commercial Sites Index lists specific services, products, and businesses. Try http://www.directory.net

If you want to set up a Web home page you'll need an editor tool. Microsoft has released a free add-on to Word for Windows called Internet Assistant, and other word processor vendors have promised versions by the time you read this. Before diving in with both feet, you should get a book on the topic (not coincidentally, the *Underground Guide to Internet Assistant for Word for Windows* (Addison-Wesley) should be available soon after this book hits the stands), or look into http://www.ncsa.uiuc.edu/demoweb/html-primer.html.

You may decide that setting up and maintaining a server is more hassle (and resource draining) than you care for. There are services to create Web pages for you, and some have their own servers.

FOR MORE INFO

Do you ever get the feeling that all the fury over the Net exceeds the bounds of reality? Does it remind you of the CB craze of the 1970s? Yeah. Us, too.

There's an amazing book written by a Net insider that should be required reading for anyone who's gone ga-ga over the whole phenomenon. *Silicon Snake Oil: Second Thoughts on the Information Highway* by Clifford Stoll (Doubleday, 1995) offers a refreshing, feet-firmly-planted-on-real-ground view of what PC technology in general, and the Net in particular, have to offer. If you understand that data is not the same thing as information, you're ready to take on Stoll.

A special note for those of you who live outside the United States. If you spend a lot of time on the phone to the States, you could save an enormous amount of money—say, half your current phone bill—by using a "callback service." The method is pretty simple: you dial a pre-assigned telephone number, then hang up the phone. A few seconds later, your phone rings. You pick it up, and you get a dial tone *in the United States*. From that point you can direct-dial anywhere in the world—including, notably, American 800 numbers.

Contact Telegroup, Inc., 505 North Third St., Fairfield, IA 52556, voice 515-472-5000, fax 515-472-4747.

That's it for me. Back over to Woody. . . .

5 The Telemployee

I have been a stranger in a strange land.

Moses
Exodus 2:22

If you're working for a company, but spend a fair amount of time outside of the central office—at home, on the road, or perhaps in customers' offices—this chapter is for you. (Telebosses may find the discussion interesting, too.)

I've broken the chapter into three sections. The first looks at points you should settle before you start telecommuting. The second examines what can get screwed up, and how you as a telemployee can avoid, minimize, or (if you're lucky) negate the problems. And the final section is for Road Warriors—those peripatetic souls who carry the telecommuting revolution to the front lines, often with little more than the electronic equivalent of a K-ration and a pea shooter.

What every telemployee needs to know

"Yes, boss, I *was* working on the Snerdly account when you called."

So here's the distilled wisdom of dozens of telecommuters, representing something like 200 person-years of telecommuting. The problems are tough, but the problem solvers are tougher. Telecommuters tend to be a very resourceful lot.

I think you'll find the solutions some of these folks have found are among the most innovative responses to vexing problems in business today.

BEFORE YOU START

> In fair weather prepare for foul.
>
> Thomas Fuller
> *Gnomologia,* 1732

Coulda woulda shoulda. Hindsight is 20-20. Be prepared. Look before you leap. Insert your favorite hackneyed homily here.

So much of what gets screwed up in telecommuting arrangements could be prevented if only the participants could've foreseen the problem and agreed to its resolution before that malodorous offal hit the rotating impeller.

Anticipate screw-ups. Sadly, foresight (some would say prescience) of that magnitude is the exception, not the rule. While this section discusses some of the predictable problems in any telecommuting relationship—and it *is* a relationship, between telemployee, teleboss, coworkers, family, and others—there will always be the unavoidable misunderstanding, miscue, or completely bollixed screw-up. It's inevitable.

Why? Because telecommuting is still largely uncharted territory. Every telecommuting arrangement is different. There are few, if any, recognized norms. Managers who have spent their lives honing their interpersonal skills discover that much of what they've learned about motivation, leadership, and discipline depends on face-to-face contact. Employees accustomed to the give-and-take of office life can overreact wildly when—rightly or wrongly—they feel they're being snubbed. And physical separation tends to exaggerate and irritate every minor inconvenience.

Welcome to Management in the twenty-first century.

Adapting Your Job

> He that would eat the nut
> Must crack the shell.
>
> Plautus
> *Curculio,* ca. 200 BC

Not all jobs are appropriate for telecommuters. Aside from the obvious ones—jobs that require a physical presence in a particular location, or ones based on face-to-face contact with the public—some other kinds of jobs just don't seem to cut it.

I'll go into some detail about Jobs from Telecommuting Hell in Chapter 6, the one for telebosses. After all, assigning a distinctly office-bound job to a telecommuter, or allowing somebody who should be at the office to telecommute, to the detriment of the job, is a management problem.

But the simple fact is that, as a potential telecommuting employee, *you know* *better than anybody else* if the work you do can be performed effectively outside the office—and how many days a week you can spend at home (or a satellite office) before the job begins to suffer. **The ultimate authority**

If you're looking into the possibility of telecommuting or are about to start telecommuting for the first time, be honest with yourself, your coworkers, and your boss. Think through the mechanics of how the arrangement will work. Will you be relying more on your coworkers? What can you do to help them, or at least lessen the burden, in return? Are there any predictable logjams in the normal flow of work that you'll be creating? What will go more smoothly?

The most important question: Can you rearrange your job, before the telecommuting starts, to make your absence less onerous? Can you shed some less-important responsibilities that would be hard to accomplish from home, or take on new ones that don't require your presence in the central office?

For example, if you're going to be relying on a buddy to look up paper files for you or answer the phone for you at the central office from time to time, can you scratch his back by offering to proofread his reports? If the current procedure is that you review and annotate claims, pass them on to the boss for her signature, and then batch them for forwarding to the next department, could you make the whole process go faster by getting verbal approval from the boss? Or instead of sending the whole file to the boss, could you fax a simple cover sheet?

The possibilities are endless. In some cases, removing yourself physically from the normal chain can actually speed up the whole process.

Consider your options well. Minor changes to your job responsibilities undertaken before telecommuting starts can save endless hours of frustration—in fact, it may well make the difference between a telecommuting arrangement that works and one that leaves you looking for a new job.

Changing your job to fit the new circumstances can be the simplest, least traumatic step in your transition to telecommuting. Funny how often the possibility is overlooked: The telecommuting books, articles, and checklists all seem to assume that your "job" is cast in concrete; that it must merely be transported, physically, from central office to the home. That ain't necessarily so. **Mutatis mutandis**

Take advantage of your assignment to the cyburbs to look at how work flows through you and around you. By simply revising the routing of a form, or changing one step in a corporate procedure, or eliminating or streamlining an unnecessary review, you may be able to make the transition much smoother for yourself, your boss, and everyone around you.

Talk with your boss and coworkers. Your move to telecommuting may solve some of *their* problems, too.

Adapting Your Boss

> The key to looking smart is to be the one asking the questions.
>
> Mark Clarkson
> *Windows Hothouse,* 1994

Have pity on your boss! Unless she has been immersed in the latest twists of flexible management methods—well in advance of her cohorts—she may not have an easy time dealing with your transition from physiocommuter to telecommuter.

Fond memories of The Boss

How does your boss manage? While every new pop business book seems to recommend a different management style—remember the facile recommendations of the *One Minute Manager*, the macho appeal of *Management By Walking Around*, or the oh-so-in-touch incarnation of *Quality Circles*?—the simple fact is that most managers (indeed, most *good* managers) go about their daily work by observing how things are going, and making adjustments where necessary. It's seat-of-the-pants management, and dammit, it's worked quite well for a long time.

Telecommuting throws a monkey wrench into the "observing" part of most managers' regimen. While physical presence has never been much of an indicator of a worker's effectiveness, absence has traditionally been a dead give-away. As a result of simple observation, a bit of intuition, and some common sense, most managers have a pretty good idea of which employees work pretty hard and which are just putting in their time.

Your mission, as a telecommuter, is to give your boss every reason to believe that you're still working just as hard as you were at the central office—more so, if at all possible. You do that by adapting the relationship you have with your boss, moving away from an emphasis on the day-to-day work you perform, toward an emphasis on final, delivered products or services.

Adapting the boss to your telecommuting is much easier said than done simply because, in most cases, measuring results can be so tricky. Yes, some bosses feel threatened. Others feel envious. Mostly, though—at least among the bosses I've talked to in the high-tech industries—managing a telecommuting employee raises questions of fair evaluation.

It's a problem you'll face every day. Best to own up to it at the get-go, talk with your boss about it *before* the telecommuting starts, and make sure both of you clearly understand the goals influencing your next performance review.

There are limits to the "adapt the boss" approach. Some bosses are incorrigible. If your boss has serious reservations about telecommuting, don't even bother trying. Find another boss, or another company, but forget trying to telecommute over the objections of an obstinate boss. The last thing you need is a quiverful of colorful flaming arrows in your back from a boss who's trying to prove a point to upper management.

> If the boss doesn't like it, ferget it.

Adapting *Yourself*

> Thales was asked what was the most difficult to man;
> he answered: "To know one's self."
>
> Diogenes Laertius
> *Lives of the Philosophers*, ca. 150 BC

It's strange, but in all the interviews I conducted with telecommuters, none of them really came out and said, "The most important changes that had to take place were with me." Granted, the theme swirled around all the conversations. But nobody laid it out quite so directly. Perhaps it's an unspoken "given." If so, it's as crucial a bit of unspoken lore as any you'll find in this *Underground Guide*.

The farther you move from the confines of the central office—be it for one day a week, ten days a month, or fifty-one weeks a year—the more important it becomes for you to act like an entrepreneur, an independent operator. It's a tough transition. And you have to be very careful because the entrepreneurial role you're thrust into will (with very rare exceptions) conflict with entrenched corporate culture.

> Entrepreneurs on their own

Many companies pride themselves on engendering an entrepreneurial attitude among employees. "Acme Widgets encourages employees to take chances," the annual report says. "We like to grow businesses within our business," says another.

Perception versus reality

Nine times out of ten, the entrepreneurial emphasis is pure hogwash—either a policy from on high that's poorly implemented where it counts most, a vision from some PR agency hired by the firm to brush up the company's image with its stockholders, or the lame pronouncement from some committee charged with reinventing the corporation. You can tell it's hogwash because the same risk-adverse, brown-nosing "team player" behavior is still rewarded; the same people are promoted; and the really revolutionary ideas still die on the vine.

Which is all by way of warning you. If you think that embarking on telecommuting represents a sea change in the corporate culture, you're probably mistaken. Not everyone in the company will appreciate your new-found independence. The entrepreneurial flashes you'll no doubt experience probably won't be well regarded back at the central office. Regardless of lofty corporate goals, direction statements, and the like, where the rubber meets the road—your work group, your department, your circle of friends—not much is going to change in your absence.

***You*, on the other hand, are going to change significantly, particularly if you've never telecommuted before. Your expectations of the job will increase steadily. Your tolerance for simple mistakes—the boss misses a meeting without telling anybody; the interoffice mail doesn't get routed to the right place, the server goes down—will diminish just as steadily.**

From what I've seen, this entrepreneurial/independence tussel is a predictable crisis that faces every telemployee—particularly telecommuting professionals. It's a problem that should be acknowledged going into the game. The only solution I've found is for telemployees to adjust *themselves*, by lowering expectations for the job, learning to put up with simple mistakes, and realizing that the folks back in the central office have to cope with a very different set of circumstances.

Do You Need a Contract?

> This is the epitome of all the contracts in the world
> betwixt man and man, betwixt prince and subject:
> they keep them as long as they like them, and no longer.
>
> John Selden
> *Table-Talk,* 1689

Telecommuting contracts are rare.

I didn't find many telemployees with formal employment contracts, much less contracts (or language in contracts) that deal specifically with telecommuting. That violates all the "rules of telecommuting," of course: The people who run the telecommuting seminars and write telecommuting books and legal books and human relations books and particularly the folks with predesigned forms for all things telecommuting would be most disappointed.

Humbug. There aren't any rules.

I would contend that there's a reason for the dearth of formal telemployee contracts. Far as I can tell, not enough is known about the specific legalities of telecommuting to make a telemployee contract worth the paper it's printed on.* The question of liability is particularly vexing. We'll look at it in Chapter 8.

Just initial pages 17, 38, and 56, then sign pages 149, 253, and 786.

While a telemployee contract may be overkill, there's enough variety in telecommuting arrangements that a written memo might be worthwhile. For example, some companies in the United States still won't provide PCs for telecommuters, even if the PCs are required for the job. (It's refreshing to know that, in some American businesses anyway, Scrooge still begrudges his lumps of coal.)

If not a formal contract, then what?

If there's even the slightest chance you might run into that kind of "who pays for what" question—and we'll talk about several possible points of contention in the next section—it's best to get it all down on paper.

> **One particularly innovative agreement I encountered was a "no fault bailout" clause in a Silicon Gulch company's telecommuting agreement. It says explicitly that the telemployee arrangement is temporary for the first three months— that either side can terminate the arrangement, immediately, during that term. Unlike many companies, which bill their telecommuting program as a "pilot" or "temporary" program, this company chose to view its arrangement with this one employee as temporary, until the probationary period was over.**

* This is a personal, not a legal, opinion, and is no substitute for competent (or even mildly incompetent) legal advice. Ask your lawyer. If your lawyer tells you differently, follow your lawyer's advice. Liability for a telecommuting project may be considerable; get a lawyer involved if you have any questions.

Who Pays for What?

Auro quaeque ianua panditur.*

Latin Proverb

The most concrete topic to sort out before embarking on any telecommuting sojourn is the pecuniary: Who foots the bill for what, and how do those bills get paid?

Telemployee with company PC (boss's view)

You might think that the answers are obvious, but they're not. I found over and over again that telemployees' expectations aren't the same as telebosses'. It's a reflection of how unaccustomed we all are to telecommuting.

The company's responsibility Few would dispute that the company should pay for any equipment specifically required by the job. (Although, as noted earlier, there are still a few companies that insist on employees footing the bill for a PC.) In addition to PCs and peripherals, that category will normally include special telephones or phone headsets, software, maintenance contracts, and repair costs. It should also include the costs of any long-distance telephone calls. All of that is pretty much standard nowadays.

You shouldn't lose any of your current benefits, of course.

Telemployee with company PC (actual picture)

* Any door is opened by means of gold.

On the other hand, you will probably be stuck with any additional electric **On your tab**
bills (which can be considerable, if you live in a warm climate and run the AC all
the time). You'll probably have to provide the physical space for your office at no
cost to the company, and most likely you'll be responsible for the desk, chair,
"normal" telephone, and other accoutrements of a typical office.

**As noted in Chapter 2, some of that stuff can get *expensive*. More than a few
telecommuting arrangements have floundered because of up-front expenses
(at least one case ended up in court because of it!), so make sure you
understand what you're getting into before you commit to telecommuting.
Sure, you'll be saving money on gas and the car and wear-and-tear on your
business wardrobe. But those savings accrue over time. These expenses hit
you on day one. Beware!**

The company may or may not foot the bill to install extra telephone lines, or **Up in the air**
the monthly charges that go with them. It may or may not pay for extra telephone
company goodies like custom ringing, call waiting, caller ID, and the like. There's
often some back-and-forth on who pays for a fax machine, if one is in the cards.

If you live a long distance from the central office (say, far enough away that
you have to fly), you may or may not be reimbursed for travel to the central office.

Similarly, the company may pay for office supplies—paper, pens, and the like—
or they may simply let you raid the office supply cabinet from time to time, leaving it
up to you to buy the more exotic stuff.

Chances are good that your new telemployee office will require additional **Insurance**
insurance. Who needs the insurance? Who pays for it? Those are complex questions.

On the one hand, your company will probably want to insure any equipment
they own, even if the equipment is located in your home office. They may do that
in one of three ways: They can require you to carry enough homeowner's insurance to cover their equipment; they can add a "rider" to their own insurance
policy, covering equipment in employees' homes; or they can ignore the whole
issue and hope that it never comes up. In my experience, the latter is by far the
most common.

Being the conscientious employee that you are, you'll want to resolve the **Taking the
problem before it occurs. Pick up the phone and call your company's Loss Preven- insurance bull
tion department (or whoever deals with property insurance). Explain to them that by the horns**
you're about to start telecommuting, and you'll have $5,000 worth of company
equipment at your home. Then say, "Okay. My house burns down. Does the
company's insurance cover it?" Chances are good the answer you'll get is, "I
dunno, nobody ever asked."

If the company says their insurance covers that kind of loss, make a note of
who you talked to, and when, and keep that note in a safe place.

If the company says their insurance doesn't cover that kind of loss, check with your homeowner's policy agent. Pose the same question, and see if your insurance would cover the loss. Chances are good it doesn't; that'll mean you need extra insurance (a "rider") to cover the company equipment. If that's the case, find out how much it will cost, and tell your boss about it. *Before* you start telecommuting. You may be able to put it on an expense account.

Remember, chances are very good your boss has no idea about what's covered and what isn't—or possibly that there's even reason to be concerned.

Worker's comp

Medical insurance is an entirely different can of worms. Worker's comp — for which the company pays premiums to provide insurance for possible on-the-job injuries—is still a big question mark. If you're running to pick up a call from your boss and trip on your home office's rug, will worker's comp pay your medical bills? Probably. If you're surfing the Web at midnight on Saturday and spill hot coffee over yourself, are you covered? Probably not. What if you take a break while working on a Tuesday morning, go out to get the paper, and slip on the ice? Nobody knows!

Life on the bleeding edge.

One last word of warning. Check before you start telecommuting to make sure your salary won't spontaneously self-destruct. Some companies automatically apply "cost of living adjustments" to employees who live away from the central office. For example, your company may pay you $5,000 a month right now, since you live in an exorbitantly high-cost part of the country like, say, San Jose. If you move to, oh, Biloxi, Mississippi, the company may "adjust" your compensation down to $4,500 a month, simply because (they say) living expenses in Biloxi are lower than in San Jose.

Historically, some companies have made that kind of adjustment to stick it to employees who work at remote plants, or to help salespeople who get posted to very expensive parts of the country. If your company has any policies along those lines, find somebody in a position of authority and get a *written* commitment that your compensation won't change. Don't trust a casual reading of the policy from your friend in Accounting: Just because the policy wasn't written to help or to shaft telecommuters doesn't mean it won't be applied that way!* Your boss might not even be aware of the policy. Go talk to the folks in Human Resources or Compensation.

---

* Did you understand that? Triple negatives are so much fun. Here it is in plain English: Say Joe Shmuck gets promoted and transferred from the San Jose central office to the Asbestos Recycling plant in Biloxi. Your company may zap ol' Joe with a cost of living adjustment, so his paycheck every month in Biloxi is actually smaller than it was in San Jose. Now say you start telecommuting from the San Jose central office. It works out so well that after a while your boss says you can move anywhere you like. You pick . . . Biloxi. What happens to your paycheck? The answer may surprise you.

What If You're Forced to Telecommute?

> Employers are finding that, unlike the voluntary part-time telecommuting programs of the past, plans forcing whole divisions into mobile offices can cause morale problems—and may even provoke valued employees to quit. Surrounded day and night by the high-tech tools of their trade, many workers burn out. And while short-term savings are significant, no one knows how the mobile office will affect long-term productivity.
>
> *The Wall Street Journal*
> August 17, 1994

For years, telecommuting advocates have been telling the big corporations that they should institute telecommuting programs because they save money. Forget happier employees. Forget higher productivity. Forget air pollution and ride-sharing regulations, reduced impact on the environment, all the "green" arguments. For years the advocates said telecommuting simply saves money—big bucks, not chicken feed. For years, the big corporations scoffed.

Lies, damn lies, and cost projections

Guess what? The advocates were right.

Pouring the foundation for that new central office

When the principles of telecommuting are applied *en masse*, the savings can be tremendous. Office space can be reduced in great chunks: Where four desks were necessary for four employees yesterday, today one shared desk may do. Cubicles can be smaller because the typical tenant won't be spending eight to ten hours a day within its confines. Low-cost or no-cost conference calls replace $25-per-square-foot conference rooms. Parking needs are decimated. Utilities. Furniture. Maintenance. Security. Lots and lots and lots of bucks.

Real savings Consider. IBM decided to convert its sales and marketing staff at the Denver Tech Center, so telecommuting was the norm, not the exception. According to published reports, 80 percent of the sales staff now telecommutes. IBM reduced its office space requirement in the Tech Center from seven floors to three, and the company is saving $1 million a year.

Contrarian view What you won't read in the published reports is that IBM "saved" some of that money by shifting office expenses from the company to its employees—not necessarily a bad tradeoff, mind you, but a fact that is all too often overlooked in the press. Conversion to telecommuting is not a zero-cost game.

Contra-contrarian view On the third hand, telemployees—even 'tho they're beset with additional home office expenses—make out like bandits in the long run. It wouldn't be unusual for an IBM Tech Center telemployee to save a thousand bucks a year or more on transportation costs (an ultraconservative estimate of 20 miles each way to work and back, 15 cents a mile, 200 work days a year, comes to $1,200); another grand or so on clothes, food, and the like; and more than an hour of time every work day. (I'll work through a financial example later in this chapter.) When it comes to dollars and sense, just about everybody wins.

What to do if your company decides it's going to save a bundle by converting everybody—little ol' you included—to telecommuting, and you don't want to? Alas, there's no easy answer. Based on conversations with a few "involuntary converts" (all of whom started out very skeptical, and ended up pleased with the change), I would suggest trying these steps.

First, make sure that you look at the situation as objectively as possible. Many people assume (and some rightfully so!) that *any* move made by their company is designed to boost profits, employees be damned. Converting to telecommuting may well be in the company's best interests—but that doesn't necessarily mean it's inimical to your own best interests, as well. In many cases, the move to telecommuting is a win-win situation for employees and companies; often, the only losers are managers who can't adapt.

Second, if you're willing to concede that a switch to telecommuting may be good for you—or at the very least that it isn't a heinous management plot to profit from the sacrifices of the oppressed proletariat—try to figure out the financial implications to you and your family. To help you, I've created Figure 5.1, the only worksheet in this book. The "Example" numbers in that figure are from a friend of mine. Put your own numbers in the "Estimate" column. Then use the other Estimate columns to push the numbers around a bit. The result may surprise you.

If you feel you're being shafted financially in the short term (that is, if your one-time expenses on the worksheet look pretty daunting), talk to your supervisor about it. Show her how the numbers on the worksheet stack up. Some companies will make funds available to first-time telecommuters, usually as a low- or no-interest loan, if relocation expenses constitute a hardship.

One-Time Expenses	Example	Estimate 1	Estimate 2	Estimate 3
1 Converting extra space to office	$750			
2 New computer equipment	$0			
3 New comm/phone equipment/installation	$600			
4 Other new equipment, furniture	$0			
5 Other one-time expenses	$0			
6 Total one-time expenses (Sum Lines 1–5)	$1,350			
New Monthly Expenses				
7 Additional insurance	$20			
8 Additional electricity	$10			
9 Additional phone	$15			
10 Other additional monthly expenses	$0			
11 Total additional monthly (Sum Lines 7–10)	$45			
New Monthly Savings				
12 Car (22 trips x 30 miles x $0.28/mile)	$185			
13 Clothes ($500/year)	$42			
14 Food (22 lunches x $4 saved)	$88			
15 Other monthly savings	$0			
16 Total monthly savings (Sum Lines 12–15)	$314			
17 Net monthly savings (Line 16 – Line 11)	$269			
18 Months to break-even (Line 6 ÷ Line 17)	5.01			
First year savings ((12 × Line 17) – Line 6)	$1,884			
Subsequent annual savings (12 × Line 17)	**$3,234**			

Figure 5.1 The only worksheet in this book

Finally, if you still don't like the idea of telecommuting, you should start some sort of formal complaint. Based on conversations I've had with involuntary converts, chances are very good you'll end up liking telecommuting—and, given the option, you should certainly consider trying it on a temporary basis—but there's no substitute for making your concerns known, right up front. At least your boss won't be able to come back six months later and say, "Gee, I didn't know Snardfarq had any problem with telecommuting."

Tax consequences   One last bit of icing on the financial cake. If your employer *requires* you to maintain an office in your home, many of the expenses associated with the office may be deductible. While there are some general guidelines in Chapter 8, if you find you're being involuntarily converted to telecommuting, a company attorney can (and should!) provide you with information about the tax consequences of the change. Not typical mealy-mouth legalese, mind you, but real advice: how much you can deduct, on which lines, using which forms. Pin 'em down before you start telecommuting. That's when you have the most leverage.

TELECOMMUTING'S ROCKY ROAD

I shoulda stayed at Microsoft.

Dee Jay
Street Fighter—The Movie, 1994

No doubt about it, embarking on a full-fledged telecommuting program is a scary undertaking. Spending a day at home every couple of weeks is one thing. Cutting the apron strings—where your physical presence in the office becomes unusual, even rare—adds an entire layer of pitfalls.

Bandwidth

bandwidth n. 1. Used by hackers in a generalization of its technical meaning as the volume of information per unit time that a computer, person, or transmission medium can handle. 2. Attention span. 3. On USENET, a measure of network capacity that is often wasted by people complaining about how items posted by others are a waste of bandwidth.

Eric Raymond, ed.
New Hacker's Dictionary, 1992

So many of the problems that confront telemployees can be traced back to this one root cause: a lack of bandwidth.

Another terrible misuse of a precise term   As you saw in the previous chapter, "bandwidth" is a technical term, used in the communications industry, with a mathematically precise definition. It's also a marvelous concept that (with a bit of liberal interpretation) goes a long way toward explaining what can go wrong with interpersonal interactions.

When you were a kid, did you ever make your own paper-cup telephones? Remember punching a hole in the bottom of a couple of cups, and tying a piece of string between them? The fancy kind used buttons to hold the ends of the string in place. Caller ID was comparatively straightforward—"Is that you, Kathy?"—and call waiting didn't cost extra. You remember.

A high bandwidth boss, with homing device

Paper-cup telephones are (you waited a couple of decades to learn this) low bandwidth. What goes in one end doesn't bear a whole lot of resemblance to what comes out the other, because the string doesn't transmit the sound very well: Much of what goes in gets "dropped out."

Let's take a look at different levels of communicating, from high to low bandwidth, and see how they apply to the telemployee.

At the high end of the bandwidth spectrum, a conversation with someone you know and interact with regularly can take place in a kind of communication shorthand: Sentence fragments may evoke entire concepts; portions of thoughts flesh themselves out without enumeration; you'll probably end up finishing each others' sentences. **Brain dumps**

If you're a design engineer, you might say to one of your codesigners, "We can't put the tab there because the center of gravity" and your buddy picks up, ". . . Shifts too far down," and a conversation that would take half an hour with a new team member becomes crystal-clear in a few seconds. If you're in sales, you might say to your boss, "We could try a joint proposal, but they might pull a Patterson . . ." and the boss would understand, ". . . and dump it back in our laps."

I call that kind of cortex-to-cortex link a brain dump, and it's pretty common with teams of propeller heads* in high-tech industries.

Communication theorists talk about "verbal" and "non-verbal" exchanges. If you can see the person you're talking to, the theory goes, you pick up visual cues that greatly enhance your ability to communicate. That's fine as far as it goes, but it overlooks this really intense form of communication.

If you've ever experienced that "brain dump" kind of high-bandwidth exchange, you know that it goes way beyond traditional nonverbal communication. There's

* A term of respect, not derision.

no need to see the other person; dumps can (and often do) take place over the telephone. It's more like a direct brain-to-brain link that bypasses the normal, uh, channels. And it never seems to happen in groups—I've only seen brain dumps take place one-on-one.

How does that affect you, as a telemployee? It's a warning sign. Several people have told me that the first sign they had of an impending screw-up in a project came when they could no longer brain dump with their old buddies at the central office. Somebody on the phone says, "Well, we could do that, but how would you get a PropAgentAccept callback?" and you don't have the slightest idea what a "PropAgentAccept callback" *is.*

Should you discover that the old brain-dump connections are weakening, I'd recommend that you finagle an immediate on-site review, with the whole group present, to bring yourself back up to speed. Team interactions can deteriorate quickly; the loss of high-bandwidth interpersonal communication should wave a red flag in front of you.

Talk, talk, talk   Climbing out of the stratosphere, the most common type of high-bandwidth communication is simply talking face-to-face, whether individually or in small groups. Telecommuters who spend long stretches of time away from the home office should plan on spending a fair amount of time back in the office simply talking. BSing. Shooting the breeze. Gabbing not only helps fill in the prodigal employee on what was happening during his absence, it helps reestablish ties, and makes future communication easier.

Based on what I've seen, gabbing—*productive* gabbing—over the phone helps, but isn't nearly as productive as the face-to-face kind. I'm not sure why, aside from the bandwidth limitation (or "non-verbal communication," if you prefer). Telecommuters who only get to the central office once or twice a year, in particular, need to refresh their face-to-face contacts, and spend quite a bit of time and effort doing it, or they start feeling alienated. Remote.

Video over the   As explained in the previous chapter, videoconferencing—the next-highest-
wires   bandwidth form of interaction—still has a long way to go. Widespread availability of full-motion video will help, but until the equipment becomes ubiquitous, and ancillary software such as whiteboard systems become more robust, telemployees should think of videoconferencing as a slight improvement over telephone, and not much more.

Phone   The telephone is not a high-bandwidth device, and telemployees have to learn quickly to take that into account in their conversations. Second-guessing the nuances of a phone conversation can sour your relationships with coworkers faster than a misrouted salary list. It's far too easy to read something into a telephone conversation.

Your boss may deliver a minor rebuke in person, but his constant smile and affable manner let you know that it's not a big deal. The same conversation over the phone, *sans* that smile and the hearty slap on the back, could be interpreted as something devastating.

Beware.

By far the lowest-bandwidth form of communication, e-mail (and its elder step-sister, fax) has to be the most convenient. Among the high tech telemployees I've talked to, the ones who made the easiest transition to telecommuting come from companies with entrenched traditions of e-mail. It's easy to see why. An e-mail message can come from down the hall or around the world, and it matters not one whit. Responding to e-mail is "asynchronous"—you read your mail when you're ready, instead of putting everything aside to talk to a coworker who drops by— and thus more in tune with long-distance communication.

Electronic mail

Most of all, it beats the hell out of telephone tag.

Many citizens of the cyburbs have advised me that the correlation between e-mail and easy (at least easi*er*) telecommuting is so strong that it would behoove budding telemployees to champion the use of e-mail in their organizations. Above all, make sure that your boss is tied in and checks her e-mail regularly. Keep the lines of communication open by sending e-mail frequently to your friends and coworkers.

There's an art to e-mail, just as there's an art to putting words on paper. Written communication is very different from telephone communication, and it takes time to get the hang of it—much less develop some proficiency. Don't be dismayed if your e-mail messages are misinterpreted. It happens to all of us. Over time, you'll get better at it.

E-Etiquette

While ambiguity and misinterpretation are inevitable, two other e-mail sins are not: flaming and pestering.

A "flame," as you probably know, is an e-mail message that tears the throat out of the recipient. People who would never dream of verbally assaulting someone else will get so ticked off, they'll compose and then fire off a vicious message in seconds—and then come back to their senses. It's a child of the medium: Flame phone calls don't pack the same punch, and face-to-face flames carry the threat of physical violence. E-mail flames take place long distance, usually between people who have never met, and often out in the open. I, personally, have posted two flames in my on-line life. And I've regretted both of them, deeply, years and years after sending them.

The traditional advice is to wait before sending a flame—wait a minute, or an hour, or a day. I don't know if that would work for most people, in most situations.

But it would certainly behoove you to consider the consequences of your act. Instant karma and all that. Even if the flame is in a private message, e-mail messages are the easiest things in the world to copy and pass along.

Thank you. No, thank YOU.

The second cardinal e-mail sin is pestering. It's rarely necessary to send a message saying, simply, "Thanks" to a posting you found on-line. Those who have been on-line long enough to be dishing out advice know that you appreciate it; hey, we started out that way, too! If you want to show your appreciation, rather than just saying, "Thanks," you might try answering another person's question. That's the nicest possible way of thanking those who have helped you. Corny, but true.

The cybernauts who say, "Nit!". . . er, "Thanks"—or otherwise fill the ether with sincere but nonessential niceties—aren't a real problem. God, I wish there were more of them! The ones who really get my goat are the guys (and they're usually *guys*) who send 500-line messages detailing their sister's boyfriend's experiences with a computer dealer's tech support line and how they would never buy anything from that lousy company again and how could you dare say anything nice about the dirty swine and what are *you* going to do about it? If you don't get a response to that kind of message, don't be too shocked!

The e-mail that I regret the most comes from very nice people who need help—but they don't realize that it would take half an hour or an hour to solve their problem. It's not really pestering: Many people (myself foremost among them!) don't realize that an easy question may not have an easy answer. Sad. If you ever ask for help on-line and get an answer like, "Sorry, but it would take quite a while to figure that one out," please don't feel snubbed. There's just so much your correspondents can do, only so many demands on their time that can be satisfied.

So much for Woody's One-Minute Netiquette and On-Line Facts of Life.*

Interlude: face on a voice

Most of the telecommuters I've interviewed insist that it's easier to talk with someone over the phone, or via e-mail, after they've met face-to-face: "putting a face to a voice" and all that. While it's certainly interesting to meet the people you talk with, and this opinion is definitely going to be unpopular in some circles, I'm not convinced that face-to-face meetings among all but the most critically wired-together teams are that beneficial.

Perhaps it's a question of changing expectations in an increasingly wired world. (Or maybe it's just me acting like a grizzled old hermit.) But when your primary form of contact with the outside business world is via phone, fax, or e-mail, over the years, the need for face-to-face interaction seems to diminish.

Over time you build mental images of your correspondents and long-distance friends, and even after meeting them, you'll find yourself thinking of them more in terms of the old images than the new reality.

* Soon to be a major motion picture starring the-musician-who-used-to-be-Prince as Woody, Tom Cruise as the e-mail vampire lestat@vlad.org, and Madonna as Ms. CyberManners.

Strange how unreal images can supplant physical reality—and a little sad, I suppose—but I see it happening more and more as folks like me spend larger amounts of time far from the madding crowd, nestled in their electronic cottages.*

Did McLuhan live in an e-cottage?

Outta Sight, Outta Mind

> Men are men; the best sometimes forget.
>
> Shakespeare
> *Othello*, 1604

Every single long-term telemployee I talked to complained about the outta sight, outta mind syndrome.

With some minor variations, the ailment goes like this. Jennifer T. Telemployee is working her butt off for the central office; everything's going pretty well. She's participating in the weekly phone conferences, staying in touch like she's supposed to, and the quality and quantity of work she's producing is outstanding. The boss loves it. Sure, her coworkers are still a bit skeptical about telecommuting, and there's still a little resentment showing through, but Jennifer churns out stuff so well that it's hard to fault her or the program.

The number-one complaint

One day Jennifer suddenly notices that a coworker, Marianne, is no longer participating in the project. Marianne hasn't said anything during the past few phone conferences, and she doesn't seem to be on any of the status reports. Curious, Jennifer shoots some e-mail to her boss, Lyle, asking what happened to Marianne.

Lyle writes back, "Oh. I thought you knew. Marianne just took over the Left-Handed Flipperhammer Project. She moved upstairs. They're still redecorating her new office, so she hasn't been on-line for a bit."

Jennifer goes ballistic. "HOW COULD YOU DO THAT?" she shouts back in an e-mail message worthy of an Internet Olympic Flamethrower. "I did my doctoral thesis on flipperhammers, and I've been using left-handed flipperhammers since I was four years old! Besides, I have seniority, ten times the experience that Marianne has, better evaluations, and my breath doesn't stink on Tuesdays. Jennifer."

Lyle's dumbfounded, of course. It isn't that he doesn't like Jennifer, or doesn't appreciate what she's done, or even that he felt Marianne was better for the job.

It'll happen to you, too.

* Marshall McLuhan cast the bandwidth issue in a slightly different way: "There is a basic principle that distinguishes a hot medium like radio from a cool one like the telephone, or a hot medium like the movie from a cool one like TV. A hot medium is one that extends one single sense in 'high definition.' High definition is the state of being well filled with data. A photograph is, visually, 'high definition.' A cartoon is low definition simply because very little visual information is provided." *Understanding Media*, 1964. If he had been a Telco engineer, McLuhan would've recognized that high bandwidth is hot.

Jennifer? Jennifer? Oh yes. Here we are.

He just plain *forgot*. On Tuesday, when the big boss asked Lyle to recommend somebody to lead the Left-Handed Flipperhammer team, he didn't even think of Jennifer. By Wednesday, it was ancient history.

There are a few tricks to keeping yourself "in play" around the office. Threatening to quit can do it, as long as you don't mind being taken up on the offer— and you don't threaten to quit so often that your boss wishes you'd just shut up and hand in your resignation. Here are a few other things that seem to work.

Make sure you get to the office often enough. If you live near the office, dropping by once a week just to shoot the breeze certainly isn't overkill. If you live far away, plan on getting to the office once a month at first, and then at least once every two (or at most three) months afterwards. Every time you drop in, make sure you have a chance to chat with the boss for a few minutes.

Figure out some sort of physical way to remind your boss constantly that you're part of the team. One telemployee I know had a poster-size print made of a photograph of her and the team. The photo featured her prominently in the foreground: You couldn't glance at the poster without noticing her. She then convinced her boss to tape the poster in the boss's office, where she would see it every time she glanced up from the desk.

Keep a constant dialog going via e-mail. Drop a message to your boss every day, even if it's something innocuous like the local weather report, or a quick "not much progress" progress report. Yeah, you'll be making a pain of yourself. But you'll also be reinforcing your presence.

Can I guarantee that any or all of those tips will work? Nope. It's the number-one problem, and it doesn't have an easy solution. Try being creative (have pizza delivered to the monthly meeting? get a coworker to put a "Jennifer says hi" note on the bulletin board? what about a singing telegram for a coworker's birthday?), and see what you can come up with.

Remember, you're competing with everything else that happens in your office for a tiny slice of your boss's mindshare.

Long-Distance Meetings

> We once thought that telecommuting might be the answer to everything from child care to traffic jams. But like so many things in our bottom-line era, telecommuting and the other office-saving measures are ending up being encouraged less by the social benefits than by the dollars they save. All the same, they represent a change-driven change made possible by the new technology, and a change that makes the traditional job a less and less meaningful concept.
>
> William Bridges
> *JobShift*, 1994

We telecommuters may be the change-driven tail that wags the corporate dog, but some things never change. Meetings place high on the immutable list. Bleccch.

Plus ça change

Welcome to the preliminary agenda planning session of the Committee to Reduce the Number of Hours Wasted in Meetings committee meeting.

Ever hear the one about the telemployee who popped into the central office for the regular weekly meeting, only to discover that it had been canceled? Hey, the boss stuck a note right next to the coffee machine. "Everybody" knew about it, right?

If you're a telemployee who physiocommutes into the central office for *any* regularly scheduled meetings, grab your appointment calendar right now, and put a big note before each of the meetings. "Call Snardfarq at the office and make sure the meeting's on." Something along those lines. Don't jump into the car and head for the central office until you're absolutely certain that your presence is needed . . . or at least anticipated.

Conducting meetings with remote participants (usually via conference call) is a real art. The telephone typically takes center stage, simply because phone conversations can only go one way: The person on the phone is either talking or listening. Unless they're carefully moderated, or highly disciplined, speakers can "step" all over each other. Overseas conference calls, where transmission time lag encourages "stepping," can quickly become unintelligible. If there's a good solution to the "stepping" problem, I don't know it.

But I have found two innovative solutions to other conference call meeting problems that bear repeating.

Many telecommuters complain that they just didn't hear what went on in teleconference meetings, particularly when more than a few people gather around the phone in the central office. One company solves that problem by imposing strict discipline on the person who sets up the meeting—essentially, the person who dials the phone. That person is responsible for writing up minutes of the meeting, and then distributing them via e-mail, shortly after the meeting takes place. The minutes have eliminated the old "I didn't know you said that" problem, and since they're distributed quickly, misunderstandings are quickly aired—if not resolved.

It's a classic bandwidth problem.

The second solution sounds a bit corny, but—my sources assure me—it works like a champ. One telemployee I know was forever being "nudged out" of conference call meetings. Since he wasn't physically present to wave his hands, raise his voice, or otherwise wedge himself into the conversations, other meeting participants walked right over him.

The solution? A sympathetic co-worker found a stuffed toy bear (rumor has it the teddy bear looks much like our tromped-upon telecommuter), and perched it on top of the conference phone, in the center of the meeting table. Now the bear does the talking. With something to "focus" on, other participants are prodded to remember there's somebody on the other end of the phone who wants to be heard. Interesting, eh?

Squeaky Wheel

The head of a dress-manufacturing firm in New York received the following telegram from his best on-the-road salesman:

```
RUEBEN SHULOVITZ,
273 WEST 48TH STREET,
NEW YORK, NEW YORK

BLIZZARD HAS HIT THIS AREA STOP COMPLETELY
SNOWED IN STOP ALL FLIGHTS CANCELED STOP
ADVISE STOP

JEFF ROGOVSKY,
HOTEL MASON,
PIERRE, SOUTH DAKOTA
```

Rueben Shulovitz did not waste a minute before replying:

```
J. ROGOVSKY,
HOTEL MASON,
PIERRE, SOUTH DAKOTA

STOP KVETCHING STOP START VACATION AT
ONCE STOP

R. SHULOVITZ
```

Leo Rosten
The Joys of Yinglish, 1989

It's a sad-but-true fact that telemployees have to be more vocal than their physiocommuting brethren. Shrinking violets don't last long.

A good manager will be able to tell by looking at you if you're displeased with the way things are going. When the manager can't *see* you, though, it's up to you to sound off, loud and clear.

To see is to understand.

> **Something bugging you? Speak up! Your manager can't tell what you're thinking. When you work away from the office, the onus is entirely on you to bring your problems up in a civilized, rational way—and the blame is yours, too, should your secret grievance go unaddressed.**

Alternative Career Tracks

> I long to accomplish a great and noble task, but it is my chief duty to accomplish humble tasks as though they were great and noble. The world is moved along, not only by the mighty shoves of its heroes, but also by the aggregate of the tiny pushes of each honest worker.
>
> Helen Keller

There's a limit. If you sneak a peek at Chapter 6, the one for Telebosses, you'll discover—and it should come as no surprise—that some jobs just aren't cut out for telecommuters, and the higher you rise in an organization, the less amenable your job will be to telecommuting.* It's a bitter truth, but one each telemployee has to face sooner or later.

Up to a certain point, in certain fields, telemployees can do everything their office-bound coworkers can do. Indeed, telecommuters can get *more* done than the average physiocommuter, and the quality of their work is often higher, as well. Front-line workers, project leaders, development team members, sales staff, writers, analysts, and many others are more effective when they telecommute a few days a week.

The cyberglass ceiling When you rise to some vaguely definable level in a corporate hierarchy—say, the level above project leader, or possibly second-line management—your physical presence becomes paramount. An occasional telecommuting day can help you deal with mountains of paperwork, sure, but by and large you have to haul your carcass to the office every day.

Some companies (including many high tech companies) offer "technical" or "alternative" career tracks: Employees can be promoted and rewarded without being forced to move into management positions. Often, the technical track isn't as lucrative as the managerial track—but then again, good techies don't necessarily make good managers, ya know?

 If you find yourself bumping up against the cyberglass ceiling, and you want to keep on telecommuting, see if your company would consider setting up an "alternative" track. You could hold onto a good job. And your company could hold onto a good telemployee.

---

* Yes, there are exceptions. We'll talk about one class of exceptions in Chapter 10, which discusses Virtual Corporations.

ROAD WARRIOR

> As the Spanish proverb says, "He, who would bring home the wealth of the Indies, must carry the wealth of the Indies with him," so it is in traveling, a man must carry knowledge with him if he would bring home knowledge.
>
> Samuel Johnson
> *Boswell's Life*, 1783

Working on the road can be enormously frustrating. In addition to all the "normal" stuff that can go wrong, there are layers and layers of obscure gremlins that can work in concert to drive you absolutely nuts.

Born to schlep

This section contains the very best of what I've learned in talking to dozens of travelers who wouldn't consider leaving home without their PCs. I make no pretense of completeness: There are enough good Road Warrior tips floating around the ether to fill another book this size. With a bit of luck, though, I'll hit a couple of ideas you hadn't heard before, and maybe save you an hour or two of extreme anguish while you're far away from home.

Top o' the tips

> I figure that people who commute from a fixed office have it real easy!
>
> Rick

Many members of the bicoastal brigade helped with their tips, but I particularly wanted to thank Rick at Aerostar, for his help on international connections. I'm told that Rick's passport weighs as much as a Clavell novel. His advice was priceless.

Portable Physical Security

> When I point out that implementing a really useful mobile-user program means exposing critical company information—probably including critical competitive information—to a substantial risk of loss or theft, I get very physical reactions. There's a lot of clearing of throats. A little coughing. . . Oh, no, that won't happen. Our people are a lot more careful than that . . .
>
> Jim Seymour
> *PC Week, 9/19/94*

The three aw-gee's If you're using a portable PC that contains sensitive company information, you have three broad security concerns:

- How to minimize the chances the PC will be stolen?

- If the portable is lost or stolen, how do you increase your chances of getting it back, more or less intact?

- If the portable is lost or stolen, how do you keep that sensitive information from falling into your competitors' hands?

Minimize chances it's stolen. In addition to all the obvious methods for staying attached to your portable (never stick it in checked luggage; don't leave it sitting on a table while you grab a cup of coffee; don't walk it through Central Park at night; hey, your Mom told you about all these things, didn't she?), there's one tip *I* overlook all the time.

Windows everywhere, street interpretation

Most hotels will let you check your portable at reception when you're headed out for a bit. While it's true that behind-the-desk security isn't absolute, in general it's much better than what little security you'll receive by leaving the portable in your room.

Once in a blue moon your portable will get misplaced, and the person who finds it will be honest enough to want to return it to you—if they can only figure out how!

Can you get it back?

For just such a situation, rare as it may be, you'll probably want to mark your portable with your name, address, and phone number. A business card taped securely on the outside of the case (don't cover the air circulation holes!) will suffice—and a Marks-A-Lot will do well, too. Some people write a little program to flash their name and phone number on the screen when the computer boots. Fair enough.

Far more difficult, though, is to build something into your portable that would convince a thief (or a fence) to return it.

I've known lots of people who have had their portable stolen. And I've yet to hear of one single person who has recovered their stolen PC because of a security device. Password protection doesn't deter theft—and, once stolen, it certainly doesn't encourage a PC's return. Sticking your business card inside the PC sounds like a good idea, but I've never seen it lead to a returned PC. (And if you put your business card inside your PC, make damned sure you stick it someplace that's cool!)

All in all, I don't know of any sure-fire deterrent to a determined thief, and, once the PC has been stolen, I don't know of any effective inducement for the PC's safe return. Bummer.

But wait. It gets worse.

Assuming your portable PC is stolen, and your arch-enemies retrieve it, what can you do to keep them from getting at all that sensitive data? Precious little, it turns out.

Keep sensitive data from prying eyes.

Some companies use their applications' password capabilities to encrypt sensitive documents and spreadsheets: Word for Windows and Excel for Windows, for example, both have sophisticated password protection capabilities. What most companies don't realize is that there are commercially available products for "cracking" that password protection. And they work. Very well. For less than $100, your competitor can "crack" and look at your on-disk bid package or price information.

What's the solution? Don't lose your portable!

On a somewhat brighter note, I've found one security procedure that works pretty well. Keep your sensitive information on diskette (or PC-card removable drive), and guard the diskette as you would your passport. You have to be careful to move sensitive files from your hard drive to your floppy (and even nuke the remnants of the hard drive files—using something like Norton File Delete—if you're paranoid), but a diskette is much easier to keep secure.

Power Conservation

> We call that fire of the black thunder-cloud electricity, and lecture
> learnedly about it, and grind the like of it out of glass and silk: but *what* is
> it? What made it? Whence comes it? Whither goes it?
>
> Thomas Carlyle
> *Heroes and Hero-Worship*, 1841

Retro Ben Franklin   Man, have there been times when I wished I could lasso a little bit of that black thunder-cloud electricity! I'm at 30,000 feet. That battery-low light starts to flicker. Down below the lightning bolts bounce back and forth—Vulcan doin' the gangsta rap. And all I need is a kite, and a string . . .

Portable battery technology is getting better, or so I've been told. Two things I've learned: Don't believe the battery "ratings" the laptop manufacturers publish (where do they get those numbers anyway?); and, don't believe the "power level" meters, no matter what the reviews say. They lie.

When embarking on any trip, I always carry an extra set of freshly charged batteries. Or two. Well, at least I try. The extra set of batteries not only protects me from the inevitable run-down just as I'm hitting my stride mid-air. It also protects me from the unforeseen: airport delays; mischarged primary batteries; once I even forgot to take my charger, and the extra pair of batteries gave me all the power I was gonna get.

And of course it goes without saying that you've looked into all the power conservation software that ships with your portable, you've installed it, and use it religiously. Of course.

Meanwhile, Back at the Ranch

> Be not long away from home.
>
> Homer
> *Odyssey*, ca. 800 BC

Leave the driving to them.   Many road warriors prefer to use the big national and international services for staying in touch while on the road—CompuServe, America Online, MCI Mail, and the like. There's much to be said for the convenience of local dialing from most major metro areas and the quality of well-maintained commercial connections.

But if you find yourself dialing back into the server at the central office fairly frequently, there are two tips I've found that may save your tail some cold winter's night.

There's nothing (well, almost nothing) worse than dialing into your office server in the middle of the night, only to discover that the server is down. If you were sitting in the office, you'd simply run over to the server, flip the power off, wait a minute, then flip it back on again. But your server is in Hoboken and you're in Hong Kong, and the best you can do is call ol' Netrovsky, your network administrator, have him jump out of bed, drive to the office, and do the power off/on shuffle for you. Netrovsky will get you for that. I promise.

C. N. E. Netrovsky, before the TOPS

If you were smart, you'd buy something called a Tone Operated Power Switch. Plug the TOPS into the wall, plug your server into the TOPS, attach a phone line, and *viola*! instant Netrovsky. You can call the TOPS, push 1 to turn the server off, wait a bit, then press 2 and the server powers back up. You can even program in a security code. Fingers never leave the hands.

TOPS systems are available for $600 to $800 from Black Box Corporation, (see Appendix B). APC has a similar device, called a "Call-UPS," that works with their UPS power supplies. At $179, it may pay for the UPS, all by itself. Oh. You can plug anything into them—they aren't limited to computers. Neat, huh?

Consider making at least one access phone number to the central office network a toll-free number (an 800 number in the United States; whatever they may be called in your country). Sometimes dialing a toll-free number is much simpler than dialing long distance (I'll show you an example momentarily). It also makes expense report accounting all the simpler. The additional cost is minimal; call your favorite long-distance carrier for a quote.

Damn the PBX!

> He would answer to "Hi!" or to any loud cry
> Such as "Fry me!" or "Fritter my wig!"
>
> Lewis Carroll
> *The Hunting of the Snark,* 1876

Watch what you're pluggin'!

I believe it was Bill Machrone who first called attention to this problem, in the pages of *PC Week.* It seems that Bill was in an office somewhere, when he decided to plug his portable's modem into a phone line. It was a regular, ol' everyday modem, with a regular ol' everyday plug that fit just fine into one of the office's regular ol' everyday phone jacks.

Except this phone jack was no ordinary phone jack, no sirreeee. It was attached to a PBX—a most unfriendly PBX, mind you—that sent about a zillion volts of electricity through his modem. Fried the sucker good. Frittered its wig.

It's by design.

What came as a revelation to me is that some PBX systems, ones that use normal RJ-11 telephone jacks, are actually *designed* to work at high amperage. While the levels are tiny compared to, say, a light bulb, they're still more than sufficient to knock out sensitive electronics—including a modem.

IBM to the rescue. Big Blue makes a little probe called a "Modem Saver" that looks like a rectangular pen with a tiny elephant nose, ending in a standard RJ-11 plug. Stick the plug in any suspect jack, and one of three LEDs on the pen will tell you if the line is normal, if it has reversed polarity (which is supposed to cause problems with faster modems), or if the line is running at more than 90 milliamps of current—considered to be the fry point for very delicate electronics, like a modem. Everything's clearly marked and easy to understand. A most impressive piece of equipment.

Best of all, it's cheap—under $30—and it's easy to get. Simply call IBM's order line (voice 800-388-7080, fax 800-766-6545, outside the United States contact your local IBM office) and ask for part 73G5395. They'll set you up as an official IBM customer (ooooh, what a tingly feeling!) and bill your credit card.

What if you find yourself in an unfamiliar office, and you forgot your IBM 73G5395? Go look for the fax machine. Ah, but that's another story. . . .

Pluggin' In Hotels

> It used to be a good hotel, but that proves nothing—
> I used to be a good boy.
>
> Samuel Clemens
> *Alta Californian,* April 19, 1867

Hotels offer their own, uh, quaint charm. While it's true that many hotels have (finally!) rewired their rooms to accommodate the portable lifestyle, far too many are still in the telecommuting dark ages.

Welcome to the Hotel California.

No matter where you are, from the shores of Papeete to the jungles of Mae Sot, there's a fax machine. When all else fails, that's where you should go. If a fax machine can use that telephone line, then by gum, your modem can too.

The fax of last resort

Don't worry if you don't speak the language. Simply walk up to the person in charge of the fax machine, point at your modem, and say, "Windows modem." Those are universal words. (Windows now comes in 20-plus languages, including two *separate* versions for Bahasa Malaysia and Bahasa Indonesia. The only terms that may be more widely understood on the planet are "taxi," "visa," "rock 'n roll," and "OK." No bull.) You may need a screwdriver and a bit of wire, but you should be on-line in almost no time.

The modem-on-a-fax-line trick isn't limited to third-world countries.

If you're dialing from a hotel inside the United States, and can't get at the phone jack in your room, you may be able to persuade the powers-that-be at the front desk to let you use the fax line during some off hour. That's when having an 800 number to access the central office network really comes in handy: It may be the trump card that lets you talk 'em into letting you use the line.

What, you're staying some place that doesn't have one of them thar new-fangled fax machines? Or the front desk insists the fax machine is all locked up until tomorrow morning? Well, it's possible that the guy at the front desk is married to his first cousin, and their son owns the place—in which case you should watch out for the shotgun sitting immediately underneath the TV on the front desk—but you still have a chance of getting connected.

Time to get devious

They take plastic, don't they? Do they have one of those swipe-through credit card readers? Bingo. Those credit card readers always have a standard phone line attached to them, and as long as they aren't running a bunch of cards through, you should be able to borrow the line for a bit. Just tell 'em that your Uncle Buford said it would be okay.

More Modem Madness

> I love to sail on forbidden seas,
> and land on barbarous coasts.
>
> Herman Melville
> *Moby Dick*, 1851

Just a few more modem tips, if you will indulge me, and then we'll move on to other Road Warrior topics.

What can go wrong

Most places in the United States and Canada, many places in Europe and Japan, and (at most) one or two places in Africa, the Middle and Far East have excellent phone service. Even in those places blessed with the highest line quality, the time will come when you get a dial tone, make the connection, and . . . your communications run at a snail's pace. Downloading a 1K e-mail message can take more than a minute. Transferring a 100K file can take longer than jumping on a plane and hand-delivering the disks. You know the tune.

Almost always, the cause is a lousy phone connection. You may think that your only option is to sit there and fume, when in fact, there are three tricks you might try.

Hang up and redial. Just because this line is a bad one doesn't necessarily mean that the next line will be bad, too. As you probably know, long-distance calls can be routed all over the place. Perhaps the next call to go through will be routed through a land line in cold, quiet Nova Scotia, instead of a tin can on Fifth Avenue.

Tried redialing a few times and it doesn't get any better? Then try dialing later, preferably when the long-distance rates trail off. Much phone line noise is "cross channel" — meaning that vestiges of Uncle Joey's voice yelling over the phone to Aunt Millie may be appearing as data bits in your file transfer. Minimize cross-talk by using the phone when humans use it least — which almost always coincides with a decrease in long-distance fares.

If calling at night doesn't help, try changing your long-distance carrier. If you aren't already dialing direct from your room, go ahead and do it. Sure, the hotel will sock you with an outrageous surcharge, but that's what expense accounts are for, eh? While you're thinking about it, you might want to sign up for

several long-distance carriers right now, and carry their access numbers with you. Start with your usual carrier, but if you get a lousy line, switch to a different carrier.

Finally, if you're dialing from outside the United States, the line may be fine, you may hear a dial tone, yet your modem may just sit there and look at you, with nary a blink in its red LED eye.

Your modem may be programmed to wait for a dial tone—but if the dial tone your modem hears isn't the standard U. S. dial tone, it may not be smart enough to proceed. The solution? Drag out your owner's manual. Usually there's an "AT" command that will disable dial-tone sensing, or some other setting you can make to instruct the modem to not wait for Godot, er, the dial tone that never appears.

> VLADIMIR: Well? Shall we go?
> ESTRAGON: Yes, let's go.
>
> [They do not move.]
> [Curtain]

Tools O' the Trade

> But lo! men have become the tools of their tools.
>
> Henry David Thoreau
> *Walden*, 1854

No doubt you've already made a half-dozen trips to Radio Shack and assembled an impressive set of traveling accessories: phone line splitters; small screwdrivers; jacks and wires with little alligator clips, needle-nose pliers, and tweezers; a single-edged razor blade and electrical tape; maybe even a *<shudder>* acoustic coupler, to drive the modem straight from a telephone handset.   **The basics**

You probably already know all about the vagaries of hooking into unfriendly phone systems, but here's a quick run-down.

Phone line splitters are handy because they turn one line into two: Plug one into the wall, and where there was one RJ-11 jack, suddenly there are two. Since few hotel rooms have two or more phone jacks, and since you're likely to want to keep a telephone plugged in, the splitter is a necessity. Just make sure you check the line with an IBM Modem Saver (see earlier) before plugging in your fancy modem.   **Beginner's course**

Far too many rooms still don't have *any* accessible RJ-11 phone jacks. That's where the screwdrivers come in (but, please, if you have to strip the wires in your hotel room outlet, make sure you've exhausted all possibilities with the front desk first—and if you can, leave things so the next Road Warrior will be able to tap into the lines easily). Sometimes you can unscrew the plastic cover on the wall; sometimes you actually have to unscrew the base of the room phone. The razor blade can come in handy if you need to strip insulation off the end of an exposed wire. Be careful, work slowly, don't pull the wire out of its connector, and be particularly cautious to avoid slicing the wire in half. Once you have the ends exposed, experiment with your alligator clips and the Modem Saver until you get a clear line. If there's any chance of the wires shorting out, be sure to wrap them with electrical tape before sealing up the unit.

Cool. Now it's time for the advanced course.

- Take a long telephone extension cord, with a couple of double-female connectors, so (if you're lucky enough to stay in a room with standard phone jacks) you can put the room's phone where *you* want it. The housekeeping staff may have a cow, but the increased convenience for you is worth almost any degree of ruffled feathers.

- Take a second extension cord with connectors, so you can put your portable anywhere in the room, or even drag it around while you're on-line. It isn't quite as nice as having a cellular modem, but it'll do until the technology catches up.

- When worse comes to worst and you find yourself monkeying around with the wiring inside the wall, use insulated alligator clips whenever you can. (Insulated clips have rubber wraps around the "alligator" part of the clip.) Working in tight spaces is never easy, and accidentally shorting out the phone line may get you in all sorts of hot water.

- Clean up after yourself. While there isn't enough current going in most phone lines to create a fire hazard, you can really zap out one of the older phone systems by leaving junk in a junction box that may some day short the wrong wires. *All I need to know about Phone Phreaking I learned in Kindergarten, eh?*

Let 'em eat cake, says I.   Yes, I've heard the screams of hotel proprietors who get all hot under the collar when you start manually tapping into the rooms' phone lines. Bah. I have no sympathy for 'em. Every hotel room that's fancy enough to have a working telephone is fancy enough to have an accessible jack. And the ones that are saddled with ancient PBX systems still have enough money to put big, day-glo stickers on all their phones saying, "We have modem jacks at the front desk. Come on down."

If they make you hook up down in the lobby, the *least* they can do is provide coffee and doughnuts. You can tell 'em Woody said so.

On the Road With Woody Ctrl+Alt

> Of all God's creatures there is only one that cannot be made the slave of the lash. That one is the cat. If man could be crossed with the cat it would improve man, but it would deteriorate the cat.
>
> Samuel Clemens
> *Mark Twain's Notebook,* 1884

If there's one thing that will make me the slave of the lash, it's business travel. I hate it. But sometimes duty calls. . . .

Anyway, let me round out the Road Warrior discussion with two more tips that you may not have considered.

Have you ever noticed how hotel rooms usually have just one usable power plug—and it's typically behind the 200-pound dresser? Fortunately, most rooms *have* to have an accessible plug, for housekeeping's vacuum cleaner.

Consider taking a short extension cord with four or more three-prong outlets at the end. A traditional "power strip," the kind you can buy for ten bucks in any hardware store, works just fine. The plug on a power strip is small enough to fit into any nook or cranny that can accommodate a vacuum cleaner plug. And the outlets on the end will provide more than enough room to keep a couple of rechargers going concurrently, with your portable plugged in, too.

Finally, a note on printers. Even though portable printers have come way down in both price and size, the quality still isn't all that great, and they're a general pain in the neck. Why bother?

Almost any hotel you'll be staying at will have a computer printer that's a local phone call away. It's called a "fax machine." If you're staying at a good hotel, you may be lucky enough to have local-call access to a plain paper fax machine, which will (arguably) produce print as good as any portable printer on the market.

Remember Rick from Aerostar? He swears that he spent a long day negotiating a big contract in one of his far-flung locations, got back to his room, made the changes on his portable, and then faxed himself the final contract that night. The next morning, final contract in hand, he closed the deal. For several million bucks.

Hey, if it's good enough for Rick, it's good enough for me.

Chill

> Travel teaches toleration.
>
> Benjamin Disraeli
> *Contarini Fleming*, 1832

On-line addiction There's some sort of crazy psychological compulsion for folks traveling away from the office that makes them insist on logging in every day. Maybe it's a fear that they'll fall out of touch. Maybe it's the loss of the usual office camaraderie. Whatever it is, the drive to get on-line can be every bit as persuasive—and every bit as destructive—as any addiction I've seen.

Chill out, okay?

The office isn't going to disappear in a day. Your e-mail can go unanswered for forty-eight hours. The folks back at the central office don't miss you *that* much. They understand that you'll be up against some major problems, trying to connect and stay in touch. And, dammit, it may do them good to figure out how to get along without you, from time to time.

The next time you're running late, there's no plug in the room, the phone lines won't cooperate, the server is screwed up, or you get a constant busy signal, don't have a cow, okay?

The demons you should be battling are the ones in the phone system. Not the ones in your head. Give up for a bit. Get a good night's sleep. Swim a few laps. Watch a hokey Star Trek rerun.

Chill.

FOR MORE INFO

> Telecommuting is a form of teleworking. In fact, if you stretch the commute distance to a few hundred miles, or whatever distance precludes frequent commuting, you have teleworking.
>
> Jack Nilles
> *Making Telecommuting Happen*, 1994

Making telecommuting happen *Making Telecommuting Happen* from Jack Nilles (Van Nostrand Reinhold, 1994, ISBN 0-442-01857-6) is the definitive source of checklists, sample forms, and organizational information for establishing a telecommuting program. Nilles coined the term "telecommuting," way back in 1972.

My only strong objection with *Making Telecommuting Happen* is its narrow definition of telecommuting—Nilles says it's the "substitution of telecommunications technologies. . . for the commute to work"—and its insistence on drawing a distinction between telecommuting and teleworking. Much like William Bridges in *Job Shift* (Addison-Wesley, 1994), I tend to think of work as something you do, not a place you go, and would submit that Nilles' definition/distinction is well on the way to becoming obsolete.* That nit aside, the book is a wonderful do-it-yourself kit for creating a telecommuting program, with all the paperwork ready to use.

If your company is telecommuting, or considering telecommuting, the best way to stay up on the latest and greatest is with the monthly *Telecommuting Review: The Gordon Report*. Edited by Gil Gordon—one of the most knowledgeable and vocal advocates of the telecommuting world—this widely quoted newsletter keeps you abreast of all sorts of important developments. The coverage of laws, government developments, and regulations in particular, can repay your company's investment many times over. $157 for an annual subscription (12 issues; $177 outside the United States) from TeleSpan Publishing Corp, 50 W. Palm Street, Altadena CA 91001 (voice 818-797-5482).

Telecommuting Review newsletter

---

* Pardon my ranting, but the telecommuting/teleworking dichotomy was a major conceptual hurdle for me while putting this book together. In *Making Telecommuting Happen*, Nilles says, "This book was produced in a home-based office. As you see it. A product of telecommuting." I agree. Creating a book in a home office, using telephones and computers, *is* telecommuting, whether you physiocommute or not.

6 Teleboss

Reason and judgment are the qualities of a leader.

Tacitus
History, ca. 100 AD

If you're in charge of a group of people, and at least one of those people is going to start telecommuting, this chapter's for you. I'm going to let you in on the predictable problems I've encountered and give you a few hints on how to resolve them.

The chapter is divided into four parts: an explanation of why telecommuting can be a good choice for you and your employees—and why it may not be; a nitty-gritty guide to setting up a program and picking the right people for the program; how to keep telecommuting working for the long haul; and finally, for those of you with TC envy, a few suggestions on how you can turn yourself into a telecommuter, too, at least part time.

Physiocommuting, employee's point of view

The art of managing organizations is changing faster now than at any time in history, and much of the change is driven by new technology: something that

The times, they are a-changin'.

wasn't even possible five years ago is going to jump out and eat your lunch this year, only to fade into ho-hum obscurity five years from now. You know that your organization has to become more competitive, more nimble, more productive.

Telecommuting can help on all those counts, and many more. That's the good news. The bad news is that *you'll* have to change to make telecommuting work. But don't be too worried: Most managers I've talked to say they prefer having telecommuters working for them. It just takes a little practice.

Put the shoe on the other foot, first.

If you want to get the full picture of what telecommuting implies from the management point of view, start by reading the preceding chapter, the one for telemployees—and take a look at the problems and opportunities your workers will face. Then, if you're accustomed to working with people one-on-one, get ready to throw out so much of what you've learned about leading people, evaluating them, interacting with them. When you lose daily face-to-face contact with an employee, you lose much of what you've come to take for granted: looking to see what they're doing; picking up those warning signs when things aren't quite going right; management by walking around. Nine times out of ten, though, you'll be repaid handsomely by how much more the employee will do for you.

Welcome to Labor in the Twenty-first Century.

WHY TELECOMMUTE?

> Tout par raison*
>
> Cardinal Richelieu
> *Mirame,* 1625

The quiz

Okay, class. Time for a little pop quiz. No peeking.

Tell me, is this statement true or false?

A good bean counter can put together a cost-benefit analysis that proves <u>anything</u>.

Time's up. Put down your pencils.

For those of you who said "True," congratulations! Your experience in the School of Hard Knocks has done you well. You may advance to the next section, the one marked Benefits.

Proof of the pudding

Those of you who said "False" need a little refresher course, I see. The plain fact is that a sufficiently talented analyst (you may substitute the phrase "professional bullshitter" if you live south of the Mason-Dixon line) can take almost any collection of numbers, and prove almost anything you can imagine.

I know. I did it for years, with budgets well into nine digits.

---

* Everything by reason.

If you, as a manager, are waiting for somebody to "prove" to you that telecommuting will save your company money, just go ahead and give up right now. Anybody you ask—consultant, lawyer, internal committee—will come up with the numbers to prove that telecommuting will save you loads of money. All of the studies in the literature come to the same conclusion: Telecommuting costs less than physiocommuting, both for the company and for the employee. Save yourself the time and aggravation. An MBA fresh out of Podunk U's B-school, who can hardly spell your company's name, will come to the conclusion that telecommuting will save you money. Lots of money. All it takes is a few hours in a business library, a pencil, and a pocket calculator—and the pencil and calculator are optional.

When it comes to numbers, telecommuting is a foregone conclusion.

As you can see, telecommuting benefits increase with time.

Trust me on this. If you're evaluating the potential for telecommuting from a financial point of view—focusing on next quarter's, or even next year's, bottom line—you're looking up the wrong end of the gift horse.

Don't base your decision on telecommuting strictly on dollars-and-cents issues. Yes, you will save money—depending on the program, maybe a little, maybe a lot. But that shouldn't be the overwhelming issue. Much more important are common business-sense questions: Will it make you more competitive? More adaptable? Will it help you hold on to key employees? Those are the questions you should be asking when considering the move to telecommuting.

If the program works, the savings will accrue, often in surprising ways. But if the program is a disaster, you'll be paying for it over and over again. Go slowly. Follow your gut instinct; don't trust the numbers any farther than you can throw them. Not every company is cut out for telecommuting. Not every boss is born to be a teleboss. And, heaven knows, not every worker makes a good telemployee.

Benefits

No one wearies of benefits received.

Marcus Aurelius
Meditations, ca. 170 AD

Telecommuting has been credited with everything from reducing the levels of air pollution (quick test: Stick your head out the window and breathe deep—is it working?) to eliminating the heartbreak of psoriasis (uh, well, lowering employee stress, anyway).

When I talk to telebosses, I always keep an ear out for their impression of telecommuting's benefits. Here's what I hear, over and over again.

Better work   Employees who *want* to telecommute and are given the opportunity are happier with their jobs. Freed from the usual office interruptions and bullshit, they get more done at home than they do at the central office. The quality of their work is usually better than it was when they were working out of the central office, although telemployees who only make it into the office a few times a month can fall "out of synch" with the latest developments.

Absenteeism   Absenteeism drops off, but it's hard to tell if that's because telemployees work at home when they wouldn't normally go to the office, or if they can just duck out for the occasional doctor's visit without "officially" taking a day off.

Ultimately, most telebosses figure absenteeism doesn't matter: It comes out in the wash. The question is whether the employee is getting the work done. If a telemployee takes Tuesday morning off to go fishing, but makes up for it by working all day Saturday, and the work is done right, and in on time, what's the diff?

Just *think* of all the people I could infect today.

Turnover   Turnover among willing telemployees drops way off: Several telebosses say they have turnover rates less than half that of the rest of the company. The conjecture is that telemployees who like to telecommute figure they could never find such a good deal at any other company—they get spoiled, and dread the thought of returning to physiocommuting.

Some day telecommuting will become much more widely accepted. Until that day arrives, though, many employees will view the opportunity to telecommute as one of their most important benefits.

A teleboss I know rates telecommuting as one of his biggest recruiting draws. Potential employees are intrigued by the existence of a formal telecommuting program and the likelihood that they will be allowed to telecommute several days a week, after they get their feet wet. Another teleboss doesn't even worry about the acclimation period. He's been known to hire workers from out of state, and have them start telecommuting immediately. "Why should I limit my talent pool, for new employees," he says, "simply because of geography?"

Recruiting

The single most important benefit in establishing a telecommuting program? Happier employees. I hear it over and over again. They work smarter, get more done, and stick with the company longer. You can try to put a dollars-and-cents figure on that, but it'd just be a SWAG* number.

Other effects of a telecommuting program can be quantified, but they're much less important than the human part of the equation.

You can generally reduce some of your central office overhead, if enough employees telecommute enough days of the week. By far the largest potential source of saving lies in eliminating square footage devoted to telecommuters' work places.

Office overhead

Shared desks are the pits. A desk-bound telemployee who is in the office three or four days a week needs a desk, a permanent desk, one that isn't co-opted by somebody else the rest of the week. You can skimp on the size of the cubicle—or even put two or more telemployees' desks in an otherwise cramped space, if they'll be out of the office on alternating days—but a personal desk is a necessity for those who spend more time working at the office than at home.

Shared desks

The Teledesk

By the time a telemployee's time in the central office tapers off to one or two days a week or less, they've already figured out how to cope with a portable "desk"—most often replacing it with a briefcase. These are the folks who can live

* Strictly Woody's Abysmal Guess

with shared desks. In fact, a converted conference room or shared table space with a phone may be sufficient. But don't push it. As you've no doubt noticed, employees can become very territorial, and the conversion to part-time telecommuting won't reduce their territorial feelings one iota. Quite the opposite, in some cases.

So if your telecommuting cost-benefit analysis relies on reduced office space, don't count your shared desk eggs before they're hatched. Put another way, people who tell you that instituting a one-day-a-week telecommuting program will save 20 percent of your current office space—even 10 percent— don't know what they're talking about.

Ancillary space

The experienced telebosses I've talked to say that their most common space-planning problem isn't with individuals' desks (it becomes pretty obvious, pretty quickly, who can make do with a shared desk, or no desk at all), but with ancillary space: storage areas, file cabinets, LAN server space, conference rooms, and the like.

The problem, of course, is that you must allow enough space in your plans to accommodate the atypical. If half of your office telecommutes on any given day, but everybody comes in for the weekly meeting, your meeting room better be big enough to handle the whole crowd—or you better have enough money in the budget to rent a meeting room nearby.

One teleboss solved the problem by drawing up his initial space plans as if all of his telecommuters were to become physiocommuters overnight. Corporate headquarters gave him allowances for overhead space: a certain percentage of the office square footage is for storage, another percentage for conferences, and so on. After calculating the square footage needed for offices and mapping out the overhead space, he then went back and eliminated the telecommuters' office space (actually, he allowed one desk for every five telecommuters).

Corporate hit the ceiling as his overhead space was way over the allowed percentages, but he countered that all that space was necessary because telecommuters take up as much overhead space as physiocommuters—and he had the numbers to prove his point. Ultimately, he didn't get all the space he asked for, but he *did* get a lot more than he might have.

The compleat carpooler

Last and least of the benefits of telecommuting are all the "blue sky" argu- **Blue sky**
ments. Yeah, telecommuting reduces driving, which reduces air pollution, rush
hour crowding, and on and on. Maybe someday 20 percent of all workers will be
telecommuting from the cyburbs, and rush hour traffic will fall commensurably. I
won't hold my breath. Literally or figuratively.

Wait a minute. Before you fire up your PC and write a nasty e-mail message to
me about conservation and being a decent citizen of the world and all, please
realize that I *do* believe that something must be done to reduce the level of crap in
the air in the world's major cities, and that we should all be doing what we can to
save Mother Earth. That's plain common sense.

It's just that I don't believe telecommuting—particularly government-mandated **Soapbox ON**
telecommuting and legislated ride sharing—will make much difference in air
pollution and crowding, at least in my lifetime. As is so often the case in virtually
every facet of governmental endeavor, regulations and mandates seem to spur
more activity directed toward circumventing the regulation and preserving the
bureaucracy that maintains the regulation than actually solving the problem.

When it comes to the net result of mandated programs—the quality of air in
major cities—I haven't seen a hell of a lot of progress in the past ten years or so.
Have you?

One final benefit of telecommuting that's come to light in the past couple of **Be prepared.**
years: emergency preparedness. It's impossible to quantify, but clearly a real
competitive advantage, should the unthinkable come to pass. When New York's
World Trade Center got hit in 1993, the telecommuters kept businesses going:
companies based in the Trade Center, with employees telecommuting from that
central office, were the first to come back online. Similarly, companies in Southern
California with well-established telecommuting programs were and are in a much
better position to recover from earthquakes.

In Case Of Emergency
Break Glass

When all else fails . . .

It's not hard to understand why the telecommuting companies fared so well. When a disaster strikes, a huge effort (second only to emergency medical care, food and shelter, and maybe electrical power) goes to restoring the telephone system.

A phone line goes back up much faster than a 16-lane highway.

Costs

> All good things are cheap;
> all bad are very dear.
>
> H. D. Thoreau
> *Journal*, 1841

Unless you get sued, the out-of-pocket costs of a telecommuting program are minuscule compared to the savings.

Start-up costs   Yes, there are some start-up costs. You can probably sketch them out on the back of a napkin, or in the margin of this book—look over on the side, and you'll see that you don't even need a spreadsheet. (Pardon my dollar-centrism: if you calculate in pounds, yen, dinari, riyals, shekels, pesetas, pesos, francs, marks, rupees, baht, rubles, krone, kyat, guilders, drachma, lira, ringgits, zloty, rand, wampum, or whatever, scratch out the dollar sign and substitute your favorite currency symbol.)

Here are the broad categories of typical startup costs:

$ _____   Meetings, committees, lost time for all the overhead of instituting a new personnel procedure, manuals, lawyers' time, courses, in-house training, consultants, and the like.

$ _____   New computer and telephone equipment for employees' home offices, unless they'll be using existing office equipment or machines they already own. Also, new equipment required to hook those people into the central office. Include maintenance costs.

$ _____   New software for employees' home office and the central office. Many software vendors will let you move the software when you move the employee and her computer at no extra charge; others will require you to buy new copies. The list of which vendors are "nice" and which are "dogs" changes from day to day; you'll have to check with the vendors to find out. (Tip: If you don't like their policy for off-site licenses, vote with your pocketbook!)

$ _____   Your people are going to lose some time—"productivity" for lack of a better term—while they get used to all the new stuff. Most telemployees probably lose three or four days getting their act in gear. The amount here is invariably offset by productivity gains; it's a rare telemployee who won't make up the loss in the first month or less. But if you want to explicitly identify the cost, do it here.

$ _____   Total all the above right here.

That's about it. With rare exceptions—say, you have to buy every telecommuter a new multimedia Pentium for their homes—the amount of money involved in setting up a telecommuting program won't even make a small dent in your budget.

The ongoing costs (and I use that term in its broadest sense) can be harder to swallow, because they involve *your* time.

Ongoing costs

Your telecommuters will be constantly pushing for bigger, better, and faster computers and networks in the central office. Your corporate IS department is, no doubt, stretched to the extremes already. The new demands from telemployees will stretch them even further—often into areas that are totally unfamiliar, and technologically challenging, for corporate IS staff. Expect a lot of friction, even more than you're refereeing now.

As your telemployees get more experience out on their own, you should expect to see more entrepreneurial ideas from them. I hear it over and over again from telemployees and telebosses: Working independently invariably leads to looking at problems from a different perspective.

If you're like most (good) managers, you'll welcome those new ideas with open arms. But, dammit, they take time. Good ideas often lead to hundreds of questions that must be answered. Lousy ideas take time, too, if only to gently let the employee know that they won't work.

The largest time sink, though, will come when you realize that you have to change your way of managing to adapt to telecommuting. It's more than the obvious fact that you can no longer look out of your office to see who's working and who isn't. You have to start thinking in terms of deliverables, and measuring people's performance in terms of what they produce—not necessarily how hard they work to produce it. That's a tricky distinction, one you'll have to master to succeed as a teleboss.

Dealing with people long-distance will take time, too. A big part of learning to be a good manager lies in learning to "read people," and it's bloody hard to read people over a telephone. How do you build *esprit de corps* when your only tool is a weekly conference call? The answer, as best I can tell, is to take the time to treat each of your telemployees well.

It's tough.

There's a reason why the biggest casualties of the conversion to telecommuting tend to be first-line supervisors: Managing telemployees is *tough*.

The real whammy, the Big Kahuna Cost, comes when you get sued for what you've done (or haven't done) while instituting a telecommuting program. As best I can tell, there are three sure ways to get sued over telecommuting—or get into hot water with the IRS, which is probably worse.

Don't hesitate, litigate.

Involuntary converts   *Force someone to telecommute, when you know that they're adamantly opposed to it.* I don't know why, but there still are workers who think telecommuting is some sort of Satanic plot. The best advice I've received from experienced telebosses: Don't even try to change 'em. Some of them finally come around, but a few will remain antitelecommuting to the bitter end. You'll spend more time and money fighting them than you will in simply giving up, arranging somehow to put them in an "office," be it ever so humble.

Sham consultants   *Magically turn employees into consultants.* Think you can send your employees home, stop paying them by the hour, and pay them by the piece? Think you can wave a magic wand and turn a salaried professional with benefits into an independent consultant with fixed-price contracts? Think again. I'll go into some detail on this topic in the next chapter, but for now suffice it to say that such devious thoughts are not only wrong, they're illegal.

Loose liability   *Overlook an important liability question.* Aunt Martha reaches over to pick up the phone while your telemployee is away from his home office, and she breaks her wrist. Who pays? Telecommuting is still in its infancy, and (as of this writing anyway) there's been virtually no enlightening activity in the courts. Do you want to be the first? Check with your insurance people and make sure your bases are covered.

Aunt Martha, five seconds before calling her attorney.

But How Do I Know They're Working?

How do you know *now*?

Pensées Pinecliffius

The last reservation   So the bean counters convince you that telecommuting will save the company money. Your employees, by and large, are chomping at the bit, ready to leave the office at a moment's notice. You've considered the problems, and come to the conclusion that, by and large, you can handle them. There's just one little question echoing around in your brain:

When my workers aren't here in the office, where I can see 'em, how will I know that they're working?

The simple answer: You won't.

It's a tough question. Among savvy and forward-looking managers, a very large majority of all the objections I've found to telecommuting boil down to that simple question. The funny thing is, they're all asking the wrong question!

Unless you've been fortunate (or unfortunate!) enough to manage people who work away from the central office—a sales force, say, scattered around the country, or maybe work crews that are always on the road—the loss of face-to-face contact will be pretty difficult. It will force you to manage in a different way, raise all sorts of unfamiliar problems, stretch you in directions you never knew existed.

The transition from physioboss to teleboss is tough, but it isn't impossible. Most of all, you have to shift your thinking to concentrate on the quality of what your employees produce, as opposed to how (or how much) they work. To put it another way, you can no longer concentrate on the process, you must focus on the result. **Focus on the result.**

Instead of asking whether your employees are working, you must ask whether your employees are producing. **The real question**

Another tough day at the office

Some people call this focus-on-the-result approach "Management By Objectives," but MBO doesn't tell the whole story. (As commonly practiced these days, MBO also tends to be monstrously intrusive, enormously expensive, and generally not worth the effort, but that's another book.)

In a geographically distributed organization, it takes a lot more than MBO forms and defined targets and formal reviews to pull a team together and make an organization work. We'll talk about the three Precepts of Remote Management later in this chapter.

Don't look so glum. You take work home, don't you? You trust yourself to get the work done. Having your employees telecommute isn't all that different, once you get over the first hump and start trusting *them* to get the work done. **Not to worry**

One teleboss I talked to said he liked his company's newly instituted telecommuting program because, for once in his life, he always knew where to find his employees.

CHOOSING WISELY

> You pays your money and you takes your choice.
>
> Caption to a cartoon by John Leech
> *Punch,* January 3, 1846

Program   Before your first telemployee walks out the office door, rarely to be seen again, you have several difficult choices to make. First, you have to figure out if you want a formal telecommuting program—or if the corporate office will require one, for that matter—and if you decide on a formal program, you'll have to get all the forms, contracts, committees, policies, and the like in place.

People   Most importantly, you'll have to pick the right people for the job. Selecting telemployees, particularly your very first telecommuters, can be a difficult process, one that can make or break the whole concept.

Do You Really Want a "Program"?

> Formalism is the hall-mark of the national culture.
>
> H. L. Mencken
> *A Book of Prefaces,* 1917

Most of the books and magazine articles on telecommuting focus on Starting a Telecommuting Program (note the capital "P"). They assume that a Project This Important needs to be defined, analyzed, implemented, monitored, and modified in a very structured way, with committees, lawyers, meetings, training sessions, reports, reviews, and on and on.

Structure does not equal success.   Guess what? The most successful telecommuting relationships I found—ones where telebosses were happy with their telemployees' work, and the telemployees weren't threatening to quit every day—were, by and large, informal arrangements between a boss and an employee. The one-on-one agreements engendered trust, transcending and obviating what lawyers could put down on paper.

Among the telemployees I talked to who do work within the structure of a formal telecommuting program (they're generally employees of large, multinational corporations), the happiest ones had all but forgotten that a formal program exists. In one case I talked to a telemployee who insisted there was no program, only to discover that her teleboss was of the opposite opinion!

My conclusion—and it'll be unpopular in many circles, but *hey!* that's what makes this an *Underground Guide!*—is that a formal telecommuting program is almost irrelevant to the success of a, uh, telecommuting program. At least in my experience, adding structure doesn't seem to add substance.

Certainly there are situations where you'll *have* to institute a formal program. **Sometimes you gotta.** Unions are wary that employers may use telecommuting to gouge unionized employees. Wholesale switches to telecommuting—where an entire department or division is suddenly pushed out to the cyburbs—can raise all sorts of thorny issues. If the switch to telecommuting involves major shifts in the company's technology, or if it raises big liability or security questions, coordination with the affected departments is mandatory, and the easiest way to implement that coordination may be via a formal telecommuting program. Compliance with the local air quality regulations may require a formal program, too.

YIPPEE! I get to be on another committee!

But if your IS department already supports dial-up access to the corporate LAN, a quick check with the Legal Department and the Loss Prevention/ Insurance people uncovers no major questions, and Human Resources and your boss don't really care, you may be able to turn a rather complex, expensive, time-consuming Problem (with a capital "P") into a simple one-on-one agreement. Many companies have.

Establishing a Program

What have I done to deserve such a fate,
I who have tried to walk in meekness and righteousness all my days?

Bram Stoker
Dracula, 1897

If you've decided to (or even been coerced into) establishing a formal telecommuting program, your first impulse may be to get the committees formed, and kick off the meetings as soon as possible. Resist the urge. **Wheels and their reinvention**

There's an enormous body of work out there devoted to telecommuting— much of it amassed by government organizations, thus free for the asking. Start by taking a look in Appendix A, where I've culled what I feel are the "best of the best" resources for instituting a telecommuting program. Send away for the brochures, get a few books, and take advantage of all the ready-made telecommuting info that exists: from multistep plans, to the composition of committees, to employee contracts, it's all been done before—many, many times.

Depending on your budget, personnel availability, and tolerance for pain, there are three general approaches to establishing a telecommuting program that seem to work.

Soup to nuts First, if you're willing to buy into a pre-fab (and highly successful) all-encompassing vision of how to set up a telecommuting program, there's a company called Smart Valley that has developed a detailed 26-step implementation plan. The plan goes from *Step 1: Prepare and present a Telecommuting Proposal* to *Step 26: Make adjustments where necessary.* You get the idea.

These folks understand the politics, the pitfalls, and the technology, too—"ISDN" is not a foreign word. They'll sell you resource material at a very reasonable rate—they'll even come in and set up your entire telecommuting operation, from beginning to end. Highly recommended. (Smart Valley, Inc., 1661 Page Mill Road, Suite 200, Palo Alto, CA 94304-1209; Internet lesliek@svi.org).

A la carte On the other hand, if you prefer the home-grown approach, there are three sources of information you'll find indispensable. Start with Smart Valley's Telecommuting Guide: It has an excellent overview of how to structure the plan. Add to that the Caltrans Telecommuting Handbook, which has loads of forms, agreements, and the like (California Dept. of Transportation, 680/24 Public Information Office, 1910 Olympic Blvd., Suite 160, Walnut Creek CA 94596; voice 510-680-4636, fax 510-938-0327). Top it all off with Jack Nilles' book *Making Telecommuting Happen* (Van Nostrand Reinhold, 1994, ISBN 0-442-01857-6), which should fill in all the remaining gaps. Pages 108–118, in particular, contain a ready-made discussion of telecommuting called "The Telecommuting Guide" that could be used as the basis for an employee pamphlet—with the author's permission, of course.

Courses Finally, if you want to develop and maintain some in-house expertise on the subject of telecommuting, consider sending some of your people to a telecommuting workshop or series of classes. The City & County of Denver conducts seminars and courses year-round. Single-day sessions cost about $125; the full suite of telecommuting seminars runs four days. Courses are regularly scheduled in Denver, or they can be taken to your site (Judy Rapp-Guadagnoli, City & County of Denver, Travel Reduction Program 2000, Career Service Authority, 110 Sixteeth St, Fifth Floor, Denver CO 80204; voice 303-640-1108).

Should you find yourself mired in some sort of telecommuting cesspool, there's one person uniquely qualified to pull you out. Gil Gordon is widely regarded as the United States' top consultant on telecommuting problems and their resolution: If you have a telecommuting problem, Gil's the person most

likely to solve it. He takes on corporate clients, 'tho heaven knows how he finds the time (Gil Gordon Associates, 10 Donner Court, Monmouth Junction, NJ 08852; voice 908-329-2266, fax 908-329-2703).

Winging It

> As long as I live I'll spit in my parlor.
>
> Thomas Fuller
> *Gnomologia,* 1732

Starting your own telecommuting "program" (with a lowercase "p") isn't all that difficult, if the lawyers, insurance folks, employee relations people, and your own boss will give you the latitude to go it alone.

It's so *easy* getting new ideas through the Legal Department.

Aside from having a good working relationship with your prospective telemployee (more about that later in this chapter), there's only one crucial step, really: The two of you have to iron out who's responsible for what.

Deciding up front

Sit down with your telemployee and make sure the two of you understand all of the points in the following list.

- Who's going to pay for computer and comm equipment, including its repair, and how to submit bills for reimbursement

- If there will be any change in the telemployee's pay or benefits

- Whether the company's insurance policy covers equipment in the employee's home, whether the employee needs to get more insurance, what kind of additional liability the company can and can't cover, and what the telemployee should do if there's an accident in their home office

- Which days the employee is expected to be in the office, and if the employee is expected to be home to answer the phone during any "core hours"

- Who's going to pay for phone bills, additional utility bills, added insurance, travel (including travel to the central office for regular meetings), and other miscellaneous expenses

- What it takes for either of you to bail out of the agreement

Providing you and your telemployee are on the same wavelength on most other topics—you know the telemployee won't let a competitor sit down at his home computer and pull up sensitive corporate information, for example—that short list should just about do it.

Sure beats thirty hours of committee meetings, a budget cycle, two teams of lawyers, and a ten-page contract, eh?

One last bit of advice on setting up a program, one that's particularly important if you're winging it and don't have the time or the patience to formally monitor how well the program is going: Use volunteers. If the program is working from the telemployee's point of view, you'll get more volunteers. If your volunteers suddenly dry up, you can bet your bottom dollar that something's going haywire.

Think of it as a zero-cost feedback loop.

Jobs from Telecommuting Hell

> Ah, Tam! Ah, Tam! Thou'll get thy fairin';
> In Hell they'll roast thee like a herrin'!
>
> Robert Burns
> *Tam O'Shanter,* 1790

What they dare not tell

The "soft" telecommuting books go crazy when they start discussing which jobs are amenable to telecommuting and which aren't. You'll find checklists, weighting schemes, threshold points, charts, and all sorts of fancy stuff. What percentage of an employee's time is spent doing Task "A"? Multiply this number by that number and add them all up, divide by the geometric mean of the hypotenuse, and you'll get an objective view of which people can telecommute, and which can't.

Yeah. Sure.

What makes a good telejob?

One article that lists good jobs for telecommuters says that one of the top jobs is "computer programmer." Uh-huh. Fact is, most programmers *can* do their thing at home just as well as they can at the office. But there are other programmers who can't venture more than a few feet from a specialized piece of hardware. Still others in crucial positions are needed on site, or on call. Tarring all those people in all those different positions with one "computer programmer = telecommuter" brush is a gross oversimplification.

Don't believe everything you read.

Nine times out of ten, you'll know right off the top of your head which parts of your employees' jobs can be accomplished at home. And the rest of the time, a few minutes spent with the target employee should clarify any lingering questions. Trust your instincts and your experience.

That said, there are a couple of job situations I've bumped into that seem like **The exceptions** they should be amenable to telecommuting, but for one reason or another never seem to work out. I call them jobs from telecommuting hell.

High-tech brainstorming—the kind of collaborative work you'd find at the **Brainstorming** beginning of a major software development project, say, or in the design of complex new electronics gizmos —always seems to come unraveled when one or more key team members spend a lot of time away from the office. Yes, I know that it should be possible to do all the brainstorming with videoconferencing, whiteboard systems, and other fancy group interaction technologies. But I've never seen it happen. And I've seen several big, expensive projects go down the tubes because the design team didn't have a chance to really hash out the potential pitfalls before the gruntwork started.

The successful high-tech projects I've seen undertaken by telecommuters took one of two different tacks. In both cases, the potential problem has to be identified before the project starts (or very, very early in the cycle), and the telecommuters' jobs are actually retrofitted to accommodate the circumstances.

The first approach that seems to work is to reduce the sheer volume of team member intercommunication by anointing a "Super Designer": one person who's charged with putting all the pieces together, and parceling out the component pieces to people who have both the talent and temperament to handle them.

That's a high-risk approach, of course: All your project's eggs are in one basket. If the Super Designer quits in the middle of the project, or (more likely) suffers a complete nervous breakdown, the whole project goes with him. The Super Designer job itself is the pits, combining the worst characteristics of a first-line management position with the pressure-cooker responsibilities of a lead designer.

The second approach to brainstorming that seems to work is to bring the whole crew together early in the project, and keep them together until they feel comfortable with breaking away. By relegating the most intense part of the brainstorming activity to a face-to-face-to-face encounter, and building consensus with all members of the team present, you'll stand a better chance of keeping the project on track.

Another type of job from telecommuting hell is one I call a COTS: a Central Office Time Sink. It's the kind of job that seems to be perfectly suitable as a telecommuting job, but either the job itself, or (more commonly) the specific combination of the job and one particular employee, turns into a massive time sink. With apologies to Ross Perot, that sucking sound you hear from south of the border may just be a COTS job that's ready to go belly-up.

COTS Consider the plight of Charlie, a hard-working clerk who spends almost all of his time reviewing claims on his computer, but occasionally needs to look up something from the central (noncomputerized) files. After considerable thought, Charlie and his boss decide that telecommuting wouldn't be such a bad idea—after all, 'most everything Charlie does can be accomplished at home, and on those rare occasions (once or twice a day) when he needs information from the central files, he can call good ol' Dorothy in the office and get the information he wants.

After a week or two—and completely without realizing it—Charlie is calling Dorothy eight or ten times a day. Sure, he could poke around and find the information he needs on-line, or start keeping his own files at home, but it's *so* much easier to just have Dorothy do it. Besides, looking things up only takes Dorothy a couple of seconds. Where's the harm?

Good ol' Dorothy

Bombarded by constant interruptions, poor Dorothy can't get her regular work done. Charlie's become a pest, but Dorothy isn't the kind of person to say that to his face; besides, it doesn't really take that much time. And she would *never* complain about a fellow employee to the boss.

The boss sees the quantity and quality of Charlie's work exceed his wildest expectations. *Hey! this telecommuting really works!* But the boss is vaguely troubled by Dorothy. She just isn't working out very well.

Hmmmmm . . . maybe it's time to let Dorothy telecommute?

The Best Telemployees

> More will be accomplished, and better, and with more ease,
> if every man does what he is best fitted to do, and nothing else.
>
> Plato
> *The Republic,* ca. 370 BC

Another one of those tough management problems: how to choose the "right" people for telecommuting, especially when the program is just starting.

A trick question

Ah, but the answer is so simple! Your best telemployee candidates are, simply, your best employees.

The qualities you seek in a telemployee—motivation, self-discipline, high achievement, reliability—are precisely the same qualities you've always sought in your employees, in general. With a few unusual exceptions (say, an employee with an exceptionally distracting stay-at-home spouse), excellent employees make excellent telemployees; mediocre physiocommuters remain mediocre in the cyburbs.

When you choose your pioneer telecommuters, look first among your best employees.

Involuntary Converts

> Wayne Wolfinger, a former Perkin-Elmer service representative in Fairbanks, Alaska, grew frustrated when the company refused to compensate him for the cost—about $120 a month—of setting up a home office and storing the parts he wanted to keep there. He left the company in December 1993 as a result of the dispute.
>
> "It was as if they were saying, 'We need to save money, so we'll make our employees pay our bills,'" Mr. Wolfinger says. Noting that his office required not only space in his house but also extra insurance, he adds, "If this is the trend, I'm looking at a cut in pay that's going to last forever."
>
> *The Wall Street Journal*
> August 17, 1994

The sad fact is that not all telecommuters are volunteers. It's particularly vexing, considering millions of people would much rather be working at home. But it does happen.

De gustibus

Take my advice. Keep your telecommuting program all-volunteer, particularly if your employees were hired with the implicit understanding that they would be working in a central office. Stay flexible enough to provide office space for people who can't hack it at home. Think creatively. You'll come up with something.

Brass tacks   What if the brass is bound and determined to turn everybody out? Ah, that's why they pay you the big bucks, *nicht war*?

Here are the best tips I could uncover for any boss put in the uncomfortable position of forcing an employee to telecommute.

- Set an example. Start telecommuting yourself.
- Warn the people above you that they could be in for some interesting times, legally.
- Try to find out what's *really* bugging the employee. Sometimes the objections given have little or nothing to do with the root cause of the problem.
- Make a genuine effort to ensure that the employee isn't hurt financially—either short term or long term—by the switch.

Home versus Telecenters

> Every bird likes its own nest best.
>
> Randle Cotgrave
> *French-English Dictionary*, 1611

I'd like to discuss one last decision you may face while setting up a telecommuting program: the use of telecenters.

Telecenters and satellite offices   Generally telecenters come in one of two flavors. Either your company will set up a satellite office, presumably located closer to your employee's home than the current central office; or, a group of people (possibly using government subsidies) will establish a telecenter specifically designed for telecommuters who, for any of a variety of reasons, won't be working from their homes.

Satellite offices are often established by large companies in an attempt to move their operations closer to employees' homes, and/or to reduce expenses for office space, by moving offices to the suburbs. They're created and maintained by the employer, at the employer's convenience and expense.

Shared equipment at the telecenter

Telecenters, on the other hand, generally accommodate telemployees from several different companies. They exist primarily to reduce the per-employee cost of equipment: Ten or twenty telecommuters can share a copier, or a printer; dozens or more can spread the expense of a teleconferencing system, making that kind of technology more affordable.

The track record for telecenters thus far has been quite good. In Appendix A you'll find resource material that covers telecenter experiences in Hawaii; Washington, D.C.; and several other places around the United States.

They work well.

Over the long term, though, I tend to be skeptical about satellite offices and telecenters. Why? They're bucking a long-established technological trend. If your company is considering establishing a satellite office or using telecenters for telemployees, keep two things in mind:

But don't bet the farm

If your primary reason for using a satellite office or telecenter is to share the expense of fancy office equipment, you may find it much less expensive, in both the short and long term, to equip your telemployees with scaled-down versions of the same equipment in their homes. The price of high-tech equipment falls, precipitously, every year. The price of office space generally increases. (More or less, anyway.) If you're going to bet on your future telemployee needs, bet on the fact that equipment costs will go down, and office space costs will go up.

The other point to remember is that telecenters are already being set up for you, and you don't need to spend a dime. The telecenters are cleverly disguised as photocopy and business service companies, and have signs on them that say "Kinkos" and the like.

As the need for expensive telecommuter services increases — teleconferencing, high-quality color copying, exotic computer printers — the corner copy shop will continue to evolve into a pay-per-use telecenter. The business model hasn't changed: The "copy shops" buy expensive office equipment and charge by the piece for its use. All that changes is the type of equipment they offer. Why build your own telecenter, your own teleKinkos, when you can rent a tiny piece of one whenever you need it?

KEEPING IT GOING

Inner development is not easy and will take time. External progress . . . has not reached its present level within a short period, but over centuries, each generation making greater developments based on those of the previous generations . . . Inner development is even more difficult since internal improvement cannot be transferred from generation to generation.

H. H. the Fourteenth Dalai Lama

The program is in place. The telemployees have been chosen. Everything is ready for the grand roll-out. Congratulations! You're over the easy part. . . .

It's different.   The day-to-day management of people working offsite is an art. If you have experience managing a dispersed group of people—say, a sales force that's scattered across the country, or around the world—you have one leg up. But for most managers this telecommuting stuff takes some serious acclimation.

A long-time telemployee I know says that successful telecommuting is based on three precepts: trust, communication, and results. Skimp on any of the three, and the whole relationship goes to hell.

Trust

> Leadership is not something you do *to* someone . . . It is something you do *for* them. If you try to exercise power and control over people, you are doing something *to* them. You are inflicting your will on them and you are making them rely on you. When people are distant, this approach is deadly. On the other hand, if you build trust, you are doing something *for* them. You are helping them to rely on their own unique talents, abilities, and perspectives. You are trusting them to tap into the power and control within themselves. –Merlin
>
> Jaclyn Kostner
> *The Knights of the Tele-Round Table,* 1994

The cornerstone   So much can (and will!) go wrong with a long-distance working relationship that you must, above all else, trust your telemployees. They, in turn, must trust you as well—and you have to prove yourself, continuously, to be worthy of that trust.

I'm not talking about some abstract touchy-feely kind of concept. I'm talking about regular, old-fashioned, day-in-and-day-out trust. The kind of trust that lets you listen to somebody's complaints about a telemployee, lets you weigh the problem, but prevents you from jumping to a conclusion until you have a chance to hash the details out with the telemployee. The kind of trust that presupposes your telemployee is working hard, even if you call in the middle of the day and he doesn't answer the phone. The kind of trust that you would want from your boss, should you start telecommuting.

Jumping to conclusions   When you lose constant daily contact, all the normal reinforcement goes with it: You don't catch a glimpse of Reggie as he walks by, heading off to a meeting; you don't hear his voice swearing at the jammed copy machine; he doesn't drop by the office with a cup of coffee and an idea to bounce off you. All the little things that tell you *Reggie is working his butt off* suddenly disappear, and it's a very natural jump from "I don't see him working" to "I don't think he *is* working."

Trust has to fill the gap. If you can't honestly trust your telemployee—if you can't, categorically, give your telemployee the benefit of *every* doubt—then your relationship is doomed to failure.

You have to force yourself to trust your telemployees until there's incontrovertible evidence that your trust is misplaced. And even then . . .

Conversely, your telemployees have to believe that you are willing and able to represent them in their absence. They have to trust that you won't forget them at crucial times (even when, inevitably, you do). They have to believe they're getting the same kind of consideration they would be receiving if they were physically present.

On the other foot

Communication

> I don't want any yes-men around me.
> I want everybody to tell me the truth,
> even when it costs them their jobs.
>
> Sam Goldwyn

Communication walks hand-in-hand with trust. It's up to you, as a teleboss, to open the lines of communication with your telemployees, and to keep them open.

Start by making sure that your telemployees stay in the loop. If you have a weekly staff meeting, let them join in on the phone, or at the very least make sure they get minutes. (What? You don't keep minutes of your weekly meetings? It's time to start!)

Earning their trust

Encourage your telemployees to call their central-office-bound coworkers, even if there's nothing specific to talk about. Catching up on office scuttlebutt is a perfectly legitimate business reason to make a long-distance phone call.

Insist on your telemployees dropping by the office, physically, from time to time. For a local telemployee, once a week is certainly reasonable. For those who live farther away, strive to get the whole group together at least once a month at first, and then a minimum of once every few months afterwards.

Keep up the personal interaction.

Of course, *every* time your telemployee drops by, you should encourage her to come into your office (be it ever so humble) and talk—about the job, about the telecommuting, about nothing in particular. That one-on-one time is most important.

If your telemployee participates in meetings—be it physically, by driving into the office, or via phone—make sure they're kept up to date: background information, agendas, and especially notification of any changes. There's nothing a telecommuter likes more than slugging through an hour of traffic only to arrive at the central office and discover that the meeting has been canceled.

Equally important to communicating freely is communicating *fairly*. Give your long distance employees as much time as you would give to the locals: Listen to their suggestions, spend as much time with them hashing over alternatives and

Fairness

exploring nuances as you would with somebody sitting across the table from you. When you fill everybody in on the latest changes, make sure the telemployee is included, too. When you solicit opinions from the group at large, make sure the telemployee is not overlooked. Communicate fairly.

A big part of communicating fairly is to allow plenty of time and opportunity for a telemployee to give you all sides of a story. If you have to deliver bad news, or even a reprimand, there's no substitute to doing it in person. Bad news over the phone is bad news, indeed.

Priorities   Finally, make sure that your telemployees can tell when you need an answer, like, *right now*—and when it can wait. Folks commuting from the cyburbs have a different set of priorities to juggle, a different set of problems to handle. Often it's impossible to tell by the tone of voice on a phone message recorder if something is "Drop Everything, Do It Now" important. You'll help your employees immensely if you'll let them know, explicitly, when you need something right away.

I'll get to the Extremely Urgent stuff after the Cosmic Must Do Yesterday pile is cleared out, okay?

Results

Results are what you expect, and consequences are what you get.

Schoolgirl's definition
Ladies' Home Journal, 1942

All of this high-falutin' telecommuting stuff doesn't mean squat, of course, unless you get some results out of it. You should expect results—good, solid results—from your efforts, and you should hold your telemployees to a higher standard than your other employees. After all, the telecommuters have been freed from much of the normal office distractions and overhead: That alone should improve the quantity and quality of work they produce.

Your telemployees should reinforce the trust you've shown by producing. The quantity and quality of work produced, ultimately, is how you have to gauge the success of a telecommuting program, and whether it should be permitted to continue.

Closing the loop

You, as a teleboss, can help improve your employees' results by using a few simple tricks:

Start out with a bang. Set early goals for your first-time telecommuters that can be achieved quickly and rather easily. Then raise the bar and extend the scope as your telemployees get the hang of it.

Schedule periodic meetings with each telemployee individually—preferably in person—to review specifically how telecommuting is going. You can conduct a telecommuting review in conjunction with a performance review, but if so, make sure the subject of telecommuting is a separate topic, covered independently of performance discussions.

Finally, figure out a way to recognize superior performance from your telemployees. "Employee of the month" awards and "take the team to lunch" kinds of recognition don't play the same way when you're working away from the central office. But little things with a personal touch—a snapshot of the group holding a banner with the telemployee's name on it; a nameplate inscribed "Joe Schmuck—Syzynrgy Team Leader"; a bottle of champagne— can mean a lot.

IF YOU GET THE BUG

> Ka* me, ka thee; one good turn asketh another.
>
> John Heywood
> *Proverbs*, 1546

Sooner or later, you're probably going to come to the conclusion that these telemployees have a pretty good deal.

What's good for the goose

If they can do it, you can, too!

Should you be bitten by the telecommuting bug, you may be surprised to know that many bosses—and I'm talking first-line and second-line supervisors, not necessarily top corporate brass—telecommute.

While it's true that you'll (usually) have a hard time justifying more than a couple of telecommuting days a week, those couple of days can make an enormous difference in your effectiveness as a manager.

* Ka means "help."

Boning up to join the ranks of the telemployed

If you find yourself in the position of trying to convince *your* boss that you should be allowed to telecommute one or two days a week, consider these tips.

Getting away from the office gives you a chance to concentrate in a way that's never possible with all the day-to-day distractions. You'll actually get more worthwhile work done in ten solid hours at home than a whole week at the office. Try it. You'll see.

Leaving office fire-fighting to one of your employees not only gives you a chance to see how well that employee performs under fire, it also gives your substitute an excellent glimpse of the corporate world from *your* point of view.

All in all, telebosses I've talked to are very enthusiastic about the opportunity to telecommute themselves. I, and they, recommend it highly.

GETTING HELP

Thank you for calling MEI.
All of our representatives are currently assisting a customer.

Recorded message
MEI Micro Center

Must be a hell of a customer.

Pensées Pinecliffius

In addition to Jack Nilles' book, covered in the previous chapter, I've found two very interesting products that should prove beneficial to most telebosses.

First, of all things, is a Windows-based software package called OpenCollar
Manager from Forward Systems Inc. (And who says the cobbler has no shoes?)
OpenCollar isn't exactly a scheduling package, but it does keep track of which
days telemployees will be in the office. It isn't exactly a job prioritizing package,
but it helps telemployees and telebosses keep track of assignments and their
status. It isn't exactly a cost-benefit analysis package, but it can cough up reports
on travel time savings, environmental improvement, telecommuting costs, and a
whole bunch more.

It's the only special-purpose telecommuting management software I've seen,
and — while the interface is a bit clumsy — it seems to touch many important
bases. Definitely worth looking into, particularly if you'll be handling more than a
few telemployees. The package costs $695, or you can call and they'll send you a
demo disk. (Forward Systems, Inc., 853 Sanders Road, Suite 330, Northbrook, IL
60062; voice 708-509-1255, fax 708-509-1254)

Any metaphor that's extended for more than a few paragraphs tends to put
me to sleep, but with that caveat *Knights of the Tele-Round Table*, by Jaclyn Kostner
(Warner, 1994, ISBN 0-446-51879-4), offers a thought-provoking look at what it
takes to manage long distance. The book's shtick — modern corporate manager
meets King Arthur, who's revered as the ultimate teleboss — wears thin by page 3.
But who am I to knock an offbeat writing style? Talk about the pot calling the
kettle black . . . .

KT-RT dishes up plenty of insightful observations and useful tips, like any
good pop business book, but it doesn't lose sight of its goals. Instead of trying to
be all things to all managers (like, oh about 10,000 pop business books I could
mention), it concentrates on those who must manage geographically dispersed
groups. Some of the book's points are pretty obvious, and some seem contrived,
but there are dozens of gems to decorate your corporate Avalon, in anticipation of
Arthur's return.

A must-read for telebosses and teleboss wannabes.

7 Transitions: Beyond Telemployee

Taken together, the weight of the decisions we must make can seem terrifying, especially since we're bound to make mistakes. Just as those who tried to imagine the effect of the automobile failed to visualize that it would create the suburbs, a phenomenon that would shift the political and economic landscape, we are clueless as to the eventual results of the Bit Bang. But ultimately, the process may prove exhilarating, as we learn to exploit our newly augmented ability to remake the world with the products of mind and the tools of collaboration. As we grapple with the unanswered questions, we're in for the ride of a lifetime.

Steven Levy
Newsweek, 2/27/95

There comes a time in every telemployee's life when the corporate crap suddenly turns from merely irritating to utterly infuriating. You'll find yourself wondering over and over again why you suffer such fools, gladly or not, and what it would take to break out on your own.

Those impulses aren't necessarily bad for you or (surprisingly!) your employer. They're the natural result of becoming more independent, of looking at problems and their solution from the outside in.

I've spoken about the importance of tolerance from the telemployee's point of view, and the importance of telebosses listening to their telecommuters' ideas. But what happens when—for whatever reason—the traditional employer/employee relationship begins to break?

Fortunately, telecommuters and their bosses have options that aren't readily available to physiocommuters. In an age where permanent lifetime employment is a joke—the boss who promises you a job "for as long as you want to work" is every bit as likely to be given the boot as you are!—telecommuting gives you an opportunity to try different alternatives to traditional one-on-one employment, without compromising your current job.

Far from the madding crowd

Permanent lifetime employment

237

Put a slightly different way, telecommuting lets you take your own career by the horns. If that career happens to be with your current employer, all the better. But if you and your current employer come to a parting of the ways, your experiences as a telecommuter may prove far more important to your real "career" than anything you did back in the central office.

Plug me in, turn me loose.

Particularly in high-tech areas, where a job's life expectancy is more like twenty months than twenty years, the skills and contacts made while telecommuting will save your neck over and over again. Simply put, keeping abreast of developments in your field by connecting with others in cyberspace is the single greatest source of job security available to you.

The three transitions This chapter covers the three predictable transitions in a telecommuter's life, should the telemployee burden become too heavy to bear: from a traditional employee to a contractor; from a contractor to a consultant; and from a consultant to a freelancer. Each marks a big step in your development. Each has its own problems, opportunities, tricks.

If you've ever wondered what it's *really* like going out on your own in a digital-dog-eat-dog world, this is the place to look.

EMPLOYEE TO CONTRACTOR

> A man who qualifies himself well for his calling
> never fails of employment in it.
>
> Thomas Jefferson
> 1792

Leap of faith— in yourself The first stage of weaning yourself from the corporate umbilical cord—the step that almost every independent worker, and almost every self-made millionaire, has taken at one time or another—is to break away from the company that bore you.

Uh, bored you. Whatever.

Office workers of the world unite!
You have nothing to lose but your . . . oh, nevermind.

Telecommuters are in a unique position to make the break. Freed from the shackles of physical presence, telemployees can experiment on their own time, try new approaches, solve problems in innovative ways, make a few mistakes, without incurring the wrath of an omnipresent boss.

Note that this kind of inventiveness can take place *with your current employer*. You needn't leave the employment of Acme Widgets to devise a better Widget-making process. Indeed, if the powers-that-be at Acme Widgets are smart and you're very good, they'll embrace your experimenting with open arms: This is the stuff of "internal entrepreneurship" and "reinventing the corporation" and all those other buzzwords.

It can be a logical, not necessarily physical, break.

Telecommuting—the ability to get out of the office, look at things differently, and network with others in the know—provides the catalyst.

Why Change?

> Change can be very exciting.
>
> Mario Cuomo
> Doritos ad, 1995

> And mighty lucrative, too, eh Mario?
>
> Pensées Pinecliffius
> On learning how much Mario made for the ad

In many cases the new skills and knowledge you'll acquire while telecommuting can be put to good use with your current company. Many telemployees find that their companies appreciate and are willing to act on ideas from their physically liberated workers.

Don't overlook the obvious.

Sometimes, though, it doesn't work that way. Combined with a natural tendency for high-achievers to change jobs just to "try something new" and an extreme adversity to boredom and corporate politics, many talented employees tend to move on every few years anyway.

Hold onto 'em by letting 'em go.

Converting those peripatetic high-achievers from employees to contractors may actually help a company hold on to their most talented workers. It's a strange fact, but true: The best way for a company to keep top-notch employees may be to help them go out on their own!

Once again, telecommuting—physical independence—holds the key.

Let's start with the first step most telecommuters toy with.

Moonlighting

Many telecommuters moonlight. That is, they take on small contracts, freelance gigs, or even assume long-term (but generally part-time) employment with a second company.

As long as your employment contract doesn't forbid moonlighting, and work for your primary employer doesn't suffer because of it, there's no reason to avoid moonlighting. In fact, the experiences you gain moonlighting can be beneficial to your primary employer! Many's the time that a problem solved for one company can have immediate application in another—even when the companies are in two completely different fields.

Avoid being one of the eaten digital dogs.

Should you decide to moonlight, keep a few things in mind:

- If you have an employment agreement, follow it. If your employee manual has policies on moonlighting, obey them. Equivalently, always assume that their sharks are smarter, hungrier, and *much* better paid than yours;

Shark? Did somebody say shark?

- Your primary employer may not like the fact that you decided to moonlight. Discretion may be the better part of multiemployer valor;

- Unless you have a binding agreement to the contrary, ideas and specific products developed for one employer are their property. As several recent lawsuits have amply demonstrated, you can get in serious trouble if, for example, you try to sell the same software—even just a lousy couple dozen lines of code—to two different companies.

- Be very aware of your obligations to your employers. Don't run up long-distance phone bills on one employer's account to benefit the other. When in doubt about the ethics of a situation involving two different employers, and in the absence of legal advice to the contrary, use the *Wall Street Journal* rule— if all of the facts of the situation were to appear on the front page of tomorrow's *Wall Street Journal*, could you and your employers live with it?

Once you've moonlighted a bit, typically for several different customers, the siren song of self-employment will doubtless turn your head. Why devote all your time and considerable talents to just one company, or even two? Can't you do better (make more money, learn new skills, take on different challenges) by selling parts of yourself to several different companies? **Contracting**

Those are tough questions. It helps to know some of the hard facts.

First, as you'll learn through the rest of this chapter, self-employment has a downside. It's called starvation. Remember that well. Unless you manage your transition from employee to contractor carefully, and provide for plenty of cushion while the inevitable hard times roll, you'll find yourself in a classic double bind: looking for a new job while not being currently employed. With rare exceptions, that usually leads to a cut in pay and benefits, not to mention more stress than you'll ever experience while employed. **Self-employed in the land of milk and honey**

Second, unless you can provide something people are willing to pay for—in high tech industries, that means you're constantly learning (nay, mastering!) new and difficult technologies—your business will turn to mud in short order. For example, ace DOS PC consultants flying high in 1991 could hardly make a living by 1994, and will be virtually extinct by 1996. Freelance nuclear engineers could write their own ticket in 1985, but by 1990 they were lucky to be writing epitaphs. If you think you're on a corporate treadmill now, the intellectual treadmill of self-employment will leave your head positively dizzy. **Give 'em what they want.**

This time, let's get a *Windows* consultant.

Work, work, work   Third, no matter how much time you're spending on the job now, while working for someone else, you will be spending considerably more time on the job while self-employed. Success as a contractor, consultant, or freelancer doesn't come overnight, and you'll pay dearly with all those long hours along the way.

Boo   What, I didn't scare you off?

Good. Maybe you have what it takes.

If you're currently a traditional telemployee and want to try your hand at telecontracting, talk to your boss. It's relatively easy for everybody involved to make the change to contracting, with your former employer serving as your number-one client. You should be able to offer your current company a greater diversity of services (that is, you can work for several departments), at a lower overall price. In many companies, reducing the "headcount" — the number of "real" employees — by one can be significant, too, as it may let your employer hire on a new employee without losing your services. That's particularly true in companies that budget separately for employees and outside consulting work. You may actually be doing your boss a favor by offering to move the cost of your work from one part of the budget to another.

Beware the bogeyman.   In one important respect, though, changing from a telemployee to a telecontractor can be fraught with peril. Even if your former boss embraces the change with both arms, other eyes are watching. Mean, beady eyes. The eyes of the taxman. And that brings us to IRS Publication 937. (If you live outside the United States, you probably face an equally pivotal — and equally ambivalent — set of regulations.)

Vive La Difference

> He ketched a frog one day, and took him home,
> and said he cal'lated to educate him;
> and so he never done nothing for three months
> but set in his back yard and learn that frog to jump.
> And you bet you he *did* learn him, too.
>
> Samuel Clemens
> *The Celebrated Jumping Frog of Calaveras County*, 1865

Warning!   Read this section carefully. There's a quiz at the end.

The transition from telemployee to contractor is the toughest jump of all because there are specific legal ramifications to being an "employee" and entirely different ramifications for "independent contractors." Run afoul of the IRS (or the, uh, taxing authorities in other countries) and you or your employer could find yourself liable for thousands of dollars in taxes and fines — or even find yourself in prison.

While most of the concerns of moonlighters tend to be merely ethical, contractors are held to a higher standard: IRS Publication 937.

What's an employee?

Ah'm from the IRS an' ah'm here ta help.

Should you and your employer decide that it's best for you to change from a full-time employee to a contractor, you must both keep an eagle eye on the regulations, and make sure that both the letter and intent of the law are followed. Otherwise, both you and your employer-*cum*-client can find yourself in a never-ending stream of hot water, one that makes navigating the River Styx seem an idyllic pleasure cruise.

The IRS is trusted with evaluating, almost on a case-by-case basis, whether a specific individual is an employee of, or a contractor to, any given organization. If the IRS decides that you are an employee, *the burden of proof is on you and the client company* to prove otherwise. Remember that the IRS has . . . shall we say . . . extraordinary powers for a democratic institution in a free society.

The ball's in the IRS court.

The distinction between employee and contractor is important. As an employee, you will generally have few if any employment-related tax deductions. As a contractor, many deductions for business expenses come "off the top." As an employee, your employer is required to provide benefits and withhold taxes. As a contractor, you're responsible for your own benefits, you generally need to file quarterly estimated taxes, you'll pay self-employment taxes, and you'll be eligible for several tax-deferred retirement options that aren't available to employees.

Why does Uncle Sam care?

Before you set yourself up as an independent contractor, make sure you get IRS Publication 937, and make sure that you understand it. (Inside the United States you can call 1-800-829-3676 to receive any tax form or publication.)

Be prepared for a long excursion into inscrutable knee-deep jargon, and utterly obsolete pronouncements. As is so often the case with IRS regulations, Pub 937 sounds like it was written in the 1960s to apply to conditions prevalent in the 1940s.

Clear-as-mud criteria

Until Congress rewrites the law (and the sooner the better, I say), these are the general criteria used by IRS in determining whether you are an employee or an independent contractor:

- An employer usually "provides tools and a place to work." As a telecontractor, you got 'em by the *cojones* on that score, bucko. Unfortunately, this isn't the only criteria.

- An employer has "the legal right to control both the method and the result of services." This is where you start splitting hairs. Most contractor-style agreements, whether they're in writing or simply understood, give the client the right to control much of the method and result of services, particularly when the services depend upon the knowledge and experience of specific individuals.

- By contrast, an independent contractor's client usually has "the right to control or direct only the result of the work and not the means and methods of accomplishing that result." Of course, the client is bound to get pretty upset if they contract for you, Mr. Expert, to provide 1,000 hours of spelling consulting services, and you hire Dan Quayle to fill in.

Living in the past

IRS Pub 937 made some sense in the days when independent contractors crafted long-tailed buggy whips at home and "real" employees assembled Model Ts on sweat lines at the factory. It makes no bloody sense at all when applied to highly skilled individuals who happen to be peddling their unique services from the cyburbs. Yet, those are the rules, and you'll have to live with them.

The quiz

Now for the quiz. It's a tough one. Is Mark Twain's celebrated jumping frog of Calaveras County an employee or an independent contractor? The answer is at the end of this chapter.

Look Before You Leap

> Keep the munition, watch the way,
> make thy loins strong, fortify thy power mightily.
>
> Nahum II
> ca. 625 BC

Trusting your career to your own devices is always a scary prospect. But, when you get right down to it, you don't have anything else *to* trust, so what the hell, eh?

How much
does it take?

The general rule of thumb dictates that you should have at least six months' income in the bank before you try to step out on your own. I take exception with the rule of thumb: It's both too little, and too much. If you have several contracts in the bag, and you've been telecommuting for a while so all of your equipment and backup systems are in place, six months' income overstates the case. On the other hand, if you're making the move to self-employment suddenly—or, perhaps, not of your own volition—and need to establish your business, possibly in a new location, six months' income can be woefully inadequate.

Besides, if you take six months' income from Silicon Valley or New York City, sell your house and move to Biloxi or Bozeman, you may have enough to live comfortably for the rest of your life!

Instead of the conventional six months' wisdom, I prefer to think in terms of workload. After watching dozens of friends and family members successfully make the transition to telecontracting, I've come to a very simple conclusion: If you have 1,000 billable hours' worth of contracts over the next year absolutely, positively, in the bag—and you're good enough to stay abreast of new developments in your field—you're ready to start working for yourself.

That's four billable hours.

Let me put that 1,000-hour goal in perspective.

Most contractors can eke out a living by billing 500 hours a year. The typical highly successful contractor/consultant bills between 1,000 and 1,500 hours a year. A busy contractor will bill 2,000 hours a year (say, 50 weeks at 40 hours per). A very, uh, creative contractor might get away with billing 2,500 hours a year. Some lawyers bill 4,000 hours a year, but *you* wouldn't do that, would you?

There's a sort of critical mass factor at work here. If you have much less than 1,000 hours in the can when you make the leap, you're going to have a hard time making the contacts and establishing the reputation—the "references," if you will—to keep the ball rolling. That's why I prefer to think in terms of hours, instead of months' salary, or actual income (which I'll discuss later, under "Contractor to Consultant").

Expenses   Income is only half of the equation. Before you consider branching out, you must also carefully examine your expenses.

If you've been telecommuting for a while, you know how much it costs to run your office: In fact, you've probably absorbed most of the expenses into your normal household expenses, with hardly a second thought. The other office expenses like long-distance telephone and equipment maintenance—the ones your boss currently pays, but which will become your responsibility when you're on your own—will probably be pretty obvious, too.

But as an independent contractor in the United States, you'll have three additional expenses that may make the difference between survival and a trip to the unemployment office.

Taxes   First, if you're successful, your taxes are going to increase significantly. The so-called "Self-Employment Tax" (which is really just the other half of Social Security and Medicare taxes—the part that used to be paid by your employer— that you now have to pay for yourself) takes a whopping 16 percent right off the top of your contracting income. For those of you who do well as independent contractors, and just happen to live in highly taxed cities, counties, or states, taxes may consume 50 percent or more of your income. Bang. Wimper.

Success hath its price.

Benefits   Second, when you go out on your own, benefits rarely follow. Some of those benefits—the matching tuition grants, or 401(k) plans—are nice, but hardly necessary. The real killer is health insurance.

 If you live in a third-world nation like Myanmar, Albania, or the United States, you will find that the single greatest obstacle to breaking away as an independent contractor is the lack of decent, affordable health insurance. I would call the lack of pooled-risk insurance in the United States a national disgrace, but that isn't strong enough.

Health insurance for the self-employed   I've heard of four approaches to health insurance in the United States that seem to work for some of the people, some of the time:

- See if an HMO or PPO* available to you as an employee will extend the same coverage to you, uninterrupted, and at a reasonable price, should you leave your current employer. If you find a plan like that, join it *now*, and get the promise in writing. Sometimes HMOs and PPOs will accept applicants straight off the street, so if you're stuck without a policy it may pay to drop by Kaiser Permanente or a competing HMO or PPO and see if they'll take you.

---

* A Health Maintenance Organization is a company that provides all of your health care for a single, set monthly fee. With rare exceptions you must use the HMO's doctors, hospitals, etc. A Preferred Provider Organization contracts with a group of physicians and other health care providers to give you care at a greatly reduced cost (often with a relatively small coinsurance payment), if you use those providers.

- Use your spouse's insurance. In my experience, well over half of the self-employed people in the United States who have health insurance get it through their spouses.

- Move to a civilized state or country. Many states have filled in the gap left by spineless national politicians. If your state doesn't offer pooled-risk insurance for the self-employed, find one (like Hawaii, Oregon, or Colorado) that does. Unfortunately, the laws are changing constantly, so any list I might publish here would be obsolete by the time you read this. Instead, you'll have to call the state Division of Insurance in the capital city of any state that may interest you.

- Join an organization that has a good group health insurance program. Many professional organizations offer health insurance, but the quality varies widely. Make sure you understand the benefits and limitations of the offered policy before you sign up.

You may qualify for a limited-time "transition" policy—often called a COBRA plan—after leaving your current employer. From what I've seen, COBRAs are pretty good as long as they last, but they never seem to last long enough. **COBRA**

Finally, beware of "Group Conversion Plans." Some insurance companies offer these plans to suckers . . . uh, people who leave group health plans when they quit a company. When I left my job with a big oil company many years ago, Travelers Insurance offered to sell me a "Conversion Policy" based on the oil company's plan. I bought it, and paid the premium religiously.

Eight years later, when I really needed the insurance, I discovered that it was a sham: Travelers would pay a whopping maximum of $2,000 per hospitalization. Don't know if you've seen emergency room prices nowadays, but I went through that $2,000 in my first *ten minutes* in the hospital. Travelers didn't give a damn. The state insurance commission didn't give a damn. The only people who cared were staffers in a U.S. Senate committee who were examining shady health insurance practices—and look at all the success they had with a national health insurance plan.

The insurance companies get away with this kind of fraud because the marketing of health insurance policies is largely unregulated: anybody can sell you anything, by and large, and call it "health insurance." If Travelers sold a $2,000-cap policy and called it "car insurance"—which *is* regulated, defined, and subject to all sorts of oversight—somebody would be in jail. **Flame ON**

They fooled me. Don't let 'em fool you.

The other kind of new expense you'll have is Errors and Omissions Insurance. It's the kind of insurance you need to protect yourself from lawsuits should you screw up on a contracting gig. If you'll be producing products or providing **E&O Insurance** services that could go awry and cause one of your clients enough grief to sue you, E&O insurance should save your tail.

Insurance companies base E&O policy rates on historical experience: You can expect to pay anywhere from $1,000 annually up for a policy that covers the kinds of claims common to your consulting business, for example. Should the nature of your business change, it's a good idea to review that change with your E&O insurance agent.

Talk with your home insurance agent. Chances are good they'll know somebody who can set you up with E&O insurance at a reasonable price. Some professional organizations also offer E&O insurance.

The $64 questions   A quick recap. If you're thinking about making the jump from telemployee to telecontractor, with your current employer as your major client, these are the questions you should be asking:

- Can your current employer guarantee, oh, 500 billable hours of work in the first year? Any less than that and you may find your current company something less than a reliable client.

- Is your knowledge valuable enough to draw 500 billable hours of work from some other source?

- Can you keep the IRS off your tail? Note that, if you can split your billable hours out so a fair percentage of them come from some company other than your previous employer, chances are good you won't have any problems.

- Where are you going to get health insurance?

Those are the problems that will dog you in making the transition.

A Real Business

> Money is life to us wretched mortals.
>
> Hesiod
> *Works and Days,* ca. 700 BC

Get off the fence.   If you're going to make the break and become an independent contractor, don't dilly-dally with it. Make up your mind and, if you feel so possessed, take the plunge, and start acting like a *real* business—for if you don't treat yourself as a real business, nobody else will, guaranteed.

If you walk through any library or bookstore you'll find dozens, maybe hundreds, of books on starting a business. Those 500-page tomes can get mighty intimidating: business plans, small business administration, startup loans, double-entry ledgers.

Bah. Humbug. Starting a business is easy.

Here's Woody's 10-Point Underground Checklist for Forming a New Business (more accurately, a sole proprietorship with no employees). Follow these steps in order and you'll have a "real" business up and working in a week or so, with a minimum of hassle.

1. Order a telephone line (or two; see Chapter 4) for the business. Have it listed in your name. Unless you really want to get a listing right away in the Yellow Pages, don't tell the phone company that it's a business line.

2. Pick a company name. Call your state's Department of Revenue and order the forms necessary to register the name (it's often called a "trade name affidavit" or a "DBA name application"). While you have the Department of Revenue on the horn, tell them exactly where you live, and ask them how to go about getting a Sales Tax License. Finally, check with the Revenuers and make sure your state doesn't require anything more than a trade name and a Sales Tax License for new businesses.

3. Fill out and submit the company name application form. Don't do anything until you receive notification from the state that the company name has cleared: It's possible that somebody else has registered the name, in which case you'll have to change it, reapply, and wait for the new name to clear.

4. Apply for a Sales Tax License, even if you won't be selling anything—the license itself is often useful as proof that you have an ongoing business.

5. Start a checking account in the company's name and get checks printed. From the moment the checking account is started, *all* business will be transacted through that bank account, *period*. If you're of the technical persuasion, get the account set up with Quicken or Quick Books, right away.

6. Call the IRS (800-829-3676) and ask for a form SS-4, an application for an "Employer Identification Number." The EIN is, effectively, a social security number for businesses—you needn't have any employees to apply for and use an EIN.

7. When the EIN application form arrives, follow the "Tele-TIN" instructions on the back to call in and receive your EIN. Then fill out the form, per the instructions, and fax it back to the Feds.

8. Rent a safe deposit box in the company's name and put the trade name affidavit, Sales Tax License, checking account application form, and EIN application in it.

9. Update your will to include your new company. Dying intestate with a sole proprietorship in the pot would put your heirs through all sorts of hell. If you don't have a will (or, better, a revocable living trust), *now* is the time to get one.

10. Start making quarterly estimated tax payments. See Chapter 8 for details.

The corporate birth certificate

That's it. That's all it takes to make your business "official." In most states,* if you have a properly registered trade name, a Sales Tax License, and an EIN, you have all the documentation about your company's birth—and its identity—that you'll ever require.

CONTRACTOR TO CONSULTANT

It is comfortable to give advice from a safe harbor.

J. C. F. Schiller
Wilhelm Tell, 1804

What's in a name?

There's no hard-and-fast dividing line between a contractor and a consultant. I tend to think of independent contractors as people who have surpassed the IRS's infamous "employee" hurdle, but still rely on just one or two clients for the bulk of their income. Consultants, to me, are those who make a living by selling their services (and sometimes related products) to a handful of clients or more.

The unifying concept that binds all consultants—again, in my humble opinion— is a direct tie to their clients. A good consultant bears responsibility not only for her actions, but for the results of her actions. When a consultant writes a computer program for a client and the program blows up, the consultant is on the next plane to get it running again. When a consultant recommends an organizational change, and sales drop off precipitously because of the change, the consultant is all over the organization, right now, trying to find a solution. In short, a consultant is always on call. It's the consulting tie that binds.

Your company's in good hands with Furbish & Freemish Assoc., P.L.C.

---

* If you live in a state with some bizarre licensing requirement, the Department of Revenue would've told you about it in step 2.

A consulting company lives and dies on its reputation. Building a successful consulting company requires Herculean effort, a sterling reputation, excellent marketing ability, and a constant stream of success stories that can be used to bring in new business.

Piece o' cake, right?

What It Really Takes

> When I hear artists or authors making fun of business men
> I think of a regiment in which the band makes fun of the cooks.
>
> Anonymous
> *H. L. Mencken's New Dictionary of Quotations*, 1942

What does it take to be a successful consultant? That's easy. You need to have a modicum of business sense, you must possess some sort of knowledge that people are willing to pay for, you should be willing to learn about the tools of the trade, and you must have a high tolerance for pain.

Four nitty-gritty qualifications

Perhaps I'm showing my biases, but I maintain that the number one qualification demanded of a budding consultant, outside of the obvious rudimentary business sense and know-how others are willing to pay for, is a willingness to learn how to use computers.

While it's certainly possible to start a consulting business with nothing but a telephone and a pencil, the key to doing well in the nineties lies in using machines to make the most of your time. Computers, fax machines, modems, phone systems—in short, the entire telecommuting panoply—have become something of a prerequisite to making a consulting business work.

Telecommuting is where it's at.

A consultant is just a telecommuter who works for herself.

Guess which one is the consultant?

Technology-driven

Many contractors, and most successful consultants, are deeply involved with telecommuting technology: They use computers to run their businesses; they keep in touch with their best customers on-line, often delivering products, proposals, and bids electronically; they use the wires to keep on top of new developments in their field and to establish a "presence" that often leads to new business (see Chapter 9).

The traditional Achilles heel of the consulting industry has been exposure—making sure people, particularly the *right* people, know where to find you. The ability to tiptoe through the cyburbs is the greatest advance for consultants in the past decade. If the I-way didn't exist consultants would have to invent it, if only for their own selfish interests!

If you're seriously considering becoming a consultant, it would behoove you to get to know a consultant in your field, preferably one who works in the same town that will be your home base. Take him to lunch. Offer to do some scutwork for him for free. Learn from his experience the ins and outs of consulting on your home turf.

Talk to an expert.

Do you think consulting is glamorous? HA! Your local wizard should be able to relate tales of horror and abuse.

Consulting combines the worst of many professions. Like a physician, consultants are always asked to give diagnoses, free, at any gathering. Like a volunteer firefighter, a consultant can get calls any time of the day or night, with demands that she immediately drop everything and attend to the disaster at hand—real or imagined. Like an architect, consultants constantly face clients who haven't the slightest idea what they really need and, when shown something that can actually solve their problem, go into apoplexy at the projected cost. Like a waiter, consultants all too often get stiffed on their fees—but unlike waiters, one lousy client can sink a consultant's entire business.

Not all doom 'n gloom

Of course, consulting has its good points. If you're successful, you can expect to spend sixty to eighty hours a week working. . . and another ten hours a week worrying. The few weekends that you don't spend in your office will probably be punctuated by calls from panicked clients. You'll be forced to spend many weeks on the road every year. And then one day you'll realize that all the effort you've put into your company hasn't built any "value": Cornelius Furbish and Associates is nothing without Cornelius Furbish—and if good ol' Cornelius gets sick, or burns out, or has to take time off for an ailing relative, the company's entire revenue stream vanishes with nary a whimper.

Hey, some people call that "freedom!"

Gig Taxonomy

> Let us work without protest;
> it is the only way to make life endurable.
>
> Voltaire
> *Candide,* 1759

Yes, I know the question you want to ask: *How much do I charge?* That's why you're reading this whole chapter, isn't it: *What am I worth per hour?*

I can see the question on your lips . . .

Hold your breath for a second. I'll get to the money question in the next section. First, we need to take a look at how you can structure your consulting work, what kinds of jobs are available, and what kinds of fee arrangements pertain.

Whaddya expect from the low bidder?

By far the most common arrangement between contractor and client is the flat hourly fee: your client agrees to pay you a fixed number of dollars per hour. You submit a bill to the client monthly, detailing your hours (typically listing the total number of hours billed each day), and they pay within 30 days (so-called "Net 30" billing).

Flat hourly rate

It's important that you establish which hours will be billed, and for how much. Will you charge for travel time? If so, do you get your full fee? What happens if you get stuck in a snowstorm in Grand Rapids? If the gig is for a presentation or a course, will you charge for preparation time?

A few cautionary notes on hourly rate billing. First and foremost, you, the consultant, must keep accurate records of the time you've spent, and what you spent it on. Computer programs such as TimeSlips may help, although a

simple hand-written or machine-based log will suffice. Make sure you update the time log every day. Second, if you have clients that are always late with their payments, assess them a 1.5 percent or 2 percent late fee every month they fall in arrears: Think of it as an incentive program. Third, don't become over-exposed to one client. If Acme Widgets is overdue on their bill, simply tell your client that you can't do any more work until the account is made current. You'd be surprised how many small consultants go under when their big clients declare bankruptcy.

You'll often see two common variations on the flat hourly rate method of billing: the retainer and the sliding hourly rate.

Retainer   A retainer is a fee paid in advance by your client, to reserve a fixed number of hours of your services. Typically, a client will contract for a set number of hours—say, 250 billable hours—over a specific time span—say, during the next six months. In exchange for the security and convenience of the retainer, you give the client a discount—10 to 20 percent is not unusual. The client pays for the hours up front, occasionally on an installment plan. As you perform the work, you submit monthly invoices showing how many hours have been consumed, and how many remain.

The retainer is a good deal all around. You know you're going to get paid. The client gets a break on your fee, and will often get top priority on demands for your time.

The only downside I've seen to a retainer arrangement is the question of what happens when the initial block of time is used up. In the example above, what happens when the client uses the 250 hours in less than six months? Do you bill the client at the "retainer" rate? If so, what incentive does the client have to write another retainer? It helps to have that problem ironed out—even put in a contract—before you hit it.

Sliding rate   Another common variation on the fixed hourly rate theme is to give your clients a break if they start using your services a lot. For example, you might give a 10 percent discount to any client with more than 500 hours in a calendar year, or 20 percent for 1,000 hours or more.

If you do give a discount, make sure you show it explicitly on the invoice. For example, if your regular fee is $60 an hour, but you're giving the client a 10 percent volume discount, bill the whole thing out at $60 an hour. Then list the discount, separately and very explicitly, at the bottom of the invoice. Doing so has two benefits: First, the client doesn't start thinking that your standard rate is 10 percent less than it really is; second, the client is constantly reminded of the benefits of using your services so heavily.

The primary alternative to an hourly consulting arrangement is the so-called fixed price contract. Typically, the client creates a formal description of the work to be performed (often called an **RFP** or **Request for Proposal**), and several consultants are invited to bid. The low bidder often receives the contract, and is obligated to perform whatever is described in the RFP.

Fixed-price bid

More consultants have lost their shirts on fixed-price bids than on all other forms of contracts combined. With rare exceptions, it's virtually impossible to construct an RFP that adequately describes a complex consulting gig. If you bid on a sketchy RFP, particularly for high-tech consulting services, you're begging for problems.

Occasionally when you look at a well-written RFP, you'll discover that it has adequate safeguards for both the bidder and the client. For example, the RFP may call for a bid based on 1,000 hours of consulting service, but allow for additional hours, under certain conditions, at a pre-determined rate. Projects with well considered pressure-relief valves of that ilk can work out well.

Fixed price, with escalators

It's well beyond the scope of this book to go into a discussion of contracts and contract law, bidding strategies, and all the little ways you can get shafted in the consulting biz. But there's one particularly heinous bit of contracting flim-flammery I wanted to warn you about before we look at feeeelthy lucre.

There's a type of consulting contract called an "hourly with ceiling" or "fixed maximum" contract that has Sucker written all over it. In essence, the contract agrees to pay you a fixed hourly fee, up to a maximum number of hours, to perform a specific task. For example, you might be asked to write a product manual for the Acme SuperWidget, and you'll be paid $80 an hour, for a maximum of fifty hours.

What's wrong with that picture? Simple. The designers of Acme SuperWidget may suddenly decide—after you've signed up for the manual writing gig—that the new, improved SuperWidget will include a component that automatically creates World Wide Web home pages, and you have to write about it. A job that should've taken, oh, 30 hours, is now up to 200 hours. *And you're left holding the bag.*

Avoid "hourly with ceiling" or "fixed maximum" contracts. They're every bit as bad as fixed price contracts, with the additional little proviso that you can never win!

What You're Worth

> The worth of a thing is what it will bring.
>
> H. G. Bohn
> *Handbook of Proverbs*, 1855

Okay, okay. This is why you read the chapter, eh? You want to know how much you can get away with charging on your hourly consulting gigs. In short: What are you worth?

Mirror, mirror on the wall You aren't alone. It's the first question computer jocks ask me when they discover that I've spent a few years as a computer consultant. It's the unspoken question whenever groups of consultants and consultant wannabes get together—a number that's rarely divulged, and even more rarely divulged accurately.

Well, the answer is easy: Charge whatever the market will bear, and not a penny more. Unless you can get away with it. *Heh heh heh.*

Monetary Macho: My fee's bigger than yours.

A very wise CompSci professor I know once told me that he figured the hourly consulting rate was so interesting to so many because it's a universal measuring stick—a number, like, oh, your IQ, that can be tattooed to your forehead, thereby establishing your position in the cognoscenti pecking order.

After all, somebody who charges $120 an hour has to be smarter than somebody charging $65 an hour, right?

Yeah. Sure.

Here's what I suggest for a first approximation of what to charge, by the hour, for your initial consulting gigs.

• Take last year's *gross* income, including salary and bonuses, but not including the value of any stock options you might have.

- Divide by 1,000 and round up to the nearest $10.

- Adjust the amount upward by 20 percent if you have a very, very specific talent that this particular client requires, and can't find anywhere else.

- Adjust that amount up or down by as much as 20 percent, to bring the total in line with labor costs in the locale where you will be consulting.

An example: you're an engineer in Boise who made $53,000 last year, plus a $4,000 performance bonus. You'll be moonlighting for a construction firm in Seattle, using talents that are hard to find, but not unique to you. My first guess at a reasonable fee would be roughly $60 an hour (maybe $70 an hour if engineers in your field living in Seattle make considerably more than those in Boise), with the client picking up your transportation and living costs if you have to make a trip to Seattle.

> **A rather typical example**

Another example: You're a software jock in Redmond who made $64,000 last year, no bonus. You're the world's top, published expert on floozihiggers. Your client, in New York, has to have a floozihigger expert. I figure you should start around $110 an hour (= $70, plus 20 percent for floozihigger experience, plus another 20 percent and a little bit more to adjust for New York's high cost of labor).

Not as much as you thought, I'll bet.

The formula works well on the high end, too, should you be so blessed. Say you're a recognized expert in a field, and you run a lucrative consulting business that grossed $200,000 last year. The formula here says you should be charging $200 to $250 an hour or more on your new consulting gigs—and, by jove, if you were to charge any less than $200 an hour, you'd undoubtedly have more lucrative alternatives!

> **The wealthy are different from you and me.**

CONSULTANT TO FREELANCER

> After being turned down by numerous publishers,
> he decided to write for Posterity.
>
> George Ade
> *The Fable of the Bohemian Who Had Hard Luck,* 1899

The difference between a consultant and a freelancer is one of responsibility. Consultants are responsible to their clients. Freelancers aren't responsible, period.

> **What's the diff?**

No. That isn't what I meant to say. Really.

Consultants make a living peddling their advice to specific companies. They generally have an ongoing obligation to those companies, to help the companies out when times get rough, or when their advice or products go bump in the night.

Freelancers, on the other hand, generally make a living out of advising or helping hundreds or thousands (or hundreds of thousands!) of people, all at once. While they have deep commitments to their products or their writings, freelancers rarely have the kind of one-to-one relationship with a client that can drive consultants crazy.

Freelancers *do* get free lunches.

Computer freelancers

In the computer business, the one I'm most familiar with, freelancers often write and support general-purpose software packages, or churn out newsletters, magazine articles, or even books. They tend to think of their customers in terms of audiences, or broad collections of people with similar problems, as opposed to specific companies.

Sic transit gloria

That layer of abstraction releases freelancers from the day-to-day crises that so often plague consultants. Conversely, though, freelancers are very much at the mercy of a fickle public: A popular tech writer today may find his articles lining bird cages next month. Big software companies stomp out little software freelancers with all the deliberation and grace of an elephant sliding on a cowpie.

Freelancers, even more than consultants, have to be very quick on their intellectual feet. They stay alive by identifying trends long before they're apparent to the general public, and running like hell to get ahead of the trends before they become old hat.

Telecommuting

While many telecommuters seem to believe that freelancing is the ultimate career choice for the cyber-connected, few seem to realize just how much freelancing depends on telecommuting technology—computers, modems, fax machines, fancy phones. Electronic submission of magazine and newspaper articles is the rule, not the exception. The number of books and newsletters written in home offices far outstrips the number written in "real" offices. Freelancers in almost every field these days are tied to their computers. Telecommuting technology permeates every facet of freelancing.

Freelancers are telecommuters who write for Posterity.

I know, I know. You have two questions, right? You want to know how much money freelancers make. And you want to know how to become a freelancer. Yeah, I thought so. Most people are curious about that. Well, this is an *Underground Guide,* so you're going to get the straight scoop, warts and all.

You're so predictable.

Becoming a Freelancer

> No man but a blockhead ever wrote except for money.
>
> Samuel Johnson
> *Boswell's Life,* 1776

Very few people make a living freelancing. Most freelancers have to augment their income with consulting, or even a day job. Still, I'd be willing to bet there are more full-time freelancers working in the high tech industries than in all other areas combined. So if you want to reach for the freelance brass ring, at least you're starting in the right place—the hottest part of the field.

The odds are agin' ya.

Many books have been written about writing books (note the cyclical reference) and how to become a "published author." In fact, if you're serious about freelancing, you probably own one or two of those books already.

How to "do" a book

They tell you how to put together a proposal; how to find a publisher, an agent, or both; when to pitch an idea; how to submit the proposal; when you should follow up; what to put in your cover letter; what color of shirt you should wear when mailing the proposal; how to cry over the phone; dealing with rejection; and so much more. That kind of advice sure looks good in theory, but in the harsh light of day, I'm not sure I believe any of it.

There's a whole lot of luck involved. You have to be in the right place when the publisher is looking for a book. You have to have the right topic, one that "sells" to the various factions within a publishing house. In short, I don't know of any sure way to become a book author, much less a successful one.

The magazine business is no easier to crack. Each magazine develops its own stable of writers, but all will take an occasional newcomer. An idea that flops miserably this month may suddenly become hot next month. An approach that works for one writer at a particular magazine may not work at all for another writer at the same magazine; and it may or may not work for the same writer at a different magazine.

Magazines

It's all a turkey shoot.

That said, I have some very specific advice for the would-be book or magazine freelance writer. I won't guarantee any of it will work, but these things do seem to help you get your foot in the door.

- Pick at least one area of technical expertise, and get very good at it. Faking it will get you through the occasional contracting gig or consulting assignment, but fakirs in print generally don't last long.

- Find out where the editorial staff of the book or magazine hangs out—usually an on-line forum, but sometimes a separate bulletin board system—and start participating in their discussions.

- Get to know the publisher and their publications. Every publisher has a different slant; find out what they're buying, and try to anticipate what they'll be publishing next.

- Remember that the material you see in print is at least three to four months stale by the time you read it.

- When you have a solid idea, pitch it—preferably by e-mail. A couple of paragraphs will usually suffice to let the editor know if the piece or book is right for that publisher, at that time.

- Learn to take "no" for an answer. You get one chance. If you pitch an idea and the response is negative, pitch it to a different publisher, or just drop it. But don't think you'll change an editor's mind by arguing about it. You won't.

Quién sabe?   Depending on how you count such things I've written or cowritten about ten books, edited a handful more, and I've been around the block with many, many magazine articles. The one thing I know for sure about what it takes to become a first-time "published author" is that *nobody knows*.

On that upbeat note, let's take a look at various freelancing jobs, with particular emphasis on how and how much they pay.

Software

> It's hard for me to get used to these changing times.
> I can remember when the air was clean and sex was dirty.
>
> George Burns

The soft connection   At first blush, including software as a means of freelancer support may seem a bit strange. But when you think about it a bit, offering software makes an awful lot of sense for most freelancers, regardless of their field of expertise.

While designing, writing, or installing custom software for a specific client is the domain (indeed, the mainstay) of high-tech consulting these days, creating and peddling software for the general business public is very similar to freelance writing: You're concerned about solving general classes of problems, and providing those solutions to thousands or hundreds of thousands of individuals.

I seek enlightenment, oh guru.

Just as undertaking training assignments, speaking at conventions, writing newsletters, and the like help to build your reputation as a freelancer, writing and standing behind a top-notch software product will help put you on the map. As best I can tell, Peter Norton was the first person to use his reputation as a software hack to build his freelance writing business, and vice versa. Steve Gibson did much the same thing, 'tho in a different way.

Software for recognition

Nowadays the software/writer/consultant lines are becoming more and more blurred, and the thrust of software products has gone way beyond traditional computer topics: A world-renowned authority on disposal of medical hazardous waste also offers a computer program to analyze disposal alternatives; an organizational consultant packages her training "refresher" as a computer-based course.

It's only the beginning. Soon, just about every consultant and many freelancers will include software as an integral part of what they offer, whether the software is sold separately or as part of a training seminar or bundle of services.

If you're thinking about turning your expertise into a software package, there are two general types of software you must consider—commonly called general purpose and vertical market—and three distribution methods—commercial, boutique, and shareware. Let's look at each.

Two types, three distribution methods

The type of software you're most likely to be familiar with is the type called general purpose: software intended for use by people in many different industries, to tackle problems common to many different kinds of users. This category includes operating system software, utilities, word processors, spreadsheets, databases, accounting software, and the like. Most computer jocks trying to break into freelance software development will typically concentrate on general-purpose software.

General purpose software

If your area of expertise is in the real world, though, the vertical market will probably interest you. Whether you're a retail marketing specialist with a new approach to reorder point tracking, or a crossword puzzle ace touting a different

Vertical market software

kind of word game, software designed to solve a specific problem in a specific industry—vertical market software—is the way to go.

Having a great idea for a new software package is never enough. Once you've settled on an idea, and long, long before you ever *think* about getting the idea translated into a real computer program, you must consider marketing. How ya gonna sell it? In my experience, fewer than one in five new software products survives more than two years. Far fewer. Almost always, marketing is the culprit: There's a red-hot product, a crying need, an easily identifiable audience . . . and almost no way to make the audience aware of the product's existence.

Commercial software
You'll find very few new software products (other than games, for which there seems to be an insatiable demand) released as full-fledged commercial offerings. The reasons? Competition and money.

Perhaps more than any other industry in history, the computer industry thrives on competition. While a handful of innovative software products manage to rise above obscurity every year, the trenches teem with products—*excellent* products—that didn't quite make it. Once I thought there would be room for four or five different Windows word processors. Now it looks like only two will survive the decade. Spreadsheets have followed the same path. Page layout programs (if they don't disappear entirely!) have dwindled to a handful. The companies that fold have fallen victim to vicious competition, on a scale that would've made Atilla the Hun beam.

When you can buy the top-selling word processor for $89, why would you spend $299 for a competitor? The financial equation has turned in favor of consolidation, not proliferation of new software titles.

Where the money goes
Still interested in launching a new commercial general purpose software product? You better have $500,000, minimum, in your back pocket. Consider that a full-page four-color ad in a major computer magazine—the *back* of a major computer magazine—costs at least $4,500. Per issue. Advertising's a killer.

So is distribution. In order to convince any of the major software wholesalers to carry your product—and without the wholesalers, you won't get your product on retail store shelves—you'll need to have a sizable ad campaign lined up. Then you'll pay thousands of dollars, up front, to the distributor for "co-op advertising." You'll agree to provide thousands of copies of the product, up front, without payment, typically, for ninety days. You'll guarantee to take back any of the product that doesn't sell—or, if it *does* sell, you'll agree to provide product at a rate that can bankrupt your company in weeks. (Sorry, they only pay ninety days after receipt.) Then, just to add insult to injury, the distributor will withhold a very substantial portion of the proceeds as a reserve against returns, and another chunk of change for future co-op advertising.

Even then, few distributors will take on a single-product vendor. It's just not worth their while to set you up in their system, for one measly product.

The joys of commercial software development

Most distributors will only be willing to pay 40 percent to 45 percent of the retail price: If your product lists for $49.95, say, the distributor will pay you $20 to $22 each, less the co-op advertising allowance, reserves, and all the other folderol. **The deck is stacked against you.**

Even the manufacturing will squeeze you. Designing a box will take many thousands of dollars, and the first run will cost a bloody fortune. The folks printing the manual need three months to get your job through. Duping disks costs a fortune. Assembling the boxes can take weeks, and before the shrink-wrapped boxes are ready to ship, the printer's bills will come due. Raw material costs for a typical small commercial general-purpose software package run about $3 to $5—higher for a short run of fewer than 10,000 copies.

Is it any wonder why so few new software products see light of day?

On the other end of the spectrum lies shareware distribution, a method that has become increasingly popular as the commercial end of things goes off the deep end. **Shareware**

Shareware companies distribute their products freely, and ask that those who use the software pay for it: Try before you buy, and all that. Evaluation versions of shareware products are widely available on every on-line service and from thousands of private bulletin board systems and shareware dealers (who sell the programs for the price of the disks) all over the world. The approach seems terribly naive, but it works. To a point, anyway.

The vast majority of shareware authors make just a few thousand dollars a year or less. For most of them, shareware is more than a hobby, but less than a full-time job. Since the price of entry is quite low (if you know how to program, you can easily launch a decent shareware product for under $1,000), many shareware projects are undercapitalized, and never quite manage to reach critical mass.

On the other hand, there are shareware companies that do very well, indeed, with a few grossing over $1,000,000 a year. Several big commercial products (ever hear of Doom, Mosaic, Eudora, or ProComm?) started out as shareware.

There's still a stigma attached to shareware. In some circles "shareware" is a key word for "buggy" or "not good enough for prime time." And, to be sure, more than a few pieces of shareware give the word "junk" a bad name. By and large, though, shareware can be most effective, both for the author and for the customer. Increasingly, the biggest problem shareware companies face is in making their presence known in an ever-widening sea of shareware.

Full Disclosure

Yes, I'm biased. I've been selling shareware (an enhancement to Word for Windows) for many years. Nowadays my shareware company does quite well, thank you: no Microsoft, to be sure, but not bad under the circumstances. Take my biases into account, should these words persuade you to consider shareware as an adjunct to your freelancing or consulting career. Better still, contact the experts: Association for Shareware Professionals, 545 Grover Road, Muskegon, MI 49442-9427; on CompuServe GO ASP.

Boutique

As a freelancer with a reputation in a specific area, you have a unique opportunity to develop and sell software that solves problems unique to your area. The entire market for the product may only be a few thousand users, but if it's used as a means to bolster your freelancing and consulting work, it may be one of the most effective sales techniques you'll ever see.

You can sell the software in connection with seminars, in-house courses, newsletters, magazine articles, or books. I call it "boutique" software, as it falls outside the madness of commercial distribution, and the narrow market usually puts it outside the mass-market character of shareware.

There are lots of good reasons for selling boutique software.

- It helps build name recognition and association with you and your ideas. You're no longer the lecturer with a few fancy slides and some unworkable snake oil; all of a sudden, your customers can put their own numbers into your spreadsheet program and see how your ideas work on their problems.

- It'll make your customers remember you when you aren't around. The printout says "Acme Widgets," sure, but it also says "Based on the Flooglebibble Seminar by Jonathan Flooglebibble, 800-GO-FLOOGLE."

- Software has "legs." While Flooglebibble Consulting may be entirely dependent on Jonathan Flooglebibble's physical presence at all consulting gigs, the software company can take on a life of its own.

You needn't do it all yourself. There are plenty of people and companies who will write the software to your spec. Others will provide order fulfillment, technical support, manuals, packaging—just about anything you can imagine. If you're looking for help, start with your local college or computer user's group (there's a big list in the back of *Computer Shopper*). You'd be surprised how much raw talent is available, and at reasonable rates.

Speaking Engagements

> The lecturer stands on a large raised platform, on which sit around him the bald and hoary-headed and superlatively wise. Ladies come in large numbers, especially those who aspire to soar above the frivolities of the world.
>
> Anthony Trollope
> *North American*, 1862

If you're a good speaker, taking on speaking assignments may be the fastest way to gain widespread recognition. Unfortunately, even though there seems to be a convention, meeting, or seminar every week in the high-tech fields, the speaking gigs are few, and tend to go to the same people over and over.

Talk, talk, talk

Before we get started, I'd like you to know that I inherited
this speaking slot from my great-grandfather.

I only know three ways to increase your chances of being invited to speak at a convention or seminar.

- Become very well known in a very narrow specialty, and hope that the convention gods decide that they need a session on that specialty.

- Get to know the people in the industry who are most likely to run panel sessions. Panel moderators have to draw on their own circle of experts to fill the panels, and they often have to work with very short deadlines.

- Get to know the people putting on the conference.

Money, money, money   Oh. You want to know how much speakers make? Yeah, I thought so.

If you're one of dozens or hundreds of speakers at a big convention, you'll probably draw an honorarium of a few hundred to a thousand dollars. The organizers should also transport you to and from the convention, give you free admission to the entire convention, and pay for your room.

If you're a featured speaker at a high-tech get-together, your fee should go up several hundred dollars, and you can probably multiply the fee by speaking several times. Once again, you should also be transported, wined, and dined like the celebrity you are.

The payoff   Is it worth the effort? Sometimes. It's rare that you'll make enough money in speaking fees to compensate for the time you spend on the project. But often the contacts you'll make as a speaker will lead to all sorts of interesting possibilities.

You'd be surprised how many first- and second-time convention speakers swear they'll never do it again. Creating and delivering a good talk is hard work, with very little save ego gratification to show for it.

Newsletters

> It is the greatest pleasure of the Athenians to wander through the streets asking, What is the news?
>
> Demosthenes
> *First Philippic,* 351 BC

All that's fit to print   Of all the options open to freelancers, writing a flagship newsletter probably holds the greatest potential for making a fat profit.

The operative term there is "potential," of course.

For your purposes, as a consultant or freelancer, the actual profit on the newsletter may be beside the point. Whether you concentrate on small circulation, high-price "insider" newsletters, or the mass circulation, low-price pedestrian kind, newsletters bring your name and smiling face to your customers' attention month after month.

The other shoe drops.   That's the upside. It's hardly a secret: every Tom Dick 'n Harry, from college alumni associations to Joe's Bivalve Veterinary Shop puts out a newsletter these days. The downside to committing to a newsletter, as a freelancer anyway, comes if you can't find anything new to fill those four or eight or twelve pages every month. And *that*, my friend, is a challenge of the first degree.

Writing a good newsletter takes gobs and gobs of time. I'm a pretty prolific writer, and I have a helluva time getting more than three or four solid newsletter pages done in a day—and that's when I know the topic, cold. If I have to pick up on something new, my productivity falls down to two pages a day, tops.

You may have endless topics tucked away in that brain of yours, and you may be able to compose witty, fresh copy as fast as you can type. But in the land of newsletters you're working without a net: Fall down just once, and all your clients will see it happening, in slo-mo, with the hard copy evidence of your mental faltering available for all the world to see.

Scary, eh?

One final word of warning on newsletters: I'm still not sure why, but it's very, very rare for a subscription-based electronic newsletter to last more than a year. I've seen a lot of smart—even brilliant—people try to launch electronic newsletters, charging anywhere from $39 to $79 a year, on every type of medium imaginable. They never seem to go anywhere.

I've talked about this at length with several friends who know the business well. One of them thinks that newsletters, by their very nature, have to be hardcopy—the customer feels slighted without a piece of heavy paper in her hands. Another thinks that the temptation is too great to just copy the floppy or e-mail or file. I'm not at all convinced either point is true, but there's something . . . a hex, perhaps?. . . that keeps knocking off electronic subscription newsletters.

Electronic newsletters by subscription

Then again, maybe *you* are precisely the person who can make the concept work. If so, I wish you luck!

Writing Articles

> No author is a man of genius to his publisher.
>
> Heinrich Heine

I've already talked about various tactics you could take to having an article accepted in one of the technical magazines. The topics I dodged at the time, and will attempt to tackle now, are the ones that probably interest you most: how do you actually write an article, and how much do magazines pay?

After you've pitched an article and had your pitch accepted, you should request a copy of the magazine's "Author's Guidelines" or "Submission Guidelines." It will no doubt thrill you to discover that there is no one, single way to write or submit an article. The Guidelines are supposed to give you an idea of how to format your submission, to minimize the amount of time your editor has to spend futzing around turning your prose into something that can be understood by the magazine's page layout software.

The article shtick

In reality, the Guidelines are rarely up to date, and most editors don't give more than nodding credence to them anyway. You may find it useful to wrangle a working sample; ask your editor to send you a copy of an article that's formatted the way she wants it. That should give you a good starting point.

Most of the high-tech magazines I know about ask you to submit either a plain "dumb" text file, or a file in Word for Windows format. If the latter, they'll probably want all of the text in the Courier font—the plain, monospaced, typewriter-like characters that are so rarely used in business today—so don't even bother thinking about how the article will be laid out.

The Guidelines will also tell you how to submit artwork. Follow those instructions precisely.

The final throes That's about all there is to it. You'll send in the article, generally electronically, whether via an on-line service, bulletin board, or mailed diskette. The editor will get in touch if there are any questions. You may have a chance to see the final article before the magazine hits the streets, but don't hold your breath. The magazine has full control over what appears in the final copy. Some magazines, of course, are better than others: as one (very talented!) magazine writer once told me, "Any resemblance between what I submitted and what ended up in the magazine is purely coincidental." The very best magazines will try hard to stick to what you submitted.

Payment Almost all magazines pay by the word, with fixed fees for a few fixed-size articles (for example, a "quarter-page review" will have a set fee, whereas an "800-word article" would pay by the word).

Fees in the high-tech magazine world are the highest of any I've encountered; indeed, there are fiction writers who go into fits when they find out how much high-tech writers make. Narrow-interest technical magazines—ones with small readerships, the "niche" publications—generally pay twenty cents a word or more. The largest circulation technical magazines pay as much as $1 a word, for solid technical articles by well-known writers. (By comparison, general interest magazines may pay ten cents a word for fiction.)

There's a reason why the high-tech fees are so high. It can take days, weeks, or even months to put together a good cover story. Very few technical people write very well, and even fewer good writers understand the techy nuts and bolts. In short, good material is hard to find: The technical people who could be writing about this stuff can often make more money simply doing whatever it is they're supposed to be writing about.

Most magazines offer a kill fee—an amount paid to the writer should the article be assigned and written, but never published—but I can't recall the last time I heard of a high-tech article being killed.

In general you'll have to submit an invoice in order to be paid. The Guidelines should cover the details, but be sure to ask your editor if there's any doubt.

Writing Books

> There ain't nothing more to write about, and I am rotten glad of it,
> because if I'd a knowed what a trouble it was to make a book
> I wouldn't a tackled it, and ain't agoing to no more.

Samuel Clemens
Huckleberry Finn, 1885

There's something special about high-tech book authors. It's hard to put your finger on it. Hmmmmm . . . How do you say? Uhhhh . . . They're all . . . what you call . . . *insane.* Yes. That's it. **The driving force**

Writing a technical book combines all the fun of an extended research project (the kind where they lock you in a room for six months, only opening the door once a day to toss in a pound of raw hamburger) with the sheer exhilaration of pounding your head against the wall in synch with the natural resonance frequency of cesium.

Different kinds of books present different challenges. "Intro" books on high-tech subjects aren't too bad, particularly if you can cull from an existing user's manual, and your editor is looking for a serious, rather subdued book. Good writers, working solely on one book, can turn out 200 pages a month working under those conditions, and probably squeeze in the occasional weekend softball game. **How long does it take?**

The real "techy" books are another story entirely. If you have a job, but absolutely no life, and you know the topic well, you can probably churn out 100 pages a month. If you have no job and no life, and have spent months or years immersed in the topic, you might get up to 200 pages a month, but at that point your brain will fry like a gob of spit on a Ford radiator.

If you don't know the topic, you don't stand a chance. By the time you finish the book, it'll be obsolete.

Some publishers try to get writers to do "work for hire." A work for hire agreement gives the writer a one-time fee, in exchange for which the writer loses all rights to the work. That fee can vary all over the place, but $10 a page isn't unusual. Work for hire is like surrogate motherhood: you get paid for your effort, but the end result of all your labors is taken away from you. If the book takes off, the publisher makes a mint. Even if it doesn't, you have no claim to what you produced. **Work for hire**

Some first-time authors settle for work for hire because they see it as a way to get their foot in the book publishing door. I can't think of any other good reason to agree to it.

Most publishers pay their authors royalties: A percentage of the amount the publisher receives for each book sold is paid to the author. That's the basic idea, but the implementation gets a little complicated. **Royalties**

When you sign a contract to write a book, there are two monetary variables: The amount of the advance, and the percentage used to calculate royalties. The easiest way to explain this is with an example.

Say you've just signed on to write *The Underground Guide to Frumious Bandersnatchi*. Your contract calls for an advance of $10,000, payable half on signing and half on delivery, and royalties of 10 percent. The list price on the book will run $40.

The advance As soon as you sign the contract, the publisher sends you a check for $5,000, which is the "half on signing" part of the advance. That $5,000 is yours to keep no matter what (providing you deliver an acceptable manuscript, and you will, you will).

You spend four months slaving over a hot keyboard, and deliver a brilliant manuscript. The publisher cuts another check for $5,000, the "half on delivery" part of the advance. That money is yours to keep.*

The Underground Guide to Frumious Bandersnatchi rolls off the presses and starts selling like hotcakes. In its first month, *TUGFB* sells 6,000 copies, or about $240,000 worth at retail. Let's say the publisher's wholesale price is about half the retail price (a 50 percent discount is a pretty good rule of thumb). So the publisher brings in $120,000 this month on *TUGFB*.

Making it back You apply your royalty—10 percent in this case—to the wholesale. At the end of the first month, you've made 10 percent of $120,000, or $12,000 on the book. Here's the tricky part. The advance really *is* an advance, so the first $10,000 in royalties you accumulate goes back to the publisher. It's called "making back the advance." The publisher owes you $2,000 (that's $12,000 you've earned, less the $10,000 advance) on sales the first month. Next month, assuming the book keeps selling, you'll make more.

In the world of fiction writers, scarcely one book in ten makes back its advance. And that's not because advances are big—a $5,000 advance for a first-time novelist is very good money. In fiction (at least in theory), the one big breakaway book makes up for the publisher's losses on all the little books.

High-tech books are different. In my experience anyway, a fair percentage of all high-tech books make back their advance. They have to because the number of breakaway books in high-tech fields can be counted on one hand. Well, maybe two.

It's a little more complicated. I've simplified things a bit here. Advances can be broken into three or more payments (on signing, on delivery of half the manuscript, on delivery of the whole manuscript, on publication, on the editor's boss's birthday). Royalty percentages often have "escalators"—they increase as the number of books sold increases. All the high-tech publishers I know about pay royalties just twice a

---

* Well, sorta. Actually, the publisher theoretically could go after you, to recover any unmet advances. In practice, I've never seen it happen, in any field of publishing.

year: on April 1 for sales through the previous December, and October 1 for sales through June. There are miscellaneous charges (typically for indexing) that can be deducted from royalties, some is withheld to provide for returns, and so on. A book contract can run twenty pages of dense legalese.

Ah, I've skirted the most important question again, haven't I? **So how much?**

In the high-tech book biz, a $10,000 advance for a first book is not bad at all. Big books with experienced authors can run $20,000. ("Big" being a relative term that somehow encompasses the cover price, projected sales levels, and the popularity of the series or author.) Royalties fip-flop all over the place, but 10 percent is low, 12 percent pretty good, and 14 percent outstanding.

And now you know the rest of the story.

GETTING HELP

> The immense and ever increasing sums which the state wrings from the people are never enough for it; it mortgages the income of future generations, and steers resolutely toward bankruptcy.
>
> P. A. Kropotkin
> *Paroles d'un révolté,* 1884

If you want the IRS to tell you whether you're an employee or a contractor, file **The IRS will** Form SS-8 with the District Director of the IRS. **tell you.**

Filing an SS-8 is a bit like asking a used car salesman how much the car he's trying to sell you is *really* worth. If you file an SS-8, please let me know. I'd like to tell you about an extraordinary deal I have on some swamp land in Louisiana that's just a little bit wet, and only for a few days a year.

Seriously, if you run afoul of any of the traps in this chapter, you're going to **Hired guns** want a damned good tax lawyer, fast. Don't speak to the IRS. Don't sign anything. Don't volunteer any information. Don't do what your accountant, or your brother-in-law, tells you, and for heaven's sake don't talk to either of them about your disagreement with the tax man. There's a little piece of paper called a subpoena that can turn your world—and theirs—upside down.

Simply stall until you get the best tax lawyer you can find.

Oh. You wanted to know if the celebrated jumping frog of Calaveras County **Twitchin'** is an employee or an independent contractor? It was a trick question. *Heh heh heh.* **Twain**

He's an employee. According to IRS Publication 334 (which paraphrases and clarifies Publication 937, as amended by Revenue Procedure 85-18 in Internal Revenue Cumulative Bulletin 1985-1, page 518), the frog is a *statutory employee* for Social Security and Medicare purposes as he is "an individual who works at home on materials or goods (that is, flies) which you supply and which must be returned to you or to a person you name (presumably, uh, recycled), if you also furnish specifications for the work to be done (that is, yell, "JUMP!")." If you own said frog and the IRS determines he is a *de facto* employee—in addition to being a statutory employee, for *prima facie* reasons cited above—and fail to withhold income, Social Security, and Medicare taxes, you will not only be personally liable for the entire amount of the taxes, you are also additionally personally liable for a penalty equal to the amount of the taxes.

On the whole, it's easier to marry the frog and forget about it.

Or you could shoot him. Dead pollywogs wag no tails.

8 Taxes, Laws, and Accounting

We don't pay taxes. Only the little people pay taxes.

Leona Helmsley
Quoted in *The New York Times*, 7/12/89

These three topics cover a wide variety of evils in every telecommuter's professional life. They're complex, forever changing, and subject to a bewildering amount of conflicting interpretation.

The "hard" side of taxes, laws, and accounting

I'm not going to step you through preparation of a Form 1040, either manually or on a computer, or tell you about methods for assessing the qualifications of an accountant. There are libraries filled with books of that ilk, and if you need help with a particular piece of the tax-laws-accounting triumvirate, you'd be well advised to seek out a book that covers your specific topic—or just go ahead and hire a pro who talks the talk.

Instead of using the shotgun approach, I'm going to carve off a little piece of each of the topics, and focus on the part that applies most directly to telecommuters and those who are computer savvy. Chances are pretty good you haven't hit those parts of the topics before, and if you're of the telecommuting persuasion, they can be damned important.

"In this world nothing can be said to be certain, except
death and taxes." Ben Franklin, Nov. 13, 1789

The biggest topic, of course, is taxes. Asking me to write about taxes is a bit like asking Jerry Falwell to write about the Marquis de Sade. While I don't necessarily think of the U.S. Internal Revenue Service as The Great Satan, is there any doubt where a modern American Mephistopheles would work, given the choice?

United States versus Woody

I've only been audited once—back in 1981, several years before I started telecommuting—and it was an excruciating experience. I took a small deduction, depreciating both a house and the land it stood on, not realizing (I swear!) that, while the house was depreciable, the land was not. My first meeting with the IRS rates among the most traumatic times of my life: I couldn't sleep for days before or after; my knees felt like Jell-O; I nearly threw up outside the auditor's office. *And I hadn't done anything wrong.* We went over my return and the error stuck out like a sore thumb. I apologized profusely, offered to write a $100 check on the spot to cover my lapse, but noooooooooooo. . . .

Why not slide bamboo slivers under my fingernails and get it over with?

Over the ensuing ten months I endured six interrogations from five different auditors, each with a different set of questions and a different way of working. They went over my return with a fine-toothed comb, and didn't find a bloody thing except for that $100 mistake. I complained to the auditors. I complained to the IRS. I complained to my senators. The whole sorry experience only ended when, ultimately, the IRS ran out of time—generally the Feds have to complete an audit within a year, unless they find something worth auditing—and they had to ask my permission to extend the deadline.

The IRS sent me a letter that said something like, "Golly, gee, sorry, sir. We've been torturing you for almost a year now, and we can't find anything significant wrong with your return. According to Regulation something-or-other, we would like your permission to continue this brutal assault on your integrity. Please check one of the following boxes, sign and return this form."

Woody stands accused before the Big I.

One of the boxes said something like, "❑ YES! I am a good citizen, and I want to help my government continue to put me through seven shades of hell. Please continue the audit until all the wonderful people at the IRS think they can't wring any more money out of me." The other box said, more or less, "❏ NO, I am not a good citizen, and refuse to allow my good and kind friends at the IRS to continue their examination of my return, even though I will probably end up in jail for tax evasion because I'm obviously trying to hide something."

Guess which box I checked.

The mighty U.S. government spent something like $10,000 auditing poor ol' Woody Leonhard, and recovered a little over $100. That's the honest truth.

My roots

Little did the auditors realize that they had created a monster, the iconoclastic beast you see before you now. It's hard to believe in anything the government does after going through an experience like that audit. I think I can trace my curmudgeonly, slightly, uh, acerbic view of bureaucracy and big organizations to that year in IRS hell.

'Course, once the Feds see this chapter, they'll probably audit me again. Just for kicks. Wanna bet?

Anyway, this chapter covers U.S. tax laws and regulations as they stood in the summer of 1995. It also touches on some of the archaic, local American inanities known as zoning laws, and a bit about accounting. As such, it's specific to U.S. citizens, both living at home and abroad, and U.S. residents subject to American taxes and local laws. If you aren't a U.S. citizen or resident, you can skip the whole chapter.

It may be worse where you live.

I am not a lawyer. I don't pretend to be one. I don't aspire to be one. Nothing in this chapter constitutes legal advice, and cannot be construed as being anything more than the quasi-educated, semicoherent rantings of one individual who's been struggling with, and drowning in, these concepts for more than a decade.

IANAL

It's worse than mere inscrutability. Tax laws change from year to year, from day to day. No publication can keep up. If you need advice about a tricky tax question (say, anything more complicated than a simple choice in your favorite tax preparation software), talk to a tax lawyer.

THE TAXMAN COMETH

He is a man of thirty-five, but looks fifty. He is bald, has varicose veins and wears spectacles, or would wear them if his only pair were not chronically lost. If things are normal with him, he will be suffering from malnutrition, but if he has recently had a lucky streak, he will be suffering from a hangover.

At present it is half past eleven in the morning, and according to his schedule he should have started work two hours ago; but even if he had made any serious effort to start he would have been frustrated by the almost continuous ringing of the telephone bell, the yells of the baby, the rattle of an electric drill out in the street, and the heavy boots of his creditors clumping up the stairs. The most recent interruption was the arrival of the second post, which brought him two circulars and an income tax demand printed in red. Needless to say this person is a writer.

George Orwell
Confessions of a Book Reviewer, 1946

**Some *real*
reform**

I keep hoping that some day The People will regain control of the American government and institute a rational tax system—say, a flat 10 percent or 15 percent of all income. I'd actually *pay more taxes*, gladly, if I could reclaim the eight or ten days a year I commonly waste on tax stuff, the intellectual energy spent on that mind-numbing complexity of ludicrous, contradictory bafflegab known as "regulations," and all the money I have to spend on software, accountants, lawyers and the like, to keep track of this garbage.

Naw. It'll never happen. Too many extremely rich and powerful people wield too much influence over those charged with modifying the 100,000-plus page tax code and derivative regulations. Ah well. If wishes were horses, hackers would ride.

Home Office Deduction

What is the perfect way to happiness?
To stay at home.

Bhartrihari
Niti Sataka, ca. 625 AD

By and large the home office deduction is way overblown. I know you didn't want to hear that, but it's the truth. Only a small percentage of telecommuters will ever qualify; and even if you do qualify, the bottom-line dollar benefit of the deduction isn't much.

With that warning, here's how to figure out if you qualify.

**For most folks,
this is as far as
you need to
read.**

If you are a traditional telemployee—that is, a telecommuter who is not self-employed, but works for a company—and you are absolutely *required* by your employer to work out of your home, you may (may!) qualify for a home office deduction. Most telemployees work out of their homes because they want to, and that automatically disqualifies them for taking a home office deduction.

Traditional telemployees can only deduct home office expenses on Schedule A, as an itemized deduction. If you don't itemize deductions, you can't take a home office deduction anyway.

Chances are good that you don't need to worry about this tax stuff: Very few telecommuters even qualify. If any one of these describe your situation, skip over the tax part of this chapter, on to the "Laws and Other Absurdities" section.

- You are participating in a voluntary telecommuting program.

- Your boss isn't willing to say, in writing, on company letterhead, for IRS consumption, that she is forcing you to work out of your house.

- You don't itemize deductions.

Okay. If you're reading down this far, I assume you are either self-employed, or you are a traditional telemployee who is forced to telecommute. (And if you're being forced to telecommute, I'll assume you *never* work out of your employer's central office. If you do, you might qualify for the home office deduction, but the IRS will be all over your case.)

Roughly eight million people qualify for the home office deduction, but only four million people take it. Why? The other four million are afraid of being audited. A little bit of intimidation goes a long way. The funny thing is, if you qualify, there's absolutely no reason to be intimidated. **Scare tactics**

While it may be true that the home office deduction will increase your chances of being audited a bit, the deduction is *not* a red flag: I've been taking the deduction for years now, and (wood duly knocked) haven't been audited for it.

The requirements for taking a home office deduction got much tougher when the U.S. Supreme Court decided, in 1993, that an anesthesiologist named Dr. Soliman couldn't deduct home office expenses because most of his work was performed in the hospital, not in his home office. **The hurdle got higher in 1993.**

As a result of the Soliman decision, the IRS rewrote its home office deduction guidelines (Ruling 94-24, if you want to look it up). The way the regulation stands now, you have to use your home office "exclusively and regularly" for the business or to meet clients. Having cleared that hurdle, you must also show that the "relative importance" of the work you do in the office is greater than work you do outside the office or, if a preponderance of "importance" cannot be demonstrated (Oy! Don't you love tax regulations?), the IRS may look at how much time you spend working inside and outside the office. **Exclusively and regularly, importantly and oftenly**

What's clear in all this murky mess is that your office has to be 100 percent "office." For example, you can't let the kids play on your office computer—the kids' use of the computer may be minuscule compared to how much time you spend on the beast, but the fact that you *ever* let the kids play on it means that the office itself is tainted, and can't be claimed as a deduction.

Ah, but does the relative importance of *assembling* a buggy whip
exceed the relative importance of *testing* a buggy whip?

**The law's an
ass.**

In fact, if you take the regulations literally, placing one personal call on your home office phone would disqualify the office deduction for an entire year.* The whole thing's insane. But that's the law.

Pub 587

If you think you might qualify for the home office deduction, get a copy of IRS Publication 587 (once again, you can get any tax form or publication from inside the United States by calling 800-829-3676). And strap on your hip waders. It's sixteen pages of dense gobbledygook that's clear as the bottom of a Louisiana bayou.

Percentages

The basis for deducting home office expenses sounds pretty straightforward: Figure out the square footage of the office and the square footage of the house, and divide. (For example, if your office occupies 150 square feet of your 1,500 square foot house, 10 percent of the allowable expenses are deductible.) In practice—having seen four different professional real estate appraisers come up with four different square footage numbers for a neighbor's house—there seems to be a lot of room for, uh, creativity. There's even a rarely used IRS provision for counting the number of rooms in a house (say, one office in a five-room house, giving a 20 percent figure) that you should only use if your lawyer *guarantees* he'll bring meals to you in the joint.

I fought the law and the law won.

* Don't believe it? Read the regulations. There's no slack in the "exclusive use" provision.

Once you've calculated the percentage, you need only keep track of real estate taxes, your mortgage or rent payments (yes, renters who qualify *can* deduct rent!), insurance, repairs, utilities, and the like. You can even depreciate the house and deduct part of the depreciation. If you itemize deductions, there's some sleight-of-hand you'll have to perform to adjust for any deduction you claim on mortgage interest but that's all detailed in Publication 587.

Dollars and deductions

Traditional telemployees take their home office deduction on Schedule A. It isn't as simple as subtracting the home office deduction from your pay. Not by a long shot. Plan on spending several hours to work through all the knots and get the numbers in the right places.

Traditional telemployee deduction

It's probably easiest to show you how this incredibly tangled web works by stepping through an example. If you have a copy of Schedule A, get it out, and follow along. (The line numbers are from the 1994 tax forms, but other years should be pretty similar.) Take a look while I step you through the calculations that typically whittle away a traditional telemployee's home office deduction to nothing.

An example

- Say you have a qualifying home office that occupies 10 percent of the square footage on your home. You made $35,000 as a traditional telemployee (adjusted gross income, Form 1040, line 32). You paid $3,000 on insurance, utilities, and repairs. Your house is worth $150,000, excluding the value of the land, and you have determined, by wading through Publication 534, that you qualify for 31.5-year straight-line MACRS depreciation—believe it or not, that's the most common situation.

The baseline numbers

- Note that, as a traditional telemployee, you cannot include deductible mortgage interest or real estate taxes in your calculation for the home office deduction. Since you will be taking your home office deduction on Schedule A, and Schedule A already has spots for mortgage interest and real estate taxes (lines 10 and 6 respectively), you can't deduct them a second time for the home office deduction calculation (which goes on line 20). Got that?

Mortgage interest and real estate taxes

That's a 31.5 year straight line MACRS depreciation for
nonresidential real property placed in service before May 13, 1993.
Oh. Of course.

Deductible expenses

- In our example, you have $3,000 of partially deductible home stuff—insurance, utilities, and repair—and your office takes up 10 percent of your home. Since you can't deduct mortgage interest or real estate taxes, that means you'll end up with $300 in deductible expenses. Not much.

Depreciation

- Depreciation doesn't amount to much either. On a $150,000 house (excluding the value of the land, again, remember?), 10 percent office use, straight-line 31.5 years, you'll come to a whopping $476 (= $150,000 ÷ 10 ÷ 31.5) in depreciation.

Total deduction

- Add the deductible expense to the depreciation, for a total of $776. That's your home office deduction for the year. Stick that number on line 20 of Schedule A—the one marked "Unreimbursed employee expenses."

How the deduction flows to the bottom line

- After adding a couple of miscellaneous expenses (tax preparation fees, safe deposit box, and so on) you have to subtract 2 percent of your adjusted gross income. Assuming your other miscellaneous were minimal, you would take that home office deduction of $776 and subtract 2 percent of $35,000, for a total allowable deduction of (oooh! aaaah!) $76. See why the home office deduction doesn't do much?

- But wait! We aren't done yet! The rest of Schedule A steps you through your other allowable deductions: medical, mortgage interest, donations. The total amount of all your deductions—including that really pivotal $76 home office deduction—has to exceed your standard deduction ($6,350 in 1994 for a married couple filing jointly) or it doesn't make any sense at all to itemize deductions.

Self-employed

Self-employed people claim the home office deduction on Schedule C, using Form 8829 and possibly Schedule F as further documentation. (If you've incorporated yourself, you can only claim a home office deduction if you're a subchapter S corporation.) Since home office expenses are subtracted directly from your business income, they can be pretty significant. You can't deduct more than your company's total net income, although losses can be carried forward to the next taxing year.

Be it ever so humble, there's no place like a partially deductible home.

For most traditional telemployees, a $1,000-or-so home office deduction probably won't even put you over the top for itemizing deductions, unless you have hefty mortgage payments or some outlandish medical bills. It's unusual that going through the home office deduction hassle pays off.

Bottom-line it for me, Woody.

For the self-employed, though, the home office deduction comes straight off your company's Schedule C profits. If you're in the almost-50-percent tax bracket (including self-employment and state taxes), a $1,000 home office deduction puts $500 in your pocket. Deduct, deduct!

If you're self-employed and you normally itemize deductions (which means you can deduct all of your mortgage interest payments, whether you have a home office or not), the benefits aren't so clear-cut. It's probably a good idea to compute your taxes each way—a non-trivial task, even with a good tax preparation program—and see if the incremental return to you is worth the slightly elevated chances of your getting audited, and should that happen, the hugely elevated hassle of having to prove the legitimacy of your claim to the deduction. In the example above, you could deduct an extra $76 by claiming your home office deduction. Is that worth the extra hassle? *I* wouldn't do it.

Some folks are loathe to claim their home office deduction for depreciation on their home. The argument goes something like this: If I depreciate the office part of my house, when it comes time to sell the house I'll have to "recapture" that depreciation and pay taxes on it.

Depreciation recovery non-issue

Well, don't sweat it. There's a really dumb part of the tax code (as of this writing anyway) that works in your favor.

> **The "home office" determination is made year to year. If you're planning to sell your house in 1998, make sure that by January 1, 1998, you've done something —rented an office in town, or remodeled the room and moved in your teenage son—that absolutely, clearly disqualifies the room as a home office. If the room doesn't qualify as a home office in the year you sell it, you won't have to recapture any depreciation taken on it, ever.**

Double-check it with your tax advisor, but I repeat. The law's an ass.

Business Expenses

> Income tax returns are the most imaginative fiction being written today.
>
> Herman Wouk

If you are a traditional telemployee, the home office deduction is (at best) all you get. You can skip the rest of this section, and move on to "Laws and Other Absurdities."

Telemployees take a break.

If you are self-employed, there's a whole gauntlet of things you can do to bring down the ire of the IRS. They're called "business expenses," and they're reported on Schedule C. I'll try to hit the high points, particularly for telefolk, in the remainder of this section.

Let's start at the beginning: the structure of your company.

Why Inc.

> Corporations are invisible, immortal and have no soul.
>
> Roger Manwood
> *Chief Baron of the English Exchequer,* 1592

I've looked and looked and can't find a good reason for most telecontractors or consultants to incorporate. While it's true that some of your tax hassles disappear once you've incorporated, you lose some otherwise-deductible expenses and have lots of overhead to contend with.

Cover your assets? Some people claim that incorporation will protect your personal assets, should somebody decide to sue. Best I can tell, though, for most telecontractors, consultants, and freelancers, that just isn't true: If you're running the show, and you screw up, you are personally liable for claims. The fact that you were personally performing the work is all that matters. You can't hide behind a corporate facade. If you're a professional out peddling your talents, protecting assets is much, much more complex than simply filing incorporation papers.

It's so debonair. Some people think that the "Inc." adds a certain flair, a certain stability, to your corporate persona. I don't buy it. The "Inc." may influence some people, true, but it's like Groucho's not wanting to belong to any organization that would have him: If a client can be impressed by an "Inc." you have to wonder what other kinds of hogwash they've swallowed.*

Welcome to the international headquarters of ME, Inc.

---

* This from a guy who doesn't own a proper business suit, and hasn't worn a tie since 1979. So what do I know about creating a "professional" aura? If you believe in "dress for success" you'll probably buy the "Inc." line, too. Guess that's what makes a horse race.

Most telecontractors, consultants, and freelancers get along just fine as sole proprietors (that's what your business is called if you don't do anything specific to change it; you own the business; you *are* the business). Sole proprietors file a Schedule C to report their business income and expense. There's very little else a sole proprietor must do, aside from following the steps mentioned in Chapter 7 to establish the business, and (generally) filing sales tax returns with the state. It's easy.

Sole proprietorships

From a federal tax point of view, a partnership is only slightly more complicated than a sole proprietorship. A partnership exists as soon as a partnership agreement is executed; the agreement usually lays out the precise percentage participation of each partner. Partnerships file a Schedule K-1 (Form 1065) to report income and expenses, but other than that, the individuals involved in the partnership are treated pretty much like sole proprietors.

Partnerships

Beware of the state income tax complications of a partnership, though, should you and your partner operate out of different states, but sell to the public only through one. Some states are getting very greedy, and may lay claim to the income from both partners. Consult your tax advisor.

Two kinds of "baby corporations" are particularly popular. The subchapter S corporation retains most of the tax benefits of a sole proprietorship (including the home office deduction, which is not available to other kinds of corporations), while affording some of the protection of a "real" corporation.

LLC, subchapter S

Some states offer a Limited Liability Corporation, or LLC, as an incorporation option. The legal status of LLCs is still being wrangled out in court. If you think you might be interested in incorporating, ask your favorite accountant or lawyer if either the LLC or the subchapter S could have any advantages for you.

To be sure, "real" corporations do have a few tax advantages. They can deduct charitable contributions (all the other types of companies require you to report the contributions as personal, so you have to itemize deductions in order to take advantage of the deduction). They can set up 401(k) plans, to provide "matching" savings. They can reimburse you for all of your medical expenses, if set up properly. But they're also subject to complicated rules, difficult reporting requirements, they're responsible for separate tax payments, and they bring along all sorts of overhead that the typical teleconsultant won't want to tackle.

The real inc.

Unless you're making megabucks, have very unusual expenses, need insurance coverage that isn't available to individuals, or are starting to hire a lot of staff, there's probably little if any reason for you to incorporate.

Business or Hobby

Chacun à sa marotte.*

French Proverb

The best-laid plans

Sometimes all your efforts go to naught: With all your good intentions to the contrary, the business you try hard to put together and keep moving turns into a nonprofit organization. That can spell disaster from the IRS.

Unless you can prove to the IRS that you are engaged in this activity to produce a profit, the Revenuers may declare it all a "hobby," and thus disallow any tax benefits you're trying to accrue.

To you it's a hobby. To me it's a way of life, OK?

 It doesn't matter how much you work, how hard you try, how many clients you can snag, or even how much you've billed but not collected. It doesn't matter that you've created the ultimate mousetrap and the world is on its way to your door. When the IRS makes its decision about whether you're running a business or a hobby, all that matters is if you can show a paper profit in three of the previous five tax years.

Yes, it is possible to prove that you're conducting a business without meeting the "three of five rule." But you'll probably end up telling your story to a tax court, and if your company is swimming in red ink already, tax court is one place you don't want to be.

* Everyone to his hobby.

Should you be placed in the unenviable position of trying to show a profit on paper for the current tax year, remember that there is no law that says you must take every deduction to which you're entitled!* It sounds a little like cutting off your nose to spite your face, but you can effectively scuttle your home office deduction, for example, by moving a TV set into the office, or letting the kids play on the computer. You can decide that it isn't worth the effort keeping track of business mileage on your car. All that counts is whether your company's net profits—the money you bring in during this calendar year, less the money you claim in expenses—is in the black.

Expenses, Legitimate and Illegitimate

> There is one difference between a tax collector and a taxidermist—
> the taxidermist leaves the hide.
>
> Mortimer Caplan
> *Time* 2/1/63

By and large, if an expense feels a little flaky, it's probably not allowed. Here are just a few things that you *cannot* claim as business expenses on Schedule C: **Not allowed**

- The first telephone line going into your house. Even if you use your home phone number for business purposes, you can't deduct the charges for the line (except outgoing long-distance business calls, of course).

- Medical expenses (with a few very specific exceptions). Health insurance is one of those things that's a valid expense this year, partially credited last year, and totally forbidden the next: check to see its current status.

- Charitable deductions.

- Gifts in excess of $25 per person each year.

- With very rare exceptions, landscaping and other things that are only tangentially associated with a home office.

On the other hand, there are some things that you can deduct that may surprise you just a little bit. Well, not *that* much. I was surprised to find out that I can deduct the cost of a new passport if my first use is for a business trip. That's a whopping $20 or so saved in taxes. Ho-hum.   **Publication 535**

---

* Okay, okay. That isn't exactly, literally, true. If the IRS thinks you're under-reporting your expenses so you can ultimately qualify for greater Social Security benefits, they'll get you. 'Course if you really *are* under-reporting expenses now to gamble on the future of Social Security, you're already playing with less than a full deck.

American homage

You can deduct the cost of almost any equipment you use, providing you prorate it, deducting only the portion attributable to business use. (That's in great contrast to the home office deduction which is an all-or-nothing proposition.) Any professional services rendered to your business are deductible. Books. Magazine subscriptions. Dues for professional organizations. Seminars. All of business travel, in most cases, but only half of business meals. Postage. Advertising. On-line service fees. Your best bet is to pick up a copy of IRS Publication 535 which goes over all the details on business expenses; Publication 917 covers mileage expenses.

Section 179   You're probably aware of the fact that you can expense a big chunk of office equipment (as of this writing, $17,500 or your total net profit for the year) every year. As long as you stay within the dollar limit, items which otherwise would've had to be depreciated can be written off immediately. This "Section 179 exclusion" is a boon to those of us who hate the thought of figuring out the IRS amortization schedules, MACRS, GDS, ADS, and heaven knows what-all. Everything you need to tell the IRS about the expense—and it's pretty straightforward—is calculated and reported on Form 4562.

If you don't expense out your computers and software using the Section 179 rules, you're in for an unpleasant surprise: Computers, by law, have to be depreciated over five years; software must be depreciated over three years. Considering that the average lifespan of hardware and software are roughly half of what is allowed in the depreciation rules, giving up your Section 179 allowance can be quite painful.

Bottom-line it   If you're in the 50 percent self-employed tax bracket, every dollar you spend
again, Woody.   on computer equipment, office equipment, software, and the like, up to the annual limit ($17,500), is subsidized by Uncle Sam to the tune of fifty cents on the dollar. It's a dynamite deal you shouldn't ignore: time your purchases to take maximum benefit from it: If you're about to go over the $17,500 limit this year, hold off on your purchase until next year.

Section 179 treatment extends beyond computers and software! You can also use it to buy furniture for your office, equipment, knickknacks, all sorts of things. While you can't expense (or depreciate) the value of fine art or antiques — they're assumed to be increasing, not decreasing, in value — furniture, rugs, and the like are all quite legitimate.

Estimated Tax Payments

> Those that dance must pay the music.*
>
> John Taylor
> *Taylor's Feast*, 1638

I'm always surprised when a new teleconsultant confides in me that he doesn't know how to make estimated tax payments, and the thought of doing all those complex calculations is very daunting.

Toil and trouble

Truth be told, estimated tax payments are probably the easiest part of your relationship with the IRS. The form (1040-ES) is a model of brevity and clarity; the intent crystal clear. If only all IRS obligations were this straightforward!

Lesseee . . . how much will I make next Tuesday? Next Wednesday?

If you're self-employed, Uncle Sam wants to collect a portion of the taxes that you will ultimately owe, just as he would if you were in a "regular" job and had part of each paycheck withheld for income taxes.

You must make estimated tax payments if you expect to owe $500 or more in income taxes by the time the end of the year rolls around. If that describes you, call the IRS and get Form 1040-ES. Payments are due on April 15 (the same time you file your tax return for the previous year), June 15, September 15, and January 15.

How and when

While it's true that you can sit down and try to project precisely how much money you're going to make, and when, in the coming year — and Form 1040-ES will take you through all the steps — the brilliance of estimated tax payments is that, with rare exceptions, all you have to do is pay one-quarter of your previous

* "Pay the piper" doesn't appear to have made it into print until 1670.

year's taxes on each of the four due dates. For example, if your federal taxes in 1994 were $6,000, you would (with rare exceptions) fulfill your entire estimated tax obligation by paying $1,500 on each of the 1995 estimated tax payment due dates.

This year to next

Of course, if your income this year falls way short of what it was last year— you changed from a "real" job to self-employment, say, or you're trying to build a new business—you'll want to go through the motions of estimating your current-year income. Be happy, though. If your income this year really *does* crater, your estimated tax payments next year should be puny.

1099

> The Lord forbid that I should be out of debt,
> as if, indeed, I could not be trusted.
>
> Rabelais
> *Pantagruel,* 1533

Follow the marbles.

Just as the IRS uses W-2 forms to keep track of salaries and wages, the 1099 form follows payments made to and from telecontractors, consultants, and freelancers.

As a sole proprietor, you may use either your Social Security number or your Employer Identification Number (described in Chapter 7) on 1099 forms. Either way, the amounts will be tracked to you and (ultimately, if the IRS gets its computers working right) your income tax return.

Each company that has paid you more than $600 for your professional services over the previous year is required, by law, to send you a 1099 form, by January 31 of the following year. Typically the amount will be reported in Box 7 "Nonemployee compensation" or Box 3 "Other income" on Form 1099-MISC.

Unless the company has made a mistake—and you should notify them, by certified mail, if there is a mistake—you are responsible for reporting all of the amounts on 1099 forms that you receive as business income on Schedule C.

Turnabout and fair play

Similarly, if you have contractors or teleconsultants doing work for you, and you have spent more than $600 for their services, the IRS insists that you fill out a 1099-MISC form for each of them, and send the contractors or consultants those forms by January 31. If you have some sort of royalty arrangement with a group of collaborators, you'll also have to make out 1099-MISC forms, reporting the royalty payments in box 2.

IRA, SEP, Keogh

> Happy is the man who, ignored by the world,
> lives contented with himself in some retired nook.
>
> Nicholas Boileau
> *Épîtres,* 1670

If you are self-employed, there is absolutely no reason in the world why you shouldn't have an IRA, SEP-IRA, or (best of all) a Keogh retirement plan. You're simply throwing money away—and into the maw of the U.S. Givement—if you don't take advantage of the plans available to you. When it comes to tax stuff, this is as close as you'll get to a no-brainer. **Do it, do it.**

The tax advantages of each of the plans are twofold. First, you get to subtract the amount you put into plan from your income—if you contribute $2,000 to your IRA or Keogh this year, and you made $50,000, you'll only pay taxes on $48,000 of income. That isn't an ordinary itemized deduction, pilgrim: We're talking reduced tax obligation, right off the top. **Off the top**

Second, once the money is in the plan it accumulates interest tax-free. You only owe taxes on the money as you take it out of the plan—presumably after retirement, when you're in a lower tax bracket. Sure, it makes sense to put money away for when you retire. But if you have any extra money left over at the end of the year, it makes even more sense to get it sheltered from income taxes. **Keeps on going**

The downside? If you have to withdraw money in a retirement plan before you retire, the government will sock you with a sizable penalty.

Its never too early to plan—or practice—for retirement.

Each of the three common types of plans for the self-employed (IRA, SEP-IRA, and Keogh) has its benefits and drawbacks. See Figure 8.1.

Figure 8.1 Retirement Plan Quick Look

Plan	Max Contribution	Last Day to Establish	Hassle Factor
IRA	$2,000	Day you file 1040	Very Low
SEP-IRA	about 13% of earnings, max about $20,000	Day you file 1040	Low
Keogh	25% of earnings, max $30,000	December 31	Moderate

IRA Establishing an IRA is as simple as starting an IRA account (look in any newspaper or ask at any bank), making the right choices on Form 1040 (there are extensive instructions), and cutting a check payable to the IRA account. You don't have to set up anything in advance: As long as you write that check on or before the day you file your 1040, and you file on time of course, the IRA deduction will be allowed. There are no annual reporting requirements for the IRS. You have no ongoing obligation: Should you decide next year that you don't want to contribute, it's no big deal. As tax things go, an IRA is like falling off a log.

SEP-IRA The SEP-IRA is almost as simple as an IRA. You have to file a form, but any bank or mutual fund house will fall all over itself helping you with the details. You have to futz around with part of self-employment tax that you calculate on Form SE (that's why the Max Contribution numbers in Figure 8.1 say "about"), but once again the bank or brokerage will help, and gladly. You can wait until the day you file your return to write the check, the IRS requires no annual reporting, and as long as you have no employees you have no obligation to contribute every year.

Keogh The Keogh constitutes a horse of a completely different color, or actually two different colors. The "defined contribution" flavor of the Keogh forces you to establish a percentage of your net income (to a maximum of 25 percent) that you will commit to the plan each year. The "defined benefit" flavor starts with a determination of what kind of benefit you'll get on retirement, then works backward to calculate how much you have to put into the plan. Some folks would have you believe that a Keogh is too complicated for normal people. They're only half right. The "defined benefit" plan *is* complicated; I wouldn't recommend it to any but the most anal-retentive of tax dodgers, uh, thrifty citizens. The "defined contribution" plan, though, isn't tough at all, if you have good help. More on that in a moment.

A Keogh plan involves creating a real-live Trust, with a capital "T." Unlike an IRA or SEP-IRA account, this Trust lives as an independent entity—thus it carries with it various reporting requirements. When you commit to a Keogh, you make an ongoing, year-after-year commitment: If you decide to put 20 percent of your net profits into the Trust this year, you must do so next year, and every year thereafter.

Not a seat-of-the-pants thing The Trust must come into existence in the year it will be used. For example, if you want to start a Keogh plan for the 1995 calendar year, you must form the Trust by December 31, 1995—you can't wait until April 15, 1996, as you can with IRA and SEP-IRAs. Once the Trust springs to life (typically with a small initial deposit), you will have until the day you file the 1040 to write your contribution check. In other words, you might start the Trust with a $500 check on December 31, 1995, but you have until April 15, 1996, when you file your 1040 for 1995, to calculate the total contribution you can make for 1995, and to put that money in the account.

The bottom line? If there's any chance you'll net more than $15,000 this year, go ahead and set up a SEP-IRA with your local bank or favorite investment house. (If your net is below $15,000, you'll get maximum benefit from an IRA; the SEP-IRA is overkill.)

What's it all about, really?

If you have more than, oh, 15 percent of your anticipated annual net income lying around, and it looks like you'll continue to have a fair amount of cash kicking about for the foreseeable future, look into setting up a Keogh. There's no faster way to grow a sizable, tax-free nest egg. Yes, there's some paperwork involved, although the annual reporting requirement—something called a Form 5500-EZ—only comes into play when your assets in the plan go over $100,000.

A defined contribution Keogh isn't nearly as tough as some people would have you believe. If you hook up with a company that does Keoghs regularly, they'll do all the hard paperwork for you. Once a year you have to fill in a few blanks, sign the form, and send it to the Feds. Big deal. My Keogh at Fidelity Investments (voice 800-544-5373) takes all of ten minutes a year to administer.

One important caveat: If you have employees, or expect to hire any, there are significant differences in your obligations to them with SEP-IRA and Keogh. If you have employees, make sure you understand those differences before establishing a Keogh.

States Want Their Piece, Too

In the present state of the world it is difficult not to write satire.

Juvenal
Satires, ca. 110 AD

We, uh, TeleTypes, should count our lucky stars that the states haven't really caught on to the implications of the telecommuting revolution. States are scrambling for every penny of revenue they can claim—witness the attempt by several states to recover sales tax on purchases made through mail order firms outside their borders—but they have not, yet, extended their incursion to the ranks of the telecommuting.

Gimme, gimme.

Want to know my vision of Telecommuting Hell? Imagine a telemployee or teleconsultant working in Utah for a company in California. Utah wants to charge him state income tax on all of his earnings. California does, too. Each state has some legitimate claim to the poor telecommuter's hide—but which state deserves how many pounds of flesh? There's no easy answer.

My guess is that the U.S. Supreme Court will render judgment on a case like that sometime in the next ten years. It seems inevitable. How will they decide? Heaven only knows.

Coming soon to a court near you

I hate to keep picking on California, but it's arguably the worst offender. One telemployee I know has to keep track of her time in California, *down to the hour*, to calculate the percentage of her income that's due the California Cæsar. I wonder how the California tax authorities would react if they knew that, even when she was physically located outside California, nearly all of her work was being done on computers located in the state. Ah, the mind boggles.

In the meantime, keep your head down and your powder dry. Don't volunteer any information to state tax authorities. Insist on literal application of the "physical presence test"—if you're physically located outside the state's boundaries, you don't owe the state any tax. And if a state starts making untoward advances on your income, find a good tax lawyer.

Filing

> Pass the hat for your credit's sake, and pay—pay—pay!

> Rudyard Kipling
> *The Absent-Minded Beggar*, 1899

Filing bit by bit The electronic filing of federal income tax returns—where the information is sent via modem to the IRS, with backup hardcopy of a verification signature coming later—continues to unfold across the country, with different states in various stages of development. Electronic filing has received a lot of attention, first as a cool toy, then as the single largest source of new cases of tax fraud.

WHOOA! Now *there's* a fast return! COOL!

Ars gratia rip-off artiste If electronic filing points to the future of the IRS, we're in for a rocky ride, indeed. With all the new time-consuming antifraud safeguards in place, the only really good reason for using electronic filing—speedy deposit of any tax refund due to you—evaporated. Unless the IRS comes up with a brilliant way to authenticate returns (which I don't anticipate happening in my lifetime), electronic filing will never become more than a novelty, only making sense for those who want to borrow immediately against their refund or those who are hopelessly enamored with technology for technology's sake.

All the hype about electronic filing, though, overshadowed a very important development for the computer savvy: Form 1040PC. Stripped down to its basics, Form 1040 is just a bunch of boxes, with numbers that you place in some of the boxes. Form 1040PC, which is only generated by tax preparation packages on (you guessed it) PCs, does away with all the verbiage, instructions, and the like, and produces a bare-bones hardcopy return that can be scanned directly into the IRS computers.

1040PC

By sending the IRS a machine-readable 1040PC form, printed by your computer, duly authorized with your signature, you're saving the government (and ultimately yourself) a heap of money, minimizing the chance of mistakes, and streamlining the whole process. Pretty good results for such a small effort. Personally, I always use the 1040PC, and recommend that my computer-enabled friends and clients do the same.

There's one little hitch, though: The form is so terse, it's virtually impossible for a human to read. So, after I'm done with my tax preparation program and am about to pack it away for the year, I always print out one copy of the long form and save it. 1040PC is great for computers, but humans will go nuts without a full 1040.

Audits

> Who steals my purse steals trash; 'tis something, nothing;
> 'Twas mine, 'tis his, and has been slave to thousands;
> But he that filches from me my good name
> Robs me of that which not enriches him,
> And makes me poor indeed.
>
> Shakespeare
> *Othello*, 1604

With the sole exception of compliance audits (which are conducted on a very small percentage of randomly selected taxpayers every year, primarily to verify the IRS's automated cheater-catching algorithms, and require an intense examination of every detail of a tax return), a tax audit is an affront on your good name. The IRS thinks you cheated—more frequently, the IRS's *computers* think you cheated—at best accidentally, and the auditor will start with the supposition that you have something to hide.

They want your tail.

Even when conducted with the utmost courtesy, and in spite of all the IRS's protests to the contrary, a tax audit is a vicious thing. That's the nature of the beast, and no amount of sugar-coating can change it.

The targets Unfortunately, the self-employed have been targeted by the IRS for special audit attention. If you're a telecontractor, consultant, or freelancer, you stand a much greater chance of being audited than the average wage earner. There's a reason why. Since the beginning of time, self-employed individuals have tended to under-report income (especially cash), and exaggerate expenses. I bet you never thought of that, did you?

As you can see in Figure 8.2, the chances of your being audited increase enormously as your gross self-employment income grows.

Figure 8.2 Chances of Getting Audited in 1993

Schedule C Gross Receipts	Number of Taxpayers Audited per 100 Filers
No Schedule C	1
Under $25,000	2
$25,000–$100,000	2.5
Over $100,000	5

What can you do about it? Don't make so much money! Sorry. Couldn't resist.

Audit anatomy The IRS conducts two very different kinds of audits: Office Examinations and Field Examinations. (There are also correspondence "audits," but those are just computer-generated forms that inform you of discrepancies in forms that have been filed, typically 1099 forms. They're almost always resolved with a simple letter.)

If you are called for an Office Examination, it would behoove you to find representation before you stick your foot in your mouth. Almost always, your representative can appear in your absence, and if they're good they'll make the most of your position.

If you are advised that the IRS is conducting a Field Examination, it's time to bring in the big guns. If the Field Examination is for anything other than establishing the existence of your home office (which can be rather innocuous), you're in deep doo-doo. Get a lawyer—a good lawyer—quick.

In general, you needn't be physically present at an audit, and I would recommend strongly that you *not* attend unless your tax advisor is insistent that you be there. The chances of you screwing up things with some dumb comment are simply too great. Leave it to the pros, take your lumps, and pay your bills.

Oh. The best way to avoid an audit, or at least avoid an enormous amount of anguish should you be audited? Don't take any "iffy" (the technical term is "aggressive") deductions. And tell the truth.

LAWS AND OTHER ABSURDITIES

> Ancient laws remain in force
> long after the people have the power to change them.
>
> Aristotle
> *Politics*, ca. 322 BC

If you think tax regulations place a heinous burden on law-abiding citizens, you ought to talk with a few telecommuters who have run afoul of zoning laws.

Perhaps it's human nature to want to force your neighbors to look, act, and behave as you do. Heaven knows the law books brim with "if you don't behave the way the majority behaves—or at least the way the majority wants to *believe* it behaves — you'll be punished" laws. But you'd think American legislatures would've learned something in the past 200 years.

Monkey see, monkey say you do, or else.

Ah well. I won't start foaming at the mouth about victimless crimes. Or the gross misuse of public funds to pursue morbid fantasies of legions of tight-assed busybodies who have nothing better to do with their time than sit in judgment of folks who do no harm. That's another book. Another time.

Woody's ranting again; ignore him.

However, I do want to touch on two legal topics that concern many telecommuters. For good reason.

Zoning

> Satirized for your protection.
>
> Bill Maher
> *Politically Incorrect*, 1995*

If you're a telecommuter, chances are good that you're working illegally.

Yes. You. A scofflaw. A petty criminal.

Most telecommuters work from homes in areas zoned "Residential" (variously called "R," "R-1," "MR-1," or any of a plethora of similarly meaningless acronyms). Most zoning authorities prohibit or restrict the operation of a business from "Residential" locations.

Zoning the cyburbs

---

* Have you seen *Politically Incorrect*, on The Comedy Channel? When Maher gets going, he's brilliant. The guy should run for President. No. For Dictator of the Known Universe. If you dittoheads want to see a very entertaining and informed counter-point to your regular fare—whether you agree with Maher's politics or not—give *Politically Incorrect* a shot. Rush may be right. But Bill Maher is what's left.

"But wait!" you protest, "surely they don't mean *me?*"

Ah, but they do. They do.

Nostalgia   Like tax laws, many of the U.S. zoning laws were created to deal with the exigencies of buggy whips and Model Ts. They exist to keep you from erecting a spiffy billboard in your front lawn, or to restrict the number of horses that can be hitched to the neighbors' posts. Few zoning regulations have been rewritten to reflect the realities of the electronic age; some haven't even been updated since the time the dodo walked the earth. You laugh, but it's true.

And as long as those archaic laws remain on the books, they can make your life miserable.

No paper tiger   In the hands of a neighbor bent on revenge for offenses real or imagined, zoning laws can force you to choose between your business and your home. In the hands of a bureaucrat who feels the necessity of enforcing every regulation, no matter how noxious, obsolete zoning laws can land you in Zoning Board hearings, or even before your County Commissioners, or the court.

What can you do? Glad you asked.

First, find out your home's zoning code — R or MR or A-1 or B or heaven-knows-what. Do so without tipping off the zoning board, the neighbors, the housing inspector, building office, or any of the officious folks who might take it upon themselves to wonder why you're asking.

Generally, that isn't too hard. If you bought your house from a Realtor, and the house was listed in the Multiple Listing Service, chances are good the listing includes the zoning code. If you rent an apartment or own a condo, the super might know, but it's probably a good idea to avoid asking the owner, particularly if it's possible that the owner will get ticked off if she learns that you're working out of your apartment.

If you can't find the zoning code the easy way, hop on down to your county or city zoning office (often called a "planning department"). Ask to see the zoning maps for your neck of the woods. You don't have to tell them a thing, except for the general geographic area that interests you.

Second, using the zoning code, find out precisely what's permitted and what's forbidden on your property.

Generally the easiest way to do this is to drop by the zoning office and ask to see the zoning regulations. Some zoning offices have pamphlets. Others will fax the information to you.

You may discover that there's no problem at all with running a business out of your home. If so, congratulations! Outward appearances to the contrary, some open-minded communities do exist. Congratulations on living in one of them. You may also discover that the restrictions aren't particularly onerous—no retail sales from the house, for example, or no employees. Should that be the case, bend over backwards to adhere to the restrictions. If the zoning board has met you half way, you should be ecstatic. Many other telecommuters aren't so lucky.

Where I live the zoning laws aren't too bad, they're just . . . dumb. Your laws may be similar.

The zoning laws say my home-based business cannot have any employees. (Fair enough—but there are no restrictions about on-site contractors.) I'm not allowed to have any business signs on my property that are visible from the street. And no more than one business-related vehicle can be parked on the streets. I can live with that.

The "primary use of the structure" must be residential, not commercial. (That's a little flakey: Is making a living a "primary use"?) The business cannot be located in an out-building. (Ridiculous! By that standard, my old 96-square-foot office was illegal.) Finally, the home-based office cannot exceed 400 square feet. (Even *more* ridiculous! What difference does it make how big my office is?)

Third, if you think you're violating zoning restrictions, don't hang a sign on your front door that says, "I am breaking the law." Have your business mail delivered to a rented post box. Arrange things so no more than one or two clients' cars are parked on the street at any given time. Keep business-related junk (like the cardboard box your monitor came in) out of sight.

Far be it from me to encourage you to break the law, but hey! this is an *Underground Guide*. Whaddya expect? Besides, there's no sense in making a nuisance of yourself. A bit of discretion may be all that's necessary.

Fourth, if you think you're violating zoning restrictions, avoid tripping any hot wires. If you're adding an office onto your home, for example, you needn't tell the building inspector that you run your business out of the house. If you're having a phone line installed, order it as a regular residential line; later, if you want to have your business listed in the Yellow Pages, you can have it changed to a business line.

What to do if you get dinged for a zoning violation? You can apply for a variance; the zoning office will tell you how. You might drag a lawyer into the picture. But, by and large, you're probably better off moving somewhere with a more laissez faire attitude.

Covenants

> Covenants are ever made according to
> the present state of persons and of things
>
> John Milton
> *The Tenure of Kings and Magistrates,* 1649

The road to hell

Homeowner's covenants are often constructed with all good intentions, then become set in concrete, find themselves subject to interpretation by increasingly intolerant individuals, and ultimately lose their usefulness.

But a contract's a contract, and if the deed to your home includes a covenant that restricts your ability to run a business from your house, and the people in charge of interpreting the covenants decide that telecommuting is a "business," you may be in for a fight on a grand scale.

The whole thing's absurd, of course. Telecommuting out of your home—an activity that requires a bit of electricity and a telephone line—is no business of a condo committee. Still, the same people who can force you to lower your fence by three inches, or change the color of stain on your siding a smidgen to the orange, wield enough power to throw a monkey wrench into your legitimate enterprise.

There's only one trick I've seen that may—may!—keep a telecommuter away from a collision course with her covenant committee. Many covenants prohibit running a "business" or an "enterprise" from the home, yet they have no such restriction on a "profession." If you can convince the committee that you are merely pursuing your "profession," as opposed to running a "business," you may be able to slip the surly covenant bonds.

All too often, though, covenant fights turn into first-class spitting contests, where the facts serve merely to confuse the issues. My advice, should you find yourself embroiled in such a contest is simple: Move. You can fight it. You can take 'em to court. You can kick and scream and swear till your goldfish is blue in the face. But in the end, a covenant fight will only alienate you from your neighbors. Why bother? Life is too short.

THE COUNTIN' O' THE BEANS

> In your report here, it says that you are an extremely dull person. Our experts describe you as an appallingly dull fellow, unimaginative, timid, spineless, easily dominated, no sense of humour, tedious company and irrepressibly drab and awful.
>
> And whereas in most professions these would be considered drawbacks, in accountancy they are a positive boon.
>
> > Monty Python
> > *And Now for Something Completely Different*, 1971

To finish off the chapter, I'd like to make a few comments about accountants. No, really, I *do* like accountants. Well, some of them anyway.

Why You Need an Accountant

> Few have heard of Fra Luca Parioli, the inventor of double-entry book-keeping, but he has probably had much more influence on human life than has Dante or Michelangelo.
>
> > Herbert J. Muller
> > *The Uses of the Past*

You need an accountant because you can't define "double-entry bookkeeping" in one simple, short, coherent sentence. Try it. You'll see.

Why You *Don't* Need an Accountant

> A beggarly account of empty boxes.
>
> > Shakespeare
> > *Romeo and Juliet*, 1594

You're a computer-savvy telecommuter. There's no sense in hiring an accountant to do things that you can do yourself. Once a good accountant has set up your books — preferably with a top-notch accounting program like Quicken or QuickBooks — you can do all the mundane bookkeeping yourself. By keeping on top of the books, posting them yourself every week or every month, you'll stay in direct touch with the lifeblood of your company: money.

Use the tools.

The same comment applies to doing taxes. When you first set up your business, it's probably worthwhile having a 1040 nut prepare your first tax return, from the bottom up. But once you've seen how it's done—particularly if you have a good tax preparation program at hand, like TurboTax or TaxCut—there's no need to hire an accountant to fill in the empty boxes.

Choosing an Accountant

> All professions are conspiracies against the laity.
>
> George Bernard Shaw
> *The Doctor's Dilemma,* 1906

It's much easier than you think. Most people don't have the slightest idea what kind of an accountant they want or need. As a computer-literate telecommuter, though, the choice is easy. You want an accountant who will:

- Set up your books on a mutually agreeable software package, like Quicken or QuickBooks, then let you take over the actual bookkeeping.
- Help when you, inevitably, get stuck posting some weird expenditure.
- Prepare your first year's tax returns.
- Review subsequent years' tax returns, which you will produce on your own with the aid of a mutually agreeable tax preparation software package, like TurboTax.

In addition you want an accountant who understands telecommuting and all the folderol surrounding home offices, so you absolutely, positively want an accountant *who works out of her home.*

There. I've narrowed down the list of potential accountants in your area by 90 percent or more. Now all you have to do is look through the Yellow Pages, pick up the phone, and find someone you feel you can trust. Ask the potential candidates if they would be comfortable with the four points above. (Hint: If you get a response like, "Our clients don't usually keep their own books," you're barking up the wrong tree.) And be very pointed when asking if they have a home office.

FOR MORE INFO

If you're concerned about protecting your assets from lawsuits, there's a book that covers the whole gamut, from the illusory "protection" of incorporation to the nearly bullet-proof Family Limited Partnerships. *Lawsuit Proof: Protecting Your Assets from Lawsuits and Claims* by Robert J. Mintz and James J. Rubens (O'Brien & Sons, 1994) not only shows you what to do, it warns you about what to avoid. These are two guys you definitely want on your side of the table.

9 Making Big Bucks on the I-Way

Note: Internet users can access "Welcome to Astro-2" on the World Wide Web by typing:

http:/aastro-2.msfc.nasa.gov
or
http:(slash, slash)astro-2.msfc.nasa.gov

Associated Press
From the *Denver Post*, 3/6/95

When the Associated Press gets a Web page address wrong twice, back-to-back, in the same article (it should be http://astro-2.msfc.nasa.gov—and any regular Web user would pick up the typo in a microsecond), you have to stop and wonder how many people really understand very much about the Internet.

Cutting through the I-way hype

Roadblock in the cyburbs

Lots and lots of business people who are new to the on-line world—especially telemployees, teleconsultants, their bosses and clients—think there's a pot of gold at the end of the Information SuperHypeWay. Countless books, magazines, and newspaper articles would lead the uninitiated to believe that the streets in cyberspace are paved with gold.
NOT!

Newbie alert

Well, not unless you're a multi-billion-dollar corporation, an Internet service provider with a handful of huge mainframes in your back pocket, or a couple of shysters from Arizona with the chutzpah to plaster an ad in a thousand different "news" groups—a gross violation of netiquette, not to mention simple human decency—and then write a book about the whole scummy event.

Where's the money? Let's start with one simple premise: If you think you're going to make big bucks on the Internet—at least any time soon—you're sadly mistaken. While it's true that the Internet stands as a nonpareil source of information (*if* you can find the information you seek), and it's certainly true that e-mail via the Internet can streamline your company's operations (as will e-mail in almost any form), I found very few companies that claim they're deriving *any* significant income from the Internet, and no more than a handful that claim to be making a reasonable profit.

So why all the brouhaha?

Uh, have you ever speculated in futures?

DRAGNET

> A crowd is not company,
> and faces are but a gallery of pictures.
>
> Francis Bacon
> *Essays,* 1612

Inertia Don't get the impression that I'm trying to convince you to stay off the Net. Nothing could be further from the truth. I am, however, pleading for a bit of sanity, asking you to think through what the Net is, what it does, how it works, and how that fits into your telework.

For the Net may change you, but you will not fundamentally change the Net.

What the Net Does Well

> Can anyone desire too much of a good thing?
>
> Shakespeare
> *As You Like It,* 1600

Connections As a loose, anarchic collection of hundreds of thousands of computers and millions of computer users, the Internet excels at providing reliable connections between people—just as reliable as the international voice telephone network; more so, in some cases.

For most telecommuters, that immediately translates into e-mail access, not only to the central office, but to customers, collaborators, and assistants. Now that every major on-line service is connected to the Internet, it's easier than ever to send e-mail to a large percentage of all computer users on the planet.

Fifteen or twenty years ago, we all saw the same thing happen with fax machines and fax numbers: They started out as something of a novelty, but before long, every business had one. Nowadays it's hard to imagine running a business without a fax machine. The same thing will happen—indeed, may already *have* happened—with e-mail IDs. They're an enormously valuable competitive tool, one your business should be using.

Without any doubt, the Internet contains the most amazing collection of information ever, uh, disassembled anywhere. There's so bloody much of it that you could sit glued to your screen until eternity freezes and never begin to absorb a small part of it. Merely keeping track of the available sources of information is a full-time job, and then some.

Information

Several publications will help you keep up with the tidal flow—the *Internet Yellow Pages* is a good place to start—and if you can find what you're looking for, there's no better source of information. Except, maybe, a good library.

The third thing the Internet does extremely well—and this is a bit hard to describe—is to keep you in touch with the future. While the Internet abounds with insufferable bores and people whose idea of a good time begins and ends with emitting electronic flatulence, a great many smart people are active on-line. Very, very smart people.

Future

If you want to keep your finger on the pulse of where this world is headed—in commerce, politics, technology, heaven knows what-all—the Internet is a very interesting place to start.

What the Net Does Poorly

> Nothing is orderly till man takes hold of it.
> Everything in creation lies around loose.
>
> H. W. Beecher
> *Eyes and Ears,* 1862

There's precious little organization on the Net. Even the tools that were created to help you find things have become overwhelmed by the sheer volume of information available.

Organize, organize.

It's a congenital defect. The Net was envisioned by its founders as a means of interconnecting diverse computers, systems, and people. By its very nature, the Net is anarchic. Bringing structure to the Net would destroy it—or at least turn it into something that isn't the Net.*

If you're looking for organization, you should be working with an on-line service. At least the big services (CompuServe, AOL, Prodigy) make an attempt to

---

* Surely in some parallel universe there must be an Anti-Net, where everything is organized, and answers to all questions are at your fingertips. Sounds like a great conspiracy theory, anyway.

organize their information. They succeed in various degrees. There's no similar attempt on the Net, and if pure, unfiltered chaos intimidates you, the Net is not the place to be.

What You Need to Do

> Man is by nature fond of novelty.
>
> Pliny the Elder
> *Natural History,* ca. 79 AD

Before I get into some specifics about money-making possibilities on the Net, I wanted to give you three tips on getting started. Think of these as necessary prerequisites to mastering the Net.

Get a good access provider. First, find a good access provider, and stick with them. There's much more to a good access provider than simply having a phone number available for you to get onto the Net. You should be receiving solid technical support, with a minimum of waiting. Your access provider should be helping you with ancillary products and services — training courses, software, on-line storage space, high-speed phone lines. If your access provider is falling down in any of those areas, get a different provider!

Register a domain name. Your domain name — the name to the right of the @ sign — says a lot about you and your roots. Newbies might as well hang signs around their necks that say kickme@aol.com, and it's hard to take an Internet-aware business seriously when employees have IDs like 70038.1446@compuserve.com or 5551212@mcimail.com.

If you're serious about doing business on the Net, get your own domain name. It's good, cheap advertising, and it shows that you're serious about your Net presence. Your access provider should be able to help you register a domain name, for much less than $50.

Silence is pre-golden. Third, keep your mouth shut until you get the lay of the land. While on-line services encourage people to dive in and participate in conversations from the get-go, Internet news groups in particular are infamous for their insular ways. When you first join a news group, you're not so much sitting in on a grand meeting of the minds as you are jumping into the middle of a secret society, replete with its own handshake, rituals, and obscure codes of conduct.

Many of the predilections of each group can be found in the appropriate FAQ (Frequently Asked Questions) file, but nothing beats a few days of reconnoitering, waiting to get the "feel" of what's happening.

WEB FEET

I can swim like a duck.

Shakespeare
The Tempest, 1611

Much of what I've discussed in this chapter has simple analogs in the pre-cyber world. One Internet capability, though, stands apart: the World Wide Web, or (as most people call it), the Web.

Web as billboard

Webbin' it at ya

Some day, advertising on a billboard on the Web—or whatever the Net evolves into, over the next decade or two—will be as common as advertising today on TV, radio, or a billboard.

Why a Home Page

Next month I am certain to be on my legs for certain sure.

John Keats
Letter to Taylor and Hessey, June 10, 1817

A Web home page probably won't bring you or your company fame or fortune, but it may help get the word out about the products or services you have to offer. If you're very clever, it may also give Web surfers an incentive to actually purchase said product or service—but don't bet the farm on it.

Not a storefront

Some people liken Web home pages to storefronts, but that overstates the case. Until there are secure means of placing orders and verifying payment, or perhaps delivering products or services over the Net, there's no "store" at all: A Web page is all "front."

Think of a home page as advertising. Perhaps advertising in an unusual and challenging medium, but advertising nonetheless.

How Much?

> He that cannot pay let him pray.
>
> Randle Cotgrave
> *French-English Dictionary,* 1611

Some business people log on to the Web, see fancy home pages with effective graphics on provocative topics, and automatically assume it's much too expensive for the small-time telewonk.

Not so! Not so!

Yes, you can afford it. While it's true that a professionally designed and implemented home page can cost tens of thousands of dollars—indeed, some of the best-known pages actually sell advertising on their pages for tens of thousands of dollars!—the means of producing a top-notch home page are not beyond the lone teleconsultant, or a telefreelancer seeking to sell a product.

All it takes is a few tools (more about which momentarily) and a spot to hang your page. Many service providers will lease you that space for a few dollars a month, and plans are afoot among all the major on-line services to set up the Web home page space for a mere pittance.

Ideal for telefolk If you have a bit of time between telecontracting gigs, creating a home page can be the least expensive bit of advertising you'll ever stumble into.

How?

> Art is a higher type of knowledge than experience.
>
> Aristotle
> *Metaphysics,* ca. 322 BC

Leverage your word processing know-how. If you can lay out a page with one of the major word processors—Word, WordPerfect—translating that page into a Web home page is as simple as a couple of clicks.

The mechanics are comparatively easy. The content . . . well, that's another story.

Web pages are quite different from any other form of advertising. They must stride the fine line between having enough gimmicks to attract attention, and not having so much that people turn old and gray waiting for the page to appear.

More than that, though, a Web page has to suck people in, and keep their interest, preferably attracting them to come back again and again. You can only do that by designing a page that's interesting, and keeping it constantly updated so it's fresh.

Coming soon . . . It's a topic near and dear to my heart. So much so that we're coming up with an entire book on the topic, *The Underground Guide to Internet Assistant,* which should be available shortly after this book hits the stands. If you're going to be building your own Web home page using Word for Windows, that's the book you need.

Once you've created and posted your Web page, you have to get the word out. **Register.**
The best way to do that is to make yourself known to one of the "registry" home
pages. Three that are worth approaching:

- http://gnn.com/gnn/wn/whats-new.html
- http://www.directory.net
- http://www.commerce.net

Remember to keep your page fresh and lively, and the world just might beat a
path to your door.

FINAL THOUGHTS

> What I make on d' peanut I lose on d' damn banan'.
>
> Italian fruit vendor in New York
> to Teddy Roosevelt, 1890

There are many ways other than Web home pages to try to make money on the
Net, of course.

Perhaps the most likely to work is to "advertise" your consulting services by **Teleconsulting**
not really advertising at all: Many a teleconsulting gig has arisen from someone in **on the Net**
the know voluntarily helping a hapless Net denizen looking for help. But don't
get your hopes up too high. Based on personal experience, I'd guess that fewer
than one in a hundred instances where a consultant gives freely to a person in
need leads to an income-producing gig.

In other words, helping people on the Net is nice, and I recommend it
unreservedly. But it can take over your life; you can starve if you don't have
another source of income.

If you have a product to peddle, the Net can provide an excellent place for **Tech support**
delivering tech support. That won't really make you any money, but it can help
build a presence that might lead to some sales.

When it comes to real business transactions—the exchange of money, credit **Business**
card numbers, delivery of a product—the Net is still in the Wild West stage of **transactions**
development. I won't knowingly put my credit card number on the Net, and I
recommend that you don't either.

Remember that, even now, a fair percentage of folks on the Net are bored,
intelligent, inquisitive students, and their professors. That should help put your
Net efforts in perspective.

Oh. My ID? woody@wopr.com. Drop a line sometime.

FOR MORE INFO

There's one problem with those "Making Money on the Internet" books. They don't have a whole lot to talk about. With that caveat, you might find *Doing Business on the Internet* by Mary J. Cronin (VNR, 1994), useful—particularly if you aren't really familiar with the nuances of e-mail, ftp, and the like. The case studies should be taken with a grain of salt: a useful exercise might be trying to determine whether the showcased companies are still in business, and of the ones that are, whether their use of the Net has changed wildly since the book was published. Still, there are plenty of interesting ideas in this well-written book that are worthy of your consideration, should you be poised to jump into the Net's rocky commercial waters.

10 The Virtual Corporation

A corporation is just like any natural person, except that it has no pants to kick or soul to damn, and, by God, it ought to have both!

Attributed to a Western judge
Ernst and Lindley, *Hold Your Tongue*, 1932

I'd like to devote this short chapter to an important concept, one that's been ridden roughshod in the past few years, the infamous virtual corporation.

The virtual CEO

Nowadays it seems that any group that wants to appear trendy to the outside world calls itself a "virtual corporation." In the popular press, the term has lost, uh, virtually all its meaning.

The Ambra experience

309

Perhaps the ultimate insult to struggling virtual corporations came when IBM announced the formation of its Ambra division, and the press insisted on calling Ambra a "virtual corporation" within IBM.

Bah. Humbug. You can no more have a virtual corporation inside IBM than you can have a virtual whale in the belly of the Titanic.

In the parlance of the retail industry, Ambra was nothing more than a private label—a product generated by contractors, with a label slapped on the front that's supposed to reflect the prestige and marketing prowess of the parent company. Sears has been doing that with its Kenmore and Craftsman lines for a century or so.

Welcome to Virtual McDonalds. May I take your neo-order?

How to lose your shirt   IBM went a little further in that it not only farmed out the manufacture of the machine, but its sales and support, too. The IBM employees who ran the company—the virtual corporation within IBM, to hear the press tell it—consisted of nothing but overhead. The net result was a botched operation that bled red ink from its inception.

Virtual corporation, indeed.

A *REAL* VIRTUAL CORPORATION

> The sum of Plato's wondrous wisdom is,
> This is not that, and therefore, that not this.
>
> Robert Dodsley
> *Modern Reasoning*, 1745

Definition   As far as I'm concerned, a virtual corporation is a group of professionals who band together, informally, to keep the wolves from the door.

Yeah, yeah, I know. There have been books and journal articles written about virtual corporations, and they don't agree with me. That's OK. They're wrong.

Webster's* says that "virtual" means "being such in essence or effect though not formally recognized or admitted." That's a good starting point. The key is the

---

* *Webster's New Collegiate Dictionary*, 1979. Still the best under-50-pound dictionary on the market. Too bad it's only available in hardcopy.

lack of a formal bond: informal associations, dissociations, and reassociations keep virtual corporations fluid, vital, adaptable.

A virtual corporation isn't a division within a larger corporation. It isn't a "matrix management"-style team assembled to solve a specific problem. It isn't a joint task force formed to bring together disparate entities within an organization. In short, if you're drawing a paycheck, you aren't part of a virtual corporation.

I think real virtual corporations form the most exciting core of the new job scene. They're characterized by individuals with exceptional skills—people accustomed to pulling their own weight, and then some—who put together a team that's somehow more than the sum of its parts.

Where the action is

And the one characteristic almost all virtual corporation participants share? They're telecommuters!

Virtual Work

> When the gods like a man they throw some profit in his way.
>
> Plato
> *Persa*, ca. 200 BC

Virtual corporations, by their very nature, aren't well adapted to handle the bulk of businesses in the industrialized world: It's hard to imagine a virtual manufacturing organization, say, or a virtual retailer or jobber.

But virtual corporations are tailor-made for the high-tech services business.

What would a virtual players' strike look like?

By far the most common type of virtual corporation today consists of two or more teleconsultants who get together for specific kinds of projects. Sometimes the pairing stems from complementary skills in a similar field—two computer jocks, say, get together to build a custom system; one consultant knows Visual Basic, the other knows SQL Server. Sometimes the consultants come from completely different fields—one may know hazardous waste disposal techniques, the

Two-by-two

other might be a shipping logistics expert. In any case, the virtual corporation lasts just as long as the participants feel comfortable with the arrangement. Each participant is free to pursue other business opportunities—or do nothing at all. If the workload gets too heavy, the participants may seek to enlarge their virtual corporation; if the project dries up, the virtual corporation is dissolved just as informally as it was formed.

Producing a product
Another type of virtual corporation—one that's very important to me, personally, because it describes how my virtual corporation works—is the kind that makes a product and offers it for sale.

The B-school books will tell you that you that a successful start-up organization has to have a strong take-charge leader, a formal business plan, and lots of capital. Well, that just isn't true any more: virtual corporations are rewriting the rules.

In a virtual corporation that produces a product, participants can be hand-selected for specific skills they bring to the team. Since they're equity participants—they own a piece of the company, and their income rises or sinks with the fate of the product—they have enormous incentive to make the best product they can, and to market and support it far beyond what might be expected of a "normal" employee.

Something to be proud of
More than that, there's no small amount of ego and pride involved, and for good reason: The participants don't drown in the obscurity of a cubicle on the 34th floor of a nameless office building; they're out front and on the line, visible and responsible for what they've created. You don't get better incentive than that.

Predictably, this kind of visibility isn't for everybody: To be a good participant in a virtual corporation, you simply have to be extraordinarily capable, and be secure enough in your ability to stand behind the products you create.

Cream o' the crop
Assembling a virtual corporation is much simpler than you might think: You simply go for the top experts in the field, people with an overwhelming drive to "do things right." Few experts refuse an opportunity for equity participation in an organization dedicated to "doing things right"—especially when the only thing they risk is their time, and they don't have to quit doing anything they're currently doing to join on the team.

Which brings me to the tough part of putting together a virtual corporation: the structure.

Organization

> The people's government [is] made for the people, made by the people, and answerable to the people.
>
> Daniel Webster
> Speech in the Senate, January 26, 1830*

* Antedated by Thomas Cooper's "The government is of the people and for the people" (*Some Information Regarding America*, 1795) and postdated by Abraham Lincoln's Gettysburg Address, November 19, 1863.

The overwhelming question in forming a thriving virtual corporation is, "How do you organize it?" After several years of struggling with the question, I think I've come up with some answers. Or, at least, suggestions.

The most successful arrangement I've seen with consulting gigs is for one of **Consulting**
the virtual corporation's members to volunteer to be lead consultant. The lead consultant takes on contract negotiation with the client, apportions work among the virtual corporation participants, and commits to completion of the project—in some cases a rather scary proposition that, in and of itself, deserves some sort of financial consideration from the other consultants involved in the arrangement.

The client, to all intents, is contracting with the lead consultant, who then subcontracts to other members of the virtual corporation. The lead consultant bills the client, and maintains any supporting documentation (expense reports, time sheets, status reports) required by the client.

As the checks come in from the client, the lead consultant writes checks to the other members of the virtual corporation. At the end of the year, the lead consultant declares the entire amount from the gig as income, and then deducts the payments to the other participants as "consulting services" expenses. (In the United States, the lead consultant would show the entire income on a Schedule C and would be responsible for filing Form 1099-MISC for each participant.)

The actual amount of the split—the percentage accorded to each participant—may vary over time, depending on how much work each participant contributes, or any other criterion the participants agree is fair. If one of the participants actually brought in the client, a "finder's fee" (typically 10 percent) may be reasonable. There are lots of variables.

Virtual corporations that produce a product, though, are in a very different **Product**
position. There are invariably costs associated with bringing the product to market, distribution fees, and a host of problems that simply don't crop up in consulting arrangements. Here's what I've found to be an equitable arrangement.

With a virtual corporation that produces a product, the participants—I call 'em "contributors"—put in a certain amount of sweat equity. Capital requirements, which run orders of magnitude less than those of traditional start-ups, become the responsibility of one individual—for lack of a better term, the "sponsor."

The sponsor enters into agreements on behalf of the group for distribution, advertising, foreign rights, and any odd thing that might come along. The sponsor takes in all income (typically from the distributor) and cuts checks for each of the contributors. At the end of the year, the sponsor reports the total income for the product, and treats each contributor's share as a "royalty" expense. (In the United States, the sponsor would show the entire income on a Schedule C, and would be responsible for filing Form 1099-MISC for each contributor.)

Here's the tricky part. I firmly believe that contributors should be paid a **Percentage of**
percentage of the *gross* receipts, not net. Most distribution arrangements in the **gross**

software industry, anyway, are calculated based on net receipts—that is, gross income less advertising and distribution expenses, cost of goods, and overhead—and contributors take a hit on items (advertising, distribution) over which they have no control. That isn't fair, and it leads to resentment among the contributors: Why should they pay for a mass mailing, say, when they don't think a mass mailing will be worth the effort?

Good for the goose, too
On the flip side, by paying contributors a percentage of gross, not net, the sponsor is freed to pursue whatever marketing, advertising, and distribution techniques seem most appropriate: There's no need for accountability to the contributors on the expenses, and thus no second-guessing about what might or might not fly with the contributors. Or, to put it another way, if you're the sponsor, you're free to make mistakes without harming anybody's profits but your own.

If I want to type 50,000 direct marketing letters, its my own damned business.

As long as the sponsor holds back a large enough slice of the pie to keep the product afloat, and the contributors are happy with their piece of the action, a virtual corporation can thrive with a minimum of capital, and virtually no traditional overhead.

RUNNING A VIRTUAL CORPORATION

> Boldness, in business, is the first, second and third thing.
>
> H. G. Bohn
> *Handbook of Proverbs*, 1855

Solving problems
When you approach a client's problem or business opportunity from a virtual corporation's point of view—not "which of my employees can do this work?" or "do I have a budget slot free to hire someone to take care of this?," but "what kind of talent needs to be brought to bear?"—many traditional business problems

disappear. Aside from the occasional client hand-holding session, the physical location of your participants rarely becomes an issue. Even their current employment status doesn't matter much. You can go for the best hired guns and, using common telecommuting technology, concentrate on solving the problem, instead of worrying about all the corporate artifice that only gets in the way.

A virtual corporation gives you lots of latitude. Surprisingly, it does so, by and large, without bogging you down in a lot of extraneous garbage.

If you put it together right, a virtual corporation practically runs itself. You have no personnel department: Consultants are motivated to do a professional job not only for the good of the current project, but also for future work with the client and with you. If you produce a product, the contributors take care of themselves, and the distributor handles all the rest. Accounting can be performed, as Thoreau suggested, on a thumbnail. Or at most a wimpy PC. There's no office politics. No back-biting. Everybody fills their own coffee cups, because everybody works wherever they like.

Under its own steam

All in all, it's a good arrangement.

The Achilles heel of most virtual corporations lies in marketing: Consultants tend to seek additional work for themselves at the expense of the informal group; contributors with a product can rarely afford the time that joint marketing demands. Indeed, if there's one thing that will force my virtual corporation to "go legit," establish as a formal entity, and hire employees, it will be the need for more extensive marketing.

When all is said and done, the great advantage virtual corporations offer is quality. There's no "deadwood"—and if any crops up on this job, he won't be around for the next one. Virtual corporations are flexible enough to add new talent as it's required, quickly—even if the need for that talent wasn't foreseen at the beginning of the project.

It's all about quality.

Products developed by virtual corporations can reflect the absolute best an industry has to offer: Contributors come in, solve a problem and "do it right," and then move on to other pursuits. There's no second-guessing, no design by committee. It should come as no surprise that some of the most innovative new ideas and products in the high-tech industries originated with experts under just those no-compromise conditions.

Whenever I talk to clients or customers of virtual corporations, I hear about one big concern over and over again: continuity. What happens if the virtual corporation crumbles away in the middle of a consulting assignment? How do customers know that this looseknit group of hired guns, uh, this virtual corporation will be around a year from now, when they need help with the product?

The downside

The answer, of course, is that there are no guarantees. Customers should exercise the same sort of caution they would with any other type of vendor: How long has the group been together? What's their track record?

Most of all, though, I think it's important that customers take a look at what they're getting. There's no guarantee the John Smith Informal Consulting Emporium will exist next month—but if John Smith has been doing this kind of work for the past five or ten years, you can feel pretty secure. You could hire the Big Six Accounting Company Consulting Branch, and have them bring in their hotshot. But who's to say the same hotshot will be around next month? And, if she leaves, where does that land your project?

I'm Snerdly. Mr. Deloitte, Mr. Touche, and Mr. Ross all send their regards.

Virtual corporations aren't immune to the same problems that plague the rest of the industry. But if you have reason to trust the "lead consultant" or product "sponsor," you're in good hands: after all, it's their business on the line. The fact that virtual corporation participants are working together because they *want* to work together speaks volumes.

11 Crystal Ball

We know what we are, but know not what we may be.

Shakespeare
Hamlet, 1601

Not to put too fine a point on it, but telecommuting and telecommuting technology are rapidly transforming the nature of "work" as we know it. Freed from the surly bonds of physical presence, telemployees can get more done, in less time, and of a higher quality than ever before—while making better use of the 250 hours that the average physiocommuter wastes every year driving to and from the office.

What the future holds

As telecommuting becomes more common, office-bound employees will first ask, and then demand, that their companies permit them to work at home more frequently. The option to participate in a telecommuting program will become a much-sought job perq. As is so often the case, though, the extraordinary will become commonplace. By the end of the century, the *lack* of a telecommuting option will be viewed as a major drawback to any high-tech job.

Concurrently, those who oppose telecommuting—typically midlevel managers accustomed to monitoring their employees by watching them—will either adapt or disappear.

But you don't need me to tell you any of that. All of those conclusions are straightforward extrapolations from what is happening right now; they're as inevitable as air pollution. Let's take a look at a few predictions that aren't quite so obvious.

THE JOB

Oh, how full of briers is this working-day world!

Shakespeare
As You Like It, ca. 1600

The job as we have known it for the past century or so is rapidly vanishing. As the economy of developed nations shifts from a reliance on manufacturing and

Decentralization

317

physical production to the provision of information and services, the necessity for centralized jobs—"work" as a place to go—decreases.

Given an option, the most capable, most talented, most productive employees—in short, those in highest demand—aren't going to sit idly by, wasting a good portion of their quality time, and no small portion of their sanity, driving back and forth to a downtown location that's increasingly irrelevant. Instead, they'll decide to live where they *want* to live, dammit, for reasons that have nothing to do with jobs. The smartest companies will chase those ultra-qualified people into the cyburbs. Laggard companies won't even know what hit them.

I told 'em, either I telecommute, or they can take their job an' shove it.

Job security   There's another force at work, concurrent with this massive potential for job decentralization: the growing instability of the workforce. The days of lifetime job security are long gone, and employees realize it. One of their best defenses—perhaps the single best way to protect against career disruptions—is to take their career into their own hands, developing skills and taking on gigs that simply would never appear in their regular jobs. Telecontracting and teleconsulting are excellent ways of doing precisely that, a fact that is not lost on legions of high-tech professionals.

Telecommuting holds the key.

THE COMMUNITY

> I reckon I got to light out for the Territory,
> because Aunt Sally she's going to adopt me
> and civilize me and I can't stand it.
> I been there before.
>
> Samuel Clemens
> *Huckleberry Finn,* 1885

None of this bodes well for large cities, their tax bases already eroded by the flight to the suburbs, their cores caught in a never-ending downward economic spiral.

Brain drain

You've heard of the "brain drain," where inner cities and third world countries lose their best and brightest to more attractive locales? You ain't seen nothing yet. The brain drain to the cyburbs over the next decade or two will deal a devastating blow to physiocommuting centers. Unless cities can transform themselves into places where telecommuters and their families would willingly live, regardless of the location of the breadwinners' jobs — or they can effectively attract businesses that are immune to telecommuting — they're going to wither on the vine.

The family of the future, with 2.4 kids.

The boonies

On the other hand, if you've ever had a hankering to invest in small-town real estate, now may be the time. Medium- and small-sized cities with high "quality of life" and low cost of living will doubtless be the major benefactors of the shift to telecommuting.

Places far off the beaten track will see more settlers, too. A pity.

THE TECHNOLOGY

> The dogmas of the quiet past are inadequate to the stormy present...
> As our case is new, so we must think anew and act anew.
> We must disenthrall ourselves.
>
> Abraham Lincoln
> Message to Congress, December 1, 1862

Push-pull

Many people see the advances in home computers and telecommuting technology pushing this move away from physiocommuting. I don't agree. In fact, I think the opposite is true: I tend to think of the move to the cyburbs as being an inexorable drive of humankind, a rational reaction to the irrational demand that all people work in the same place. Technology merely permits telecommuters to do what they naturally want to do.

In the end it may be a chicken-and-egg argument. The fact is that technology continues to change at a breathtaking pace and—whether the technology pushes demand, or demand pulls technology—we're in for some mind-boggling changes over the next few years. Let's take a look at some of those changes.

Computers   The foundation of telecommuting, the PC, is in for some big changes. The power of computing available for a given price continues to double every eighteen to twenty-four months. Computing power we can only dream about today will become commonplace in three to four years. Everything stored on your central office's LAN right now will fit on your home PC's hard drive in four or five years. The economic balance between central sites and home PCs will continue to tip in favor of home. Telecommuters are, and will continue to be, on the right side of the price/performance curve.

Software   Applications and capabilities that we can't even imagine today will be common in five years. Microsoft, likely, will continue to dominate the desktop. If suites exist at all (their function may be absorbed into, oh, Windows 99 or Windows 00), they'll be so cheap that price won't even be a significant consideration. But the bugs! Oy! The bugs!

On-line services   For-profit on-line services are likely to become indistinguishable from the Internet (more about which next). Following Microsoft Network's (MSN's) lead, the major on-line services will move to fixed monthly pricing, with little or no charge for connect time. Content will become key, and MSN will be the game to beat. Look for a bloody consolidation among the major on-line services in the next few years.

The Internet   Somehow, some day, somebody will have to pay for the Internet. Deciding exactly how and how much will consume hundreds of thousands of Net-hours over the next few years. I have no idea how it will turn out.

The immediate hot items for the Internet are security and finding a way to grab all that Web data in an intelligible way. With security, more commercial applications will emerge. Industrial strength Web search engines should also be around the corner. Servers will crop up to do all the cataloging and correlating of large Web network sections ahead of time.

A few blocks beyond that will be new Net protocols to replace the Web protocol. Hyper-G is being developed in universities. It is multimedia like the Web, but stores the connections (the links) separate from the document. You don't have to wade through many pages and hypertext links to locate the information you need. More importantly, search software doesn't have to. These links can be scripted together to form a "tour." The audience just sits back and watches the presentation on the Net unfold.

Other groups are working on Net videoconferencing. CUSeeme is one such experiment. The problem with videoconferencing, as with voice, is that gaps in delivering the data can throw a monkey wrench in the works.

The cable TV industry isn't sitting still. Cable is being challenged by wireless satellite and is reacting by branching into a dizzying number of areas. One product to watch for is a cable box that is supposed to connect to the Internet at anywhere from 100 Kbps sustained to 10 Mbps (yeah, well, I'm not holding my breath). Cable is also taking on the local phone companies—a move that can only be good for competition, and thus for telecommuters everywhere. **Cable industry**

Cable has many hurdles to overcome, some the size of the old Berlin wall. The cable industry, while it has potential to reach 95 percent of the American households, is crippled by a large one-way problem. That is, most cable companies' entire infrastructure (hardware, billing, software, protocols, you-name-it) is geared for one-way communication, from the cable company to your TV set. Their ability to overcome that bias may well determine whether the cable companies even survive the next couple of decades.

The ATM protocol has been heralded as the solution for cable, corporations, telecommuters, and anything else ATM bigots can think of. The protocol is packet technology like X.25 (wait a minute, wasn't that heralded as the protocol of the future a decade ago?) and Frame Relay (wait a minute, wasn't that heralded as the protocol of the future a few years ago?). ATM beats ISDN and Frame Relay at delivering synchronized video and sound because its packets are compact and thus don't bottleneck the network. ATM also allows multimedia, including voice, in a well-integrated way. ATM's downfall is its small packet size, which causes high overhead. (Every packet has a little over 9 percent overhead, so it isn't very efficient.) **ISDN alternatives**

Will ATM take over ISDN? Hell, I can't even get the phone company to admit that it *has* ISDN. So what's to take over?

Desktop videoconferencing will progress, but I don't think it's going to be the big smash many companies think it will be. The primary use will probably be telecommuter desktop to company meeting room. With 100 Mbps LANs and steadily decreasing costs for desktop videoconferencing equipment, that may ultimately extend, in a limited fashion, to desktop-to-desktop videoconferencing. But even with all the kinks ironed out, the camera will still be sitting above your head or below your chin—either way, there's no eye contact, and the angle is unflattering at best. **Video-conferencing**

IN SUMMARY

Telecommuting is the way of the future. Go out and do it. Proudly.

Appendix A
For More Info . . .

Here's my short, short list of the most important sources of additional information targeted to the telecommuter, telecommuter wannabe, and teleboss.

SETTING UP A TELECOMMUTING PROGRAM

CalTrans—*Runs one of the most advanced telecommuting programs in the United States. Their* Telecommuting Handbook *is a good intro to setting up a telecommuting program.* Leah Zippert, Public Info Coordinator, 680/24 Public Info Office, 1910 Olympic Blvd., Suite 160, Walnut Creek, CA 94596. Voice: 510-680-4636, Fax: 510-938-0327.

Los Angeles County—*Believed to be the largest telecommuting program in the United States. Extensive reports on the results of dozens of individual programs.* 500 West Temple Street, Room 588, Los Angeles, CA 90012. Voice: 213-974-2616 or 213-974-2394.

New Ways To Work—*Information and publications on telecommuting and many other "flex" options, including job sharing, flextime, and the like.* 785 Market Street, Suite 950, San Francisco, CA 94103. Voice: 415-995-9860.

Smart Valley—*Runs a telecommuting program in the San Francisco Bay Area. The* Smart Valley Telecommuting Guide *costs $7, available by check only.* 1661 Page Mill Road, Suite 200, Palo Alto, CA 94304-1209. Voice: 415-328-4575, Internet: lesliek@svi.org.

Washington State Energy Office—*A very aggressive and highly successful government agency involved in encouraging the shift to telecommuting. If you're going to set up your own telecommuting program, get their guidelines,* Telecommuting: An Alternate Route to Work *(2 volumes, $50).* 935 Plum St SE, Bldg. 4, P.O. Box 43165, Olympia, WA 98504-3165. Voice: 206-956-2230, Fax: 206-956-2217.

TELEWORK CENTERS

General Services Administration—*Federal government contact point for telecommuting in general, and the D.C. telework center in particular.* 18th & F Streets, NW, Washington, D.C. 20405. Voice: 202-501-1580.

Hawaii Department of Transportation—*Pioneers in the telework center concept.* 600 Kapiolani Blvd., Honolulu, HI 96813. Voice: 808-548-6526.

Smart Valley—*Info on telework centers in the San Francisco Bay Area.* 1661 Page Mill Road, Suite 200, Palo Alto, CA 94304-1209. Voice: 415-328-4575.

HOME OFFICE

AT&T Home Business Resources — *Interesting, free service. The* Home Office Computing Handbook *(developed by the editors at* Home Office Computing *maga- zine) may be useful, particularly if you're new to the game.* Voice: 800-383-6164, Fax: 800-341-8888.

U.S. West—*A new program called Home Office Consultants can help you choose among the bewildering array of phone company services. Ask for a copy of the* Home Office Resource Guide. *(While I take great issue with several of their comments about comput- ers, the magazine has some general business information that you may find useful.)* Voice: 800-898-9675. *Other local phone companies are starting similar programs targeting the home office customer; call your local phone company for the latest information.*

CONSULTING

Gil Gordon Associates—*Gil provides consulting and advice, writes a monthly news- letter, and conducts an annual seminar on setting up telecommuting programs. Widely regarded as one of the top experts in the field.* 10 Donner Court, Monmouth Junction, NJ 08852. Voice: 908-329-2266

BOOKS

The Internet Companion Plus: *A Beginner's Start-Up Kit for Global Networking* by Tracy Laquey (Addison-Wesley, 1993) ISBN 0-201-40837-6. *Concise, straightforward guide to the Internet. With disk. List $19.95.*

Making Telecommuting Happen by Jack Nilles (VNR, 1994) ISBN 0-442-01857-6. *Complete guide to setting up a telecommuting program, including many of the forms and supporting information you'll need.*

Working from Home: *Everything You Need to Know About Living and Working Under the Same Roof* by Paul and Sarah Edwards (Tarcher/Putnam, 1994) ISBN 0-87477- 764-X. *Indispensable, encyclopedic compilation of advice for anybody who works at home. List $15.95.*

COURSES AND TRAINING

Denver City and County—*Judy Rapp-Guadagnoli is the Telecommuting Program Manager for the City and Country of Denver. Her office produces many brochures and runs a comprehensive series of courses year-round.* Denver Dept. of Public Works, 220 W. 14th #302, Denver, CO 80204-2700. Voice: 303-640-1108, Fax: 303-640-2088.

NEWSLETTERS

Gil Gordon Associates—*Gil's* Telecommuting Review, *the monthly newsletter for the industry, is available for $157 (or $177 outside North America) from* TeleSpan Publishing Corp., 50 West Palm Street, Altadena, CA 91001. Voice: 818-797-5482.

SOFTWARE

Forward Systems, Inc.—*Purveyors of a software package that will help you manage a telecommuting program.* 853 Sanders Road, Suite 330, Northbrook, IL 60062. Voice: 708-509-1255, Fax: 708-509-1254.

Appendix B
Phone Book

Reducing the huge number of telecommuter-support phone numbers to a concise ten-page list proved most diffucult. Apologies to all of those who didn't make it onto the list.

HOME OFFICE

Here are a few suppliers of some of the more exotic products for the home office mentioned in this book and some hard-to-find phone numbers.

Specialty Paper

Image Street—*Colorful preprinted papers, designed to be used in laser printers. Letterhead, envelopes, brochures, business cards, your photo on self-adhesive labels, and more.* Moore Business Products Div., P.O. Box 5000, Vernon Hills, IL 60061. Voice: 800-462-4378, Fax: 800-329-6667.

Paper Direct—*More top-notch paper, of every imaginable stripe.* P.O. Box 618, 205 Chubb Avenue, Lyndhurst, NJ 07071-0618. Voice: 800-A-PAPERS, 201-507-1996, Fax: 201-507-0817.

Telephones

Hello Direct—*The only place you'll find cordless headsets. Wide variety of products in their catalog, many of which are hard to find.* 5884 Eden Park Place, San Jose, CA 95138-1859. Voice: 800-444-3556, Fax: 408-972-8155, CompuServe: 74577,425, Internet: xpressit@hihello.com. *Or take a look at their Web home page,* http://www.hello-direct.com/hd.

HB Distributors—*Plantronics doesn't sell directly to consumers, and it can be very difficult to find their entire product line locally. HB Distributors carries the full Plantronics line, and they'll send you a catalog, too.* 8741 Shirley Ave., Northridge, CA 91324. Voice: 818-882-0000, Fax: 818-700-1808.

Internal Revenue Service

IRS—*To get any form or publication the IRS offers to the general public, in particular, you can apply for an Employer Identification Number by calling and asking for Form SS-4.* Voice: 800-829-3676.

PC PRODUCTS

PC Connection—*In general, the easiest, fastest, most reliable place to buy general PC stuff is from* PC Connection, 6 Mill Street, Marlow, NH 03456. Voice: 800-800-1111 (24 hours a day, 7 days a week) or 603-446-1111, Fax: 603-446-7791. *If you call before 3:00 a.m. Eastern Time, they'll ship* that night *for delivery the next day.*

Computer Shopper—*The magazine with the latest on what to buy, and how much to pay, in each issue. Absolutely indispensable.* Available at any computer store, newsstand, or grocery store near you.

Business Software

Image Club—*All the cartoons in this book are from ImageBase clipart, available through Image Club.* 10545 West Donges Court, Milwaukee, WI 53224-9985. Voice: 800-661-9410, Fax: 403-261-7013.

METZ Software—*Makers of solid, down-to-earth Windows software. I use Metz Phones, a simple single-purpose program, to keep track of names and addresses. It's all the PIM I need.* P.O. Box 6699, Bellevue, WA 98008-0699. Voice: 206-641-4525, Fax: 206-644-6026, CompuServe: 75300,1627, America Online: METZSoft, GEnie: A.METZ

OsoSoft—*Rockford! Pro For creating business cards on your PC. Shareware.* Voice: 805-528-1759.

PKWare—*PKZip. The de facto standard for compressing files before sending them over the wires. Shareware.* Voice: 414-354-8699, Fax: 414-354-8559.

WinZIP—*If you use PKZip with Windows, be sure to get Nico Mak's WinZIP, which makes PKZip easy to use.* CompuServe: 70056,241.

Supplies

MEI Micro Center—*From cheap disks that always work to no-name CD-ROM drives, this is the place to get your generic supplies.* 1100 Steelwood Road, Columbus, Ohio 43212. Voice 800-634-3478, Fax 614-486-6417.

Global Equipment Company—*My favorite for mail-order office furniture and the big stuff.* 2318 East Del Amo Blvd., Compton, CA 90220. Voice 800-645-1232 or 516-625-3456.

Hardware

Black Box Corp—*Interconnectivity specialists, from LAN stuff to phone stuff.* P.O. Box 12800, Pittsburgh, PA 15241. Voice: 412-746-5500, Fax: 800-321-0746, To order a catalog: 800-552-6816.

Cables To Go—*More than just a cable store: If you need to connect anything to anything, these are the folks to call.* 1501 Webster St., Dayton, Ohio 45404. Orders: 800-826-7904, Fax: 800-331-2841, To order a catalog: 800-826-7904.

Gateway Keyboards—*An excellent alternative to Northgate keyboards, if the Northgate click drives you to distraction.* Voice: 800-846-2000 or 605-232-2000.

IBM—*The "modem saver," part number 73G5395, checks to see if a phone line will fry your modem.* Voice: 800-388-7080, Fax 800-766-6545, outside United States, contact the local IBM office.

Northgate Keyboards—*While Northgate computers may be hard to find, their keyboards live on at this phone number.* Voice: 800-526-2446, Fax: 612-943-8332.

Specialized Products Company—*For telephone equipment, telephone, and test products.* 3131 Premier Dr., Irving, TX 75063-9969. Orders: 800-866-5353, Fax: 800-234-8286, To order a catalog: 800-866-5353.

COMMUNICATION VENDORS AND SERVICE PROVIDERS

And for those who wish to comparison shop . . . here is a list of vendors and service providers to call. They will gladly send you a brochure on their product and answer questions.

Fax Software

If you need more features than a "Lite" version of fax software bundled with other products, try one of these on for size:

American TeleRep—Fax/PM (for OS/2). Voice: 203-648-9587.

Cheyenne Software—BitFax Pro/FaxPro (Mac version). Voice: 800-243-9462.

Delrina—Winfax Pro. Voice: 800-268-6082.

Phoenix Tech—Eclipse Fax. Voice: 800-677-7300.

Smith Micro—QuickLink II. Voice: 800-964-7674.

Sofnet—FaxWorks Pro. Voice: 800-329-9675.

Softkey International—Ultra Fax. Voice: 800-323-8088.

Thought Comm—FaxTalk Plus. Voice: 800-532-2825.

Trio Info Systems—DataFax+. Voice: 800-880-4400.

WordPerfect—ExpressFax. Voice: 800-451-5151.

Voice Mail Management

If you have shopped for answering machines/voice messaging services/answering services and found them wanting, or if you just like the idea of making your PC take messages, then this list of voice messaging software companies will come in handy. Many are bundled with voice fax modems, voice messaging boxes, and some multimedia boards. Unlike fax software, they are usually not "Lite." The voice messaging software companies listed here can send you information, answer questions, and most importantly, give a list of hardware vendors that bundle their product.

Cheyenne Communications —Bitfax Pro. Voice: 516-484-5110.

Kalman Technologies —Ancilla. Voice: 604-684-3118.

Pacific Image Comm.—SuperVoice. Voice: 818-457-8881.

Smith Micro—Quickline Msg Center. Voice: 800-964-7674.

Sofnet —FaxWorks with Voice. Voice: 404-984-8088.

Voice Boxes and Multimedia Boards with Voice Messaging

Best Data—Ace. *Board with messaging.* Voice: 800-632-2378.

Boca Research—Soundexpression. *Board with messaging.* Voice: 407-997-6227.

ClearWave Communications —Intellect. *This is a softphone/box.* Voice: 404-984-8088.

Interactive —Communicator/SoundXchange. *Board with messaging.* Voice: 800-292-2112.

Octus—Personal Telephone Asst. *This is a softphone/box.*Voice: 619-452-9400.

Spectrum—Envoy. *Board with messaging.* Voice: 604-421-5422.

Modems

This is a short list of modem vendors. There are all kinds represented here, including voice fax/modems. Remember to choose all the software you need first, and then match the modem to the software. Modem vendors like to put people on the interminable hold. Be forewarned!

AT&T Paradyne —Voice: 813-530-2000.

Best Data Products —Voice: 800-832-2378.

Boca Research —Voice: 407-997-6227.

Computer Peripherals —Voice: 800-854-7600.

Digicom —Voice: 800-833-8900.

Etech Research —Voice: 800-328-5538.

Hayes —Voice: 800-964-2937.

Interactive —Voice: 800-292-2112.

Media Magic —Voice: 800-624-8654.

MultiTech —Voice: 800-328-9717.

Prometheus —Voice: 800-477-3473.

Practical Peripherals —Voice: 800-225-4774.

US Robotics —Voice: 800-845-0908.

Zoom —Voice: 800-666-6191.

Peer-to-Peer LANs

These LANs are easy to connect and allow a telecommuter kingdom with multiple computers to share and share alike.

Artisoft—Simply LANtastic. Voice: 800-233-5564.

CBIS—Desk to Desk. Voice: 800-835-3375.

Microsoft—Windows for Workgroups/Win '95. Voice: 800-426-9400.

Performance Technology—PowerLan. Voice: 800-327-8526.

At-Home Routers

Telebit—Netblazer Voice: 800-835-3248.

COMMUNICATION SOFTWARE

If you need to gesticulate electronically, download a file at the Central Office, or just want to shoot the digital bull with a colleague, here's a starting point for finding the ideal communication software:

Remote Control Software

Avalon Technologies—Remotely Possible/DIAL. Voice: 800-441-2281.

Microcom—Carbon Copy. Voice: 800-822-8224.

MobileWare Corp.—Mobileware. Voice: 800-260-7450.

Norton Lambert—Close Up. Voice: 805-964-6767.

Ocean Isle Software—ReachOut Remote Control. Voice: 800-677-6232.

Smith Micro—Remote Disk. Voice: 800-964-SMSI.

Software Corp. of America—PolyPM/2 (for OS/2). Voice: 203-359-2773.

Symantec Corp.—pcAnywhere. Voice: 800-441-7234.

Traveling Software—LapLink for Windows. Voice: 800-487-4313.

Triton Technology—CoSession. Voice: 908-855-9440.

Data Communication Software

DataStorm Technology—ProComm Plus. Voice: 800-315-3282.

DCA—Crosstalk. Voice: 800-348-3221.

Delrina—WinComm Pro. Voice: 800-268-6082.

MediaPoint—Zipcomm. Voice: 800-783-6355.

Mustang Software—QmodemPro for Windows. Voice: 800-999-9619.

Traveling Software—Commworks for Windows. Voice: 800-343-8080.

Document Conferencing

Many document-conferencing software packages are poor cousins to videoconferencing. You may wish to ask videoconferencing vendors if they have document-conferencing packages and vice versa.

AT&T—Vistium Share SW Professional. Voice: 800-637-2600.

Databeam—FarSite for Windows. Voice: 800-877-2325.

Eden Systems—The Meeting Room. Voice: 800-459-6338.

Eyetel Comm.—Communicator I. Voice: 604-984-2522.

Fujitsu— Desktop Conferencing. Voice: 800-446-4736.

FutureLabs Inc—TalkShow. Voice: 800-933-8887.

Intel—Proshare Premier Edition. Voice: 800-538-3373.

IBM—Person to Person for Windows. Voice: 800-426-9402.

Vis a Vis—Vis a Vis for Windows. Voice: 800-263-9673.

Videoconferencing

Doceo Publishing—Video Sampler CD. *This CD has a tutorial on videonconferencing and a product guide.* Voice: 404-564-5545.

AT&T —Vistium Personal Video. Voice: 800-225-5627.

Intel —Proshare Video System. Voice: 800-538-3373.

PictureTel —PictureTel Live PCS. Voice: 800-715-6000.

ISDN

This is where to start if you want to get ISDN service.

General Information on ISDN

Intel—*ISDN general info.* BBS: 503-645-6275, Fax: 800-525-3019.

ISDN Phone Service

Ameritech — Voice: 800-832-6328.

Alpha Telecom Inc. — Voice: 205-881-8743.

Bell Atlantic — Voice: 800-570-4736, 800-245-9780.

BellSouth — Voice: 800-858-9413.

Cincinnati Bell — Voice: 513-397-5151.

GTE — *GTE has some ISDN access.* Voice: 800-888-8799, 800-448-3795.

NYNEX — Voice: 800-GET-ISDN.

Pacific Bell — Voice: 800-995-0346.

Rochester Telephone — Voice: 716-777-1234.

Southwestern Bell — Voice: 800-792-4736.

US West — Voice: 800-945-9494, 800-603-6000.

If you need to telecommute long-distance, you will also need long-distance ISDN service.

AT&T — Voice: look in the Yellow Pages for a local representative.

MCI— Voice: 800-MCI-ISDN, 214-701-6745.

Sprint— Voice: 913-624-4162.

STENTOR (Canada)— Voice: 800-578-ISDN.

WILTEL— Voice: 918-588-5069.

ISDN Products

ISDN requires several pieces of equipment. There are NT-1, Terminal Adapters (TA), Power Supply (PS), and ISDN bridges/System Adapter cards. Which piece of equipment the vendor retails is indicated. Contact your ISDN service provider for ISDN phone and Group IV fax products, if you are interested.

AdTran—NT1. Voice: 205-971-8000.

Ascend Communications—Pipeline 50. Bridge.Voice: 800-272-3634.

Combinet —Everywhere 160/400. Bridge. Voice: 800-967-6651.

ControlWare Comm Systems—TA. Voice: 908-919-0400.

CSI Connective Strategies—TA. Voice: 410-931-7500.

Digiboard — PC ImacImac/4. Bridge. Voice: 800-344-4273.

Extension—Long Distance Lan Adapter E-101. Bridge. Voice: 800-856-2672.

Gandalf—LANLine 5240I. Bridge. Voice: 800-426-3253.

IBM—WaveRunner. Bridge (limited). Voice: 800-426-4968.

Intel—RemoteExpress. Bridge. Voice: 800-538-3373.

OST—PC SNET. Bridge (Mac version also). Voice: 703-817-0400.

TelePower—TA. Voice: 818-587-5540.

PRODUCTS FOR THE CENTRAL OFFICE

For you traditional telemployees, here is a start on your wish list—all the cool stuff you might want the folks at your central office to consider. (And you IS types can sneak a peek, too.)

Security

Security Dynamics—SecureIDcard ACE/Server. Voice: 800-732-8743.

Remote Node Servers/Bridges/Routers

3COM—AccessBuilder. Voice: 408-764-5000.

DCA—Remote LAN Node Turnkey Server. Voice: 800-348-2221.

CISCO—AccessPro PC Card (NT router). Voice: 408-526-4000.

IBM—LAN Distance. Voice: 800-342-6672.

Microcom—LANexpress. Voice: 800-822-8224.

Novell —Netware Connect. Voice: 800-453-1267.

Shiva—LanRover Plus. Voice: 617-270-8300.

Stampede—Remote Office. Voice: 800-763-3423.

Telebit—Netblazer. *Router.* Voice: 800-835-3248.

Xylogics—Annex Software. Voice: 800-225-3317.

ISDN Hubs/Routers

Eicon—SO/HO. Voice: 214-239-3304.

Network Express—*ISDN hub.* Voice: 800-553-4333.

Teleos —AccessSwitch. Voice: 908-544-6432.

Teleconferencing

Latitude—Communications Meeting Place. Voice: 408-988-7200.

Electronic Whiteboards

Microfield—Graphics Softboard. Voice: 800-334-4922.

Smart Technologies—Smart 2000. Voice: 403-233-9333.

E-MAIL, CYBERSURFING, NET

If you ever wanted to get connected, here's the ultimate shopping list.

Company E-mail

Banyan—Beyondmail. Voice: 800-828-2404.

Lotus—CC:MAIL Mobile. Voice: 800-343-5414.

Microsoft—Microsoft Mail. Voice: 800-426-9400.

Novell/WordPerfect—Groupwise. Voice: 800-861-2507.

On-line Services

America Online—*These folks have had a reputation in the past for oversubscribing (1-800-busysignal). Try to get a "trial" subscription first.* Voice: 800-827-6364.

CompuServe—Voice: 800-848 8199.

Delphi—Voice: 800-695-4005.

Genie—Voice: 800-638-9636.

MCI Mail—Voice: 800-237-9383.

Prodigy—Voice: 800-776-3449.

Internet Services

Best bet is to get the e-mail list from somebody already on the Net. If you can't, here are some providers that can offer national access.

Colorado SuperNet—*Woody's favorite.* Voice: 303-296-8202; Fax: 303-296-8224.

Netcom—*Netcruiser is the front end. Another notorious oversubscriber, you may get frequent busy signals when trying to connect.* Voice: 800-353-6600.

Pipeline—Voice: 212-267-3636.

PSI Inc.—Voice: 800-827-7482.

Internet Email Add-Ons

ConnectSoft—Email Connection. *E-mail consolidator, but has potential deadly bugs, unfriendly support.* Voice: 206-827-6467.

Qualcomm—Eudora. *Good general e-mail package.* Voice: 800-2-Eudora.

Swfte International—The Wire. *MCI Mail add-on.* Voice: 800-237-9383.

Internet Browsers and Net Access Package Software

Ameritech—NOTIS WinGopher. *Gopher browser.* Voice: 800-55NOTIS.

Booklinks Technology—Internetworks. *Web browser.* Voice: 800-453-7873.

California Software—Software InterAp. *Package viewer.* Voice: 714-675-9906.

Frontier Technology—WinTapestry. *Web browser.* Voice: 414-241-4555.

FTP—Plus. *Package viewer.* Voice: 800-282-4387.

IBM—WebExplorer. *Package viewer for OS/2.* Voice: 800-342-6672.

MicroMind—Slipknot. *Web access for shell accounts.* E-mail: slipknot@micromind.com.

MKS—Internet Anywhere. Voice: 800-265-2797.

NetManage—Chameleon. *Package viewer.* Voice: 408-973-7171.

NetScape—Navigator. *Web browser.* Voice: 800-638-7483.

Spry—Air Mosaic. *Web browser.* Voice: 800-777-9638.

Spry/O'Reilly & Associates—Internet in a Box. *Package viewer.* Voice: 800-557-9614.

Spyglass—NCSA Mosaic. *Web browser.* Voice: 708-505-1010.

Web Publishing Software and Servers

The "do-it-yourself" way to stake a claim on the Web requires a Web server and publishing software to create a home page. Here's a list of contacts to get you started.

Ameritech Library Services—Netpublisher. *Web publishing/server for NT.* Voice: 708-866-0150.

Biap Systems—MacHTTP. *Mac-based Web server.* Web: http://www.biap.com/

HTML Assistant Pro.—*For making Web pages.* Voice: 902-835-2600.

Hot Metal—*For making Web pages.* Voice: 800-387-2777.

Process Software Corp—WWW for Windows NT. *For creating your own Web server.* Voice: 508-879-6994.

Quadralay Corp—WebWorks. *For creating your own Web server.* Voice: 512-346-9199.

Web Consulting Services

These companies help you establish a presence on the Web. Services run the gamut. Everything from Web page design, creation, Web Server set up, to leasing space on an existing Web Server.

Active Window Productions—Voice: 617-497-4011.

Connect Inc.—Voice: 800-262-2638.

Internet Presence—Voice: 804-446-9060.

Tag Online Mall—Voice: 800-824-8281.

Index